Mass- ...on and Literacy Practices

LANGUAGE & SOCIAL PROCESSES
Judith Green, editor

Shards of Glass: Children Reading and Writing Beyond Gendered Identities
  Bronwyn Davies

Children as Researchers of Culture and Language in Their Own Communities
  Ann Egan-Robertson and David Bloome (eds.)

Constructing Critical Literacies
  Peter Freebody, Allan Luke and Sandy Muspratt

Constructing Gender and Difference: Critical Research Perspectives on Early Childhood
  Barbara Kamler (ed.)

Preschoolers as Authors: Literacy Learning in the Social World of the Classroom
  Deborah Wells Rowe

Writing Ourselves: Mass-Observation and Literacy Practices
  Dorothy Sheridan, Brian Street, and David Bloome

forthcoming

Teaching Cultures: Knowledge for Teaching First Grade in France and the United States
  Kathryn M. Anderson-Levitt

Life in a Preschool
  David P. Fernie and Rebecca Kantor

Narrative Sign Making and Classroom Literacy
  Joanne Golden

Funds of Knowledge: Theory, Research and Practice
  Norma Gonzalez and Luis Moll (eds.)

Early Childhood Classroom Processes: A View through an Ethnographic Lens
  Rebecca Kantor and David P. Fernie (eds.)

Interprofessional and Family Discourses: Voices, Knowledge, and Practice
  Marleen McClelland and Roberta G. Sands

Reading to Children: Developing a Culture of Literacy
  Carolyn Panofsky

Learning Written Genres
  Christine C. Pappas

Writing Ourselves
Mass-Observation and Literacy Practices

Dorothy Sheridan
University of Susex

Brian Street
King's College London

David Bloome
Vanderbilt University

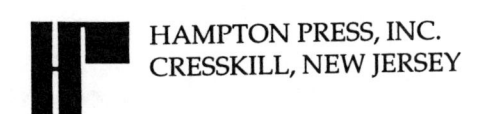

HAMPTON PRESS, INC.
CRESSKILL, NEW JERSEY

Copyright © 2000 by Hampton Press, Inc.

All rights reserved. No part of this publication may be reproduced, stored in a retrieval system, or transmitted in any form or by any means, electronic, mechanical, photocopying, microfilming, recording, or otherwise, without permission of the publisher.

Printed in the United States of America

Library of Congress Cataloging-in-Publication Data

Sheridan, Dorothy.
    Writing ourselves : mass-observation and literacy practices / Dorothy Sheridan, Brian Street, David Bloome
       p. cm. -- (Language & social processes)
    Includes bibliographical references and indexes.
    ISBN 1-57273-277-6 (cl) -- ISBN 1-57273-278-4 (pb)
       1. Literacy--Great Britain--History--20th century. 2. Great Britain--conditions--20th century--Historiography. 3. Social sciences--Research--Great Britain--History--20th century. 4. Public opinion--Great Britain--History--20th century. 5. Social surveys--Great Britain--History--20th century. 6. Mass-Observation. I. Street, Brian V. II. Bloome, David. III. Title. IV. Series.

LC156.G7 S44 2000
302.2'244--dc21

                                            00-040744

Cover photo: A canvasser from the Bolton Labour Party talking to a Bolton resident, 1938. Photograph taken by Humphrey Spender as part of the Worktown Study of Bolton carred out by Mass-Observation, 1937-40. Reproduced with permission of Bolton Art Gallery and Museum.

The letter from Tom Madge, Tom Harrisson and Humphrey Jennings which was published in the *New Statesman* on 30 January 1937 has been reproduced with the permission of Dr Vicky Randall (for Charles Madge), the trustees of the Mass-Observation Archive (for Tom Harrisson) and Mrs Mary-Lou Legg (for Humphrey Jennings). Mrs Legg would like to record that the lettter was drafted in Humphrey Jennings' absence and he did not agree with its contents (personal communication with D. Sheridan, 7 November 1999).

Hampton Press, Inc.
23 Broadway
Cresskill, NJ 07626

Contents

Foreword Shirley Brice Heath	ix
Series Preface	xv
Acknowledgements	xvii
About the Authors	xxi
Introduction: Literacy Theory and Mass-Observation	1
Literacy Practices and Social Life	3
Invisibility of Literacy Practices of Ordinary People	5
Literacy Practices and Mass-Observation	8
The Mass-Observation Project	12
Theorising Literacy: Mass-Observation Project as a Telling Case	13
Outline of the Book	15
How We Have Used the Words "Mass-Observation" and Related Terms	15

SECTION I: AN HISTORICAL CONTEXT OF MASS-OBSERVATION

Introduction to Section I	19
1. Mass-Observation from 1937 to 1981	21
The Historical Origins: Social and Political Contexts	21
The Recruitment of the Panel of Volunteers	32
The Years Between 1950 and 1980	38
The Rehabilitation of Mass-Observation	39
2. Mass-Observation Revived: Writing Britain	43
The Re-Launch	43
Publicity and Funds, 1981-85	47
After the Hiatus, From 1986	51
How People Join Mass-Observation: Advertising and Recruitment	52

Becoming a Mass-Observer	60
The Directives	64
Organisation and Classification of Data	70
Changes and Developments	71
Connections with Other Projects	73
The Contemporary Mass-Observation Project and the Original Mass-Observation	73

3. Mass-Observation and Anthropology — 79

British Anthropology in the Early Twentieth Century	80
Mass-Observation as Anthropology at Home	82
Malinowski and Mass-Observation	85
Firth and Mass-Observation	88
Limitations of the Anthropologists' Critiques	93
Pocock and Mass-Observation	95
Contemporary Anthropology: The Reflexive Turn	103
Mass-Observation as Case Studies	106
Mass-Observation as Literacy Practices	108

SECTION II: DIALOGUES AND WRITING PRACTICES

Introduction to Section II — 115

4. Framing the Dialogues: Literacy Practices — 119

Reading Mass-Observation and the Nature of Knowledge	121
Gathering, Analysing and Writing Up the Data	127
Constructing the Dialogues	132
Final Comments on Constructing Dialogues	134

5. Dialogues About Literacy Practices and the Mass-Observation Project — 137

Mrs Wright (W632)	139
Mrs Friend (F1373)	145
Mr Barrow (B1106)	156
Mrs Safran (B2197)	163
Mrs Martin (M1498)	173
Mr Richards (M1593)	180
Ms McPhail (M2493)	187
Mr Russell (R1671)	195
Mr Reed (R450)	201

SECTION III: ORDINARY PEOPLE WRITING

Introduction to Section III	211
6. The Uses of Writing	213
7. Power, Personhood and Crossings	237
8. Writing Ourselves and Writing Britain	281
Bibliography	293
Appendix Ai: Bibliography of Original Mass-Observation Books	305
Appendix Aii: Recent Anthologies and Edited Material	307
Appendix Aiii: Mass-Observation Occasional Papers Series	309
Appendix Aiv: About the Mass-Observation Archive	313
Appendix Bi: Lists of Topics Covered in Directives Since 1981	315
Appendix Bii: Sample Directives	319
Appendix Biii: Introductory Information for New Recruits	331
Appendix Biv: Pseudonyms and Numbers of Correspondents Cited	335
Appendix C: The Spring Directive 1991	337
Appendix D: Interview Guidance Sheet	343
Author Index	347
Subject Index	351

Foreword

Shirley Brice Heath

> There is no direction. Whither? I
> cannot say. I cannot say
> more than how. The how (the howl) only
> is at my disposal (proposal) : watching—
> colder than stone .
>
> (William Carlos Williams, *Patterson*, Bk. II)

The American poet, William Carlos Williams, penned these lines as an opening to his poetic attempt to capture the present and the past of the ordinary everyday lives that make history. He worried that his work might put onto these lives a direction that was not there in the intentions of the individuals he described. His was a painful process—one in which he often tried to think of himself as simply the observer, the recorder, "watching—colder than stone," and uninvolved in the pace of the ordinary. In the end, Williams' long poem leaves no doubt that all of us are ordinary and the ordinary is history. The irony is that when historians write history, they often try to dispose of the ordinary while also recognizing that any proposal for the future rests very much with what lies in the ordinary.

Had Williams known of the Mass-Observation Archive in Britain, he would have been exceedingly curious about how a group of ordinary people could agree to record daily life around them and capture it in archives. Williams would have applauded this project as one that "watchers" could return to again and again in order to understand both their own links to the ordinary and the evolving patterns of change in daily living. Williams would have further been delighted by the emphasis on "writing ourselves" that centers this book, for detailed here are the almost invisible literacy practices that give lasting meaning to daily events, thoughts, and response of ordinary individuals.

But this book does much more than detail the writing practices, contexts, and values of such individuals. Given here is the intellectual history of the project that has managed for more than six decades to catalogue and make available written correspondence from volunteers in the United Kingdom who detailed their observations on everything from local pub life to the 1981 wedding of Prince Charles and Lady Diana Spencer.

Opening the book is a history of the pioneering efforts of the founders and sustainers of the M-O—a *denkcollectiv* or "thought collective." This term was coined by the scientist Ludwik Fleck in the 1930s in an account he wrote on the "genesis and development of a scientific fact" (Fleck, 1979). In his little monograph, Fleck gave an account of how the modern concept of syphilis and links between syphilis and the Wassermann reaction originated and how the thought collective around these issues worked in the 1930s. His work makes clear what is taken for granted at the end of the twentieth century—every scientific method and stance resulting from research belongs to the community of researchers involved, and its members cultivate a certain kind of exclusiveness that relates both to method and content.

The thought collective behind the Mass-Observation (M-O) was an evolving eclectic community of individuals who exchanged ideas and maintained their intellectual curiosity about how the British were carrying out their daily lives and interpreting the impact of national and international affairs on local life (see Chapter 4). Like members of all thought collectives, those who, since its inception in 1937, have provided the special carrying force for the collection, have often disagreed among themselves about its purposes, direction, and motivations. Too rarely have these individuals stopped to reflect on their own roles in the project. This volume pulls together much of what we know about the zigzag history of M-O and its relations with the public, the media, and academics.

Behind the origin of the Mass-Observation was the view that the project would represent anthropology brought home (see Chapter 3), away from the exotic isles and villages of the far-flung British empire and back to the pubs, factories, streets, and homes of British citizens. Asserting the value of recording the ordinary lives of such individuals represented a dual challenge to anthropologists who had previously focused very much on the exotic or different behaviors of faraway groups. This book lays out just how the perspective on the value of this double focus fared over the years and how changing views on methodology, "science," and uses of research both moved the project along and threatened its existence.

In many ways this book offers an intellectual case study of how a research project can become embedded in national politics, economic market pressures, and the ebb and flow of personal relationships between academics and journalists. Particularly useful in this intellectual history, however, is the unique perspective it offers on the social genesis of the thought collective as participants over the years maintained relations with mass media interests as well as to the curiosity of the public at large about the lives of ordinary British citizens. Fleck characterized the layers of a thought collective as those of a concentric circle moving out from the center of scientists who conceive and direct the project to layers that lead eventually to (often distant) others eager to learn just how science might have some practical value or local interest. The history of the M-O reminds us just how the genesis of any collective evolves, has its own internal inconsistencies and disagreements, and seemingly "matures." Moreover, both contemporaneously and subsequently, individuals framing that history continue to shape and reshape origin myths and subsequent tales about its genesis. This ongoing history and involvement of individuals contributes to current reception and maintenance of the project. Periodic remakings of the M-O—in the popular press and in academic rumor circuits—have made the artifacts and words of the project continue to give off messages of difference (see Chapter 2).

Clear also within this book is the extent to which the workings of a group of researchers and their reception by the public and by members of different professions that may seem related result, in large part, from acts of serendipity. A combination of accidents created M-O as a major repository of historical materials, but through the years, unplanned actions and connections among individuals have given it shape and have made it very much a part of British awareness. Over the years, readers of the British press have become accustomed to seeing notes about M-O in their newspapers, and those who have participated have themselves helped spread word about the Archives. The continuous recruitment of individuals to write for M-O—as *correspondents* and not as *respondents*—also ensures that this project of history remains alive and ever-changing. Its periods of inactivity and near-closure illustrate the familiar story of how pragmatic demands for government funds and foundational support so often over-power requests for support of archival collections and the processes necessary to sustain these.

Myths, other than those of its origin, have grown and been reshaped around M-O. The quirks of particular personalities, as well as the expansive reputation of some, such as Humphrey Spender whose genius for photography was part of M-O, have helped set the project in the public collective memory and current view. The actual historical development of this thought collective has, over the decades, been subject to particular career ambitions of individuals as well as to the goals of adopting institutions. From being claimed by anthropologists at the outset, M-O evolved as a sociology project and a mass marketing tool. Today, it combines these various historical shapings and meets the needs of several institutions and discipline-based groups of scholars. Various groups have, according to their sense of the usefulness of M-O to them, claimed different degrees of responsibility for the materials.

However, this volume gives us not only a retrospective view on the ways of social science and the interaction of any such project with public media and public opinion. It also illustrates just how academic disciplines have developed a need to assert particular claims over the priority of certain methods and types of data. Just what M-O is has often centered, as it still does today, on debates about the methods used to collect the materials. Some view the detailed writings and reflections of individuals as relatively useless, because these individuals were not chosen randomly and cannot be reduced to a quantitative entity. Others regard the data as skewed, because of the self-selection bias inherent in those who chose to respond to M-O requests for material.

Still others, closer to the discipline of anthropology, regard M-O as intensely valuable precisely because of the self-selection. Literacy (and several other topics) turn in on themselves here to give us a view of particular phenomena from the inside out: participants use their own writing to reflect on their uses of reading and writing. In keeping with this focus on participants' own voices, practically half of the present volume is given over to the writing of M-O correspondents, (see especially Section 2). Autobiography, case study, memoir, and ethnography all come together to make up the corpus of M-O writing. Individual accounts have often become parts of autobiographies, and, in some cases, the primary material for biographies and historical studies. For other scholars, the materials offer opportunities for comparative case studies of individuals within groups rarely treated in "standard" accounts of British history—women, gays, and workers, for example. Always, these individuals present themselves with regard to their particular spaces and time, giving further indication of the extent to which accidents of place and chronology shape individual lives and the character of a community, as well as the writing practices that surround remembering and reacting.

Finally, this book lets us recognize what we need to be told often: materials of the past do anticipate many issues we believe we have only recently discovered. Chosen for illustration of this point in this volume is the theme of literacy, but with primary emphasis here on writing rather than on reading. Here, especially in sections two and three, we see just how social literacies emerged over the decades and how individuals contributing to M-O then and now view their own productions of texts and the uses of their materials by those producing still other kinds of writing. Reflections on the value of literacy for lifelong learning come through in the variegated patterns of time in which individuals perceive writing to be important to them. As tools of mediation and activity, the journals or M-O responses to directives enabled individuals to reflect on their own learning across several decades as well as types of occasions for learning and for using knowledge and for incorporating direct experiences (see Section 2). The writings of M-O participants, more often than not, need to be strongly linked to what the individual correspondents say about their own perceptions of themselves as represented beings, as individuals within a larger collection of people. The sense of what it means to be heard and read for ordinary people comes through again and again in the accounts of social literacy given here.

It is useful, particularly for readers from the United States and Europe, to speculate on how it is that nothing directly comparable to the M-O project exists within their national treasures. What was it about Great Britain in the late 1930s that turned the interests of a few men to collecting the thoughts and ways of ordinary people? Was this original interest sustained over the next two decades by the sense of vulnerability Britain suffered in World War II and the ensuing struggle to compete within a rapidly developing global economy? Did fixed patterns of linkage between levels of schooling and possible employment outcomes contribute to the comfort with which Britishers write and speak of social class—such a frequent topic within the M-O archival materials? It has long been possible for residents of regions of Britain or even sections of its cities to speak with pride of their long and strong ties to working-class culture; many aspects of British life best known around the world derive from well-known institutions and habits identified with such workers.

The ease with which M-O correspondents lay out their class backgrounds and their sense of distinction from those above and below them will strike American readers as odd. No nation has been as uncomfortable with social class as the United States, because of the nation's persistent claim to equal opportunity for social and regional mobility by all its citizens. Hence to take pride in location within any class except the middle is to express a kind of self-satisfaction that seems to defy the myth of equity. Archives within the United States have only pockets of memories from the ordinary people about whom the poet William Carlos Williams wanted to write. Individualism and the cult of the individual hero, leader, or spokesperson as prime material for creating histories of events make up the bulk of American archival materials. Second to this mass are records of groups, often voluntary and formed to meet special needs, but even here, such groups or organizations often center around key individual members or leaders. It has been left to local historical societies to locate, catalogue, and maintain (generally with little or no governmental support unless linked to a prominent figure or event) small versions of collections that resemble those of the British M-O. Only the occasional small-town library or historical society will have long-running writings done by farmers, teachers, factory workers, housewives, sailors. Hence the librarians in every small town across the United States, as well as every social historian who has tried to find records to reconstruct the thoughts and actions of ordinary people, will read of the M-O with envy.

Europeans have tended to write and speak of social class in terms of particular occupations or societal niches linked to region, language, or dialect. But they have also had perhaps greater success than the United States in keeping archives of organizations and groups that embrace the ordinary in membership and types of activity. Traditions of social history that capture the mundane and the magical of daily routines, as well as the rhythm and pace of country or city life, have long been of great attraction to European social scientists. Thus European readers will find in the M-O primary materials, as well as within many secondary writings these made possible, a familiar ring. But social scientists across Europe will also find in this volume and others from the M-O an abundance of perspectives and a system for organising and storing such records that is to be envied. Most evident to both Americans and Europeans reading this book will be the impossibility within their own nations of creating the rich stories of writing given here for Britain.

The poet William Carlos Williams would surely see the M-O as a combination of the dilemmas surrounding disposal/proposal. The materials of M-O, though part of a *proposal*, that is, written in response to public requests as well as directives regarding content, resulted from a *disposal* of will and time from correspondents: hence women and retirees have contributed a large proportion of the archived records. Furthermore, many of the writings over the years show how certain *proposals* that individuals made for relationships, life courses, or organizational changes aborted or went astray (see Chapter 6). More often than not, what became available to one's *disposal* determined the course of individual *proposals*. Furthermore, particular historical and economical conditions disposed individual correspondents to choose one or another slant on a topic at one point in time, while several years later, they themselves found their earlier responses quite curious and even inexplicable. The pinch between extreme contingency and planned consistent pattern catches all of us, and in our reflections about ourselves, we are forced to take note of both. The focus of this volume on writing by individuals who both create and derive social meaning from their literacy enables us to see clearly just how important the "taking of note" is to the complex process of self-knowledge. We come here face-to-face again with William's lament that we cannot know the "whither" of our direction. We can, however, know much about the *how*—those ways in which as writers, we find a measure of temporary control over direction, and we move closer to accepting our ability to be "watchers" of ourselves.

Series Preface

LANGUAGE AND SOCIAL PROCESSES

Judith Green, Editor
University of California at Santa Barbara

Associate Editors

Ginger Weade
Ohio University

Carol Dixon
University of California
at Santa Barbara

Language and Social Processes provides a forum for scholarly work that makes visible the ways in which everyday life is accomplished through discourse processes among individuals and groups. Volumes will examine how language-in-use influences the access of individuals and culturally, ethnically, and linguistically diverse groups to social institutions, and how knowledge construction and social participation across diverse social settings is accomplished through discourse.

Studies in education and other social institutions are invited from a variety of perspectives including those of anthropology, communication, education, linguistics, literary theory, psychology, and sociology. Manuscripts are encouraged that involve theoretical treatments of relevant issues, present in-depth analyses of particular social groups and institutional settings, or present comparative studies across social groups, settings or institutions. Send inquiries to: Judith Green, Series Editor, Graduate School of Education, University of California, Santa Barbara, CA 93106.

Acknowledgements

Our first acknowledgement and deepest appreciation are to the Mass-Observation correspondents who allowed us to interview them and who joined with us in exploring the nature of reading and writing both in the Mass-Observation Project and in everyday life. In order to maintain their privacy and in accordance with their wishes and the policies of the Mass-Observation Project, we do not reveal their names. It is, of course, their words and their insights—along with those of the other seven hundred plus Mass-Observation correspondents—that make up the heart of this book.

We want to give special thanks to those whose interviews and writings we have highlighted in Chapter 5: Mrs Wright (W632), Mrs Friend (F1373), Mr Barrow (B1106), Mrs Safran (B2197), Mrs Martin (M1498), Mr Richards (M1593), Ms McPhail (M2493), Mr Russell (R1671) and Mr Reed (R450). We greatly appreciate the extra effort that you have given and your tolerance of what must have seemed to be endless questions and conversations. We hope that we have fairly and respectfully represented you. We have appreciated your feedback on our efforts.

We also owe a debt of gratitude to the Friends of the Mass-Observation Archive whose financial support has made the continued existence of the Mass-Observation Project possible. Most Archive Friends are also correspondents—that is, they not only send money but also their writings; others are researchers, too. Their contribution has been invaluable.

We also want to thank the University of Sussex, which gave Brian Street and Dorothy Sheridan sabbatical leave during the period when we were setting up the research and conducting interviews; and the Economic and Social Research Council, whose award for the one-year project, "Literacy Practices and the Mass-Observation Project" [R000 23 3728], supported the research during 1992 and 1993. We also acknowledge King's College for their support of Brian Street's involvement in the research project since 1997.

Several institutions helped support David Bloome's involvement in the research project and in co-authoring the book. David Bloome began working on the research project during a sabbatical leave from the University of Massachusetts at Amherst, where he was a professor in the School of Education. The U.S.-U.K. Fulbright Foundation provided a grant to David Bloome during his sabbatical leave, and the University of Sussex Institute for Continuing and Professional Education provided an intellectual "home" during the sabbatical leave.

Over the years, there have been many people who have worked at the Mass-Observation Archive or been closely associated with it at the University of Sussex and they have all, in different ways, made this book possible. We would particularly like to thank Joy Eldridge and Judy Pickering, who have been part of the present Archive team for many years now, and Tim Graves, who has come to the Archive more recently; thanks, too, to Julie Applin, Raymond Hickman and Becky Garrett for their analytical work on the Mass-Observation data; Anna Jarvis, Emma Nash, Spencer Gasson and especially Susan Hutton for transcribing interview tapes; Shirley Stay and Pat Fuller for photocopying assistance; and Ian Budden, William Alexander, Sheila Shardlow and Michelle Viccars for computing advice and support. Adrian Peasgood, the University Librarian and Trustee of the Mass-Observation Archive, has consistently championed the work of the Mass-Observation Archive and we are grateful for his kind support and interest. We have also benefited from the friendly support and encouragement of our academic colleagues and friends at the University of Sussex: Alistair Thomson, Jenny Shaw, Janice Winship, Alun Howkins, John Jacobs, Rod Kedward, Peter Dickens and Sue Wright (now at the University of Birmingham).

During 1992 and 1993, Brian Street and Dorothy Sheridan organised a series of seminars, many of which addressed issues raised in this book and which provided a forum for us to discuss our ideas and plans as well as hear about complementary and related work from our invited guests and speakers. In particular, we would like to mention Jane Mace, Hermine Scheeres, Dorothy Jerrome, Harold Rosen, Martin Hammersley, Liz Stanley, Celia Roberts, Roger Hewitt, Gunther Kress, Mike Baynham, Roz Ivanic, David Barton, Tony Kushner and Gemma Moss. There are also many colleagues who have been interested in Mass-Observation for many years and whose ideas have influenced and informed our work: notably Angus Calder, Penny Summerfield, Nick Stanley, Tom Jeffery and, of course, David Pocock, who initiated the new Mass-Observation Project in 1981.

We also appreciate the support of Peabody College of Vanderbilt University and the Department of Teaching and Learning for supporting David Bloome's continued involvement in the research and writing. Special thanks to Rosemary Washington for transcribing data, typing and many other clerical and supportive activities that are important to the research project and to the writing. We also want to acknowledge the contribution of Sara Hill, who helped co-author parts of Chapter 6 and contributed in many other ways to the writing of the book; and we want to acknowledge Stephanie Power and Sheila Otto, who helped proofread the book manuscript.

We have deeply appreciated the support and encouragement of Shirley Heath and Judith Green. Shirley Heath met with us several times to help us identify issues and put the research project and book into perspectives that helped highlight contributions to a broad range of fields. We are honoured that she agreed to write the foreword to the book, and in so doing, helped us make clear that the insights offered by the Mass-Observation correspondents and the issues raised do not just have "local" importance but are significant to people anywhere who are interested in the social and cultural dynamics involved in writing, defining knowledge, and the conduct of inquiry. Judith Green, the editor of the series within which this book is published, immediately saw the potential contribution of our research and of the Mass-Observation Project to broadening definitions of writing and education. We also appreciate her careful editing and her help in clarifying our often muddled explanations.

Finally, we want to acknowledge the support, encouragement, and advice of our close friends and families whose lives we constantly disrupted and whom we imposed upon in many ways in order to accomplish the research and writing that has resulted in this book: Barry Stierer, Laurie Katz and Chloe, Alice and Nicholas Street.

About the Authors

David Bloome is a Professor of Education in the Language and Literacy Program of Peabody College of Vanderbilt University. His interests include literacy practices in classrooms and communities, and young children's spoken and written narrative development. He is the co-editor of *Linguistics and Education: An International Research Journal* and the co-author of *Discourse Analysis and the Study of Classroom Language and Literacy Events* (in press, with B. Morton, N. Shuart-Faris, S. Otto and S. Power) and *Reading Words* (1994, with B. Stierer) and editor of *Classrooms and Literacy* (1989), *Literacy and Schooling* (1987) and *Students as Researchers of Culture and Language in Their Own Communities* (1998, with A. Egan-Robertson).

Dorothy Sheridan is the Archivist at the Mass-Observation Archive and joint Director of the newly established Centre for Life History Research, both at the University of Sussex, England. Her interests include life history "research," women's history especially the period of the Second World War in Britain, and non-élite writing and autobiography (she is President of the European Association for Autobiography). She is a member of the editorial board of *Women's History Review* and *Family and Community History* and teaches on a variety of courses at Sussex and elsewhere on life history, research methods and the use of archives, including the MA programme: Life History Research. Publications include *Speak for Yourself* (1984), *Among You Taking Notes: The Wartime Diary of Naomi Mitchison* (1985), *Mass-Observation at the Movies* (1987), *Wartime Women* (1990 to be re-issued 2000).

Brian V. Street is Professor of Language in Education at King's College, London University and Visiting Professor of Education in the Graduate School of Education, University of Pennsylvania. He undertook anthropological fieldwork on literacy and education in Iran during the 1970s, and has since written and lectured extensively on literacy practices; in South Africa, Australia, Canada, the United States, and so on. He is best known for *Literacy in Theory and Practice* (1985), edited *Cross-Cultural Approaches to Literacy* (1993) and brought out a collection of his essays with Longman under the title *Social Literacies* (1995), which was cited in his receipt of the David S Russell award for distinguished research by the National Council of Teachers of English in the United States. He has been involved in writing/editing 10 books and has published over 60 scholarly articles. He is currently editing *Literacy and Development: Ethnographic Perspectives* (2000) as part of a commitment to link ethnographic-style research on the cultural dimension of literacy with contemporary practice in education and in development.

He has been awarded a number of research projects in the area of literacy practices: 1992-1993 (with D. Sheridan and D. Bloome) "Literacy Practices and the Mass-Observation Project" (ESRC); 1995-1996 (with Mary Lea): "Perspectives on Academic Literacies: An Institutional Approach" (ESRC); 1999-2002 (with D. Baker) "School and Community Numeracy Practices " (Leverhulme Trust); with D. Baker & Eve Gregory (2000-2002) "Literacy Practices at Home and at School."

Introduction:
Literacy Theory and Mass-Observation

> The category of research—like the canons of knowledge in general—is by no means a transparent one. It is highly constructed, often authoritarian, and has a hidden political agenda. . . . All in all, I would prefer a broad definition of research, one that recognises it can be done by people other than professional academics and for different types of audience . . . (Deborah Cameron, 1992, p. 124)

We are interested in the Mass-Observation Project as a way of understanding the nature of writing in Britain in the late twentieth century. Our interest in writing is inseparable from our interest in the social conditions within which people write, the social purposes they use writing for, and how writing fits in with their life histories, all of which define writing itself. We are also interested in how writing is implicated in power relations, both those involved in the daily lives of people and those among people and the dominant institutions of our society. We are interested in how writing is used to establish identities and to transform social situations and relationships.

We view the Mass-Observation Project as a unique institutional context for writing. Mass-Observation began as an attempt to establish an "anthropology of our own people" (Madge, 1937). From the beginning, Mass-Observation involved ordinary people observing and writing about life in Britain, and collecting those writings for future use by researchers, the media, students and the public in general.

Anthropologists in Britain had already been studying foreign people and cultures for many years before the emergence of Mass-Observation. As part of the intellectual, social and political milieu of the times, the founders of Mass-Observation believed that the methods of

2 INTRODUCTION

anthropology might be used to provide representations of life in Britain beyond the portrayals of the press and other establishment media. Although anthropology was one of the most important influences, throughout its history Mass-Observation has been influenced by a broad range of disciplines and intellectual movements including sociology, life history, literary theory, feminist social theory and political theory, as well as social anthropology. Thus, Mass-Observation was and still is positioned in a way that forces it to grapple with the contradictions among various disciplines and the different ways they define knowledge. Mass-Observation also had to grapple with the difficulties involved in using ordinary people as observers and writers of field observations and reports. In some cases the observations were self-observations and reflective; in other cases, observations of others. To what degree could the observations, interpretations and writings by untrained ordinary people be trusted? What kind of knowledge was being produced by the efforts of Mass-Observation? Mass-Observation has found itself grappling with some of the most difficult and problematic issues facing social science research. Thus, our interest in the writing people do for Mass-Observation cannot be separated from questions about the nature of research and knowledge.

Although the Mass-Observation Archive contains hundreds of photographs and other visual material, Mass-Observation is primarily about writing. Writing is what people do and it is also the product of their efforts. On the one hand, what people write and how they do it is influenced by Mass-Observation itself, by the directions it gives, the demands it makes on people, and by what people perceive Mass-Observation to be. On the other hand, Mass-Observation is defined by what people use it for, how and what they write, and by the demands people make on it, especially those who write for it. Thus, Mass-Observation, both historically and contemporarily, exists in a space that is both part of dominant academic institutions (it is housed at the University of Sussex, used by academics, and claims contributions to the accumulation of academic knowledge) and yet is also outside dominant institutions. It is constituted by the writings, observations and insights of ordinary people who both individually and collectively make claims about the purposes, practices and policies of Mass-Observation. Such an institutional position makes inquiry about literacy practices and Mass-Observation a particularly useful telling case for gaining insights into the nature and relationships of writing, knowledge, power and social life in Britain. We have approached our inquiry about literacy practices and the Mass-Observation Project by acknowledging the intimate relationship between literacy practices and social life.

LITERACY PRACTICES AND SOCIAL LIFE

The word "literacy" conjures up images of people struggling with written words, teachers giving lessons in the alphabet, and pupils reading the classic texts. But this is not what we mean by literacy. By literacy, we mean the ways that people use written language in their daily lives. As people conduct their daily business, whether at home, at work, at school, or elsewhere, they use written language to get things done, to communicate with others, to establish and maintain social relationships, to enact rituals, and to create meaning. Literacy is not a thing or a skill separable from life nor, given our definition of literacy does it make sense to talk of illiteracy. The term "literacy" is a heuristic, a way to focus attention on one aspect of social life.

We are not alone in viewing literacy in this way. Indeed, over the past few decades there has been a movement away from viewing literacy as a decontextualised, psychological skill toward viewing it as a social phenomenon—a set of social and cultural practices. Sometimes referred to as the "New Literacy Studies" (cf., Gee, 1990; Street, 1995), the study of literacy has become the study of particular social and cultural events and practices that vary both within and across social groups and societies. One implication of the New Literacy Studies is that one can never just study literacy, one is always studying literacy and social life. And, as we argue throughout this book, the study of social life cannot be reduced to abstract structures, but must lie close to what people do, what social meanings it has for them, and what social consequences it has for them.

How, when and where people use written language depends a great deal on their shared expectations and on how social institutions "embody" written language. That is, in any specific situation, people will have shared expectations—a shared cultural model—about what is an appropriate use of written language, how the written language should be interpreted (what interpretative framework should be brought to bear on the writing), who should play what role in the writing event, and the implied social positions and relationships created among the people in the writing event. But at the same time, the social institution within which the writing or reading is taking place influences how it is done by structuring the physical and interpersonal environment; or more simply put, who is likely to be there and what materials and tools one is likely to find. For example, in classrooms, one is likely to find many children and an adult, generally constrained to stay within the room, using crayons, pencils, paper. At home, at church, in the workplace, there are different configurations of people, different material resources available, and different expectations about how and when people should use written language. As importantly, there are different expectations about who is authorised to do what: to write, to read, to establish an authorised interpretation, and so forth. A great deal of work often goes into the structuring of institutional environments to support certain ways of using written language and constraining others. We use the term literacy practices as a shorthand way of noting two important dimensions of uses of written language. First, reading and writing are always social and cultural events. Whether there is a group of people present or a single person, whether the written language has an audience or not, reading and writing are always embedded in and defined by what is happening socially. Second, there are established social practices for the use of written language in particular types of situations; and thus, there are similarities in how written language is used over time and across different people within a particular type of event. A literacy "event," then, may be any event involving written language (Heath, 1982, p. 93), but it only takes on meaning with respect to the literacy practices that it draws upon and gives expression to. A single literacy event, as we shall see, may draw on a number of different literacy practices.

An important dimension of the "New Literacy Studies" is analysis of how written language is used to assign social identities or social positions to people within such an event. The term social position is often used instead of social identities, as the latter suggests a more permanent identity independent of situation, while the term social position emphasises the socially constructed and situation-specific nature of identity. Whenever people engage in a literacy event, they do so from a social position (Besnier, 1993; Brodkey, 1987; Clark & Ivanic, 1997; Fairclough, 1992; Ivanic, 1994). The social positions that people take up depend upon the various social positions available within the particular literacy practices and event. In a classroom reading group, for example, the positions available are usually teacher or pupil group member and the practices usually include academic literacy practices and school literacy. They are both taken up and assigned by others. Social positions are often negotiated and contested, and may evolve and change as an event progresses. While the positions available and the nature of the positions are not wholly determined "a priori," neither are they newly invented. Both as a group and as individuals, people may contest what positions are available, how they are assigned, and what their nature is. Such contesting, however, does not negate the thesis that people engage in writing events from social positions associated with the event and the various literacy practices and texts involved.

The social positions from which people write provide warrants and constraints for what they may and may not do (including what and how they write), and also constitute part of the interpretative context for both the texts created and for the writing event itself. The availability of social positions within a literacy event and a set of literacy practices, who may take them up, and what warrants and constraints are imposed, may involve issues of gender, race, sexual orientation, class and other broad-based social dimensions by which people are frequently defined (cf., Egan-Robertson, 1994; Rockhill, 1993). However, even these more broadly based social identities are socially constructed (or reconstructed) within specific events.

One of the problems with the term "literacy practices" is that it may give the impression that the practices are static or deterministic. There certainly may be efforts to stabilise a set of literacy practices. The people in the event may hold each other accountable for using written language in a particular way. However, people are continually modifying established literacy practices, adapting them to new situations, and, at times, straightforwardly challenging and sabotaging established literacy practices (for example, see Clark and Ivanic's work, 1997, on how students challenge their tutors' notions of academic literacy practices by contesting the use of impersonal and stuffy language). Mass-Observation writing provides a classic case of such contestation over what counts such as literacy in writing ourselves into history. Therefore, rather than view literacy practices as a static set of situated ways of using written language, it may be more useful to think of literacy practices as an evolving and dynamic set of social practices that are always at a nexus of processes of social change, struggle and stability.

The challenge for researchers interested in literacy is to describe the social, cultural and intellectual events and practices within which written language is used. It is not enough just to describe the forms of written language used and the immediate social context, although both forms and immediate context need to be described. The broader institutional context, its ideological impetus and history must also be described, as well as the dynamics between specific, local literacy practices and the broader institutional and ideological contexts. However, the description of both local events and practices and institutional and ideological contexts is made difficult by the complex relationships of social institutions to each other, the co-mingling of institutions, and the supplanting of one institution by another.

INVISIBILITY OF LITERACY PRACTICES OF ORDINARY PEOPLE

We focus on the Mass-Observation Project for two reasons. As we have argued elsewhere, the everyday literacy practices of ordinary people are nearly invisible (Barton, Bloome, Street & Sheridan, 1993). (In Chapter 6 we discuss the complexities in defining "ordinary people".) The mass media portrays an illiterate and aliterate population, and politicians, bordering on demagoguery, castigate schools for producing pupils who cannot read or write. Our research and that of others studying literacy practices in everyday life (e.g., Barton & Hamilton, 1998) shows that there is a great deal of writing going on in everyday life, writing outside of school, work and "established" publishing. Yet, very little is known about the scope, nature, use and social contexts of writing in everyday life. Little attention is paid to writing in everyday life—it is frequently not even considered to be writing-and the people who produce such writing are not usually considered writers. When ordinary people write, there are very few contexts in which their writing is acknowledged and in which they are acknowledged as writers The example of Mass-Observation is one of the few contexts where they become visible.

Research studies such as the writing in the community studies at Lancaster University (Barton & Hamilton, 1998; Barton & Ivanic, 1991; Hamilton, Barton & Ivanic, 1994) have begun to challenge the invisibility of writing in everyday life. However, much more work needs to be done. Our study of literacy practices and the Mass-Observation Project is part of a broader effort to make visible the writing and literacy practices of ordinary people in their everyday lives. For example, through our interviews with the people who write for the Mass-Observation Project we were able to record how people organised space and time for writing. Mrs Friend (F1373),[1] who describes her writing in Chapter 5, has a dedication to letter writing. She may write upwards of a dozen long letters a day, encouraging others to write as well. She writes in her living room, yet there is very little overt evidence of so much writing happening there: just chairs, sofa, end tables, a television, a dining table. However, hidden in the end tables are her writing supplies, and hidden elsewhere are a platform for writing, files of letters and reference books. She takes these out in the evening when her husband and she sit down in front of the television, and the room becomes a letter writing workshop. Her writing, except to a few who know her and those who receive her letters, is invisible, but it is very much a part of her life and the life of her family and friends. To not see the writing is to not see important parts of her life and to overlook ways in which she acts upon the world in which she lives.

---

[1]Mrs Friend is a pseudonym for one of the Mass-Observation writers who will appear frequently in this book. All Mass-Observation writers are given a number when they join the Project (in this case F1373), which they use when they write to maintain their anonymity.

The invisibility of the writing of ordinary people in their everyday lives is not just a technical matter corrected by better research methods, more field studies, or more sensitive researchers. It is also a power issue. We live in a society that has reserved "legitimate" writing for a select few. Novelists, journalists, academics, government officials, poets and a small number of others are viewed as legitimate writers; their writing carries authority. The power of their writing—its ability to define reality, to set before the public the questions for debate, to inscribe emotions and morality in narrative, to make law and order—derives in part from their connections with institutions of power (for example, mass media, universities, government, business) and in part from the small number of people who are allowed to claim the identity of writer.

A great deal of effort goes into making the writing of this small group visible and the writing of ordinary people invisible. The difficulties of getting a book published create an artistic hierarchy that restricts the label "author" and "writer" to a select few, and the awards, by-lines, bibliographies and reference books (for example, social science and humanities index, citation indexes, compendiums and anthologies of literature) identify whose writing is and is not worthy. A whole range of procedures and activities conducted by publishers, book distributors, shops and libraries perpetuate and promote the predominance of certain kinds of books (and authors). Schools play an important part in creating visibility and invisibility, defining long before adulthood who is and who is not a writer.

Schools have not always played the role of defining writing as something reserved for an élite. Howard's (1991) historical study of learning to write shows that many writing practices employed in the late nineteenth century in Britain eschew the dominant role of school in learning. Conversely, Street and Street (1991) analyse the "schooling of literacy" in classroom practices to illustrate how a restricted model of what counts as literacy is constructed and woven into everyday schooling practices. Grammar lessons, composition studies and educational standards marginalise all but a few who can apply those lessons, studies and standards to their writing; but most importantly it is the structure of writing education itself that makes clear that writing and writers are graded. The result is that most people feel that they are not writers and that their writing is not legitimate or worthy of note.

It takes an extraordinarily strong character and perseverance to counter the structure of visibility and invisibility, to see oneself as a writer and one's writing as worthy when few of the social institutions in society support such a view (and indeed may actively support just the opposite). Although they are few in number, organisations and programmes such as community writing projects and worker writing projects are a direct challenge to élitist views of writers and writing, asserting and supporting the efforts of ordinary people as writers of their own histories and lives (Mace, 1995). To make visible and legitimate the writing of ordinary people in their everyday lives would eradicate the privileged status given to the few, and open up another venue for people to exercise power over their own lives. And thus, the maintenance of invisibility is a matter of control and power. The data on writing in the Mass-Observation Project that we discuss in this book challenges this invisibility and the control associated with it.

LITERACY PRACTICES AND MASS-OBSERVATION

The invisibility of the everyday writing of which Mass-Observation is evidence derives to some extent from popular images of reading and writing, including the notions that reading is "in decline," that "people don't write anymore," that "standards of literacy are falling," that there is more "illiteracy" than before (OECD, 1995; Street, 1997; Wray, 1997). This image is often set against a "High Culture" view of writing as "literary" and "accomplished" that sets the standard for what it means to be "literate"—as in many cultures, the word for literate in English can mean both the practical skills of reading and writing and the cultural standards by which "civilised" society is judged (Street, 1984). However, between the "high" literacy of literary or professional endeavour and the literacy "difficulties" and "illiteracy" that dominate media discourses, there is another level of activity—the everyday social practices of reading and writing that perhaps represent a key feature of literacy in contemporary society, despite the dominant images.

The study of literacy practices and the Mass-Observation Project can tell us a great deal about the "social facts" of this everyday literacy in contemporary Britain. Many of the people who write for the Mass-Observation Project appear to write a great deal; the Mass-Observation Project gives a particular form and structure to writing processes that are already going on in other contexts. The data that we have collected in our research on literacy practices and the Mass-Observation Project do two things in relation to this phenomenon: first, they establish evidence for the social fact itself; in this sense they represent a "factual" kind of ethnography, which we discuss in more detail in Chapter 3. Once we know more about both the practices and the conceptions of literacy evident in the Mass-Observation collection, we will be in a better position to develop further research that might address how general the phenomenon of "everyday" writing is, whether the Mass-Observation cohorts are distinctive, and to ask questions about other bodies of writers in contemporary Britain who might be focused on other social institutions and procedures (cf., Barton & Hamilton, 1998; Barton & Ivanic, 1991; Clark & Ivanic, 1997).

But the Mass-Observation writing is also evidence of a different kind: it involves analytic commentary by the writers themselves on their own lives and is reflective about some of the characteristics of their own "everyday" writing itself; it asks and seeks to answer questions about what are its purposes and what are the social processes involved in its construction. This is the second set of insights provided by our data on literacy practices and the Mass-Observation Project. The people who write for the Mass-Observation Project become researchers themselves by commenting on (and theorising) their own writing practices. This usage corresponds to Cameron's broad definition of research with which we began this chapter, one that recognises that research can be done by people other than professional academics. This is closer to the reflexive ethnography that has come to dominate the discipline of anthropology in recent years. Through their personal knowledge and experience, the Mass-Observation writers provide insights into the nature of literacy that are not apparent in either the dominant discourse or in much of the academic research literature. More locally, such an analysis might also help us to "read" the Archive: if we know what kind of writing it is, then when we read responses to different directives, we might be able to interpret them in the light of what we now know about what the respondents themselves are trying to achieve through their writing.

Beyond countering invisibility and establishing the social fact of writing, there is another reason for studying literacy practices and the Mass-Observation Project that makes our study different from the studies of writing in the community cited earlier. The Mass-Observation Project occupies an unusual location among social institutions. It straddles the boundaries between establishment institutions such as the university, academic disciplines, the media (including the BBC) and what one of the original Mass-Observation founders called "ordinary, hard working folk" (Madge & Harrisson, 1939b, p. 3).

This unusual location raises epistemological questions such as the following: what is the nature of the knowledge contained in the Mass-Observation Project? Is it legitimate knowledge? Reliable? Valid? Scientific? As we discuss in detail in Chapter 3, it was exactly these questions that were raised by some anthropologists during the early days of Mass-Observation in the 1930s, and that still get asked. As is already apparent, anthropologists in particular were concerned about the nature of Mass-Observation and wrote about it, both supportively and critically, at the time. It is because of this interest and concern and the profound questions raised by thinking of Mass-Observation from an anthropological perspective, that we devote a whole chapter of this book to describing and analysing the anthropologists' views both then and now (see Chapter 3). Broadly, we conclude that Mass-Observation at its inception was very like the anthropological enterprise in attempting to give voice to people who were otherwise invisible and marginalised in academic circles, as were the non-Western societies which anthropologists usually studied.

But Mass-Observation was different from the anthropology of the day in that it not only treated ordinary people as its subjects but also collaborated with them as fellow researchers. Mass-Observers not only gave data about their own lives to the experts but were themselves responsible for the collection and analysis of social data around them; they were both subjects of research and researchers themselves. It was this that upset some anthropologists of the day, whose critiques we explore in some detail because of their importance for our understanding both of the provenance of Mass-Observation and its significance today. For some of the same questions still arise, regarding the authority over knowledge of experts and of ordinary people, and Mass-Observation can provide concrete evidence of the complexity of such issues and their salience in contemporary British society, not only in the academic world. Indeed, the academic world has been changing in regard to its claims to authority, and while many still adhere to the traditional view of academic authority over knowledge, others, particularly in anthropology, have taken a more "reflexive turn" (Clifford, 1988).

From this new perspective, traditional claims to knowledge are themselves aspects of a particular culture and its power relations and should not be taken at face value. It is from this more relativist and open perspective that the present account is written, again drawing upon anthropology amongst other disciplines as did the founders of Mass-Observation, but now a rather different anthropology in a rather different academic climate. While other disciplines have been important in the development of Mass-Observation, as we detail in Chapters 1 and 2, the particular emphasis we place upon anthropology derives from this twofold history: that anthropology and anthropologists played an important part in the emergence of Mass-Observation; and that anthropology provides an important underpinning to our own perspective on both Mass-Observation and on literacy as we research and write this account.

The questions raised by exploring literacy practices and Mass-Observation from this perspective draw attention to a boundary line between establishment institutions, in this case academic disciplines, and ordinary people. Although, as we have noted, there has been a reflective turn in the social sciences that has caused many researchers to question their own practices and writing, in general academic disciplines in the social sciences are still concerned with the accumulation of knowledge and truth. Academic disciplines develop theoretical constructs, methods and operations to claim knowledge. They separate themselves from the folk theories and methods of ordinary people by claiming "scientific" authority for their knowledge. Similarly, academic disciplines structure a hierarchy of truth; scientific truth takes precedence over folk knowledge. Thus, when ordinary people claim to provide knowledge, academic disciplines examine their constructs, methods and operations in a particularly critical way. To the extent that the constructs, methods and operations differ from those of the academic discipline, the legitimacy of the knowledge provided is called into question. Conversely, of course, academic disciplines do not themselves go unchallenged. Ordinary people, including those who write for Mass-Observation, challenge the legitimacy of researchers to construct valid knowledge about lives and worlds from which they are so far removed. So too the language of academic research may be challenged as also far removed from the language of everyday life. Knowledge is contested.

These challenges to legitimate knowledge are also a challenge to writing. It is frequently the case that writing is viewed as a transparent vehicle for communicating knowledge. From that perspective, the only question that can be asked is whether the writing accurately represents the knowledge. Scientific writing is taken as the epitome of accuracy, while the writing of ordinary people is taken as contaminated by subjective views, personalising accounts, narrative structures and emotional commentary (Olson, 1994). While these views have themselves been called into question by anthropologists and others who have treated academic practices as cultural practices (Collins, 1991; Street, 1995), it is still fair to say that academic institutions and other dominant institutions (such as the media) view with suspicion the writing and claims to knowledge of ordinary people.

Given its social "location," the Mass-Observation Project is constantly negotiating among many different social domains, institutions, definitions of knowledge and agendas. Thus, the literacy practices employed are exactly at that point of creative development that we indicated above in critiquing static models of literacy; they are located among such domains, institutions, definitions, and so forth, and the study of them holds promise for revealing how people use writing to cross boundaries and how new literacy practices evolve. It is the uniqueness of the Mass-Observation Project that makes it an important site for the study of literacy practices, an important telling case.

In the section below, we give a brief introduction to Mass-Observation; Chapters 1 and 2 provide greater detail.

THE MASS-OBSERVATION PROJECT

Started in 1937, and revived in 1981 after a break of two decades, Mass-Observation is a small but important social institution in Britain. From all over the United Kingdom, ordinary people observe and reflect on everyday life and then write to the Mass-Observation Project at the University of Sussex. Scholars and students, mostly in the humanities and social sciences, use the Mass-Observation Archive to research a broad range of topics about contemporary society and the past. In Chapters 1 and 2 we give a detailed description of how Mass-Observation works and its history. The point we want to foreground here is that Mass-Observation is primarily writing. The Mass-Observation Archive contains over one million pieces of paper; over 2,500 people have written to the Mass-Observation since 1981, not counting those who participated during its early phase. A visitor to the Mass-Observation Archive would see the staff at one end of the room recording material on cards and on computer databases, making lists and indexes, labeling and filing, as well as writing letters and notes of guidance to the people who write for Mass-Observation. At the other end of the room, researchers and students sit at tables reading the contributions, taking notes and drafting essays and articles.

The Mass-Observation Project is part history project, part anthropology, part auto/biography and part social commentary, but it is not history, anthropology, life history, or social commentary done only by those authorised to do those things. It is also constituted by ordinary people throughout Britain. Most people in the United Kingdom have heard of the Mass-Observation Project, but few know what it is or how it works. Most Mass-Observation correspondents do not publicise their participation, although few keep it a secret. Thus, somewhat like the community writing projects and the worker writing projects (Mace, 1995), the Mass-Observation Project provides a forum for those typically excluded from having a voice in writing history; but unlike those community and worker writing projects, the Mass-Observation Project relies on academics (and others in established institutions, such as the BBC) to pull together the diverse written contributions to Mass-Observation and make them public. It is this unusual institutional "location" of Mass-Observation that makes it interesting to study as a case of writing. This alone would warrant interest. But there is more to the warrant for studying writing associated with Mass-Observation—the people who write for it.

The people who write for the Mass-Observation live throughout the United Kingdom, although primarily in England. Currently the majority of correspondents are over 45 years of age and 70% of them are women. They come from a range of economic and work backgrounds. Many of the women have experienced what we call a "de-railed education" (described in more detail in Chapter 7). Educational opportunities that they could reasonably expect to have were denied or hindered. For example, the parents of one Mass-Observation correspondent would not let her take the entrance exam for grammar school because they did not believe she needed that kind of education, although her teachers encouraged her to go on to grammar school. Another ran into trouble with her school for no fault of her own other than being inquisitive, and was denied needed and earned recommendations. But these demographic descriptions and educational experiences alone are not what warrants the study. It is the correspondents' interest in and pursuit of writing. Simply put, they write, not only for the Mass-Observation—most use writing in many other aspects of their lives. Nonetheless, few consider themselves to be writers. As a group of people who write, they warrant study for what their experiences with writing can reveal to us about the nature, place and conditions of writing in contemporary British society.

THEORISING LITERACY: MASS-OBSERVATION PROJECT AS A TELLING CASE

The view of literacy we have presented above, and the task that we have taken on—namely, the description of literacy practices and the Mass-Observation Project—is useful in ways other than those claimed by traditional studies and theories of literacy. Traditionally, researchers built abstract models of reading and writing based on and tested through experimental studies. These theoretical models could then be used to guide practice—teaching, assessment, and so forth—and to generalise to reading and writing across situations and contexts. Underlying such an approach to theory building are assumptions about writing and reading as decontextualised processes and assumptions about knowledge as abstractable from the contexts of its production and use. From that point of view, descriptions and interpretations of writing and reading practices viewed as inseparable from the contexts in which they are used and defined are of little use. They do not lead to empirical generalisations, and they do not test abstract experimental models that can be applied across situations. Rather, we view the nature of theorising and the use of description differently.

We see the Mass-Observation Project as a "telling case" that informs about the nature of writing and literacy in contemporary society, not through empirical generalisation, but by revealing the principles that underlie relationships between specific writing practices, the local events of which they are a part, and the institutional contexts in which they take place. A telling case shows how general principles deriving from some theoretical orientation manifest themselves in some given set of particular circumstances. A good case study therefore enables the analyst to establish theoretically valid connections between events and phenomena which previously were ineluctable. From this point of view, the search for a "typical" case for analytic exposition is likely to be less fruitful than the search for a "telling" case in which the particular circumstances surrounding a case serve to make previously obscure theoretical relationships suddenly apparent. Case studies used in this way are clearly more than "apt illustrations." Instead, they are means whereby general theory may be developed (Mitchell, 1984, p. 239). Thus, what we provide in this book is a description of literacy practices associated with the Mass-Observation Project, which we then use to better understand the nature of literacy practices in contemporary society in general, the conditions in which they take place, and the social meanings and consequences of their use (further discussion of the use of telling cases in studying the Mass-Observation Project can be found in Bloome, Sheridan & Street, 1993).

Theorising literacy is not a process of abstracting or decontextualising reading and writing from social life, but just the opposite: it is a process of explicating reading and writing as part of social life. That is, the questions to ask about reading and writing are not, "What is reading?" and "What is writing?" but rather, "How is reading?" and "How is writing?" Such questions require describing, interpreting and explaining what particular people do with written language in particular situations and events.

By describing, interpreting and explaining, we mean a recursive and reflexive process in which a specific event or situation is described, interpreted for its social significance and social consequences for the people involved, and explained as part of a broader set of events and contexts. Each process—description, interpretation and explanation—employs a theoretical framework or set of theoretical constructs; but at the same time, the processes of description, interpretation and explanation are used to challenge those theoretical constructs. The challenge is inherent in this view of theorising. Social life continuously evolves as social, economic, political and cultural conditions evolve; theoretical constructs and frameworks that hover close enough to everyday life to be of use in addressing and understanding social life must also evolve to incorporate the changes in social life. The changes in social life are not just a matter of broad, anonymous social trends (such as the evolution of the nation-state, the development of fast capitalism), but also of reflected, conscious action of people acting at both micro and macro levels on the worlds in which they live.

OUTLINE OF THE BOOK

The book is divided into three sections. The first Section (Chapters 1, 2 and 3) describes the Mass-Observation Project, its history and controversies with anthropology. This section provides the background necessary for framing the literacy practices described in the rest of the book. It is not just a descriptive account of the history of Mass-Observation, but rather an intellectual framing of the Project helping the reader to make sense of what *kind* of knowledge and writing they will be encountering in subsequent sections. For this reason, readers concerned only with the educational or the autobiographical aspects of Mass-Observation will probably still need to address the issues raised in Section 1. Section 2 (Chapters 4 and 5) focuses on the voices of the people who write for Mass-Observation. We describe a research project in which we interviewed a number of these writers and we devote the main part of this section to detailed accounts by nine of them. These dialogues, as we call them, provide pictures of how and why people write for the Mass-Observation Project and their comments on other writing that they do. In one sense, this section, then, constitutes the raw data of the book and would therefore appeal to readers with a particular interest in everyday writing practices. However, we would suggest that, in order to locate these data in their intellectual and social context, they are read in close conjunction with Sections 1 and 3 of the book. The discussions in the third section concerning personhood, power and identity (Chapters 6, 7 and 8) draw on both the data in Section 2 and the issues raised in Section 1. Section 3, then, balances description, interpretation, and explanation, as we attempt to use the Mass-Observation experience to provide insight into the nature of literacy practices in contemporary society.

HOW WE HAVE USED THE WORDS "MASS-OBSERVATION" AND RELATED TERMS

In researching and writing this book, we have used the terms "Mass-Observation," "Mass-Observation Archive" and "Mass-Observation Project" in ways that occasionally overlap. In general, we hope that the meanings of the terms will be clear from the context. However, to avoid any confusion, we offer the following guidance.

"Mass-Observation" has been used by us as an all-embracing conceptual term to denote the whole business of "being or doing Mass-Observation." This includes everything from observing the pub-goers of Bolton in 1937 to keeping a diary during the Second World War, from interviewing people about their leisure habits in 1949 to writing in 1991 about the experience of going to school. It includes the ideas, the aims, the activities and the people, whether they are the core team or the panel of writers. In this sense, we ourselves become part of Mass-Observation in writing this book.

We usually add the words "early" or "original" to Mass-Observation when differentiating the first historical phase from the later initiative. The original Mass-Observation therefore refers to the research organisation which was set up in 1937 and continued into the 1950s. The history of this first phase in described in Chapter 1.

The second phase of "Mass-Observation" began in 1981 (with some minor activities in 1977). This is variously referred to as the "new" project, or "Mass-Observation in the 1980s and 1990s". When it first appeared, it was called "The Inflation Project". In this book, we describe it as the "Mass-Observation Project", or occasionally as the "Project". The Mass-Observation Project is based at the Archive at the University of Sussex.

The Mass-Observation Archive is at the same time a collection of papers and also an institution with staff, premises and research facilities. Although the "archive" of papers can be said to have existed since the original Mass-Observers began work in 1937, this was not a word used at that time. The Archive as a public institution and research resource has only existed since 1970 when it was set up at the University of Sussex.

Other writers, including current Mass-Observation contributors and academic commentators whose words we have quoted, have their own preferred method of referring to aspects of Mass-Observation which may differ from the usage described above. We have reproduced their usage without amendment.

SECTION I
An Historical Context of Mass-Observation

Introduction to Section I

Mass-Observation began as an effort to establish an "anthropology of our own people" and to involve ordinary people in that effort. At the time in 1937, anthropology was itself a fledgling field. As a mode of inquiry and as a body of knowledge, anthropology needed to establish itself as a legitimate field and discipline. In academia, Mass-Observation found itself circumscribed by the debate over the legitimacy of anthropology as science, while in the field, it found itself circumscribed in its early years by the Second World War. Mass-Observation became a way for the government and for Britain itself to know about and record everyday life during the war.

It is unlikely that in the beginning many of the people associated with Mass-Observation were concerned about the writing of anthropology or thought about Mass-Observation as a set of literacy practices. The "reflective turn" in anthropology with its concern for the writing of ethnography, representation and the nature of knowledge was still four decades away. Literacy studies, controversies about the nature of literacy, and government programmes to promote literacy, were unknown. Yet from the beginning, Mass-Observation can be viewed as the establishment and evolution of a set of literacy practices. These literacy practices were adopted and adapted from literacy practices in academia, journalism, fiction writing, diary writing, letter writing and elsewhere. The literacy practices established by Mass-Observation hovered close to the goals, methods, operations and content of Mass-Observation, as is true of any set of literacy practices. That is, we take it as axiomatic that literacy practices are inseparable from what people are doing, where, when and with whom they are doing it, the meanings they are constructing, and the material, social and economic conditions within which they live. Literacy practices are not abstractable from the social events and dynamics of which they are a part or from the meanings created. To understand literacy is to understand it in use, with all the complexities, difficulties, confusions, emotions, tensions and ambiguities of human activity.

Thus in Section 1 we provide a history of Mass-Observation—its first phase from 1937 through to the early 1950s and its second phase, which began in 1981. What we describe is an intellectual history bound up with the historical events, social and economic conditions, social institutions and personalities surrounding Mass-Observation. This intellectual history leads into a discussion of the relationship of Mass-Observation and anthropology—a relationship that was at times contentious but at other times synergistic. While Section 1 is important in its own right as illuminating the history of Mass-Observation with regard to the nature of anthropological inquiry, it also sets a foundation for the rest of the book. It provides an historical context for the evolution of literacy practices discussed in Sections 2 and 3. The description and discussion of literacy practices and the Mass-Observation Project is a "telling case", a case that helps us learn about the nature of literacy not by removing it from human activity but by keeping it part of it.

1
Mass-Observation from 1937 to 1981

> We are continually impressed by the discrepancy between what is supposed to happen and what does happen, between law and fact, the institution and the individual, what people say they do and what they actually do, what leaders think people want and what people do want. (Charles Madge & Tom Harrisson, 1938, p. 32)

THE HISTORICAL ORIGINS: SOCIAL AND POLITICAL CONTEXTS

In his literary history of Britain in the 1930s, Samuel Hynes argues that Mass-Observation can be seen as precisely encapsulating the mood of a young and politically radical generation. Within Mass-Observation, we can see the desire to reconcile artistic and political preoccupations with, at one level, the struggle against the spread of fascism across Europe (and especially its then recent and violent expression in the Spanish Civil War) and, at a more personal level, ambivalence about class position and privilege. "It was at once literary and scientific, realist and surrealist, political and psychological, Marxist and Freudian, objective and salvationist. In its confusions of methods and goals it is a complex example of the confusions of young intellectuals at the time" (Hynes, 1976, p. 278).

It is easier in retrospect to identify the contradictions and inherent limitations of the Mass-Observation project, but this "confusion" which Hynes describes would not have been acknowledged by the founders of Mass-Observation. In their various public statements, they were consistently defiant, single-minded and unambiguous. They aimed, they said, to create "an anthropology of our own people" (Madge, 1937), to challenge the assumption that the press could genuinely represent public opinion and, above all, to bridge a gulf of ignorance between what they called "the establishment" and the ordinary working people of Britain. The founding group was led by a triumvirate of young men—Tom Harrisson, Charles Madge and Humphrey Jennings. Tom Harrisson had only just returned from Malekula, an island in the New Hebrides. His early interest in natural history, especially ornithology, had been replaced by an interest in human social life and, for the three years before the founding of Mass-Observation, he had lived with the people of Malekula as a self-taught anthropologist. Charles Madge was already a published poet by 1937 and was employed as journalist with the popular, left-leaning newspaper the *Daily Mirror*. Humphrey Jennings was an artist, photographer and writer, but is remembered now, above all, for his acclaimed work as a film-maker. He was, at that time, a member of the GPO Film Unit, the pioneering British documentary group led by John Grierson. Looking back twenty years later, Harrisson described the late 1930s as a time of "European squalor". "Mass-Observation did at least throb", he wrote, "and felt undefeated. Perhaps it was its peculiar contribution and why so many people who were young and tortured then still think of it kindly today" (Harrisson, 1959, p. 162).

The three made contact through the letters column of the weekly political journal *The New Statesman*. There had been a letter in the issue of 12 December 1936 from a Mr Geoffrey Pyke remarking on the public reaction to the abdication crisis. The decision of Edward VIII to abdicate as King rather than give up his marriage to the American divorcée, Wallis Simpson, had provoked a national crisis which Pyke suggested deserved critical analysis.

THE NEW STATESMAN AND NATION December 12, 1936

Correspondence

KING AND COUNTRY

Sir, How far the press reflected, and how far it evoked and moulded, public opinion during the last ten days it is impossible to say. Thousands of letters have poured into the offices of newspaper and other organisations from obscure and eminent people alike. It is most important that these should be preserved and made accessible.

Anthropologists and psychologists all over the world are studying the reactions of primitive tribes to sexual situations. There have been concentrated within the last ten days the reactions of the people of the British Empire to a sexual situation. Here in a relatively limited form is some of the material for that anthropological study of our own civilisation of which we stand in <u>such</u> desperate need.

It would seem that the majority of the inhabitants of the Empire are unable to tolerate the image of a Queen—whose chief function together with her Consort would be to be an object of idolisation—who has previously been married to two men who are still alive. Attempts have been made by various interests to use this primitive reaction to their own ends. Nothing could now be more important than the widespread public realisation of how they thought that this could be done.

It is equally important, particularly from now on, that similar investigations should be set on foot in the United States. It is not impossible that in a similarly primitive way the treatment of Mrs. Simpson, in whom Americans have taken an interest almost as great as that taken in England in the King, may there be felt by some Americans, however mistakenly, to be an aspersion on themselves.

Should this be so we may expect, on some future occasion, a compensatory manifestation of anti-British feeling, showing itself in an irrational refusal to co-operate and perhaps a revengeful suspicion of motive.

It will help our understanding and sensible behaviour towards this if we have obtained in some measure an understanding of our own recent psychopathic reactions.

We must now be prepared, too, for that Puritan reaction here, which seems to accompany all Fascistoid movements.

  6 Gordon Square,   GEOFFREY PYKE
    W.C.I.

Charles Madge could not resist the gauntlet thrown down by Pyke (Pyke himself apparently made no further contribution to the debate). A letter from Madge was published three weeks later to say that such a study—"an anthropology of our own people"—was already in the making.

THE NEW STATESMAN AND NATION January 2, 1937

ANTHROPOLOGY AT HOME

SIR,—Mr. Geoffrey Pyke suggested in your columns the other week that the constitutional crisis had begun to produce material for an anthropology of our own people.

Some days before the precipitation of the crisis, a group was formed for precisely this purpose. English anthropology, however, hitherto identified with "folk-lore," has to deal with elements so repressed that only what is admitted to be a first-class upheaval brings them to the surface. Such was the threatened marriage of the "Father-of-the-people" to Mrs. Ernest Simpson. Fieldwork, i.e., the collection of evidence of mass wish-situations, has otherwise to proceed in a far more roundabout way than the anthropologist has been accustomed to in Africa or Australia. Clues to these situations may turn up in the popular phenomenon of the "coincidence." In fact it is probable that in the ultra-repressed condition of our society they can only materialise in this form, so mysterious in appearance. But the "mystery" is part of the mechanism of repression. It can be reduced scientifically into the constituent terms of the hidden wish, and referred back to the accepted principles of anthropology. These principles and those of psycho-analysis, and the sciences dealing with the behaviour of man, have been applied by the group to the Crystal Palace-Abdication symbolic situation.

The real observers in this case were the millions of people who were, for once, irretrievably involved in the public events. Only mass observations can create mass science. The group for whom I write is engaged in establishing observation points on as widely extended a front as can at present be organised. We invite the cooperation of voluntary observers, and will provide detailed information to anyone who wants to take part. CHARLES MADGE 6 Grotes Buildings, Blackheath, SE.3.

He called for "mass observations" to create a "mass science" and invited volunteers to help in the research. At that time, Madge was living with his wife, the poet Kathleen Raine, in Blackheath in London. The GPO Film Unit was not far away, and the Madge/Raine flat was already the meeting place for a group of like-minded friends, including Humphrey Jennings, and was soon to become Mass-Observation's first headquarters. Tom Harrisson was not at this stage part of the group of friends in London. On his return to England, he had gone north to the town of Bolton in Lancashire. He supported himself partly by taking labouring jobs in the Bolton cotton mills and partly from his earnings from *Savage Civilisation*, the book he wrote about his time in Malekula (Harrisson, 1937). Bolton, once a flourishing town made rich by the cotton industry but in decline by the late 1930s, had appealed to Harrisson because it was the seat of the Levers, the wealthy soap manufacturing family, who had connections with the New Hebrides through the export of copra from the islands back to Britain.

Harrisson said that he saw Madge's letter in the copy of the *New Statesman* he was reading in Bolton Public Library. As it happened, and as a startling example of the coincidences which so fascinated the Mass-Observers, the letter appeared opposite a poem he had written about Malekula, "Coconut Moon." Harrisson made contact with the London group, and the third published letter in the sequence was signed by all three men and was headed "Mass-Observation." The letter represented the launch of the organisation. It called for 5,000 observers and included a curious list of subjects to be studied.

THE NEW STATESMAN AND NATION, January 30th, 1937

ANTHROPOLOGY AT HOME

Sir,—Man is the last subject of scientific investigation. A century ago Darwin focused the camera of thought on to man as a sort of animal whose behaviour and history would be explained by science. In 1847, Marx formulated a scientific study of economic man. In 1865, Tylor defined a new science of anthropology which was to be applied to the "Primitive" and the "savage." In 1893, Freud and Breuer published their first paper on hysteria; they began to drag into daylight the unconscious elements in individual "civilised" man. But neither anthropology nor psychology has yet become more than an instrument in the hands of any individual, which he applies (according to his individuality) to primitives and abnormals.

By 1936 chaos was such that the latent elements were crystallised into a new compound. As so often happens, an idea was being worked out in many separate brains. A letter in THE NEW STATESMAN AND NATION from Geoffrey Pyke, arising out of the Simpson crisis, explicitly mentioned the need for an "anthropology of our own people." A fortnight later a letter called attention to a group centred in London for the purpose of developing a science of Mass Observation, and this group effected contact with other individuals and with a group working in industrial Lancashire which had so far concentrated on field work rather than formulation of theory. These interests are now united in the first, necessarily tentative, efforts of Mass Observation.

Mass Observation develops out of anthropology, psychology, and the sciences which study man—but it plans to work with a mass of observers. Already we have fifty observers at work on two sample problems. We are further working out a complete plan of campaign, which will be possible when we have not fifty but 5,000 observers. The following are a few examples of problems that will arise:

Behaviour of people at war memorials.
Shouts and gestures of motorists.
The aspidistra cult.
Anthropology of football pools.
Bathroom behaviour.
Beards, armpits, eyebrows.
Anti-semitism.
Distribution, diffusion and significance of the dirty joke.
Funerals and undertakers.
Female taboos about eating.
The private lives of midwives.

In these examples the anthropological angle is obvious, and the description is primarily of physical behaviour. Other inquiries involve mental phenomena which are unconscious or repressed, so that they can only be traced through mass-fantasy and symbolism as developed and exploited, for example, in the daily press. The outbreak of parturition-images in the press last October may have been seasonal, or may have been caused by some public stimulus: continuous watch on the shifting popular images can only be kept by a multitude of watchers. The observers will also provide the points from which can be plotted weather-maps of public feeling in a crisis.

The subject demands the minimum of prejudice, bias and assumption; the maximum of objectivity. It does not presuppose that there are any inexplicable things. Since it aims at collecting data before interpreting them, it must be allowed to doubt and re-examine the completeness of every existing idea about "humanity," while it cannot afford to neglect any of them.

Equally, all human types can and must assist in this work. The artist and the scientist, each compelled by historical necessity out of their artificial exclusiveness, are at last joining forces and turning back towards the mass from which they had detached themselves.

It does not set out in quest of truth or facts for their own sake, or for the sake of an intellectual minority, but aims at exposing them in simple terms to all observers, so that their environment may be understood, and thus constantly transformed. Whatever the political methods called upon to effect the transformation, the knowledge of what has to be transformed is indispensable. The foisting on the mass of ideals or ideas developed by men apart from it, irrespective of its capacities, causes mass misery, intellectual despair and an international shambles.

We hope shortly to produce a pamphlet outlining a programme of action. We welcome criticism and co-operation.

TOM HARRISSON
HUMPHREY JENNINGS
CHARLES MADGE

Short histories of the organisation, which some have also called a "movement" (see Summerfield, 1985), have been written (Calder, 1985; Jeffery, 1978; Sheridan, 1984, 1993a; L. Stanley, 1990; N. Stanley, 1981), but no full history of Mass-Observation has ever been completed. Nor is this book such an undertaking. The absence of a history may partly be the result of the complexity of the organisation and its refusal to be placed too firmly within the strictures of a single academic discipline. An additional challenge is the difficulty of doing justice to the diversity of motivations and investments brought to Mass-Observation by the people who created and ran it. Just as the Mass-Observers themselves imbued the organisation with particular but often disparate desires and meanings in the 1930s and 1940s, so subsequent commentators have tended to read Mass-Observation within a single frame. It has been characterised variously as a documentary or photographic project (Laing, 1980), as a deeply flawed social survey (Abrams, 1951), as a middle-class adventure at the expense of the working class (Gurney, 1997), as salvationist (Hynes, 1976), as a people's history (Calder, 1985), and as a life history project which was a precursor to, for example, present-day oral history (Sheridan, 1996).

The absence of a comprehensive history may also be a result of Mass-Observation's own failure, despite its meticulous documentation of *other* people's lives, to record systematically its own activities. Reconstructing even the composition of the core membership of Mass-Observation—who did what, when and how—is not easy. There are no minute books, or salary records, few records of research plans and proposals, and the correspondence about their research, though it has survived, is patchy and one-sided, often interfiled within the papers of a specific study. This makes it hard to develop a chronological and inclusive overview of how they operated. The absence of office records is consistent with a disregard for the bureaucratic and the formal; Mass-Observation received very little funding and, in its enthusiasm to get out into the streets to observe and document everyday life, was more likely to spend what it earned on gathering information rather than on improving its administration. In its early years, financial help was given by the socialist publisher, Victor Gollancz, who was promised four books out of Mass-Observation's pre-war study of Bolton. Only one book eventually emerged (*The Pub and the People*, 1943) and that long after the team had left Bolton. Additional funds in this early phase came from northern wealthy benefactors whom Tom Harrisson cajoled into supporting the work, apparently without strings. Otherwise, Mass-Observation relied on its meagre earnings from the occasional commission, supplemented by income from book publications (25 appeared between 1937 and 1950; see Appendix Ai) and articles in the press. Many of those employed as observers and investigators, especially in Bolton, worked for almost nothing.

Before war was declared in September 1939, both Bolton and London provided the bases for Mass-Observation activities. Harrisson led the northern wing and rented a small house in Davenport Street, Bolton, from which to direct his small and frequently changing team of observers. For over two years, the citizens of Bolton were scrutinised and described, counted and followed; when they took their annual holiday in Blackpool, they continued to be the subjects of study. The

28 CHAPTER ONE

themes of the research included work in the cotton mills, pub life, street scenes, shopping and markets, religious and political meetings and celebrations, sporting events and leisure activities, especially dancing, going to the cinema, belonging to clubs and joining in a variety of social occasions. From time to time, the investigative team was augmented by artists, including William Coldstream and Julian Trevelyan. The photographer, Humphrey Spender, who, as a friend of Harrisson, came up to Bolton on several occasions, took over 800 photographs (see Spender, 1982).

Meanwhile in London, similar research was taking place—on the music industry, including dancing and dance halls, on London's East End and the Jewish community, on people's fears and expectations about the imminence of war. The first of the London-based studies owed much to the involvement of Humphrey Jennings. It was concerned with George VI's Coronation on 12th May 1937. Despite the fact that the abdication crisis had originally brought Mass-Observation into existence, it had been too soon for Mass-Observation to be in a position to undertake research on the crisis. The team only began working in February 1937, so Coronation Day was their first opportunity to explore public feeling about the monarchy. Observers were sent into the streets of London to record the behaviour of the crowd; in addition, a questionnaire was distributed "Where were you on May 12th?" and, supplementing the information obtained in this way, Mass-Observation also requested diaries of the day to be kept by the volunteers who had responded to the first appeals for help. An anthology of the resulting material, in which the day diaries from the volunteer writers predominated, was published later the same year as May Twelfth (Mass-Observation, 1937).

Although it is this group of volunteer writers (the "National Panel")[1] and their present-day counterparts who provide the focus for this book about writing and Mass-Observation, it is useful to see the Panel within the context of the wider organisation. The use of the Panel writers (who kept diaries and responded in detail to regular questionnaires) was never conceived of as a separate method of research by the Mass-Observers; it formed part of a broader endeavour to use trained observers or field workers. In the rest of this chapter, we sketch out very briefly the development of Mass-Observation after its inception.

---

[1] In the 1930s and 1940s, Mass-Observation used various words interchangeably to describe its volunteer writers, including "Mass-Observers", "Observers", "Respondents to directives" and "Members of the National Panel". The people recruited to the new phase of Mass-Observation from 1981 onwards are now called "Mass-Observation correspondents" or just "correspondents".

When Britain declared war on Germany on 3 September 1939, Mass-Observation began to wind down its work in Bolton, and centralised its activities in London. There had always been an interest in the implications of war, and now Harrisson especially saw possibilities for Mass-Observation as an instrument for research on civilian life in wartime conditions. By then, Humphrey Jennings had moved on. The GPO Film Unit became the Crown Film Unit, and Jennings was to direct some of the most important British wartime documentaries under its auspices. Madge also decided to leave in 1940. Many years later, he said that he was uncomfortable with what he saw as "home front espionage" (Madge, 1976), but there had already been serious disagreements and differences in approach between him and Harrisson before the war. Harrisson succeeded in putting the services of Mass-Observation at the disposal of the state through his friendship with Mary Adams, whom he had met when she was Head of Talks at the BBC. At the start of the war, Mary Adams was appointed to the Home Intelligence department at the Ministry of Information and was keen to use what she saw as the more subtle and sensitive methods of Mass-Observation as a way of gaining information on the ways in which people in Britain were coping with the rigours of wartime life, and perhaps importantly, how they were responding to the Ministry's public information campaigns. Harrisson seems to have had no reservations about working for government, and perhaps shared with some other members of the wartime team of investigators a sense that monitoring the mood of the country (the nation's morale as it was termed), as a precondition for the effective mobilisation of labour, was essential war work. He certainly argued this case in trying to prevent members of the team being conscripted into the armed forces.

The relationship with government was relatively short-lived, however, and by 1941 when Mary Adams was replaced at Home Intelligence, the formal arrangement ended. Mass-Observation continued to undertake work for individual government departments, but it also accepted commissions from other bodies, charities and pressure groups, and commercial organisations. The emphasis on general social issues remained strong throughout the war and in the immediate post-war years, with studies on health, education, social welfare and employment, the family, having (or not having) children, industrial production, propaganda and the media, political opinion and practice, religion, sexual attitudes, leisure activities and a host of other subjects which were either commissioned as studies or which the organisers of Mass-Observers themselves chose to study.

Eventually, Tom Harrisson himself was drafted into the army in 1942. His specialised knowledge of Southeast Asia was put to use in the Special Operations Executive. He was parachuted behind enemy lines in

30 CHAPTER ONE

Tom Harrisson (left) and Humphrey Spender at Humphrey Spender's studio in the early 1970s. They are making selections for a book of Spender's Worktown photographs. Photograph reproduced courtesy of the Trustees of the Mass-Observation Archive.

Tom Harrisson with the Mass-Observation papers when they first arrived at the University of Sussex in the early 1970s.

Borneo to organise guerrilla warfare against the Japanese. Extraordinarily, his influence on Mass-Observation remained strong and he returned at the end of the war to resume his directorship for a few more years. In all, Mass-Observation's first active phase can be seen to have continued for over a decade; most of this time, it was the work conducted by the full and part-time team of investigators (and not the writing by volunteers) which predominated and which made up the greater part of Mass-Observation's published books and reports. The early observational work, employing mostly ethnographic and documentary methods was gradually superseded by larger scale quantitative surveys using door-to-door interviews and the distribution of hundreds of printed questionnaires. In the next section, we shall turn to the people who contributed to Mass-Observation as "untrained" observers (the members of the Panel), whose writings about their own lives constitute about a fifth of the total Archive, and whose enthusiasm and commitment in the 1930s and 1940s provided the inspiration for the present-day Mass-Observation Project and our own interest in what it can tell us about the meanings and uses of literacy.

THE RECRUITMENT OF THE PANEL OF VOLUNTEERS

Charles Madge and Humphrey Jennings, rather than Tom Harrisson, were mainly responsible at the outset for recruiting the volunteer Mass-Observers. Tom Harrisson was much more concerned with direct observation; his work in Bolton for what they called the "Worktown Study" was very much a case of "us" (the Observers) looking at "them" (the Boltonians). It was Harrisson, however, who kept the Panel going long after Madge and Jennings had left Mass-Observation. Harrisson recognised its value in supplying information from all over Britain, on a regular basis, when difficult wartime conditions risked interfering with the activities of his team of field workers.

If Harrisson came to see the Panel as a useful vehicle for fact-gathering, Madge and Jennings started out with rather different conceptions of what the Panel might achieve. Madge's fascination with the quality of the writing itself and his belief in its capacity to transcend social barriers, especially those of class, are evident from an article he wrote in the literary journal, *Life and Letters*:

> The reports which are written for Mass-Observation come largely from people whose behaviour, language and viewpoint are far removed from academic science or literature. Sociologists and realistic novelists-including proletarian novelists-find it difficult if not impossible to describe the texture of this world. (Madge, 1937, p. 37)

Madge began recruiting volunteers early in 1937. He relied partly on word of mouth and partly on the press to reach people. The Panel grew rapidly during 1937—from 25 respondents in the first month to 257 by September. By the end of the year, 592 people had taken part. The first instruction to these volunteers was to record everything they did on the 12th day of February. The exercise was repeated on the 12th day of March and thereafter on the 12th day of each month until January 1938. Reports were also submitted on other themes—smoking habits, personal appearance, reactions to advertisements, and on other days—Armistice Day and Christmas Day.

Madge speaks of giving both middle- and working-class people a voice. In practice (and with some notable exceptions), the project was not very successful in gathering first-hand working-class experience. The majority of Panel members were drawn from the less affluent layers of the middle classes—teachers, librarians, secretaries and clerks, shopkeepers, students and housewives. Insofar as they were preponderantly quite young, politically to the left and without access to more public channels of communication, however, it can be argued that they *were* a relatively "voiceless" group in pre-war Britain. Just under half the recruits at that stage were women of all ages, and the enthusiasm with which they participated in Mass-Observation is another indication that Madge achieved some success in offering a voice to the voiceless, though perhaps not in ways that he had first anticipated.

The publication in 1937 of *May the Twelfth*, mentioned earlier, represented the first public exposure for the material from volunteer writers. As an anthology, it was composed of fragments from the one-day diaries written on 12 May 1937, the Coronation Day of George VI. The extracts were cut together without editorial comment by Madge and Jennings. As well as extracts from diaries, *May the Twelfth* contained on-the-spot reports, written mostly by students who mingled with the crowd on the London streets during the Coronation parade and recorded what they saw and heard. The distinction between those required to observe others and those required to observe themselves was not made clear in *May the Twelfth*, and this seems to have prompted at least some of the heavy criticism from social scientists, whose comments we discuss in Chapter 3. Among the critics were Raymond Firth (1939), T. H. Marshall (1937) and Marie Jahoda (1938). It remained a central ambiguity in Mass-Observation and was to some extent a result of Mass-Observation's *deliberate* collapsing of categories between the expert and the non-expert.

> The Observers are cameras with which we are trying to photograph contemporary life. The trained Observer is ideally a camera with no

> distortion. They tell us not what society is like, but what it looks like to them. (Madge & Harrisson, 1938, p. 66)

The fact that the observer as *investigator* was probably paid, while the observer as *diarist* was unpaid, may have clarified the distinction at the time for those involved but cannot always be inferred retrospectively. A highly self-conscious and intellectual investigator could be more unintentionally self-disclosing than a diarist who restricts his or her writing to "factual reporting" in the cause of greater objectivity. Jahoda complained in *Sociological Review* that the Mass-Observers were not "scientifically trained".

> I have little doubt that every observer was enthusiastic about his task and wished to be quite objective and unbiased. As, however, they are all casual and untrained observers, they must show bias in their observations. They cannot be . . . quite representative of the mass of people for they are themselves a selected group of people whose types require examination. (Jahoda, 1938, p. 209)

And, as Jahoda and other critics of Mass-Observation argued, if the observers as the subjects of the study are not "trained" as professional social investigators, then they and their writings must be seen as the *objects* of study, in which case, they must somehow be representative. This anxiety to define observers as either one thing or the other, as either "objective" or "subjective", continues to preoccupy some of the users of the Archive today as well as some of the current correspondents themselves, as does the anxiety about "representativeness". Ironically, Mass-Observation's attempts to refute the charges of being unscientific only served to perpetuate the ambiguity. Two years after the project had begun, Madge was defending the amateur while still confirming the essentially outward direction of the observational process, for example in his use of the words "vantage point" below:

> It immediately puts us in touch with a section of people in the population who were at one and the same time ordinary, hardworking folk and also intelligent and interesting enough to want to help us. We did not regard these people as being themselves scientists studying the mass, nor did we consider them as being a random sample of public opinion. Their position was something different. They were observers, untrained but shrewd, placed at vantage points for seeing and describing in their own simple language what life looks like in the various environments which go to make up England. (Madge & Harrisson, 1939b, p. 3)

Madge wrote the above as part of a BBC script which was broadcast on 1 June 1939. It illustrates the shift away from the original desire to capture a certain authenticity of experience and feeling as it was expressed in diary-writing and a shift towards a more pragmatic interest in enlisting "key informants", people who would be sufficiently motivated to supply Mass-Observation with the kind of information which might be difficult or impossible to obtain using professional investigators. Mass-Observation differed from other bodies using key informants, however, in its preference for what Madge calls "ordinary, hardworking folk"—that is, not, in the first place, "respectable" (i.e. middle-class professional) members of the community.

Wartime brought changes in the role of the Panel. The diaries became a useful vehicle for collecting information about day-to-day civilian life in wartime, partly because they could be written with only minimal guidance from Mass-Observation, and partly because they could be stored in the diary-writer's home if emergency conditions interfered with communications and other more direct fact-gathering by employed Mass-Observers. In late August 1939, Harrisson invited all the volunteer writers to send in full, continuous daily dairies. Over 150 people responded by sending in a diary installment for the month of September 1939. Although numbers dropped as the war continued, over 500 individuals have been identified as having at one time or another written a diary for Mass-Observation between 1939 and 1945. A larger group of people responded to monthly prompts sent to them by Mass-Observation. These prompts, which were called "directives", consisted of a series of open-ended questions inviting full and detailed opinions and experiences on pre-determined themes such as the evacuation of children, attitudes to politicians, accounts of the blackout, coping with food shortages and so on. Over 2,500 people took part in responding to directives during the period of the Second World War, although in any one month there were never more than 500 individual replies.

When Harrisson joined the army, the work of collecting and caring for the diaries and directive replies fell to H. D. (Bob) Willcock, a quiet and unassuming member of the core team who had joined Mass-Observation at the start of the war. Willcock took a more rigorous approach to the work and was much more concerned about the public acceptability and the demonstrable validity of Mass-Observation's findings. Nevertheless, he was committed to the acquisition of autobiographical material, seeing it not primarily as "fact gathering" but as a way of "recording social change at . . . deeper and more significant levels" than had hitherto been possible because it tapped "their subjective feelings, their worries, frustrations, hopes, desires, expectations and fears" (Willcock, 1943, p. 456). Two years later, John Ferraby, another Mass-Observer who specialised in the analysis of the material, echoed Willcock's view in a note on his paper on the falling birthrate:

> Figures do not form the main part of the report; in the present survey most of the figures are given in an appendix. The basis of the report is the verbatim comments made by the contacts . . . or from the written replies of the Panel. . . . They bring dead figures to life and make the abstract concrete. Without unlimited financial support, it is necessary to sacrifice either a degree of numerical accuracy or a degree of accuracy in interpreting the figures obtained. We believe that in most cases the interpretation of results is more important. (Ferraby, 1945, p. 6)

Despite a spirited public defence of the qualitative material, however, there were reservations within the ranks. The diaries proved especially impenetrable (Kertesz, 1993). A Mass-Observer charged with the task of analysing the diaries in 1944 wrote in an internal memorandum:

> The longer I work with the diaries the more definite becomes my opinion that they should not be used on their own. They are essentially supplementary to more detailed investigations. Used thus they provide invaluable quotations, sidelights etc. But when you use them by themselves you are continually up against the fact that you can't prove anything from them. (M-O A File Report No. 2181, Nov 1944)

By 1947, the debate had become bitter and Harrisson, temporarily back in Britain after his wartime experiences, inveighed:

> If I have criticised what I call the "quantitative obsession", it is not because I am unaware of the great importance of statistical work, but because I am concerned at its undue dominance at present. One or two methods should not be mistaken for the only "scientific" ones, especially by those outside sociology who are now increasingly interested—and at last more aware of its value to the community. It is clear that in most sociological research we require an adequate admixture of words and numbers, of penetration and tabulation, representation and interpretation, understood situations and unimpeachable correlations, the raw material of life with the authentic statistic of validity. But we must not be afraid to explore problems not at once open to quantitative measurement. To limit sociological research to what can be measured quantitatively is to perpetuate a vicious circle and to delay by decades the probing towards principles, permanent laws and scientific generalisations which can literally alter the whole basis of future planning and the organisation of world society. (Harrisson, 1947, p. 24)

MASS-OBSERVATION 1937 TO 1981   37

Despite Harrisson's characteristically combative defence of qualitative work in sociology, the continued criticisms about "proof" and "scientificity" took their toll on Mass-Observation's interest in the diaries and directives. By 1949, Mass-Observation had all but abandoned the members of its Panel and was placing a much greater reliance on quantifiable information. The process was accelerated when Mass-Observation became a limited company in the same year. Len England, who had joined Mass-Observation as a schoolboy in 1939 and had carried out some of Mass-Observation's most extensive observations on cinema audiences in the early years of the war (see Richards & Sheridan, 1987), became the Managing Director. He wrote

> Mass-Observation stands unreservedly by its original principles expressed in its very name observation as opposed to questionnaire. But what those of us working in the organisation have come to realise is that this method of approach has its own particular limitations. It provides quality and depth but no automatic indication of quantity. (England 1949-50, p. 594)

The criticism of Mass-Observation reached a crescendo in 1951 with the publication of *Social Surveys and Social Action*. Its author, Mark Abrams, devoted an entire chapter to Mass-Observation in what must have been one of the most searing indictments of its achievements, describing its methods as "inchoate and uncontrolled" (Abrams, 1951, p. 112).

The criticism was serious and not only for its academic implications. Since becoming a limited company, Mass-Observation was compelled to take account of its reputation in the commercial world. A number of competitors in the public opinion business had now emerged in response to the boom in consumer production. The government departments, once Mass-Observation's most regular wartime customers, had access to their own social research organisation (as the Wartime Social Survey, later the Social Survey). There was a pressing need for Mass-Observation to compete with these organisations and earn its living by selling its services to commercial customers. The late 1940s and early 1950s saw a shift from social history concerns to research on consumer behaviour. There was also another important factor which facilitated the shift; the technological innovations in computing opened up the possibility of processing much larger amounts of data quantitatively. Evidence of Mass-Observation's recourse to computer analysis can be found in the Archive in the form of sheets of largely undecipherable zeros and ones and sets of early punch cards. Most of those diarists who had continued after 1945 now gave up. They were no longer receiving any kind of encouraging response from Mass-Observation. No doubt many of them felt like the teacher who gave up in 1949:

There I give up. I've done it since March 1940. Recently I wrote and asked for information. As I lead a very uneventful life, I wanted to know which . . . items in my diaries were of use and whether anything different was desired and what could be omitted. I received a polite reply in such general terms as to constitute no answer. It was as if one man said to another in an office "What shall I say?" "Oh, keep the old girl at it, some of it may come in handy". Soon after that I lost interest. It took a bit of doing and now its gone flat on me, and I'm giving up. It was clear to me that the man who replied to me hadn't looked at the diary I sent with my request for information. (Mass-Observation Diaries, 1949)

THE YEARS BETWEEN 1950 AND 1980

In the three decades following the appearance of Abrams' book, social scientists paid scant attention to Mass-Observation. In her paper on Mass-Observation's work in Bolton, for the British Sociological Association conference, Liz Stanley (1989) reports that she could not find a single reference to Mass-Observation in the previous ten years' worth of *Sociological Abstracts* and she comments, "the lack of current interest in M-O from sociology and anthropology is surprising perhaps only because of its completeness" (L. Stanley, 1990, pp. 2-3). Two references in sociology textbooks (Easthope, 1974, p. 102; Kent, 1981, pp. 119-120) dismiss Mass-Observation as an historical oddity.

Given this silence among social researchers, the resurrection of a practice which even the original proponents have forsaken might seem doomed. It would not be possible at all, perhaps, if there had not been substantial shifts in concerns and methods within both the social sciences and the humanities generally. Autobiographical writing has become a key issue within feminist literary and historiographical debate (Bell & Yallom, 1990; Sheridan, 1993c; Steedman, 1986, 1992; Swindells, 1995). These changes have provided the conditions for a cautious re-evaluation of some of Mass-Observation's achievements.

The beginning of the process was the re-discovery of the early papers in the cellars of Mass-Observation UK Ltd in London at the end of the 1960s. Paul Addison and Angus Calder, both researching the period of the Second World War, drew attention to the collection (Addison, 1975; Calder, 1969). Asa Briggs, then Vice Chancellor at the University of Sussex, offered it a home at the University. Tom Harrisson was invited to Sussex to establish the papers as a public archive. It was officially opened by Asa Briggs in 1975 (see Appendix Aiv for more information about the Archive).

The emergence of radical interest groups and civil rights campaigns in this period produced a parallel search for new sources in social history which would shed light on the experience of people who had hitherto been hidden from history (Rowbotham, 1973). The proliferation of oral history groups, of worker-writer and community publishing groups, of women's history groups, of black and working class groups, challenged the existing orthodoxies not only of history but of all the social sciences. The editorial in the first issue of *History Workshop* proclaimed:

> The great bulk of historical writing is never intended to be read outside the ranks of the profession, and most of it is written only for the attention of the specialist groups within it. Teaching and research are increasingly divided, and both divorced from a wider or explicit social purpose. In the journal we shall try to restore a wider context for the study of history, both as a counter to the scholastic fragmentation of the subject, and with the aim of making it relevant to ordinary people. (*History Workshop*, 1976, p. 1)

Here is a striking echo of Charles Madge's "ordinary, hardworking folk" of 1937, but the new more exploratory climate did not mean a completely unequivocal embrace of Mass-Observation. There were, and still are, understandable reservations about Mass-Observation's upper-class provenance. The snobbery which imbues some of the early observational accounts is striking and occasionally offensive. The Worktown project in which mostly upper-class male southerners subjected the "natives" of Bolton to intensive scrutiny has been singled out for particular criticism (Gurney, 1997). The fascination with the "otherness" of working-class culture is explicit in the early descriptions. Interestingly, the autobiographical material, which was relatively free of this "us" and "them" taint (or where such a tendency could sit more comfortably with the expected subjectivity of the diary form), was much less often consulted by researchers when the Archive was first opened. Two main approaches to Mass-Observation have been taken by researchers: either Mass-Observation is studied historically as a product of the documentary movement of the late 1930s, or its surveys and reports are trawled thematically for primary historical evidence or as colourful "illustrations" for themes already chosen.

THE REHABILITATION OF MASS-OBSERVATION

The increasing popularity of the Mass-Observation Archive as a historical resource since the mid-1970s, while gratifying in itself, is less relevant for the purposes of this book than the process which Nick Stanley has described as the "rehabilitation" of Mass-Observation as a method, a process which he himself begins in his thesis on the first three years of Mass-Observation's history (N. Stanley, 1981). Stanley takes on the task of re-evaluating the entire enterprise within the context of other contemporary literary, artistic and social scientific movements and succeeds in reinstating Mass-Observation creditably within the British sociological tradition. In his chapter on the volunteer Panel, he painstakingly reconstructs the Panel's shape from the surviving diaries and directive replies, producing for the first time a reliable profile of the kind of people who chose to write for Mass-Observation. He acknowledges that any statistical breakdown of Panel responses should be viewed with caution, but suggests that the Panel material may yet have other merits:

> This is not an argument about the representativeness of the data as a true profile of the general population. In one respect, even if the sample, on inspection proved highly skewed it might yet provide useful information about this particular population. . . . This point is further supported by a second line of argument which maintains that the Panel material gives (as do, in greater depth, the wartime diaries) a "thickness" of data precisely because it is not confined by the normal narrowness of the printed questionnaire. (N. Stanley, 1981, p. 149)

Angus Calder has raised a similar point. The prediction of Churchill's defeat in the post-war general election at a time when "most people in politics and the press would have found the idea unbelievable" was perhaps Mass-Observation's "finest hour" (Calder, 1985, p. 180). The very bias of the Panel composition, Calder suggests, far from producing a distorted view of political currents, may have "made it a better instrument for detecting long term tendencies than a more perfect sample of the population could have been". A more systematic comparison of Mass-Observation's results with those of the British Institute of Public Opinion on the question of Churchill's popularity during the war was carried out by Diana Parkin. She concludes that "Mass-Observation has a more sensitive ear to pick up nuance and contradiction which gave it a much greater predictive ability [than BIPO]" (Parkin, 1987, p. 86).

There is the another intriguing and unusual dimension to Mass-Observation which has appealed to the post-1968 historian—the sense of participation expressed by the volunteer observers. Several writers have picked up on the significance of having an identity as a "Mass-Observer". Penny Summerfield has suggested that this commitment, which depended upon shared objectives, means that Mass-Observation itself can be considered a social movement rather than solely a social research organisation (Summerfield, 1985). One of Mass-Observation's earliest claims to originality was that it offered a democratic form of social science in which everyone could be authors of their own history. Volunteers questioned about their motives for joining Mass-Observation in 1937 confirmed the meaning of this participation for them. It was an activity with immediate personal satisfactions and was consistent with their social and political inclinations.

> I joined Mass-Observation as a result of reading an article in the newspaper asking for observers. I had for some time been convinced that many of those who supply the people's needs . . . are a long way out of touch with what people really desire and need. (quoted in Sheridan, 1990, p. 22)
>
> I am doubtful if the people who do Mass-Observation are representative of the population as a whole in spite of their different classes and jobs, because it isn't everybody who would take the trouble to write their impression, even though they may be good at observing. They must all be people willing to work for a cause. (quoted in Sheridan, 1990, p. 18)

Janet Finch picks up on the same theme in *Research and Policy* (1986):

> . . . the approach to data-creation goes beyond concepts of unproblematic fact-gathering: there is a more explicit recognition of the process of undertaking research as a political activity in the broadest sense, and the knowledge thereby created as intrinsically political. (Finch, 1986, p. 94)

Finch's chapter on "Mass-Observation and the 'Alternative' Tradition" is a further contribution to the rehabilitation of Mass-Observation. She takes Mass-Observation's treatment of one subject, the documentation of the impact of war on children, and argues that in spite of the fact that it was insufficiently systematic, the particularly "imaginative techniques" used by observers and Panel members produced much richer data than that produced by quantitative methods and that this enabled Mass-Observation to challenge the "blandness of official rhetoric". For all its weaknesses, Finch concludes that Mass-Observation can legitimately be seen as a form of alternative and oppositional social science.

If Mass-Observation has been more or less enthusiastically reclaimed as a resource by social historians and reservedly "rehabilitated" by sociologists, where does that leave a present-day revival? Some of the weaknesses of the original work (lack of systematic research plans, incomplete field work, widely varying approaches taken by the field workers, dubious statistics) can be conveniently attributed to the constraints of the historical period, to the embryonic stage of contemporary social research methodologies and to the exigencies of wartime.

It is much too simplistic to claim today, as did the original Mass-Observers, that "ordinary people" do not have a voice. It is also unrealistic and patronising to suggest that "voices" can be "given". We are surrounded by cultural reflections of ourselves: in the press, on television and radio, in the alternative histories from the newer publishing houses and in the smaller scale projects of local and oral history groups, in our own videos and photograph albums, in the burgeoning heritage industries and in the now highly sophisticated opinion polls and market research. Can there be any role for the particular collection and interpretation of autobiographical writing represented by Mass-Observation in the task of social understanding? Nick Stanley (writing in 1981 just before the Archive launched its new project) was cautiously optimistic:

> ... what of the prospects of renewal? I think it is important to distinguish between making a case for the reintroduction of some of the concerns of Mass-Observation and arguing for a resurrection of the organisation. Here only the first is suggested as a possibility for sociology—namely the exploration of an "amateur sociology", taking the example of the national Panel in different directions. The notion of a self-reflective observer offers a genuinely interesting possibility for a hermeneutically informed account. (N. Stanley, 1981, p. 272)

In Chapter 2, we shall go on to describe the revival of Mass-Observation, or more precisely, the revival of one of its central features, the recruitment of the "self-reflective observer" to a new national Panel. The context of this revival, and the way in which it has evolved since 1981, are intimately related to the kind of writing which is now produced for the Mass-Observation Archive. Chapter 2 will therefore cover both the historical origins and development of the new phase of Mass-Observation, and also the practical details of its operation in order to describe the cultural and social framework within which the writing is done, read and understood.

2
Mass-Observation Revived: Writing Britain[1]

Understandably, we assume, without examining the assumption, that, minor differences apart, everyone else (apart from those whom we 'simply can't understand') is much the same as ourselves. It comes as a surprise then, and often a fascinating one, to discover that within a few miles of oneself, or sitting next to one on a bus for all one knows, there are others, no less ordinary than oneself and to all appearances normal who are living in a radically different world and viewing a shared world with very different eyes. (David Pocock, 1987, p. 420)

THE RE-LAUNCH

From his notes and from conversations which he had with Sheridan at the Archive at the University of Sussex, it was clear that Tom Harrisson often considered the possibility of reviving Mass-Observation in the 1970s. Sadly, however, he was never to realise any of his plans. He was killed suddenly early in 1976 in a road accident in Bangkok. His role as director of the Archive was adopted by David Pocock, at that time Professor of Social Anthropology at Sussex.

---

[1]Sheridan had already been working at the Mass-Observation Archive with the older material since 1974, and was therefore intimately involved with the 1981 initiative. From 1991, she became solely responsible for directing all aspects of the new Project. Chapter 2 relies heavily on her knowledge of the history of this phase. Although co-authored, the account in Chapter 2 is in effect an "insider" view. For the sake of clarity, we felt it was important to make Sheridan's particular role clear.

But Harrisson's influence continued. Shortly after his death, the historian Philip Ziegler attempted the first revival of some of the original ideas of Mass-Observation, using the Archive itself as a base. Ziegler was working on the early papers in the Archive for his study of the monarchy. He planned to publish his research as a book (Ziegler, 1977) to coincide with the Silver Jubilee of Queen Elizabeth in 1977. Ziegler had been a friend of the late Tom Harrisson and, in his capacity as a senior editor at Collins Publishers, had overseen the posthumous publication of Harrisson's last book, *Living Through the Blitz*, in 1976. He was sympathetic to the Mass-Observation approach and decided to augment the early Mass-Observation material on royalty, which he was using for his own book, with contemporary accounts of the Queen's Jubilee. This involved enlisting the help of assorted friends, acquaintances and former Mass-Observers—anyone, in fact, who could be persuaded to write something about their feelings towards, or participation in, the Jubilee celebrations. It was then that the notion of re-establishing a Mass-Observation-style panel of volunteer writers on a more ambitious scale first began taking shape.

Philip Ziegler's book acted as a stimulus to David Pocock. He decided to invite people (through the press) to send in accounts of Jubilee street parties. About 500 descriptive accounts of street parties, accompanied by photographs, printed ephemera and some memorabilia, were received from people all over the country as a result of this request. It is reasonable, with hindsight, to reflect that both this initiative, and the subsequent launch of the "Mass-Observation in the 1980s" Project, which took place the same year as Prince Charles married Lady Diana Spencer in 1981, were influenced by Mass-Observation's much earlier preoccupation with the place of the royal family, and especially the significance of major national events such as coronations and weddings, in the cultural fabric of British social life. The public controversy over Edward VIII's abdication in 1936 had been the spur which brought Mass-Observation into existence, and the first substantial Mass-Observation publication was *May the Twelfth*, a collage of accounts of the day George VI was crowned in 1937. In his new Afterword to the re-issue in 1987 of Mass-Observation's *May the Twelfth* (1937), David Pocock wrote:

> Some explanation must account for my continued interest in May the Twelfth because I am still surprised every time it occurs to note not just similarities but apparently identical features on that Coronation Day and those reported in the Day Diaries written for Mass-Observation on 29 July 1981, the wedding day of Their Royal Highness, the Prince and Princess of Wales. (Pocock, 1987, p. 420)

Similar observations and one-day diaries were collected by Mass-Observation during the 1953 Coronation (used much later in the 1966 publication, *Long to Reign Over Us*, by Leonard Harris). There certainly was a sense in which the 1981 Wedding, with all the inescapable media hype and the ubiquitous debates about its value and meaning in British society, seemed to demand some kind of documentation which might reflect a different, more nuanced perception of the ways in which people were responding to the event than that which was available in the British media at the time.

The Royal Wedding, planned for 29 June 1981, was set to be the biggest royal jamboree since the Coronation of Elizabeth II in 1953. However, it was taking place against a particularly demoralising backdrop, and the extravagance of the preparations set up stark contrasts. High levels of inflation had been a continuing cause for concern and discord in the immediately preceding years. Unemployment was escalating: in 1980, 2.78 million people in Britain were officially recorded as out of work. The degree of civil unrest in the six counties of Northern Ireland was acute. In May 1981, the MP Bobby Sands had died after being on hunger strike with fellow Republicans in the Maze prison. During the summer months, several British cities, notably Bristol, London, Manchester and Liverpool, were the scenes of a series of disturbing riots. According to the polls, the popularity of the Prime Minister, Margaret Thatcher, and her Conservative government, was at its lowest since coming to power in 1979; the success of the new political alliances in Parliament was causing consternation within the established parties. 1981 was a watershed year for Britain. A year later, much had changed. With the advent of war with Argentina over the Falkland Islands, Margaret Thatcher consolidated her power and Britain embarked on the period which has become known as "The Thatcher Years".

This was the context for the social and political re-birth of Mass-Observation in 1981. At first, David Pocock called it "The Inflation Project." It was only later that it became known as "Mass-Observation in the 1980s" (and then "and 1990s"). Pocock was interested in the way in which factors such as the cost of food and amenities, the experience of unemployment and redundancy, and the cut-backs in public services affected people in their day-to-day lives, and the relationship between this and the wider political mood of the country. In 1985, when justifying the Project's first four years in an application for funds, he wrote:

> The material we collect is unique because it describes the concrete and specific contexts of particular lives, details which are lost in large-scale summations. Our collections prior to the 1984 General Election, for example, would have predicted the outcome, but unlike

any public opinion poll, we preserve the record of the mood, the motives and the immediate factors (by no means always political) which dictated voting and non-voting. Similarly the diaries kept by our panellists during the Falklands War will be an essential source for anyone investigating the complexities and turn-arounds of public opinion of that time. (Application to the Nuffield Foundation, 1985, p. 2)

In Chapter 3, we discuss the links that can be made between David Pocock's interest in people's "personal anthropologies" and the self-reporting activities which were the cornerstone of early Mass-Observation's work. Would people be as ready to write about their lives in Britain in 1981 as they had been in 1937 for the original Mass-Observers? Had writing, especially letter-writing, been superseded by the telephone and the more visual forms of communication?

I was confidently advised in the 1980s people would not be as interested in writing as an earlier generation had been; but what started as an attempt to bring in some contemporary material very rapidly grew to twice the size of the original enterprise. . . . (Application to the Nuffield Foundation, 1985, p. 3)

The initiative did not begin life as a formal, funded research project with clearly defined academic objectives and an explicit research methodology. The primary aim was to extend the existing Archive and to provide future historians with information about life in Britain in the 1980s which would be roughly comparable to the documentation of the period 1937-49. By now, it was evident from the demand for access to the Archive that the results of Mass-Observation's early work were becoming widely recognised as an important historical resource for scholars of the period. It was also clear that the material contributed by volunteers in the form of diaries and answers to open-ended questionnaires (known as directive replies) constituted a unique collection of "amateur" or non-élite writing. The potential research value of an equivalent collection for the 1980s promised to be considerable, but of course the re-launch opened up old questions as well as new ones. The new activities soon attracted publicity and the interest of researchers, which in turn led to demands for accounts of the Project and for some kind of intellectual rationale for its existence. Whereas once, it was possible to locate Mass-Observation safely as an historical phenomenon with no special implications for present-day knowledge about ourselves, the new Project placed the whole nature of "doing" Mass-Observation, whatever that might mean, back on the academic agenda, and it put those associated with the Archive in the firing line.

Just as the original Mass-Observation cannot be regarded as a monolithic enterprise but rather the embodiment of a volatile mix of interests and influences, so the fledgling "Inflation Project" grew and developed in response to a wide variety of pressures and demands on it from within the Archive itself, from the academic community and from the community of writers who were busily building the new Archive.

PUBLICITY AND FUNDS, 1981-85

In 1981, a small donation of £7,000 (originally promised by Denis Foreman, of Granada Television, to Tom Harrisson and Asa Briggs when they were setting up the Archive) suddenly materialised. As the University of Sussex seemed prepared to fund Sheridan's salary and the running costs of the Archive at least for the time being, it was decided to use the donation to cover the costs (mostly postage but also stationery and photocopying costs) of recruiting and maintaining contact with a new panel of Mass-Observers. David Pocock wrote a brief letter to the editors of all the national daily and Sunday papers. This was followed by the same letter to a selection of local newspapers. Some of the letters appealing for recruits began to appear in the press in late May and early June. Most of the newspapers contacted by David Pocock responded positively, except *The Sun* newspaper, which returned his letter enclosing, without further comment, its advertising rates. Other papers sent journalists to visit and, as a result, some papers carried feature articles rather than the letter by itself. In one week in July 1981, Pocock and Sheridan were contacted (and later interviewed) by Simon Winchester of the *Sunday Times*; David Pocock appeared on an afternoon television programme, "Afternoon Plus"; the associate editor of the *Times Higher Education Supplement* visited the Archive; and Pocock and Sheridan were invited to visit the offices of the *Daily Mirror* at the invitation of the then editor, Mike Malone.[2]

Philip Ziegler's Jubilee "panel" and the 1977 street party reporters—those who could be re-contacted and were still keen—became the core of the new Mass-Observation panel in 1981. They were, by definition, people who were more likely to be interested in royalty

---

[2] As a result of the discussions with the *Daily Mirror*, the Archive agreed to offer a home to the original letters sent in by readers of the newspaper. For the next five years, sacks full of letters covering every possible subject, especially those issues in the public mind in the early 1980s, arrived at the Archive and were carefully stored. As a commentary on those years, they include more working-class opinions (as far as it is possible to tell) than do the bulk of the contributions received directly from members of the new Mass-Observation panel. In this way, they offer an interestingly different but complementary perspective.

48 CHAPTER TWO

and so, in order to move beyond the focus on royalty, it was clearly essential to recruit more widely to broaden the scope of the Project. It is of interest now to look back on that early publicity and see how it engendered certain expectations within the Archive itself, and for the people who responded. The letter below appeared in the weekly social and political paper, *The New Statesman*:

> The Tom Harrisson Mass-Observation Archive is conducting a three year survey into the effects of inflation on daily life and is appealing for volunteer observers and reporters. The work is interesting and not arduous, involving only a willingness to write to the archive both about personal experience and things seen and heard in daily life. The experience of "ordinary" people is of particular interest. (5 June 1981)

The New Statesman reproduced the letter in its original form, but the Letters Editor of the *Daily Mirror* altered David Pocock's wording and published this version:

> Over the next three years we are carrying out a survey of people's reactions to inflation. It doesn't matter who you are: your views will be of interest. If you want to volunteer, write to me. (3 July 1981)

The emphasis on being "ordinary" was there from the start, as was the implication that anyone can take part—"the work is not arduous", "it doesn't matter who you are". What is especially significant, and this is also apparent in the instructions to the participants, is that while personal experience is solicited, there is also an emphasis in these early appeals on the observation of others, to record "things seen and heard". In this sense David Pocock drew not only on the idea of reporting on one's own life and experiences as one might do in a diary, but also on the methods employed by Harrisson in, for example, his pre-war study of Bolton when members of the Mass-Observation team were sent out to observe and record the behaviour of people in public places. The new Mass-Observers were being asked to be at the same time both autobiographers *and* investigators/reporters, to report on the self, but also to observe, to take notes, to be out in the community taking the pulse of the nation, to be part of a collective enterprise to create a documentary of the 1980s. In this respect, the conflation of the two roles—autobiographer and investigator/reporter—was an echo of the original conceptualisation of the "Observer" when Mass-Observation first began.

It can now be seen as both the great original strength of Mass-Observation and at the same time a vulnerability. It has meant that the critiques which accompanied Mass-Observation's birth in the late 1930s (which we shall discuss in the next chapter) could be legitimately revived. Issues of methodology, however, were not addressed in 1981 and, as the use of a word like "survey" in the letters to the press illustrates, the Project operated within an uneasy mix of paradigms: opinion polling on the one hand, participant observation on the other, with journalism and ethnography, not to mention autobiography, incongruously thrown together. However, no claims were made at the time in the academic press for any kind of scholarly credibility. In any case, it was with this public representation of what a new Mass-Observer was that the Project took off most spectacularly outside the academic community. There was never any problem about attracting recruits. However confused the understanding of the new Mass-Observer might have been, it was a role that many people were keen to fill. Indeed, as we argue later, it was precisely the mix of social commentator and self-reporter that seemed to appeal most to the new Mass-Observers. It enabled the individual writer to choose his or her own balance between autobiography and documentary, and this balance varied not only among writers, but in relation to the subjects covered. The first "directive" (the term used to describe the questions which were sent to the volunteers) elicited 191 replies in June 1981; by Spring 1984, the figure had risen to 650. Over the next nineteen years, over 2,500 people would take part, many of them writing at great length and over many years.

In view of the number of years which have elapsed since the new Mass-Observation Project began, it is ironic to recall that the "Inflation Project" was originally intended to run for only about three years. That is what was conveyed to the press at the time, and that was the understanding on which the new Mass-Observers joined the Mass-Observation Project. The material which they sent in was to be stored in the Archive for future generations of researchers to discover at some unspecified but distant point in time when they came to study what it was like to live in Britain in the early 1980s. Most of the Archive's systems of administration, recruitment of writers, collection and storage of material and arrangements about public access were initially based on this assumption. However, as more people joined and as the Mass-Observation Project became better known, it seemed to gain its own momentum and somehow funds were found to keep it going.

There was never any attempt in those early years to analyse the material as it came in, or to use it as a basis for any kind of research; all resources were absorbed in simply handling the material as it flooded in, keeping records of who wrote and when, and ensuring that their contributions were sorted and filed. It must be borne in mind that this work—the correspondence with the new Mass-Observers and

50 CHAPTER TWO

responding to the consequent influx of new material—was only one part of the work of the whole Archive. The primary function of the Mass-Observation Archive, and the one for which the University of Sussex foots at least most of the bill, is to offer an historical resource for visiting scholars and others who wish to consult the papers. Priority must be given to filing and preserving material, to maintaining regular opening times and to ensuring that the kinds of services expected of any public archive (including supervision of the search room, retrieval and return of material, copying facilities and other forms of researcher support) are consistently available. As references to the early material began to appear in print, and also in radio and television programmes (see Appendices Ai-Aiii for a full list of publications), demand for access to the Archive grew; the publicity generated by the new Mass-Observation Project undoubtedly added to the Archive's fame. As a result, the whole Archive, always a small unit in terms of staff resources, was becoming much busier.

The pump-priming donation from Granada Television was followed by a succession of government-funded job-creation schemes. The schemes were originally intended to support the work of sorting and listing the early material, which was in poor condition, but the new Mass-Observation Project created an immediate and pressing demand for attention, and the newly employed archive assistants were asked to work on the new as well as the old material. Thanks to those schemes, which at first were relatively generous, the Archive was able to benefit from the skills and hard work of large number of young people who left their own mark on the work. However, the drawbacks of these schemes, which could be no more than a cosmetic attempt by the government to massage the unemployment figures, soon began to outweigh the advantages. The build-up of experience, so essential in archive work, was lost because of the ruling that no one could stay for more than a year, and by the end of the third year, the rules had become so restrictive and mean-spirited in terms of the rate of pay that trade union approval was withdrawn and the schemes were abandoned as a source of support. At that stage, in 1985, it seemed as if the Project would have to fold. The sad letters flooded in from the new Mass-Observers:

> I am desolated to hear there will be no more directives, but not surprised. [G1041]
>
> I am really upset that I will no longer be receiving directives from you. Although when no summer directive came I knew in my heart of hearts that the end was nigh, as it were. I will return to my usual unobservant person that I always was ... [D156]
>
> This reversal won't put me off sending broadsides of drivel periodically so you are not off the hook ... [O406]

Very sad about poor old Mass-Obs, but you have managed to keep it afloat for longer than I at least had feared. The material is all there and I am sure that a lot of us will start our diaries whenever something exciting happens-assassination of Mrs T? Fine weather? All these unlikely things which may yet happen and which we must catch like flying joys. Anyway, I hope one day someone will leave you an enormous legacy. Meanwhile thank you for all the work and worry you have put into it. It has become part of true history. [M380]

AFTER THE HIATUS, FROM 1986

Help came in the form of a grant of £50,000 from the Nuffield Foundation in 1986. The grant was remarkably and generously open-ended and simply provided for the resumption of the Project. It provided enough funds to employ two part-time clerical assistants and to cover the material costs of maintaining the work for at least three more years. During the interval (known as "the hiatus") when funds dried up, many of the correspondents had refused to stop writing despite clear warnings that the Archive could not keep receiving their contributions. These people, delighted with the restoration of activities, once again became the core of a new and enlarged panel. Appeals for new recruits were made once again through the press, and the Autumn 1986 directive was sent out inviting the correspondents to comment on what they considered were the main events of 1986 (personal or political, or both) and to keep a diary for 25 December 1986 whether they celebrated Christmas or not. By 1987, the mailing list contained over 1,200 names.

Because there were no formal stipulations about the way the grant from the Nuffield Foundation should be spent, it was possible to make it last over five years and to supplement it with income from other sources. One of these sources was the Archive's own publishing programme, consisting primarily of edited anthologies based on the wartime material (see Appendices Aii and Aiii). Much later, in 1991, the Archive was able to benefit from small but regular charitable donations made possible by the establishment of a "Friends of the Mass-Observation Archive" scheme. The Project also began quite early in its life to earn small amounts towards its own upkeep. As it became better known, the Archive was approached by researchers about using the panel of correspondents to explore a particular topic which interested them. During these early years, the London Office of the European Community commissioned a project on British membership in the European Community (Special Directive, 1982), BBC Television asked the Archive to solicit material on work and unemployment (Summer 1983) and a firm of freelance anthropologists commissioned material on electronic developments in banking (Summer 1984).

These "commissions" have remained a significant source of funding for the Project in the absence of any large external grants. Although researchers can request that a topic is covered, and can gain access to the resulting material, they do not acquire the material itself (it remains within the Archive and the usual rules governing access to the collection continue to apply), nor is any form of analysis or summary of results offered by the Archive staff. The researchers must undertake the analysis themselves. What they "buy" is access to data produced by a panel composed of people with a high level of commitment to the project itself, which ensures that however popular or unpopular the theme of the directive might be, it still yields a response. Most commissioning researchers are from academic institutions who have received funds from sources traditionally supporting academic research, such as the Economic and Social Research Council and the Nuffield Foundation. The BBC has also made substantial use of the contemporary material, including commissioning directives.

There are tangible benefits to be gained from the occasional collaboration with outside researchers. Not only do they make a financial contribution which allows the Project to continue, but they also demonstrate the usefulness of the material to present-day research. Considerable care is always given to the balance between the short-term interests and requirements of the researchers (and their funders) and the long-term interests of the Mass-Observation Project. This balance is not always easy to achieve. Evidence from interviews with selected Mass-Observation correspondents in 1993 (described later in the book) suggests that at least one of the commissioned directives was unpopular with the Mass-Observation correspondents and that it was only because of their abiding loyalty to the Mass-Observation Project as a whole that they bothered to reply to that commissioned directive. A selection of directives, including the contentious Summer 1993 directive on the Environment, is included in Appendix Bi.

HOW PEOPLE JOIN MASS-OBSERVATION: ADVERTISING AND RECRUITMENT

The kinds of people who have volunteered to take part in the Mass-Observation Project-their backgrounds and their motives for getting involved—have varied in relation to the extent and form of publicity the Mass-Observation Project has received. Images of what "Mass-Observation" is, could be, or should be, have been conveyed to potential correspondents in a variety of forms, but the most powerful representations are conveyed by the media. There has been substantial media coverage over the years not only of the contemporary Mass-Observation Project, but also of the early Mass-Observation papers and publications arising from their use.

[Letter From M1498 Volunteering To Write for Mass-Observation]
[Original Letter was handwritten in pen on blue paper]

10TH November 1986

Dear Prof. Pocock,

I read in the Evening Argus that you wanted ordinary people to write about their lives. I was brought up in Polegate but moved to Wigan eleven years ago as my husband comes from Lancashire. We moved back here in July, partly to be nearer my family, but mainly to improve our job prospects as my husband has been unemployed. I think our difficulties are fairly typical of many ordinary families at the moment and I think I could find plenty to write about e.g. our search for work, differences between North + South etc. We are both 32 and have two sons at junior school. I realise you are probably more interested in the content than the writing but I did get a Grade A 'A' level in English at Wigan college of Technology, again in the hope of finding a better job later on, and I like writing. I hope you will consider me.

Yours sincerely,

A distinction needs to be made between direct and active recruitment by the Archive (in the form of appeals through the letters pages of the press), and indirect recruitment resulting from articles in newspapers and magazines, books, book reviews and interviews on radio or television. No attempt to buy advertising space has ever been possible. Press coverage over the years has always been mixed. Some of it has taken the form of news items containing variations on the theme of "ordinary", "everyday" and "people's" history. These include "Everyday Stories of British Folk" (*The Sheffield Daily Star*, 18 November 1986), "Grant Brings History to Life" (*Brighton Evening Argus*, 7 May 1986), and "An Invitation to Write Tomorrow's History Books" (*The Wolverhampton Express*, 8 November 1986). Some have also included less positive images-for example the unfortunate "Curtains for Peeping Toms" in the *Observer* (30 June 1991), which headed what was otherwise a sympathetic article about the Archive's constant quest for funds. The references to spying and eavesdropping are also constantly evoked: "Look Out Britain, They're Eyeing You" (*Sunday Times*, 2 November 1986), "Peeping on Tom Again" (*Today*, 27 November 1986), "We Know What You're Doing!" (*Brighton Evening Argus*, 14 October 1986). Other press coverage includes reviews of the more recently published Mass-Observation books, or articles by Mass-Observers themselves.

Items on the radio, on television and in the press have always produced the largest number of interested responses, but the Mass-Observation books have also encouraged people to join. Two edited wartime diaries, *Nella Last's War* (Fleming & Broad, 1981) and *Among You Taking Notes: The Wartime Diary of Naomi Mitchison* (Sheridan, 1985), are often cited by women in particular as the inspiration for their getting in touch with the Archive. Other books which have appeared since 1981 and have attracted volunteers, perhaps because they include extracts from diaries and from the writings of wartime contributors, are *Speak for Yourself* (Calder & Sheridan, 1984) and *Wartime Women* (Sheridan, 1990).

A smaller number of people volunteer to take part after making personal contact with a member of Archive staff, either on a visit to the Archive (some correspondents are also researchers) or as a result of meeting someone away from the Archive. These contacts occur in a variety of settings: academic seminars and conferences are perhaps most common but also academic courses, day schools, evening classes, exhibitions, trade union and adult education groups, after-dinner speeches and public lectures. Some more specialised groups of writers have been recruited in this way—for example, classes of school-age correspondents. In general, attempts to recruit school children through their teachers and visits to the Archive result in batches of writing (for example, replies to one particular directive) being donated to the

Archive, but very few recruits found in this way stay with the project for more than a year.

Publicity is also generated from time to time by the correspondents' own activities. Individual Mass-Observers have been interviewed by journalists from both radio and the press on their own initiative about their participation in Mass-Observation (the Archive could never give out names because of its promise of confidentiality); others have written articles for magazines and newspapers or for the newsletters of the organisations to which they belong. Very often, someone has joined as a result of a recommendation from a friend, colleague or relative.

The first wave of letters in the press appealing for new Mass-Observers in May 1981 attracted about 400 interested writers. In response to directive No. 2 (on the Royal Wedding), 347 people sent in a diary for the day. This was followed, eight months later, by a second similar appeal to 30 national and local papers. As a result, 800 copies of the Spring 1982 directive were sent out to everyone who expressed an interest, resulting in the return of 205 replies (52 men and 153 women). By the end of 1983, there were 677 people on the regular mailing list.

It was clear from the start that the new Project, unlike the original 1937 initiative where men predominated, was attracting a much larger number of women than men. Part of the reason for this was that the Project recruited heavily in the latter half of 1983 from an article by an existing Mass-Observer in the newsletter of the *Housewives Register*, an organisation of women. However, as the figures in Table 2-1 indicate, the imbalance was already present from the start of the new recruitment drive.

The disproportionate number of women in relation to men continues to be a characteristic of the new Project, and proves to be extraordinarily resistant to manipulation, despite some small efforts

Table 2-1. Responses to Directives from November 1982 and November 1983.

Directive	Total Replies	Men	Women	Overall Response
Winter 1982	309	68	241	55% (estimated)
Spring 1983	370	83	287	57%
Summer 1983	386	90	296	62%
Autumn 1983	333	72	261	52%
Winter 1983	399	93	305	58%

over the years to recruit more men. In 1983, for example, existing correspondents were asked if they would try to recruit new male correspondents for the Project. This was known as the "Man Appeal". Thirty-seven men joined as a result of the initiative. The Spring 1984 directive (on health issues) was sent out to 235 men and 551 women. Responses were received from 156 men and 494 women, 63% response rate and 89.6% response rate respectively. So even when more men were recruited, they seemed less likely to respond.

The next wave of publicity was triggered by the anthology of wartime Mass-Observation material *Speak for Yourself* (Calder & Sheridan, 1984), which appeared in March 1984 in hardback, and a year later in paperback. It was widely reviewed in the national and local press (over 24 reviews), and resulted in considerable radio and television coverage, although a high proportion of people asking for information did not follow through by joining the project. Of the 1,378 people who were sent the Summer 1984 directive on electronic innovation in financial services, fewer than half replied. By the time the Winter 1984 directive was mailed out, the mailing list was pruned down to 880 people, and 472 replies were received. It has been Archive practice since then to remove the names of people from the mailing list after a period of about a year during which nothing has been heard from them. This practice of "weeding" the mailing list has made it difficult to monitor the relative popularity of different directive themes, but it seems reasonable to assume that some subjects appeal to more people than others. It may be the large numbers of people who enquired but decided not to become regular Mass-Observers in the Summer of 1984 were put off not by the nature of the Mass-Observation Project as a whole, but by the request to write about banking and financial services, which would have been the first directive they received.

From time to time, correspondents write in to say that they have decided to leave the Project. The reasons they give are usually related to ill health (often failing eyesight or difficulty in typing and writing, especially as they grow older) or to the fact that they have suddenly become too busy to answer directives. About half a dozen people have left because of becoming disenchanted with the Project itself. The kinds of complaints they voice include feeling that the project has become "commercial" or market research oriented, or alternatively, that the questions have become too personal. Their criticisms usually relate to what they perceive to be a change in policy or practice since they joined the Project.

Very few names were added to the mailing list in 1985 and no directives were mailed out between Spring 1985 and Autumn 1986 when there were no funds. The last directive (Spring 1985 on religion and morality) to be mailed out before the break between 1985 and 1986 was answered by 403 people. People who spontaneously volunteered during this period were either rejected or put on indefinite hold. When the injection of funds from the Nuffield Foundation facilitated the re-starting of the project from 1 October 1986, the mailing list was re-activated, people on hold were contacted, and a new set of letters was dispatched to the press. At the same time, considerable publicity was attending the Archive's other activities, including an exhibition at the Watermans Arts Centre in London to commemorate Mass-Observation's 50th anniversary, the publication of *Mass-Observation at the Movies* (Richards & Sheridan, 1987), the showing of a film about Mass-Observation, "Stranger than Fiction", directed by Ian Potts, on Channel 4, and a major Thames Television series, "The People's War", which drew on the Archive's early material. Levels of recruitment reached the highest point ever with 1,333 on the mailing list in Spring 1987, but with a response rate of only 51% (182 from men and 494 from women). A comprehensive "weed" reduced numbers to 998 in Summer 1987, and the total hovered around the 900-1,000 mark until the end of 1989.

With the project on a firmer financial footing from 1986, it was possible to start to look more closely at the composition of the panel. Women continued to outnumber men and people over 40 years old predominated. The Project had also been unsuccessful in recruiting many people from Afro-Caribbean and Asian backgrounds. In order to diversify the composition of the panel, a special recruitment campaign was organised in 1987. Lists of specialist publications were drawn up, targeting, in particular, potential male volunteers (the armed services, prisons, men's hobby magazines, trade unions), younger people and ethnic minorities (through specialist newsletters and papers). There was no previous connection between the Archive and these publications, and no insider contacts.

The response to this initiative was patchy; a few excellent new volunteers were recruited. One of the main problems was that only a few of the publications actually published the letter. The highest response rate came from readers of the *Rambler*, a magazine for people who enjoy walking in the countryside (an interest not especially confined to men of course). Of the 47 people recruited through the *Rambler*, only fifteen were men.

The panel continued to grow, reaching a new peak of 1,233 on the mailing list in Spring 1990.

58 CHAPTER TWO

> Dear Sir/Madam
>
> I understand you are looking for volunteer mass-observers. I would be interested in joining your ranks. I am a male aged 34. I have been married a year. My wife lives and works in London and will join me sometime next year once my house (a council house bought in my grandmothers name) has been totally refurbished with the help of a housing repair grant.
>
> My wife is of West Indian and Irish descent so our son is a wonderful mixture of races, cultures, and for that matter languages. I speak to him in Welsh and he will be educated through the medium of Welsh.
>
> I have only lived in Taffs Well two years. My parents come from the village but because my father was in the RAF we lived all over the world. My mother lives in the village again as do my brother and sister, grandmother, uncles, aunts and cousins. My fathers parents live in the next village.
>
> I am a Plaid Cymru community councillor so get to know a lot about what goes on in this changing part of the world. In the next local elections I may stand for the Borough if it still exists, or for Cardiff if we are taken over by the city.
>
> I mention all these things in the hope that you may find me an interesting observer of the local scene.
>
> Yours

Until 1994, all unsolicited volunteers were accepted unconditionally. During this period, media attention remained constant if unpredictable. *Wartime Women* (Sheridan, 1990) was published in hardback, and then in paperback in 1991, and was widely reviewed, particularly in the women-orientated media (e.g. "Woman's Hour" on BBC Radio). The Nuffield money ran out in 1990 around the same time as David Pocock retired from the Project. A small internal grant from the University of Sussex assisted the Project over the period of a year. This was instrumental in updating computer support and in improving the Archive's ability to become at least partly self-financing, but no dedicated funds were available for the Project.

Active recruitment lapsed after 1990 and the overall numbers on the mailing list were deliberately allowed to drop. The Archive was struggling to sustain such a large mailing list with limited resources. In any case, high numbers on the mailing list did not guarantee a good response rate. The response to the Spring 1990 directive was low, 42% (160 men and 362 women), only rising to 52% in response to the Summer directive and to 55% in response to the Autumn directive. It was clear the Project was carrying a lot of people who no longer wished to write, and this triggered a major "weed" before the Autumn 1991 directive was sent out, bringing numbers down to 664. Replies from that directive were 118 men and 302 women (63% response rate), followed by a 74% response rate to the directive on personal hygiene commissioned by BBC Radio (Spring 1992 Part 1) and a 70% response rate to the Part 2 (pace of life) commissioned by Jenny Shaw, a sociologist at the University of Sussex. Unexpected publicity attracted 300 new recruits in the first three months of 1991. About 250 of these resulted from a feature article in the *Guardian* in January 1990. Additional recruits responded to an article in *Plus* magazine, and to the reviews of *Wartime Women* the same year. By the end of 1991, the Project had attracted 427 new recruits, but in 1992 only 54, and in 1993 only 42, most of these being recruited through word of mouth. Despite the absence of active recruitment, however, there always remained a trickle of enquiries and new recruits. The composition of the panel, despite the fluctuations in size, remained remarkably constant, namely the ratio of men to women, and the high proportion of older people. Researchers using the collection were often dismayed and puzzled at not finding writings from younger people within the collection.

In 1994, for the first time since the Project began, and in a spirit of experimentation, Sheridan introduced a policy of rejecting certain categories of volunteers, that is, women over 35 and men over 50. Announcements of the new policy were made to the existing panel which, perhaps not surprisingly, provoked some negative reactions from older people, especially women, who found it hard not to think of the restriction as insulting. A comparison between the age and gender ratios in 1992, before the policy was introduced, and in 1996, when it had been in operation for two years, is shown in Tables 2-2 and 2-3. The restriction appears at first glance not to have had much effect, but it is clear that if it had not been in place, the uncontrolled acceptance of all the people who volunteered between 1994 and 1996 would have produced an even greater preponderance of older people and women. It seems likely that whereas deliberate recruitment campaigns are capable of attracting younger people and men, the more passive and low-level recruitment policy of accepting people who happen to hear about the Project is predisposed towards attracting older women.

When figures are compared over a longer period, there is some evidence that without intervention, the gender balance had shifted. In 1984, for example, about a quarter of the "active" correspondents were male. In 1992, the proportion had grown to a third. These figures relate exclusively to the composition of the mailing list in any given year. The characteristics of the groups responding to any given directive might demonstrate quite different patterns (although preliminary explorations

Table 2-2. Women Active in Mass-Observation.

Women Active in The Project	Total	Under 35 yrs. Old	% Under 35 yrs. old
In 1992	493	58	11.76%
In 1996	329	44	13.37%

Table 2-3. Men Active in Mass-Observation.

Men Active in The Project	Total	Under 50 yrs. Old	% Under 50 yrs. old
In 1992	192	65	33.85%
In 1996	132	43	32.57%

of directive response rates suggest that the pattern of the composition, at least in terms of age groups and gender, remains remarkably stable for most directives). The other important factor in determining the composition of the panel is the drop-out rate. There is some evidence to suggest that different categories of volunteers behave differently within the Project. Younger men, for example, stay involved for less time than older men or women, which means that the Project would need to be continually replacing the younger men in order to maintain their presence in the Project.

BECOMING A MASS-OBSERVER

What then is involved in becoming a Mass-Observer in the present-day? This section will concentrate on the information provided by the Archive to the correspondent. We especially highlight how literacy is implicated in becoming a Mass-Observer. Later in the book, we shall be discussing the ways in which the correspondents understand the Project and interpret the task of taking part.[3]

The pattern of contact between the Archive and a new recruit typically begins with an initial letter or phone call (patterns of recruitment and the ways people hear about the work are covered later

---

[3]Discussions on the nature of the Archive/correspondent relationship have already been published by Sheridan. See for example "Ordinary hardworking folk: Volunteer writers in Mass-Observation 1937-50 and 1981-91" (1993a), "Writing for . . . Questions of representation/representativeness, authorship and audience" (1993b) and "Writing to the Archive: Mass-Observation as autobiography" (1993c).

Open day at the Mass-Observation Archive, 1992

in this chapter). They are then sent a package of information describing the Project and outlining what taking part would entail. Apart from a request that they sign a copyright form, they are also asked for a "Self-Portrait" which would serve as an introduction to their participation in the Project. This request is relatively non-prescriptive, leaving the correspondents to find their own preferred level of self-disclosure. As a result, the portraits vary widely in both length and coverage. Most people respond with a few pages about their life to date, their family and work, their neighbourhood and their education. A few send in something which closely resembles a curriculum vitae (indeed it may well have been produced for job applications and only slightly revised, if at all, for the Archive). For several years, these portraits were the only form of background information about the writers in the Archive. However, researchers consulting the collection increasingly wanted "harder" information. The introductory self-portraits are not available to

62 CHAPTER TWO

researchers because they are identifiable. In any case, the variation in form and content (or more precisely some of the omissions), and the "embeddedness" of items of information, makes it time-consuming for Archive staff to unearth the required details for researchers. In 1991, a more structured Biographical Information form (see Appendix Biii) asking for age, place of residence, occupation and living/marital situation was introduced. This does not replace the discursive self-portrait, but is an addition to it and could be sufficiently impersonal to be made available to researchers.

The new recruit is also asked to supply a recent photograph. Again the response is varied. A few people decline to provide any photograph at all. Some say that they do not like to be photographed and have nothing suitable to send. Some worry about being more easily identified from a photograph. Most do send prints that range from elegant studio portraits to the tiny passport photos taken in photo-booths, from grainy indoor family shots to glamorous sunlit seaside poses. Photographs of people on holiday are very common, perhaps because that is when most people use cameras; it is also a time when people are able to create pictures of themselves looking healthy and relaxed—that is, images that they feel comfortable about placing with their writing for posterity.

Every new volunteer today receives a copy of the "How To Take Part" booklet. This advice has grown out of much shorter introductory leaflets dating back to the beginning of the Project which were prepared in response to the questions the Mass-Observers themselves asked. By 1989, the booklet had become eight pages long and illustrated with cartoons and drawings. It opened with an explanation, reproducing text which had been written by David Pocock in 1981, "How Did Mass-Observation Begin?":

> Mass-Observation began in the late 1930s. At the time of the "Abdication Crisis" (as it was called) Tom Harrisson, Charles Madge, Humphrey Jennings and their friends were struck by the gap between what the papers were reporting and what people in buses, streets and pubs were actually saying.
>
> Mass-Observation was founded to chronicle the "voice of the people", to record day-to-day life in the United Kingdom-what we sometimes call "the real history". Mass-Observation is not a public opinion poll intended for immediate publication. We are creating, rather, a unique "time capsule" for the historian of tomorrow.

The booklet goes on to describe, briefly, the present Archive and the fact that it is consulted for research. Information about the way the project works is given under the headings "Protecting the Mass-

Observation material", "What it's all about", "How to join the project" and so on. In a section headed "Some thoughts on writing", guidance is given on what might be expected:

> First of all, don't feel pressured. We well understand that not everyone is interested in everything and also that the range of people's experience can be limited for all sorts of reasons. Therefore you must feel free to pick and choose and to write in the light of your own experience. But do remember that "negative" reporting is always valuable; when we had a directive on cars and driving, for example, it was important to have the views of non-drivers.
>
> It is always useful to widen your report by asking for the reactions of relatives and friends. Also you may observe a little scene or overhear a little snippet of conversation which reveals an aspect of life in our times and is worth recording. However, please do not identify people by name but do identify gender, approximate age and (if you happen to know it) occupation. THIS IS NOT AN INVITATION TO EAVESDROP. THERE IS ALL THE DIFFERENCE IN THE WORLD BETWEEN REPORTING SOMETHING CASUALLY OVERHEARD AND DELIBERATELY LISTENING TO A PRIVATE CONVERSATION...
>
> When you receive your directive do not rush to reply. Read it through, discuss it with family and friends as occasion offers, see whether news or features in the media have any bearing on it. There is no virtue in speed and no need at all to apologise for a gap of a month or two between the receipt of your directive and your report.

The version of the booklet in current use, last modified in 1991, runs to fourteen sides, and takes a question-and-answer format. Some of the questions are: "What is the Mass-Observation project?", "If I join, what will I have to do?", "Can I send in other writing or contributions?", "What kind of paper shall I use?", "Must reports be typed?", "How much should I write?", "Is there a deadline?", "Who sees my contributions?", "How can I be sure that my privacy is protected?", "Can members of my family read what I send to you?", "Can my Mass-Observation writings be published?", "Can I visit the Archive?" and so on. The section "Some thoughts on writing" remains as above with only minor amendments. The answers to the questions are intended to provide just enough guidance to give people a sense of the whole endeavour while at the same time ensuring that they should feel free to develop their own forms of contribution, particularly in relation to how often and how much they should write.

THE DIRECTIVES

Throughout the time that the correspondents remain involved in the Project, they continue to be exposed to, and negotiate with, representations of the Archive as a whole and the Mass-Observation Project. The main form of contact takes place through the "directives" and the accompanying letters which they receive three times a year. How the directive has been written, who has written it, which themes it covers and what kinds of respondent it assumes, are all key elements in the forging of the relationship within which the writing takes place.[4] The directives, and more particularly the letters that accompany them, reinforce and develop many of the themes of the introductory booklet. A full list of the directives since 1981 is included in Appendix Bi. From the start, the emphasis is placed on personal experience, and on writing as much or as little as the writer is inclined. In 1981, there was an explicit emphasis on the observation not only of other people's behaviour, but also of objects and events. Some of the questions require no more than a list or chronological account. The very first directive, sent out in May 1981, includes requests that the Mass-Observer "look out for reactions" to newly introduced coins, that they note down local events in the run up to the Royal Wedding, that they record the number of local shops which have closed down in the past twelve months and that they describe a typical day's meals. The same directive goes on to ask for personal experience of unemployment, personal experience of holidays and the price of vegetables ("this is obviously connected to the weather we've had this year"). The tone is casual, friendly and the topic relatively "safe". No-one is expected to bare their soul, unless of course they wish to. The experience of unemployment was perhaps the only question which touched more closely on an autobiographical and personal area.

The second directive took the form of a short letter, and requested only that people keep a diary for the day of the 1981 Royal Wedding. It was headed "Celebration or bore?". Directive no. 3 in 1982 returned to the same varied mix of themes which were covered in the first directive: house prices, including observations of properties in the local area, lists of unsolicited mail received, experiences of the winter weather, effects of the rail strike, knowledge about the local elections among friends and acquaintances and more on shop closures. This

---

[4]Hermine Scheeres of the University of Technology, Sydney, undertook a linguistic analysis of both a set of directives and the forms of responses which they elicited. She presented her findings, "Writing, reader/texts relations: Reading the M-O directives and Responses" in a seminar at the University of Sussex (Mass-Observation seminar series) on 19.10.93. The paper is unpublished, but a tape of the seminar and subsequent discussion is available in the University of Sussex Library.

directive resulted in a vast amount of printed material being sent to the Archive (mostly estate agents' material and copies of unsolicited mail). The repeat request for shop closure information set a few correspondents, who were to become regulars, on a particular path of response, and their detailed accounts of their local high streets continued to arrive long after the requests for such reports had ceased. The balance between the one-theme directive and the mixed directives continued for another year. Single-theme directives included the Falklands War in 1982 and the tenth anniversary of British membership of the European Community (also 1982). The Winter 1982 directive on food, meals and eating habits generally was the first of a more focused set of directives, and with the focus on a theme came a greater emphasis on self-reporting. For example: "please be as specific as possible e.g. specify whether you are a vegetarian, vegan . . . if you object to particular additives, please say which . . . please do add other reasons which occur to you for not eating things . . ." (Winter 1982). The response was rate was high and the replies very detailed. The correspondents seemed quite willing to speak of their own activities and preferences, and in many ways, it was easier than the earlier tasks, which involved observation and counting, which took them out of their ordinary everyday routines, and which a few felt uncomfortable about since it did smack of eavesdropping or spying.

By 1984, the pattern of producing three directives a year, each one containing at the most three areas for discussion, was set. The subjects (see Appendix Bi) included current events (elections, strikes, disasters, wars, reactions to international and national news), but they also called for more personal accounts of opinion and experience, including retrospective accounts of childhood and early adulthood. Although the directives contained questions, there was a deliberate effort made to avoid producing short and uninformative answers. This was not only a question of framing the questions in an open-ended fashion but also of ensuring not very much space was left on the directives, which would encourage correspondents to shorten their answers so that they could be squeezed onto the same pages as the printed directive. In almost every directive there is an injunction to regard the questions as prompts to get them writing:

> As usual I have listed some topics, as usual many of them are in the form of questions and, as usual, I beg you not to treat them as such; they are there to provoke and stimulate thought. (Spring directive on morality and religion, 1985)

The quotation above also illustrates the emphasis on the specific author. The directives until 1990 were authored and signed by David

66 CHAPTER TWO

Pocock, although the texts became increasingly a collaborative production involving Sheridan and other members of the Archive staff. Very occasionally, Sheridan's voice would be included. For example both signatures appeared on the Winter directive 1984. The use of "I" remained dominant, however, and there is no doubt that when the Mass-Observers replied, it was to a University Professor of Social Anthropology. The Autumn 1982 directive, which dealt with the question of children's pocket money and its relation to the contribution children make to their households, included the following paragraph:

> *An anthropological note*: In a trading caste of western India a boy of 7 or 8 would regularly be given the equivalent of 50 pence and be told to go and buy some household need, vegetables, say. On his return, his father would quiz him: how many vegetable stalls had he visited, what was the range of prices . . .

In the next paragraph of the same directive, the voice shifts:

> Nearer home: My grandfather in Sheffield before the 1914-18 war told his sons that the cost of their education was to be regarded as a loan from him to them which they should repay as soon as they could afford to do so . . .

And then there would be the more commonplace, shared voice which Pocock used in the Summer 1981 directive, revealing an author who also went shopping, visited the post office, met people in the street in an everyday sort of way:

> Last week two men ahead of me in the Post Office collected their pensions and I saw them again in the greengrocer's. . . .

The backup team, once described by one Mass-Observer as "the Ladies of the Archive", remained a shadowy presence, both in terms of their representation in the directives and (judging by the replies to a direct question on the subject in the Spring 1991 directive) in the minds of the Mass-Observers. Since 1991, there has been a deliberate shift towards greater visibility in the way staff at the Archive are represented. Individual members of staff are named and their roles sometimes described. The more collaborative production of directives is made explicit.

The directives themselves have a different look to them since 1990. The headings are larger, the typeface larger and bolder; there is more "white" space and the occasional graphic or illustration is included. This has been made possible by having access to more sophisticated word-processing packages and a high-quality laser printer, but it also stems from a desire to move away from what some Mass-Observers have described as the "exam paper" look of the directives. The directive remains discursive, but the use of "I" in the actual text is rare (it continues to appear in the covering letter but not in the body of the directive), and the amount of explicit self-disclosure by the author of the directive is less. Astute correspondents, however, have enjoyed picking up on all kinds of clues about Sheridan's opinions and proclivities. Attitudes to, among other things, the legalisation of cannabis, the relations between men and women, homosexuality (as revealed by the use of the word "gay" in the Summer 1990 directive), and a number of other controversial topics have been commented on by many correspondents, sometimes with approval and sometimes with disapproval.

Irrespective of the amount of autobiography in the texts of the directives themselves, the choice of the subject matter of the directives has always been a personal matter. Until 1990, the themes, and the treatment of the themes, were exclusively decided by David Pocock, even when he was responding to ideas and suggestions of a potential commissioner. The same situation pertains today. The choice of themes evolves out partly from Sheridan's own research interests[5] and those of colleagues at the Archive and at the University of Sussex, and partly from the ideas and suggestions of the writers themselves. There has also been an attempt, over the years, to cover contemporary social and political issues, but the constraints of time and resources permit only three directives per year and therefore do not provide a structure for rapid response to current events. The directive on the war over the Falkland Islands, sent out on 19 April 1982, was a response to the number of people already writing to the Archive about it. A second directive on the same topic "The Falklands War Aftermath", was sent out later the same year (there were six separate mail-outs in 1982) to invite comments on the various military parades and celebrations that occurred when the war ended. These directives asked for on-the-spot reactions to the war, but many years later, when war again threatened over Iraq's invasion of Kuwait in 1990, Sheridan tried a different approach. The Autumn directive was sent out in October 1990, over two

---

[5]These interests include writing itself—autobiography, diary-keeping and reading, for example—but also women's studies, life stories, feminist history, gender relations, the home and family, sexuality and politics. Some of the themes have been chosen because they result in material for courses at the University of Sussex based on the Archive (an adult education course, the Certificate in Life History Work, an undergraduate course, Social Investigation and Mass-Observation, and a Masters-level course, "Critical Approaches to Mass-Observation").

68 CHAPTER TWO

months after the invasion. One of the key items of news at that point was the release of hostages held by Saddam Hussein, the Iraqi leader, and the visit by former British Prime Minister, Edward Heath, to Iraq for negotiations. The Autumn directive invited correspondents to chart their reactions to developments over the following weeks:

> It would be very helpful if, even after you have sent us your initial responses, you could continue to keep a kind of log of your reactions to events. This could take the form of a "Gulf Crisis" diary which you could either send in instalments or keep until you are returning the Spring directive next year.

By the time the Spring directive was sent out in February 1991, Operation Desert Storm was well under way, and the correspondents had recorded their reactions to the expiration of the UN deadline and the commencement of Allied bombing of Iraq on 17 January 1991. The directive contained thanks for the instalments already received and a request to keep recording while the conflict continued. As a result, a very large amount of material was received covering the whole period of the Gulf War. Similar, though less extensive, coverage has been obtained for other national events: the Royal Wedding of 1981, the political scene in 1982 including party political changes and local elections, the General Elections of 1983, 1987 and 1992 and reactions to strikes and industrial unrest in 1982 and 1983. In 1984, comments were invited on a range of topics: the Miners' Strike, rate-capping in Liverpool, the teachers' union activities, rail strikes, the European Parliament and the visits to the United Kingdom of President Botha from South Africa and President Reagan from the United States. In November 1987, soon after a strong gale hit the south of England and parts of Wales experienced flash floods, reactions to the appalling weather conditions were invited.

Over the same period, wider social issues were touched on, including reactions in 1987 to the government health campaigns about AIDS, and more recently to public controversies: public food scares about salmonella in eggs and listeria in cheese (1989), the environment and ecological issues (1992), personal security and crime (1993), the Lottery (1985), the crisis over British beef and Bovine Spongiform Encephalitis (1996). Many major events have been captured by general requests for opinions which give the correspondents the opportunity to select those issues and events which they deem to be important, or which have a particular resonance for them personally. In the Spring of 1990, they were asked for a "Retrospective of the Eighties", and in the Winter 1992 directive and the Summer of 1993, they were asked for similar reports for 1992 and 1993 respectively. The 1993 directive included some suggestions of possible topics: "conflicts in the former Yugoslavia and in Somalia, the European debate, the British education system, the National Health Service, the monarchy and crises within the Conservative government".

In addition to the topics suggested, many correspondents send in unsolicited reports, and it has been possible in this way to gather material which has not been tackled in a directive. For example, one of the most important issues of the 1980s, people's reactions to a new and highly unpopular tax, the Community Charge (Poll Tax), did not appear in a directive, but was still covered by some correspondents, who often wrote at length about their own experience spontaneously—that is, without needing to be prompted by a directive. One such account is discussed in Bloome, Sheridan and Street (1995, p. 21).

When a directive arises from a suggestion by an outside researcher, every effort is made to "convert" the text into the Mass-Observation house style: to use a colloquial style, to avoid "closed" questions, to stimulate and provoke the writers, and to be as inclusive as possible so that everyone feels they have something to contribute on a subject. For example, when Alia Al Khalidi approached the Archive in 1995 about doing a directive on the production and consumption of women's sanitary products for her doctoral thesis, Sheridan suggested that her theme be extended beyond the narrow focus on consumption to produce a directive which would elicit women's experiences of menstruation in the context of their life stories, and in addition, to produce a differently-worded directive for the male correspondents which would invite them to write in an area in which men are very rarely asked for their views and experiences. Since 1990, there has been a greater emphasis on reflection, life story narrative and self-reporting: "How do you feel?", "What do you think?", "Have you changed . . .?", "What has been your experience of . . .?" but the topics range over what might traditionally be described as both "personal" and "public", and the correspondent is encouraged to respond by crossing and re-crossing the same boundaries. The Spring 1991 directive was one of these later directives, asking first for an educational life history, then for a personal account of the correspondent's writing practices, and then for a log of literacy events and practices. The replies to this directive are discussed more fully later.

The forms of response requested include the diary or log format, often a record of one day's activities, or a longer one (as for the directive on the Gulf War), or a specific request to log activities: which television programmes watched, what meals eaten. Sometimes, lists have been requested: books read, money spent, posters seen, shops closed down, the clothes in your wardrobe. Some requests are for thematic life stories.

Replies to those are usually chronological in form: growing up, growing older, menstruation, close relationships, educational history. Most ask for stories: accounts of celebrations, memories of childhood and youth, or for descriptions: what your living room looks like, what your neighbourhood is like. Questions are often specific: not "what did you usually do?" but rather, "tell us what you did when..."

The aim is to ensure a variety of themes, to stimulate, amuse and provoke the correspondents into replying, and to create as far as possible a diverse set of multi-layered, multi-faceted life stories on a whole range of contemporary concerns.

ORGANISATION AND CLASSIFICATION OF DATA

There has no doubt been a shift towards greater formality as the Project evolved, and this was consolidated when Sheridan took over full responsibility for the Project in 1990. The most visible result of the change-over from the correspondents' point of view (or at least the one that has raised some comments from a few of them) was the replacement of personal, often hand-written, thank-you letters by standard acknowledgements. This gradual change was not occasioned by any legal or ethical obligation, but simply by the pressure of work, and the need to change priorities in the allocation of scarce resources. During his involvement with the project, David Pocock acknowledged the receipt of every piece of writing, usually responding individually to personal news or items of special interest, with Sheridan occasionally helping out when the task grew overwhelming. This succeeded in ensuring that people felt valued, and many wrote to say how sorry they were when he left the Project.[6] One writer expressed it quite poignantly:

> ... this [change] has had a marked effect on my writing the diary everyday and on my feelings about writing it. It has also affected my attitude to writing my response to the directive. I find myself wondering if the change of director is going to affect the writing of other correspondents. ... I find it harder to write and I miss the sense that someone I know personally is on the other end listening to me speak. I have been tempted even to give up writing it altogether but I won't do that. I will keep on but it may take some months before a new sense of confidence and intimacy develops ... my feeling is more impersonal, less trusting. I am sure that many

---

[6]Some of the reactions to the transition, and their psychological implications for our understanding of the significance of gender in the writing relationship, have been explored by Jenny Shaw (1994) in her paper "Transference and countertransference in the Mass-Observation Archive".

other correspondents feel the same sense of loss as I am suffering from so perhaps future users of M-O will notice the shift of tone that came about in April 1990. [O1364f]

When Sheridan took over in 1991, she decided to limit the amount of change that occurred all at once so she continued responding individually to as many writers as possible. The task became impossible to sustain; the more time devoted to this activity, the less time and energy there was for managing the Archive as a whole, and for writing and research. The policy had to change. The personal notes are now reserved for about a quarter of the writers, currently selected by Judy Pickering, the archive assistant who works most closely with the Mass-Observation Project. She picks out those writers who ask particular questions or who describe something out of the ordinary. Everyone else receives a standard photocopied acknowledgement letter which is revised every few weeks and which tries in a collective way to express appreciation, offer feedback and share news about the Archive.

CHANGES AND DEVELOPMENTS

The continued existence of the Project over many years has provided an opportunity to refine and develop methods of organisation and archiving, and to improve the nature of the relationship with the correspondents. Changes in the Project itself prompted the need for a review of procedures. The impact of the growth of the panel on the one hand, and the increased and unforeseen demand for access by researchers on the other, has intensified the problems of confidentiality and control. Agreements about care, especially of sensitive material, had to be as good as possible. Once contact has been lost with a Mass-Observer, it is impossible to make proper agreements. In her capacity as an archivist, Sheridan had become sensitised to questions of copyright, ownership and privacy through the sometimes frustrating experience of handling problems raised by research use of the original Mass-Observation material of the 1930s and 1940s where so much had been left uncertain. The impact of this archival aspect on the evolution of the Project is discussed more fully later in this chapter.

A growing sense of obligation towards those who wrote for Mass-Observation (both in the past and in the current Mass-Observation Project) and towards the material they had created had become part of a wider general awareness in the research community of the ethical responsibilities which are involved in all kinds of social investigation (see, for example, Cameron et al., 1992). During the 1930s and 1940s, those running Mass-Observation made no attempt to formalise the legal status of the material which was written for them, and in this they were probably no different from other social researchers of the time. There seemed to be an understanding that the privacy of the diarists and directive respondents would be protected, but unattributed quotations from their contributions would be used in reports and publications. There is no evidence in the Archive to suggest that any of the contributors were ever unhappy about this arrangement. On the contrary, some writers report checking through the books when they were published to ensure that they had been quoted! (see Sheridan, 1990). There is also evidence that writers who felt that they were not considered "useful" became disillusioned with Mass-Observation and dropped out. Being read and quoted anonymously was a *raison d'être* for taking part.

The present-day situation is rather different. The provisions of the Data Protection Act of 1984 and the Copyright Act of 1988 in the United Kingdom have introduced legal obligations which bind the Archive. The issue of privacy is of primary concern. Within the first three years of the launch of the Project in 1981, the decision was taken to allocate a number to every new recruit. This takes the place of their real name on material available to the public. This substitution was introduced cautiously, because it seemed to militate against the friendly and personal nature of the writing relationship. After having originally admonished the writers for *not* writing their names all over everything they sent in so that pages wouldn't get lost, they were suddenly being instructed to use their number. Although a few people never quite got the hang of the new idea and continued to include their name at the top of every page, most people who expressed an opinion about the new rule welcomed it, feeling that since the material was now being looked at so soon after it had been written, it was an important form of protection and allowed them to feel freer in what they wrote. A few people said that they were not at all concerned about their privacy and a very few simply preferred to be identified and thereby credited for their work.

The question of copyright was not tackled until 1987. In order that the Archive (represented formally by its four Trustees) can give permission for researchers to use the material in publications, it should, strictly speaking, either own the copyright itself, or be prepared to contact a writer every time someone wants to quote their text. The impracticality of the latter option led to the introduction of a copyright form (analogous to the agreements used by oral historians) which would give the writer an opportunity to make an informed choice about who would have rights over his or her material. Those who joined and left the Project between 1981 and 1987 did not have the opportunity to record their preference, and their papers have the same ambiguous status in this respect as the wartime diaries. Since 1987, most new recruits sign the copyright form; only a few have asked for special conditions, and about five people so far have opted to retain their own rights in full over their texts. Signing the agreement does not deprive people of the right to reproduce their Mass-Observation writing themselves in publications.

CONNECTIONS WITH OTHER PROJECTS

The contemporary Mass-Observation Project shares many common features with other kinds of projects which have at their heart a concern with the history of ordinary people in their own words. At the Nordiska Museet, the Ethnographic Museum in Stockholm, Stephan Bohman and his colleagues have been collecting Swedish life stories for some time (Bohman, 1986), and have recently also begun a Mass-Observation-style project which solicits writing on themes. Elsewhere in northern Europe, other life-story projects have flourished (see Gullestad, 1995). In Poland, the collection of life stories has a long and honourable tradition (Bertaux, 1981; Plummer, 1983). The emphasis of these projects tends to be on "whole" life stories or autobiographies told retrospectively. In this they share with many oral history projects in Britain and in the rest of the world a focus on the whole life and on the lives of older people in its primary aim of capturing memories which will soon be lost. Similarly, community writing and publishing, of which there is a strong tradition in Britain since the 1970s, combines the whole life story with shorter productions: poetry, plays and fiction writing (Mace, 1995; Maguire et al., 1982). The use of panels of respondents in the United Kingdom at least can be traced back to the early BBC audience research on listener reactions to radio programmes (Silvey, 1974) and it continues to be a method of data collection which offers a longitudinal perspective. Sociological and anthropological research which takes as its subject the individual life story or the small community or subculture can also be seen to have common patterns with the Mass-Observation approach. A very detailed account of such projects in the social sciences has been written by Ken Plummer in his *Documents of Life* (1983), though strangely he omits mention of Mass-Observation.

THE CONTEMPORARY MASS-OBSERVATION PROJECT AND THE ORIGINAL MASS-OBSERVATION

One of the significant differences between the present Mass-Observation Project and most other community or social research projects is its historical link with the earlier Mass-Observation movement. The link between the 1937-49 phase and the 1981 revival, although jumping three decades of relative silence, can be both problematic—in that it opens up again all the theoretical and methodological issues which the first Mass-Observers failed to address satisfactorily—but also advantageous in that it creates a kind of historical framework which can be made to work in its favour. There is no doubt that the physical location of the new Project within an active working archive reassures the contributors, who write so enthusiastically and frequently, that their material will be taken seriously. It demonstrates that there is less risk that their efforts will be neglected in a dusty storehouse or be consigned to the dustbin. The widespread interest in, and use of, the earlier material suggests that there will be a demand for the kind of reporting they do. Moreover, they have evidence of the way such material is used, and this helps to curb anxieties about exploitation or breach of privacy. There is a satisfaction to be gained in taking part not only in a collective history (in the sense that people from all over the country are participating), but also in a history which was begun many years earlier by the likes of the redoubtable Nella Last and her contemporaries who kept their diaries for Mass-Observation. At the same time, those with responsibility for the early material are gaining knowledge not only of the physical and administrative care of such material but also of its analysis and interpretation, and can bring to bear that knowledge and experience at an early stage in the collection of new material.

But there is a complexity to this inheritance which arises from the way working practices in the Archive continue to "borrow" from early Mass-Observation its terminology and, to some extent, its systems of record-keeping and physical order. The continued use of two important words "Mass-Observation" and "directive" causes consternation, especially amongst people who have never heard of the original organisation. Whereas once the name "Mass-Observation" might have more positively suggested a popular or democratic form of social research—the observation of everyone by everyone—and for the benefit of everyone, now both "mass" and "observation" are suspect words because of the negative connotations they have acquired in recent times for some people. If *The Masses* could once be used as the title for a radical union paper in the United States in 1917, it now evokes derogatory meanings: "mass production", "mass media", "mass hysteria", the undifferentiated rather than the collective. Raymond Williams has commented on the ambivalent meaning of the term in his *Key Words*: "a term of contempt in much conservative thought, but a positive term in much socialist thought" (1983, p. 192). Equally, "observation" is associated with surveillance, and the two terms together bring to mind "Big Brother" with all the dystopian connotations of George Orwell's *Nineteen Eighty-Four*. There is no easy way of assessing the extent to which the title "Mass-Observation" discourages people from volunteering to join the Project, but it is reasonable to assume that it does have some negative effect. In 1994, Sheridan put a question about the title to the current Mass-Observers. Of course, they had, by definition, expressed an interest in Mass-Observation despite (or even because of) the name, but it was instructive to examine their reactions. The greatest proportion of people said that while the name did sound strange, they liked the connection with the past activities of Mass-Observation, and many people expressed a strong aversion to the whole notion of name-changing which is done purely to "modernise" or make the Project sound more palatable to contemporary ears.

The other term borrowed from the earlier phase is the word "directive", which was first introduced in 1937 to describe the instructions to the writers who had volunteered to help Mass-Observation. The Directive was never a questionnaire; rather it *directed* the attention of the Mass-Observers to the subject area which Mass-Observation was studying at any one time. By the end of 1939, the Mass-Observation directive had developed into its standard form of a series of questions or guidelines, often containing a commentary and feedback on earlier directive replies. It was designed to prompt the respondents to gather information about their own lives and to observe others around them. In effect, the directives invited correspondents to produce detailed reports combining experience and opinion which would be sent back to Mass-Observation each month to be incorporated into their research together with information drawn from other sources.

Like "Mass-Observation", the term "directive" brings to mind the tools of totalitarianism at worst and those of bureaucracy at best (especially as it has been used by the European Community since the 1970s to denote prescriptive policy statements). It remains, however, a useful way of distinguishing the Mass-Observation approach from the questionnaire which in practice operates at a more structured level and risks producing short uninformative answers mirroring the questions. The discursive directive, despite its name, is capable of eliciting long reflective essays on a subject in a way a more structured questionnaire cannot, and may be responsible for ensuring that the correspondents feel able to contest and adapt the space that is created for their reply. Indeed, when a numbered questionnaire is included within a directive, the correspondent is as likely to ignore the numbering and the order as he or she is to respond directly to it. For the moment at least, then, the word remains useful and, as with the name Mass-Observation itself, has the value of constantly reinforcing the link with the work of the early Mass-Observers.

There is one change in terminology, however, which reflects a significant shift in how the Mass-Observers have been conceptualised within the Project since about 1990. Between 1981 and 1990, the members of the panel continued to be addressed as "Mass-Observers" or even "Observers" in the same way as their counterparts had been addressed in the 1930s and 1940s. This continues to be the preferred mode of direct address in letters and directives, but Sheridan has chosen to use the term "correspondents" when writing about the panel members. Pocock sometimes referred to the Project as "friendship by correspondence" and the sense of dialogue, or even of conversation and the exchange of letters, rather than the clinical and one-way supply of "data", between staff at the Archive and the people who write, remains a key element in the relationship. "Correspondent" (which also has journalistic/documentary connotations) conveys the sense of a mutual relationship much more accurately than the more usual social scientific terms such as "respondent", "subject" or even "informant". In this respect, then, the Mass-Observation tradition has been successfully reworked and some new terminology introduced.

The influence of the early Mass-Observation remains powerful, however, and not only in relation to the use of language. One much less obvious inheritance from the original work of Mass-Observation is the way in which categories are used to record and to arrange the material. The categories devised by the early Mass-Observers are replicated within the present Archive. These categories are not only reproduced in the management of the original papers but also in the record systems and arrangements used for the collection of contemporary material since 1981. For example, directive replies for men and for women are stored in separate boxed sequences. Liz Stanley has questioned the "givenness" of Mass-Observation's gender categories and their reproduction in the Archive's sorting systems in relation to one-day diaries written in 1937 (L. Stanley, 1995, p. 90). Later, in Chapter 7, we discuss how the replication of systems of organising knowledge can determine not only the ways in which researchers come to read and interpret the newer Mass-Observation material, but also how disjunctions may arise between the way the present-day writers understand what happens to their material and the way it is made available for public consultation. Similarly, readers bring their own classification to the material, as Bloome, Sheridan and Street discuss in *Reading Mass-Observation Writing* (1993).

It is important to emphasise that the replication of institutionalised systems of classification can be ascribed as much to the professional protocols of archiving as it can be to the dominant influence of early Mass-Observation.

The principle of "provenance", which is universally implemented in public archives, dictates that the physical arrangement of historical papers should retain (or reconstruct) as far as is possible the original order of the material. That is, imposed categories (such as the systems of subject classification used for books in libraries) should be avoided, and the arrangement should reflect the historical generation of the material. It is the work of the descriptive tools—inventories, catalogues, indexes, calendars and latterly of electronic retrieval tools—to represent other categories and to offer different routes of access and retrieval into the subject matter of the material which may also reflect more recent developments in the field of study or the organisation of knowledge. The principle of provenance enables the scholar to learn as much from the physical juxtaposition of papers, and from their context, as from the textual content of the papers. There is every justification (indeed, it is arguably a professional obligation) to retain the original order of Mass-Observation's papers in the process of archiving. The early diaries and directive replies from men and women, therefore, remain in two sequences according to gender just as they were filed when they were first received by Mass-Observation; both the diaries and directive replies were received in monthly instalments from their creators and remain in boxes labelled by month and year. The use made of the material by Mass-Observation did not focus on one individual's writing over time, but on issues, events and periods of time—on what people were writing in June 1940 about the evacuation of British troops from Dunkirk, or in December 1941 about the Japanese attack on Pearl Harbour, or in May 1945 about the end of the Second World War. Since 1981, most of the new material has been filed in the same way. Replies to directive themes, virtually all written during the same three-month period, are boxed together in one sequence for men's writing and one for women's, and labelled with the date and subject. Similarly, where systematic records were kept about individuals, the emphasis was on the traditional socio-economic categories: gender, age, marital status, occupation and place of residence. Records of changes over time, or of the life trajectories of Mass-Observers, were not made (although this information is available within the texts themselves), nor were other kinds of attributes formerly recorded—for example, political affiliation, sexual orientation, ethnic origin, religion, educational background, family and household details. In this area, the present-day Project differs slightly from the early Mass-Observation. Whereas the material collected by the early organisation was only seen by Mass-Observation's own personnel, the Archive places recently received material directly in the public domain. It has become necessary to make a distinction between what is "safe" to make public (i.e., what is easily rendered relatively anonymous) and what is unsafe. Diaries, letters, some photographs, various kinds of communications with the Archive, and some contributions containing sensitive information fall into the latter category, and are placed in what are called the "Personal Files". They are embargoed from public access for a specified number of years (usually 30, but sometimes longer at the request of the writer). This file is a record of the individual's participation in the Project. Researchers have no access to this file, and although the correspondents for Mass-Observation are told about it (and sometimes negotiations have to take place with them about it), it is not always easy for them to visualise exactly how the whole system works when they have never visited the Archive.

Entirely new systems of organisation and arrangement could have been instituted for the new Project but they were not, and this is no doubt due to the very strong sense in which both Pocock and Sheridan were continuing something already begun, and not beginning something entirely new. In this sense, the continued implementation of systems which seemed to work in practice, and with which researchers and Archive workers had grown familiar, seemed desirable. The power of the early Mass-Observation, then, in structuring the new initiative, must be acknowledged; at the same time, it is important to recognise that any systems of organisation of knowledge are ideologically constituted and are capable of determining the ways in which that knowledge comes to be understood. This is one of the issues which this book addresses through the lens of selected Mass-Observation case studies and through analysis of data arising from the "Literacy Practices and the Mass-Observation Project" research described in the Introduction and Chapter 4. In the next chapter we discuss the relationship of Mass-Observation to anthropology, providing a context for understanding both the place of Mass-Observation in intellectual debates of the times and for current analysis of Mass-Observation as "literacy practices."

3
Mass-Observation and Anthropology

> A radical ethnography must take ordinary persons doing ordinary things as the central issues. (Erving Goffman, 1963, cited by N. Stanley, 1981, p. 34)

> "Anthropology Begins At Home". From the start of my own fieldwork, it has been my deepest and strongest conviction that we must finish by studying ourselves through the same methods and with the same mental attitude with which we approach exotic tribes. (Bronislaw Malinowski, 1938, p. 103)

In this chapter, we address the relationship between Mass-Observation and anthropology. One of the founders of Mass-Observation, Tom Harrisson, considered himself to be an anthropologist and saw Mass-Observation as bringing anthropology home, applying the principles of research on so-called "exotic" societies to his own society. At the same time, some of the leading anthropologists of the day in the United Kingdom, Bronislaw Malinowski and Raymond Firth, took serious note of Mass-Observation's claims to be an anthropology of ourselves and delivered some powerful criticisms that have remained in the memory of the discipline and still colour its relationship to the project. The concerns of the discipline at that time with professionalisation of the study of society, with the elaboration of case study methods, with the genre of ethnography and with the relationship of objective to subjective modes of inquiry were all germane to the development of Mass-Observation. They form the ground for Malinowski's willingness to support the project by writing an introduction to the account of the *First Year's Work* as well as his criticisms of the way it claimed to handle anthropological concepts and approaches.

The revival of Mass-Observation in 1981 was also initiated by an anthropologist, David Pocock, professor of Anthropology at the University of Sussex. He was at that time interested in the idea of a personal anthropology—the models and concepts of society in which representations and experiences of ordinary people are grounded—and his interest in Mass-Observation might be seen as part of his exploration of the ways in which such models are part of everyday life, not just of professional academic inquiry. As we shall see later, he himself argues that pragmatic and policy issues as much as intellectual ones drove his involvement in the new project. The self-reporting by volunteer writers, which has always played a key role in Mass-Observation's activities, can be seen as expressions of their personal anthropology. The ways in which meaning is constructed and interpreted in daily life were a central concern of the Oxford anthropology in which Pocock was steeped, and indeed Pocock was responsible for a seminal account of the shift from function to meaning that characterised this tradition (Dumont, 1975; Pocock, 1961). It was this tradition which also influenced the recent participation in Mass-Observation of Brian Street, another Sussex anthropologist trained at Oxford, who has engaged in ethnographic studies of literacy practices in contemporary societies in different parts of the world, including the collaborative study of the literacy practices of the contemporary Mass-Observation correspondents, which is reported in Sections 2 and 3 of this book. Mass-Observation is, then, closely linked with the intellectual history of the discipline of social anthropology in the United Kingdom; different phases of the project can be linked with changes and developments in the discipline, as well as with movements in other fields such as sociology, auto-biography and history (described elsewhere in this book). This section attempts to delineate some of the features of that connection in order to locate Mass-Observation in its broader context, to dispel some of the myths that stem from the early commentaries on Mass-Observation and to consider its place in contemporary social and intellectual inquiry at the end of the twentieth century.

BRITISH ANTHROPOLOGY IN THE EARLY TWENTIETH CENTURY

Social anthropologists in Britain have been concerned with genealogies and myths of ancestry both as objects of inquiry in the societies they study and as playing a key role in the emergence of the discipline itself within the overall taxonomy of intellectual work in Britain. The story of Bronislaw Malinowski, a "founding father" of British anthropology, provides an important starting point for locating Mass-Observation on the intellectual map, as he was one of the first anthropologists to engage with the project and to see its place in the emergence of the discipline. Malinowski was a Polish émigré to England who went to the Trobriand Islands as an anthropologist to do what was then traditional survey-type social research (Kuper, 1973). At the outbreak of the First World War, as a citizen of the Austro-Hungarian Empire he was treated as an alien subject and given the choice of spending the war in an Australian prison or of living in the Islands under the jurisdiction of a British Commissioner. He chose the latter and proceeded to make a virtue of necessity by learning the local language, "living with" local inhabitants and observing their customs and practices "from the inside."

On returning to the United Kingdom, he presented this approach as a key to understanding native ways of thought and proceeded to write a number of celebrated ethnographies about the Trobriand Islands, their sexual customs, economic systems and beliefs (Malinowski, 1922). He obtained a lecturing post at the London School of Economics and helped establish the discipline of modern anthropology, running a seminar whose participants became the next generation of lecturers and eventually professors in the major departments in the United Kingdom, at London, Manchester, Oxford and Cambridge. Malinowski has a strong claim to being the founder of the profession of anthropology in Britain, for he established its distinctive apprenticeship—intensive fieldwork in an exotic community. For the fifteen years he spent at the London School of Economics after his return from the Trobriand Islands, he was the only master ethnographer in the country, and virtually everyone else who wished to do field work in the modern fashion went to work with him (see Kuper, 1973).

Most British anthropologists today can, according to Kuper (1973), trace their genealogy back to one of this generation and ultimately to Malinowski. We would suggest that the development of Mass-Observation can be linked to the intellectual movements and debates that followed the diaspora from London School of Economics to these different departments, especially to Oxford and then Sussex universities.

Malinowski's experience became the basis for a new tradition in anthropology, that of ethnographic field work. Nineteenth-century anthropologists had worked mostly through surveys, either conducted themselves or, in the case of Sir James Frazer, from accounts by travellers, missionaries and district commissioners who corresponded with him. Following Malinowski, the process of living with the "natives" became a necessary rite of passage for entering the discipline of anthropology, and the core texts of the discipline became ethnographies—accounts of their experiences written by field workers. Students in British universities today are still exposed to these early texts, though now often framed by current theoretical and ideological perspectives, and new field workers continue the tradition and provide new ethnographies for anthropology courses. Debates over the validity and nature of ethnographic inquiry were central to the view of Mass-Observation formed by its founders on the one hand and by the professional anthropologists who responded to it on the other. Anthropology claims a special prerogative over this sense of ethnography, as the experience of living with "other" peoples and learning their language, then reporting on their findings in large academic monographs. Students and researchers using the concept in other disciplines are frequently made to feel that they are not "proper" ethnographers, especially if their "field" experience is restricted to their own society or to brief studies. Green and Bloome (1997) suggest a threefold distinction that helps avoid some of the status claims evident in this background. They distinguish between *doing ethnography*, which they see as involving "the framing, conceptualizing, conducting, interpreting, writing and reporting associated with a broad in-depth, and long-term study of a social or cultural group, meeting the criteria for doing ethnography as framed within a discipline or field" (1997, p. 6); adopting an *ethnographic perspective*, by which they mean "it is possible to take a more focused approach (i.e., do less than a comprehensive ethnography) to study particular aspects of everyday life and cultural practices of a social group". Central to this view is "the use of theories of culture and inquiry practices deriving from anthropology and sociology to guide the research"; and finally, using *ethnographic tools*, which "refers to the use of methods and techniques usually associated with fieldwork. These methods may or may not be guided by cultural theories or questions about social life of group members". We shall suggest below that interpreting Mass-Observation observers as in some cases adopting an "ethnographic perspective" allows us to recognise the anthropological dimension of the project without making the kind of unsubstantiable claims about the expertise and training of the participants made by Harrisson in the early days and which upset anthropological professionals at the time.

MASS-OBSERVATION AS ANTHROPOLOGY AT HOME

The founders, as we have described above, did indeed present Mass-Observation as a kind of "anthropology of ourselves" or a "people's ethnography," and in principle anthropologists were likewise interested in applying their discipline "at home", as the quotation from Malinowski at the head of this chapter illustrates. Harrisson's particular way of representing this aim through Mass-Observation, however, led to some conflict. He had conducted anthropological field work in the New Hebrides (Harrisson, 1937) and wanted to apply the same methods to the "savages" of Britain. He had also been trained in natural science and had an interest in ornithology, so his anthropology took on a particularly positivist character; it could be seen as treating human beings like birds, to be observed and described as though they were natural specimens. In one of the Bulletins regularly circulated to volunteer Mass-Observers between 1937 and 1950, the Day Survey on the 1937 Coronation (published as *May the Twelfth*) is referred to as "aiming to apply the methods of science to consideration of an industrial culture" (M-O File Report A4, 1937, p. 1). In relation to responses to a previous Bulletin, an even grander claim is made: "We can see in them the possibility of a democratic science, and consequently in due course of scientific democracy" (p. 1). This is to be a science of the people not just of the expert. Indeed, experts come in for heavy criticism for their inability to speak the language of "ordinary" people, a view that is reinforced by some scientists themselves: Julian Huxley, for instance, in a preface to *May the Twelfth* writes that some of the reports there "would put many orthodox scientists to shame in their simplicity, clearness and objectivity" (1937, p. 6). The latter point in particular is a source of pride for the founders of Mass-Observation and equally a source of criticism by anthropologists. N. Stanley, in the fullest account to date of the relationship between Mass-Observation and the anthropology of the day, sees Mass-Observation's positivist claims as the most vulnerable to anthropological critique. He argues that "Mass-Observation discovered positivism, or rather fell into it without being aware that it had done so. Positivism was, in any case, in vogue in the thirties as there was a general confidence in what science could achieve" (N. Stanley, 1981, p. 34). That anthropology shared this faith is claimed by Kuper in his history of the discipline:

> If one were to characterise the mood of British anthropology in the first decades of this century one would have to stress the over-riding concern with the accumulation of data. The ultimate goal might still be the reconstruction of cultural history, or evolutionist generalisation, but these interests were overlaid by a strong resurgence of British empiricism ... "facts" might soon disappear.... Their collection was an urgent matter. (Kuper, 1973, p. 5)

It was in the spirit of this "scientific" approach to social life that Harrisson recruited the team of "observers", training them briefly in ethnographic methods and sending them out to observe and describe the everyday behaviour of people in the northern town of Bolton: the Worktown project.

As we discussed in Chapter 1, the kinds of people attracted to this enterprise—the first Mass-Observers—were young, politically radical and often upper-class; some, like Harrisson himself were anthropologists and sociologists; others were artists, poets, documentary film-makers, journalists, photographers like Jennings, and writers. The kind of ethnography that they employed, particularly observation of everyday details of British life, drew the attention, and sometimes the criticism, of professional anthropologists such as Malinowski and Firth, as we shall see. While the Worktown project and some of the national studies, such as the Coronation, the appearance of Jews in London, and so forth, focused mainly on observation using "trained" observers, the strand that focussed on a "panel" of observers responding to "directives" was to be increasingly important in the second phase with which this book is mainly concerned. This aspect of Mass-Observation was more evidently interpretative and subjective than that characterised by the Worktown project, which claimed to be more observational and objective.

The distinction is not, however, entirely clear cut as the organisers believed that even the more "amateur" respondents to directives were also becoming trained by their very participation in Mass-Observation: "In addition to the special scientific uses, we believe that observing is of real value to the Observer. It heightens his power of seeing what is around him and gives him new interest in and understanding of it" (Jennings & Madge, 1937, p. x). Indeed, there are frequent asides in the Bulletins and directives of the day to how the Observers can hone their skills (cf., M-O Bulletin, Autumn 1937).

That the volunteer Mass-Observers are more than "mere recorders" is emphasised by the way in which they are invited to comment on the topics and directives themselves. In the Autumn 1937 Bulletin, for instance, a list of subjects is given and Mass-Observers are asked to indicate whether they find these interesting and how they would word them. Those that attract interest would then be issued as directives in a subsequent Bulletin. Mass-Observers are involved to some extent then in design as well as in recording empirical data: they are being asked to adopt an ethnographic perspective and to become in some senses ethnographers themselves and not mere recorders or informants. This is an issue that was hotly debated in the early phases of Mass-Observation (cf., Bulletins, 1937) and remains of significance in the contemporary Project (e.g., see responses to Spring directive on literacy, 1991). The original phase of Mass-Observation work began coming to an end in the 1950s and there was a lapse of time before a new phase began with Pocock's revival of the self-reporting, "directive" approach in 1981. As described in Chapter 2, this phase developed further the reflexive accounts by "ordinary" people of their own experiences and observations and represents a different—more contemporary—view of "ethnography" than the more positivist aspects of parts of the first phase. Pocock's first directives, sent to a largely new pool of respondents, were on such diverse themes as the Royal Family and events involving them (weddings, coronations, funerals); everyday experiences of the respondents' lives (house decoration, money, family relations); and public issues of a national and international kind. A shift has been detected since Sheridan took over the Project in 1990, her directives being more reflexive and less observational, including diaries on media coverage of the Gulf War, education policy, coverage of sex and marriage in the press (see Appendix Bi for list of themes). This phase continues at present, and it was to these observers that Sheridan and Street sent a directive in 1991 on the subject of their own writing as itself a social practice, not just a means of recording observations. The responses to this directive form the basis for the analysis, in Section 3, of Mass-Observation as literacy practices. Aspects of the first phase of Mass-Observation, then, involve a view of ethnography as objective description akin to natural science, while another aspect, developed further in the recent phase, is more akin to the kind of personal anthropology described by Pocock and, more recently, the reflective ethnography characteristic of contemporary anthropology (cf., Clifford & Marcus, 1986). Amongst all these shifts and nuances in the development of Mass-Observation, it has been the claims in the first phase to be "scientific" that have remained prominent in anthropological recollections, particularly the critiques by the anthropologists of the time, notably Firth and Malinowski. It is to their commentaries that we now turn.

MALINOWSKI AND MASS-OBSERVATION

Malinowski wrote a relatively complimentary introduction to the *First Year's Work* but then proceeded to "pull it to pieces a little, for despite all its promise and the value of its results, it needs a thorough overhaul of principle and method" (Malinowski, 1938, p. 87). He rejects most of the popular and press criticisms levelled at Mass-Observation (such as that the observers were "spies", "nosey-parkers" or simply "maniacs", a perspective that persists to this day: cf., *Observer*, 1994) as not worth much attention, but chooses to focus on one serious question: "Is Mass-Observation scientific or not?" (p. 88). In order to be scientific it must be free from bias and "it has to generalise as much as is warranted by evidence and no more". The problem with social science in general, and with untrained observers such as Mass-Observation employed in particular, is "How can Mass-Observation hope to reach an objective, that is scientific, result from subjective data?" (p. 95), with its inevitable distortions. Malinowski's answer to this dilemma lies at the heart of his development of anthropology and indeed of qualitative work in social science generally:

> In human affairs the more subjective the behaviour, the more objective are the scientific data it furnishes. The Mass-Observers of the movement function as what we technically call in Ethnography "Informants". Their statements are the subject matter on which further scientific analysis is indispensable. The objective treatment of subjectively determined data must start at the very outset. (Malinowski, 1938, p. 96)

It is here that the founders of Mass-Observation are found wanting. Malinowski cites the public defences of Mass-Observation put forward by Madge and Harrisson that assert the data itself to be objective, that what the trained observers at least (if not those responding more subjectively to directives) do is report facts and that it is up to commentators not these observers themselves to interpret the facts. To support this interpretation of Mass-Observation, Malinowski quotes Madge in *First Year's Work* as saying:

> Mass-Observation is an instrument for collecting facts, not a means for producing a scientific philosophy: it is each man's job to find his own salvation as best he can, Mass-Observation merely proposes to acquaint him with the relevant scientific facts. (Malinowski, 1938, p. 95)

To the contrary, says Malinowski, it is the framing and theoretical orientation of those who design the questions and interpret the results that allows "objective" work to be carried out on essentially subjective data. This is what is meant by "ethnography" in the new discipline of anthropology. In a passage that also presages contemporary views of ethnography, Malinowski considers what kinds of data enable the scientist to achieve this aim:

> The point at which really good ethnographic material places itself beyond any argumentation or suspicion of doubt is linguistic documentation: texts characteristic of native sentiments or attitudes; stories and myths; magical spells and legal formulae. (Malinowski, 1938, p. 98)

The focus on language as an object of study and not simply the medium for research represents a major contribution by Malinowski that has been since acknowledged in socio-linguistics (Lyons, 1981) and in the work of anthropological linguistics (Grillo, Pratt & Street, 1987). It has also been highlighted from a methodological point of view, and it is interesting to find Spradley recognising that the application of ethnographic methods to our own society involves precisely such a focus on language: "To do ethnography in our own society, it would be necessary to begin with a serious study of the way people talk" (Spradley, 1979, p. 19). We would add also, the way people write.

Malinowski sees himself as having been largely responsible for such a focus on language as well as the aim of bringing it home: "From the start of my own field work, it has been my deepest and strongest conviction that we must finish by studying ourselves through the same methods and with the same mental attitude with which we approach exotic tribes" (Malinowski, 1938, p. 103). This, then, he believes, is the strength of Mass-Observation and it is in this context that its aims should be judged. In advocating this perspective, he felt it necessary to critique what he saw as the mistaken, more positivist defence put forward by the founders. Ethnography is subjective material, couched in language, rigorously and objectively gathered and analysed. In this sense, Mass-Observation could take its place as part of the tradition of ethnographic enquiry that was emerging in Britain (and in the United States) at this period. If we wish to understand Mass-Observation and its place in British intellectual and social life, we need then to take some account of the anthropological context in which it was embedded and the debates current in the discipline at that time, notably as they impinge directly on the Mass-Observation project.

N. Stanley suggests a number of aspects of the discipline of anthropology that the founders of Mass-Observation found appealing:

> Anthropology was a practical science. Its descriptions revealed new ways of organising human society undrempt of by Europeans. It was also easy to "do", and used amateurs as well as professionals. Most importantly, it was dramatic and involved a nice apparent paradox. Anthropology was traditionally performed on other . . . civilisations; to turn the whole procedure upside-down could be advanced as not just a novel idea but the basis for a popular slogan "an anthropology of ourselves". Such an approach did not just involve a turning of our anthropological vision inwards suddenly, but meant knowingly employing apparently inappropriate categories from ethnography. (N. Stanley, 1981, p. 42)

It is perhaps the treading on professional ground by the amateurs of Mass-Observation that lay behind some of the more caustic criticisms by academics and, as N. Stanley points out above, the tables would be turned on the traditional anthropologist. As we have seen, Malinowski is less troubled by the latter point, although Firth (discussed later) does appear to have been concerned by the former. It is the views of these two anthropologists regarding Mass-Observation that have tended to colour the dominant view of the project still held in much contemporary anthropology, even though both the discipline and Mass-Observation have changed considerably in the intervening period.

FIRTH AND MASS-OBSERVATION

Raymond Firth is more critical of Mass-Observation than Malinowski, mainly with respect to its methods. In "An Anthropologist's View of Mass-Observation" (Firth, 1939; subsequent page references are to this article), he writes:

> It has not clearly formulated many of its field problems, its statistics on the trends of public opinion are shoddy, its samples are inadequate, its questions are often badly framed, and it is content too often to rest on the bare answers alone instead of following them up by the much harder work of actual observation. (pp. 191-192)

He had been asked to give "a detached summing up of Mass-Observation" in which he was "naturally" interested "since this new movement is concerned to investigate in English life many of the problems with which anthropology deals in primitive life, and claims to use to some extent the same techniques of study" (p. 166). The main technique used by the anthropologist is "micro-sociological":

> In his examination of the societies classed for convenience as primitive, the anthropologist is interested to discover not only the formal structure of the society, but also how this structure actually manifests itself in the lives of individuals; he has to determine what issues are important to the people, the opinions that individuals of different types hold about them, and the ways these opinions or verbal acts are related to other kinds of behaviour. To ascertain these things, he relies largely on first-hand observation, not only of what people say, and say they do, but also of what he sees them do. (p. 166)

It is against these criteria that Firth assesses Mass-Observation, both its practice and its claims. The lack of such material from Western societies has made it difficult for anthropologists to compare their findings with life at home, and Firth cites Malinowski's own concern that the gap should be filled by an "anthropology of civilisation". Firth sets out the details of how an "anthropology of civilisation" might be conducted in a way that could provide a programmatic statement for

Mass-Observation itself and the gap it was filling in our knowledge of ourselves. With regard to our understanding of the role of religion in contemporary life, for instance, he points out that while there are church records on attendance, "we still have only general impressions about what the mass of ordinary folk who are nominal Christians really believe and how far they carry their religion into their daily life". It is this that an anthropology of ourselves would get at. There is an interesting echo here of the language used by Mass-Observation regarding its focus on "ordinary folk", a concept still prominent in contemporary representations by both participants and scholars (as we discuss later in the chapter). Similarly, Firth cites areas of inquiry that have been central to Mass-Observation, such as what people really think about Kingship and the King (rather than what formal constitutional books have to say). It is into this "breach", he suggests, that the founders of Mass-Observation have stepped.

This, indeed, had been identified by Harrisson, Jennings and Madge: the need for social scientists to spend more time "studying the normal and everyday behaviour problems of our own lives, as actually lived in the houses and factories, pubs and chapels and shops in this kind of civilisation"; and they had come up with a method of tackling it. The first phase of Mass-Observation, as we have seen, used both extensive survey of material by a network of observers all over the country and an intensive survey by small groups in "Worktown" and the East End of London. One source of the observational techniques was Harrisson's own earlier experience, to which Firth refers somewhat warily: Tom Harrisson had "spent two years in the New Hebrides, and has published a vivid account of the life of the natives and their contacts with civilisation. This study provided him with an introduction to the technique of anthropological field work" (p. 168).

While the initial publications of the findings led to criticisms that Mass-Observation was prying or snooping into people's lives, Firth, like Malinowski, rejects such a view and argues that few anthropologists would agree with it: rather, "anthropologists agree with Mass-Observation that an important series of problems awaits investigation, and that an empirical technique of an intensive kind is necessary for the collection of data" (p. 169). Indeed, Firth cites instances of "collaboration between Anthropology and Mass-Observation": Harrisson had been invited to present his findings to anthropologists at both the RAI and LSE, anthropologists had visited the Worktown survey and Malinowski, of course, had written the introduction to *First Year's Work*.

Nevertheless, anthropology, Firth argues, has some serious criticisms of Mass-Observation, not as hostility to the movement itself but "as judgement after trial, of some of its basic claims, methods and results" (Firth, 1939, p. 170). The founders, he asserts, overstated the novelty of Mass-Observation and its difference from social science survey work previously conducted in the United Kingdom. *Britain by Mass-Observation* (Madge & Harrisson, 1939), for example, states that there had been "nothing on normal behaviour" in this country, and "Anthropologists who have spent years and travelled all over the world to study remote tribes have contributed literally nothing to the anthropology of ourselves" (p. 13). Firth is plainly piqued by such sententious—and unnecessary—claims and points out the wealth of survey work previously conducted in the United Kingdom, notably the famous Rowntree and Mayhew surveys (p. 170). These, though not strictly anthropological in overall design, had attended to the minutiae of daily life, such as household budgets and data on meals eaten in working-class homes, of the kind anthropologists would be interested in and for which Mass-Observation was claiming novelty. However, once the early Mass-Observation studies began to be published (after Firth and Malinowski's criticisms) it became apparent that they were rather different from the Rowntree and Mayhew surveys, being more grounded in case studies and ethnographic perspectives. From this point of view some of Harrisson's claims for novelty were perhaps more justified than Firth would have been able to recognise on the basis of the limited material available to him at that time.

There are two kinds of data for which, according to Firth, Mass-Observation claims novelty—"the observer's first hand record of the behaviour and talk of people engaged in their ordinary occupations; and the memory record, taken down from the lips of an informant, of typical past situations, from her view, in her ordinary experience". According to Firth, Mayhew's survey of 1860 included both and "the most that Mass-Observation can claim is that it has fuller records from a wider range of observers on these matters than previously and that its data allows for the kind of comparative generalisations, including comparisons with earlier surveys, not available before" (p. 176). The data on which Mass-Observation is particularly strong are the "fields of extra-family kinship, religion, politics and public ceremonial occasions such as the Coronation of 1937" (p. 176).

However, Firth is more sanguine about the quality of these data:

> At its worst it is mere journalism; at its best, it reveals the actual working of institutions in the lives of the human beings who maintain them, gives valuable indices to thought and belief in a way statistical treatment has not yet been able to do, and provides lines of enquiry into many points of social relationships that may otherwise be overlooked. (p. 176)

However, he faults Mass-Observation for not following up these lines of enquiry: the main problem here is that there is no comparison between what people say they do and external observations of what they actually do. Questionnaires elicit interesting responses on such topics as "On what do you base your opinion?" (to which most referred to newspapers) or whether they have read and believe in horoscopes (in which one third of women but only 5 percent of men "believed"). In both cases, the data can be taken only as evidence for representations or impressions, but Mass-Observation interpreters appear to claim them as factual data and offer statistical summaries and exaggerated generalisations. Here Firth gets back at the "jibe" against anthropology "for having contributed nothing to the study of ourselves". One of the reasons, he retorts, that "has held anthropology back is just this realisation of the necessity for getting more than a simple set of answers to a couple of questions in order to be able to state what the nature of a particular belief is, and how effective it really is" (p. 183). There are various ways of doing this: one is to use large statistical samples, as with public opinion polls; another is a true random sample; and a third, more frequently used by anthropologists and which Mass-Observation could have used in arguing for qualitative data, is to study the context in which the people who expressed these opinions lived. In analysing responses to questions about military service and warfare, for instance,

> A detailed study of their home conditions, their employment, the number of their children, and the liability of these for military service ... would have enabled us to obtain a much better idea of the factors determining their views as to the possibility of war. (p. 187)

We know from a survey of the surviving papers in the Archive that this is exactly the kind of information that Mass-Observation did have about the volunteer panel—much more than was available from the surveys to which Firth refers. But knowledge about this would not have been available to Firth at the time he was writing, as Mass-Observation did not publish this data (it is now available to researchers in the Mass-Observation Archive).

Apart from these methodological problems, Firth also complains that there is not enough theory; the "raw" documentation remains unconnected to particular problems or theories. He quotes Mayhew: "facts without theory or generalisation cannot possibly teach us at all" (p. 177), and he criticises Madge's conception of putting together reports from different observers as "a cocktail conception of truth" (p. 95). While Mass-Observation has indeed presented a great mass of facts on many topics that have not hitherto been empirically studied, "much of their material is not well integrated, nor linked up with the problems they have stated to be the particular subject of their investigation" (p. 178). The theoretical positions are not well articulated and the data is not linked to them: instead "one gets the impression of a great mass of detail on individual reactions, but that the central key to these reactions is missing".

A further methodological problem lies in the position of the observers themselves, who are "expected to be both informant, giving the subject matter for the real scientific analysis, and recorder and interpreter of this subject-matter, working at a comparatively low level of abstraction and generalisation". On this, Firth quotes Malinowski, who insisted: "The objective treatment of subjectively determined data must start at the very outset. It must be embodied in the terms of reference of every specific enquiry" (p. 179). On the one hand, Mass-Observation observers need no special training since their role is as informants, whose reports will then be analysed by professional anthropologists: on the other, they are treated as "scientific observers", getting "objective facts". He gives examples from an account of Armistice Day in which an observer elicits opinions from a serving maid but doesn't indicate how his own views might have influenced her account or his representation of it in the way that a professional anthropologist would.

Despite the validity of many of these points, in general terms, one has to acknowledge that some of Firth's concern with the amateur status of the observers stems from his own interest as an academic anthropologist in establishing the discipline as a valid and credible newcomer to the social sciences in British universities. The founders' grandiose and somewhat noisy claims for Mass-Observation as anthropology might undermine that serious endeavour. Indeed, a factor in Firth's criticisms does appear to be the overstatements and abuse against social science in which they indulged, which is a different issue from what Mass-Observation itself—or even Harrisson, Madge and Jennings talking to a different audience—have to say.

After allowing for some of these factors, then, what remains of value according to Firth in Mass-Observation and how does it fit the intellectual climate of the time and in particular his conception of the role of anthropology? He concedes that "The anthropologist will at least agree that much of the raw material obtained on aspects of contemporary life is novel and important. Studies of football pools, proletarian art, dancing, all-in wrestling, a Coronation, have their place in modern sociology" (p. 188). There is also some comparative value in material collected in this way that can be set against material on similar topics obtained in other ways: "Thus one may expect that the data produced by the Worktown Survey on the 'Pub' will give in great fullness an account of an institution which can be compared with those given by Seebohm Rowntree in York and the New London Survey" (p. 188).

The problems that Firth and others have with Mass-Observation appear to lie as much in the exaggerated claims made by the authors as in the outcomes themselves. While resisting their unnecessary claim that this was the first such census of a public house population, he does acknowledge that some of the generalisations that emerged are indeed useful: for instance, regarding the cycles of the day and the week, which lead to the conclusion that "the last hour of the day is of more than economic significance owing to the importance of 'social drinking'" (p. 189). The anthropological insight in cases such as these is that drinking habits are linked with social patterns that have a class and gender dimension, something that is perhaps more commonplace now but needed conceptualising in the first place. It is to this dimension of the anthropological enterprise—in particular the use of case studies to make apparent theoretical links such as these—that Mass-Observation perhaps relates most closely and has the greatest contribution to make. It is this aspect to which we will return when discussing the recent phase of Mass-Observation and our own research on it.

LIMITATIONS OF THE ANTHROPOLOGISTS' CRITIQUES

Firstly, though, we must evaluate these commentaries and assess their significance for contemporary research on the first phase of the Mass-Observation project. The major point to make is that both Malinowski and Firth were writing at a very early stage of the project. Firth himself acknowledges that "some of these criticisms will probably not be applicable to the results of the Worktown Survey when they are published" (Firth, 1939, p. 192). His comments are based on the early publications: *Mass-Observation*, 1937; *May the Twelfth, First Year's Work*, 1938 (with its introduction by Malinowski); and the compilation *Britain*, 1939, published nine months later (and which he complains does not take account of Malinowski's criticisms), all of which he references (Firth, 1939, p. 169, footnote). The other sources of data for Firth were the Bulletins and notes for field workers occasionally issued by Harrisson and his team, and some of the programmatic statements that appeared in the press. Much of the criticism by these leading anthropologists, then, was based not on the outcomes of Mass-Observation or on the actual data, which at that time was not available outside Mass-Observation. Preservation of the material and provision of access to it only occurred in 1970, when University of Sussex agreed to house the papers collected by Harrisson from the founding of Mass-Observation in 1937 to the effective demise of the first phase in the 1950s. The scholarly view of Mass-Observation at this early period was, then, inevitably limited. Moreover, the criticisms levelled against the first phase of Mass-Observation appear to refer to its founders' claims for the "objective" and scientific quality of the observations, such as the Worktown project and the London studies, run with a team of trained observers, rather than to the other strand of Mass-Observation work, the use of a small panel of volunteer observers set up by Madge. With hindsight it seems that the anthropologists did not fully appreciate these different strands of the Mass-Observation project. Certainly, their criticisms may be less applicable to the later phase of Mass-Observation, from 1981, when David Pocock began a new series of directives that were sent to a new panel of "observers". Although this phase used the self-report technique begun in early Mass-Observation, it is not necessarily subject to the same problems or criticisms as those levelled by Firth and Malinowski at what they knew of the early phase. The issue of whether observers were "informants" or "ethnographers" will be addressed later, in relation to consideration of Mass-Observation as literacy practices, but again the problems that arise are not precisely those raised in the 1930s by Firth and Malinowski. A further problem which taxed these early anthropologists, that of professionalisation of the discipline, is perhaps less salient now than it was then. And the overstatements and sententious criticisms of other social scientists to which Harrisson was prone now look like relatively minor features of the whole project and certainly not significant in assessing the work itself and the wealth of data that has accumulated in the intervening half century.

Yet it appears that these early criticisms remain in the folk memory of the discipline of anthropology (and possibly more generally of scholars who approach Mass-Observation with some inkling of its early history and the debates it raised). When we have given seminars on the contemporary project and our research on it we invariably receive comments that cite—however vaguely—the existence of those early commentaries and raise in particular the problems of informants/observers, "representativeness", professional/amateur, and methodology. As we indicate later, aspects of these issues do need addressing in the contemporary project, too, though in a different way than that which appeared salient at an earlier period. The intellectual climate has shifted and what appeared a problem then might appear a strength now: the reflexive turn in anthropology, for instance, suggests a less rigid distinction between observer/observed and between objective/subjective than concerned the early commentators. Similarly, the relevance of the Mass-Observation data as itself evidence of writing practices is more apparent in the light of recent theoretical developments in the study of literacy, as we detail in Section 3. And there is now, of course, a considerable body of material, stored in the Mass-Observation Archive and readily accessible to scholars and the public, that provides a different data base than the few publications and internal documents with which Firth and Malinowski were acquainted.

A history of Mass-Observation, then, needs to disentangle these different levels and influences in both the presentation and criticism of it: the overblown rhetoric needs to be compared with the actual practice; the differences in views amongst its founders need setting against the representation of Mass-Observation as monolithic; the critiques by anthropologists based variously on responses to such rhetoric or to individual figures and derived from specific documents and periods in the development of the project, need to be disentangled from the serious methodological critiques that remain problematic today; and the theoretical and methodological perspective offered by early critics needs to be put in the perspective of contemporary anthropology, for which some of those views might themselves be called into question. While these early commentaries are, then, important historically in helping us set Mass-Observation in its social and intellectual context, they are less useful in themselves as an analytic framework for approaching the project today than perhaps many anthropologists continue to believe. Surprisingly, this point is still important when considering the revival of Mass-Observation in 1981 by David Pocock, who was himself an anthropologist and might thereby have offset and updated the early anthropological view. His theoretical and methodological orientation was rather different from those of Firth and Malinowski or of Harrisson himself. It is important, then, in moving towards a contemporary understanding of the project and its significance at this point in the twentieth century, to understand that orientation and to locate the new phase of Mass-Observation in relation to the anthropology of this period. So we turn now to an account of the anthropology out of which the new phase of Mass-Observation emerged and in particular to the influences that might have affected Pocock's revival of the enterprise.

POCOCK AND MASS-OBSERVATION

The later phase of Mass-Observation has not had as much attention from anthropologists as the early work. Although Pocock was Professor of Social Anthropology at the University of Sussex at the time he inaugurated the new phase in 1981, there has been less extant evidence for Pocock's views on Mass-Observation and its relation to anthropology than is available from Harrisson, Firth and Malinowski, which might explain why their view rather than his remains dominant in the discipline's folk memory of the movement. It is, however, possible to elicit something of the intellectual tradition that inspired this new anthropological interest in Mass-Observation from Pocock's own writing,

96 CHAPTER THREE

including his accounts of the concept of a personal anthropology, as well as from internal Mass-Observation memoranda and responses to Mass-Observers during his period as Director. In addition, we have had recent correspondence with David Pocock concerning the views of Mass-Observation expressed in this chapter and we include his comments in this section (Pocock, 1998, personal communication). His account provides a key insight into the contemporary link between anthropology and Mass-Observation and the continuing debates about the kind of knowledge represented in Mass-Observation writing.

In the introductory chapter of *Understanding Social Anthropology*, published in the "Teach Yourself" Series in 1975, Pocock addresses the reader directly as a potential anthropologist in whom some of the basic principles of the discipline are immanent. He describes the history of anthropology as a series of movements between more interpretative and more positivist approaches to social phenomena. In the early part of the twentieth century researchers such as Malinowski, Radcliffe-Brown (and, he might have added, Firth) rejected the nineteenth-century speculation about origins and survivals and its emphasis on physical as well as cultural aspects of human development. Instead, they emphasised anthropology's role as a scientific study of social phenomena, rooted in functionalist theory: this perspective maintained that all aspects of human activity, including those most strange to rationalist eyes, such as rituals, myths and superstitions, could be explained in terms of their functions—they all had a role to play in maintaining order and stability in social life. It was this that led to the split between different branches of Anthropology, the functionalists emphasising Social Anthropology, while Physical Anthropology, Archaeology and Cultural Anthropology developed in different directions. British Social Anthropology, for instance, with its emphasis on functions and social institutions, was at this time very different from American Cultural Anthropology, with its focus on culture broadly defined. The latter was, perhaps, less concerned with claims to being scientific and in some senses was more rooted in the humanities. Pocock goes on to develop an important critique of the so-called scientific tradition in British Social Anthropology and in so doing locates himself (and the later phase of Mass-Observation) in a more culturalist and humanistic framework than his predecessors in anthropology and in Mass-Observation, such as Harrisson, Firth and Malinowski. Pocock wrote:

> The post-war generation of British anthropologists, especially those influenced by the Oxford school under the leadership of Evans-Pritchard, was disposed to question the scientific pretensions of the inter-war years [and we would add, of the anthropology represented by Malinowski, Firth and later Harrisson. Pocock

continues:] Evans-Pritchard, wrote in 1950[1]: "It is easy to define the aim of social anthropology to be the establishment of sociological laws, but nothing even remotely resembling a law of the natural sciences has yet been adduced". (1975, p. 5)

For Pocock this view led to a significant break in British Social Anthropology during the 1960s from the earlier more empiricist and natural science based tradition, a break which he terms a shift from function to meaning. The work of Evans-Pritchard and the Oxford School, in which Pocock himself was trained, brought attention back to a more reflective and person-oriented view of the discipline. In order to understand human phenomena, Pocock argues, one has first to understand what they mean to the people concerned (1975, p. 6). In order to find this out one has to attend to people's own concepts or models of social life. That people themselves hold theories makes them more akin to the anthropologist: the split between observer and observed, on which Firth and Malinowski placed so much emphasis, appears less clear cut. Indeed, the relationship between the two is itself part of what anthropology studies: "Ought there not to be some sort of relation between a people's own theory of life on the one hand and the theory of the social anthropologist on the other?" (Pocock, 1975, p. 6). It was in answer to this question, then, that Pocock developed the concept of a Personal Anthropology—a recognition of the ideas, concepts, theories of self and society which each person holds and which inform their practice and their social relationships. This leads to a view of social anthropology as a relative theory of knowledge:

> There is a very important sense in which we can use the word [anthropology] not to designate a particular area of study but in a more general and personal way . . . the anthropologies of particular authors. (Pocock, 1975, p. 6)

That such ordinary people's models of social life are socially constructed rather than located in de-contextualised individuals is central to Pocock's view. We suggest that this intellectual concern with Personal Anthropology may have led him to Mass-Observation as a way of finding out about the social patterns in ordinary people's personal epistemologies. However, as with other dimensions of the Mass-Observation project, one has to be wary of reductionist accounts that attribute to schools of thought activities which may have arisen from the immediate practicalities of the institution and its personalities, as Pocock himself argues (Pocock, 1998, personal communication).

---

[1] The text in Pocock (1975) does not provide an exact reference for the quotation from Evans-Pritchard.

Pocock provides an interesting account of the re-launch of the Mass-Observation project in 1981 for which he was largely responsible, an account that mixes pragmatic needs of the moment with larger intellectual concerns. As Dean of the School of African and Asian Studies at the University of Sussex at the time when Tom Harrisson offered the Archive to the University, Pocock was charged with securing the gift and the arrangement for access by scholars to the material, but assumed that he would then retire from involvement. However, soon after the Archive had been successfully lodged at the University and a grant obtained to ensure the beginning of restoration work, Harrisson was unfortunately killed in a car accident and Pocock was left to decide what should be done. A Sussex graduate in Sociology, Dorothy Sheridan, had been employed by Harrisson as his personal assistant in 1974, and she continued to manage the Archive after Harrisson's death in 1976, but there was uncertainty about how to continue funding her position. A way of ensuring support for her involvement, according to Pocock, was to launch a new phase of Mass-Observation: "We decided to try the water with what later was called a Mass-Observation Special". This new activity began with a directive on inflation, followed by others on "the Royal Wedding" (Lady Diana and Prince Charles in 1981) and on "the pre-Christmas period". These "Specials" had the effect of raising the national profile of the Archive, which was now actively soliciting material from a new panel of correspondents, not just archiving the old material, which had been the main activity when the files arrived at Sussex.

There were, then, pragmatic reasons for the re-launch of Mass-Observation in 1981, although Sheridan points out that the activities themselves were contextualised, as had been the earlier ones, in ongoing debates about the nature of such social documentary. She and other Sussex researchers at the time, such as Angus Calder, Tom Jeffery, Penny Summerfield and Nick Stanley (whose research has been referred to earlier), were continually discussing and writing about the nature of Mass-Observation and exploring, as had the founders, questions of methodology, validity and distinctiveness. The new scholars of Mass-Observation were particularly influenced by the feminist and radical oral history trends at the time, including issues about auto-biography, self-representation and problems of interpretation and analysis. Pocock was exposed to these discussions in his emerging role as Director of Mass-Observation in the decade after the launch, and this also influenced the way the new Project developed, along with the previous influences from anthropology on which we have focussed, and the more serendipitous factors that Pocock suggests initiated the new phase in the first place. Indeed, he himself does record, in addition to the pragmatic reasons he gives for launching the new project, his own views about how the former phase of the project had been defined and how the new one was to be conceptualised:

> Once a relaunch was decided, there was just one thing that I was decidedly against in the earlier operation that I was going to avoid. That was the de haut en bas tone that characterised the socio-political involvement of the public school Left in the 20s and 30s. I disliked and discouraged the idea of the observer as in some way, in any way, superior. And I remember Naomi Mitchison [one of the earliest correspondents who continued to contribute in the new phase and who became a well-known author in her own right] wrote expressing the hope that I would not limit myself as, she suggested TH [Tom Harrisson] et al had, to the voluble A and B categories [the higher social classes]. (Pocock, 1998, personal communication)

Pocock presents this position as a matter of policy rather than of intellectual concern, linking his commitment to reading all of the replies to the directive to his worries about how Harrisson had treated some of the earlier correspondents:

> I had always had in mind a story about the chilly reception that a devoted fan of TH [Tom Harrisson] had after having made a journey to visit him. So although I enjoyed it a lot of it was an important policy line with me, rather than any intellectual interest, that those who wrote in should be made to feel significant. (Pocock, 1998, personal communication)

It was not only policy but also pleasure that fuelled his commitment:

> Certainly once we got started I got a great buzz out of the interaction with the people writing in. I read everything and can boast that with few exceptions when I was overloaded everyone who did write in received a personal acknowledgement. (Pocock, 1998, personal communication)

The intellectual line, though, he casts doubt upon. Where we have suggested that it was his interest in a Personal Anthropology that lay beneath his involvement in Mass-Observation, Pocock himself offers a more pragmatic explanation:

> Obviously I was the same person in both relations [Mass-Observation and Personal Anthropology] so it would have been odd if my general sense of what anthropology ought to be about is not

apparent in the Directives. . . . But there was not that direct intellectual link that you suggest. . . . Politics and pragmatics were the factors. (Pocock, 1998, personal communication)

He goes on to explain why he did not engage in much analysis of the responses to the directives in the new phase of Mass-Observation:

There was no time for more than the most superficial analysis. While I was answering the responses to one Directive I was already talking about the substance of the next one. I only wrote up one batch of material and that was the one on neighbours and neighbourhoods. (Pocock, 1998, personal communication)

Irrespective of whether or not he had time to apply such analysis himself to the data, we would nevertheless like to suggest that the design of the new Project itself may also be understood in terms of Pocock's concern for personal anthropology. While respecting his account of the history of the later phase of Mass-Observation, which indeed links with the serendipitous character of much of the earlier phase, we would like to suggest that a reading of the Project that sees it as a way of expressing and revealing the participants' personal anthropology, offers a fruitful way of making sense of the material. Taking one's cue from Pocock's own work in this area, we can ourselves read the responses to directives that Mass-Observation had sent out from its earliest days as providing a way of accessing ordinary people's personal epistemologies in ways that dominant historical records failed to do and that lie at the heart of an anthropology of ourselves. The correspondents are themselves asked to reflect on and make explicit the models that gave meaning to their social lives and, in this sense, operate as both informants in the traditional sense of anthropological field work, to which Malinowski and Firth both allude, and as observers of social life, including their own, in the sense that Pocock notes in his account of personal anthropology. This interpretation links closely with the other trends that we have noted as influential in the new phase of the Project—in feminism, history and autobiography, all likewise concerned with meaning rather than function and with recognising "ordinary" people's knowledge. This is, interestingly, a view that fits well with the role described in the early Mass-Observation Bulletins previously mentioned: correspondents were indeed being asked to adopt an ethnographic perspective, in Green and Bloome's sense (1997). If not fully fledged ethnographers, nevertheless their views were being taken seriously as co-researchers in the sense that Cameron et al. (1992) argued for research to be "with" as well as "on" or "for" its subjects. Indeed, anticipating Cameron's argument in an afterword to *May the Twelfth* (1987), Pocock writes:

the founders of the Mass-Observation movement, as it was called, all shared a belief that whether the observation was of the masses, or by the masses (it was in fact a combination of both) it was certainly for the masses. (Pocock, 1987, p. 416)

To this extent then, Pocock's position is not so far from ours, even though he wishes to stress the pragmatic and political dimension of the re-launch rather than the intellectual line. Where we would agree most with his position is in the argument that a single monolithic view of Mass-Observation is not feasible—that the participants themselves disagreed as to its purpose and value, just as did the anthropologists who criticised it. Pocock, like ourselves of course, has the advantage of hindsight in his comments on early Mass-Observation and its relationship to the study of society. Whereas Firth and Malinowski were concerned in the 1930s to protect the professional space being carved out by a new discipline from the "dilution" of amateurs and were limited in the range of Mass-Observation materials on which they could call in order to assess this threat, Pocock had access to 50 years of published materials and to detailed papers in the Archive. Apart from their variety and richness in their own right, these papers demonstrate differences of opinion amongst the founders and organisers that indeed make the movement now seem less monolithic than it had to the anthropologists of the 1930s.

Pocock notes, for instance, differences of opinion between Madge, Harrisson and Jennings about the extent to which the collection of data should be guided by theoretical questions and pre-conceptions, or be free and open, interpretation to be left to the reader. As we have seen, this was a crucial issue for the early critics, who complained that—at least according to the public statements about Mass-Observation put out by its founders—it was relatively unstructured, empirical data collection in the sense that Harrisson approached his ornithological work. Pocock notes the actual differences of view on this: Jennings, the photographer and documentary film maker, saw the *May the Twelfth* data as a kind of montage whose unity was "to be made in the mind of the reader. It was to be a serious aesthetic and moral experience" (p. 416). For Madge, who co-authored the book, Pocock suggests a more complex and split attitude. On the one hand, as a poet, he would sympathise with Jennings; on the other, as a journalist, Communist and later Professor of Sociology, he had also some scientific and political purpose, writing in *May the Twelfth*: "Mass-Observation is more than journalism or film-documentary, because it has the aim not only of presenting but also classifying and analysing the immediate human world" (p. 414; cited in Pocock, 1987, p. 416). Madge, according to Pocock, "regarded himself as combining anthropology and social psychology in his handling of the material", while from a political point of view he saw these two sciences as "potentially the foremost allies of revolution" (*The Left Review*, 1 July 1937; cited in Pocock, 1987, p. 416).

Tom Harrisson, the third founder of Mass-Observation, and the one against whom much of the criticism by anthropologists was levelled, in fact had no hand in compiling *May the Twelfth* and even complained that he did not see it until proof stage, when his comments were ignored. For him the book was not anthropology: "This book did not attempt to be anthropology, if by anthropology we mean not only the description but also the integration and explanation of a whole phenomenon in its cultural context: it was rather a detailed piece of documentation, having much in common with documentary film" (Harrisson, letter to Madge, 1940, cited in Pocock, 1987, p. 418). This criticism of Mass-Observation's lack of academic direction or theory somewhat ironically echoes those of Firth and Malinowski against Harrisson himself. Pocock brings out the ambivalence and complexity of this situation in a way that was less possible for his anthropological predecessors by showing how the differences of opinion to which they refer can actually be contained within not only the movement itself but also within a single influential individual in it. While appearing to agree with his anthropological critics in another letter: "it was a crazy idea to have it edited by a whole bunch of intellectual poets" (letter to Geoffrey Gorer, 1938, cited in Pocock, 1987, p. 418), Harrisson also donned the empiricist hat that had so irked them, stating that "he would prefer to see the movement wallowing around in a maze of fact rather than beelining for a premature conclusion" (p. 416).

The same ambivalence is evident amongst the Mass-Observers themselves. The autumn Bulletin in 1937 cites conflicting views of the role of theory that reflect those of the academic community: one Mass-Observer writes "it hardly matters where we start", and another argues " . . . amassing facts is just a waste of time unless you first have a clear purpose". As in other areas of Mass-Observation inquiry, the Mass-Observers themselves are as reflective and thoughtful about the issues raised, methodological and theoretical as well as ethical and political, as the academic commentators. One feels that this is what attracts Pocock to Mass-Observation in the first place and it suggests a way of viewing the movement that gets us beyond the sterile debate about theoretical versus empiricist orientations. It is the alternative viewpoints themselves that lie at the heart of Mass-Observation's strength; the "people's history" perspective that drew many Mass-Observers in the first place appears also to have attracted many of the academic participants.

Pocock opens his Afterword to *May the Twelfth* with a brief personal memory of his own first encounter with Mass-Observation as a schoolboy: he had picked *May the Twelfth* off the shelves in his school library at the age of fifteen, read it under his desk, and he still remembers "the initial puzzlement and then the tingle of delight that comes with real discovery" (p. 415). This was, to his teenage eye, "a magnificent subversion of authority". He goes on:

> The Coronation of George VI was "history" as far as I was concerned but it had never occurred to me before that "history" could be written in this way. If I derived anything more permanent than this first pleasure it was a critical sense that precisely such details as those that Mass-Observation had recorded were at least to be borne in mind whenever later I was to be faced with an "official record". (p. 415)

One might say much the same of the kind of anthropology espoused by Pocock and those who he describes in the shift from "function to meaning". Certainly he advises the readers of the *Understanding Social Anthropology* (1975) volume mentioned above that this is how they might write anthropology: against the grain as it were, both presenting through description their own concepts and models of social life as indicative of those held by ordinary people, and through commentary and reflection offering some analysis of them. For Pocock this is not a threat to his discipline but an expansion of it. Just as in the field he might discuss with informants their conceptions of Mind, Body and Wealth, so through Mass-Observation directives he might explore with members of his own society their conceptions of the economy, of home, of self (early directives in the revived Mass-Observation). The relationship between artistic and scientific, political and academic dimensions of early Mass-Observation, variously expressed between and within the personalities and domains of work of its founders, continue to be explored and sometimes bridged in the new project.

CONTEMPORARY ANTHROPOLOGY: THE REFLEXIVE TURN

Anthropology itself has recently become more self-conscious and critical of its early heritage, in particular the colonial overtones of Malinowski and other "founding fathers", and has begun to explore the nature of the ethnographic account itself (Asad, 1979; Clifford, 1988; Fardon, 1990). Clifford and Marcus (1986) in a highly influential volume, *Writing Culture*, have focussed on the writing up of such accounts in equally critical vein. They argue that anthropologists have paid too little attention to the process of how they write their field experiences: many treat writing as a transparent vehicle for the experience itself, whereas close analysis of their texts demonstrates how much their message was dependent on the form of language and rhetoric they adopted. Indeed, Thornton (1983) went so far as to say that what defined anthropology as a discipline at the turn of the century, as it struggled to differentiate itself from travellers tales, missionary accounts and commissioner reports, was not the experience itself—these people had often experienced longer and deeper encounters with "natives", and knew their languages better than the anthropologists—but rather the way in which it was represented in text. The academic discourse, including the tradition of the monograph, with its classic layout into chapters based on economics, politics, religion, was itself constitutive of the discipline. In this sense ethnography is only one component of the anthropological tradition, along with writing, participant observation and so forth. Conversely, other disciplines may use ethnography in different ways without having to locate it in the discourse of anthropology or its myth history. Reflection upon the nature and experience of field work has also led to some revision of the meaning of ethnography within anthropology itself.

Todorov (1988) has suggested that there is a fundamental contradiction at the heart of the ethnographic enterprise, although he suggests that this contradiction can be used in a productive and illuminating way. On the one hand, the ethnographer claims validity because he or she has some "distance" from the ideas and beliefs of the people under scrutiny. Members of a culture often do not realise what they are taking for granted; the classic introductions to anthropology state that you do not ask a fish to tell you about water—it is so immersed in the medium that it does not realise it is water. As Julian Huxley commented in his foreword to *Mass-Observation* (1937), "We live immersed in society as a fish in water, and our ways of thinking and feeling are moulded by the social framework" (p. 3). For him the role of anthropology and of Mass-Observation as a particular technique within the social sciences was essential in providing scientific knowledge of our own society. Huxley and Tom Harrisson, in his more contentious accounts of Mass-Observation, believed that this could be done through applying scientific methods, including detailed and unbiased information gathering. Todorov echoes these claims when he suggests that anthropologists have argued it is by exposure to another medium—"taking the fish out of water"—that we can identify the nature of the medium we take for granted: the outside ethnographer by dint of distance from the culture can draw attention to its fundamental tenets and epistemological presuppositions—the assumptions it makes about knowledge, how it is defined and legitimated and who has rights over it. There is, however, according to Todorov, a contradiction in the way that anthropologists value such "distancing". For the same anthropologists who celebrate distance in ethnographic accounts require their colleagues to have familiarity with the local culture derived from proximity and close everyday interaction; in anthropological circles it is important to "know your people" well and not simply to remain at a distance. This tension between distance and proximity is the defining feature of ethnography, according to Todorov. When ethnographers go to the field, they separate themselves from their home culture and enter a strange and alien one. When they leave that culture in turn, to return home, they go through a further separation and have to re-enter their home culture. At this threshold point, the returning ethnographers can see their own culture with the eyes of a stranger: the familiar becomes strange, a concept emphasised in Agar's classic account *The Professional Stranger* (1980; see also Stocking, 1968, 1983). Gradually, however, this distance, too, lessens as the ethnographers enter into closer proximity to their own everyday norms and beliefs. The likelihood is that they will return at some point to the culture they have studied and the process will happen again. Indeed, they will most likely be always mentally moving between different cultures, always shifting between proximity and distance in any cultural setting. This, then, is the essence of the ethnographic experience; proximity and distance held in tension simultaneously. The experience involves, then, epistemological relativity, reflexivity and critical consciousness. Epistemological relativity involves recognising one's own assumptions about knowledge and how it is legitimised in one's own society, so as to be able to view the knowledge of other societies with a more open mind. Since assumptions about knowledge are frequently hidden and naturalised, it is easy to simply impose them on other people as though they are universal.

The discipline of anthropology in particular has been concerned with this relativity of knowledge, and anthropologists would argue that doing ethnography involves attention to such epistemological levels and not just issues of technique and method. Reflexivity refers to the ability to reflect critically on the way in which one's own cultural background and standpoint influence one's view of other cultures. Lack of reflection, for instance, on the metaphors we use for describing other ways of life can, as Asad and Dixon show (1985), serve to impose our own views on them in subtle and hidden ways. Critical consciousness represents a newer tradition in anthropology and views ethnography not simply as a convenient tool for studying and researching, but as itself a product of particular dominant societies at a particular period. The ways in which we observe and then write up those observations need to be considered critically if they are to avoid the ethnocentrism of earlier periods of academic work.

This is equally applicable to the observations and writing of Mass-Observation observers. A key question for commentators on Mass-Observation, especially for anthropologists, has been "can the correspondents, with little or no training, adapt the ethnographic approaches used by professionals and apply them to their own, 'common-sense' lived experience?". For contemporary anthropologists this is a question not so much about objectivity and theory—although untrained observers may well exhibit differences in degree from professional anthropologists in this regard—as about reflexivity and critical consciousness. What kind of evidence are the Mass-Observation observers providing? Are they "just" informants or are they also at the same time themselves social commentators? A further question, raised by both Mass-Observation and commentators on it, is how can we apply the methods of anthropology—including the principle of distancing and proximity—to "our own culture"? We discuss some of the attempts to answer these questions in relation to actual Mass-Observation writing, with reference to the concepts of "case studies", "thick description", "communicative competence", and "literacy practices".

MASS-OBSERVATION AS CASE STUDIES

It is worth reiterating here what is entailed by considering Mass-Observation as "case studies", as this may provide a methodological solution to some of the questions raised by early commentators as well as by the new anthropology. This will then lead us in to the discussion of Mass-Observation as literacy practices. One sense in which the accounts provided by Mass-Observation correspondents can be interpreted in terms of the methodological assumptions of social science is to treat them as case studies. Mitchell's (1984) essay on case studies represents a particularly influential example of this view in the discipline of anthropology and its use of ethnographic case studies. Rather than applying "enumerative induction", as in much scientific and statistical research, as a means to generalising and for establishing the "representatives" of social data, Mitchell advocates "analytical induction":

> What the anthropologist using a case study to support an argument does is to show how general principles deriving from some theoretical orientation manifest themselves in some given set of particular circumstances. A good case study, therefore, enables the

analyst to establish theoretically valid connections between events and phenomena which previously were ineluctable. From this point of view, the search for a "typical" case for analytic exposition is likely to be less fruitful than the search for a "telling" case in which the particular circumstances surrounding a case, serve to make previously obscure theoretical relationships suddenly apparent. . . . Case Studies used in this way are clearly more than "apt illustrations". Instead, they are means whereby general theory may be developed. (Mitchell, 1984, p. 239)

This represents a way of viewing Mass-Observation as ethnography: the correspondents' writing can be seen as providing telling accounts of specific aspects of the culture they both inhabit and observe. Another way of viewing such accounts is as what Geertz calls "thick description". Again, knowledge is built up from local experience and not just the province of high theory. Geertz writes:

The major theoretical contributions not only lie in specific studies—that is true in almost any field—but they are very difficult to abstract from such studies and integrate into anything one might call "culture theory" as such. Theoretical formulations hover so low over the interpretations they govern that they don't make much sense or hold much interest apart from them. That is so, not because they are not general (if they are not general they are not theoretical), but because, stated independently of their application, they seem either commonplace or vacant. One can, and this in fact is how the field progresses conceptually, take a line of theoretical attack developed in connection with one exercise in ethnographic interpretation and employ it in another, pushing it forward to greater precision and broader relevance, but one cannot write a "General Theory of Cultural Interpretation" [cf. Asad's claim (1979) that there can be no "general theory of ideology"]. Or rather, one can but there appears to be little profit in it, because the essential task of theory building here is not to codify abstract regularities but to make thick description possible, not to generalise across cases but to generalise within them. (Geertz, 1983, pp. 25-26)

Walter Benjamin made a remarkably similar comment on the role of photographic representations: wary of high theory imposing its meanings, as indeed was Mass-Observation, he pointed out how photographs may generate unexpected connections that subsequent observers recognise in ways unnoticed at the time.[2] Pocock's comments on the unexpected similarities and differences generated by the May 12th material suggest some commonality of approach across the

---

[2]We want to acknowledge and thank J. Lowry for this point.

MASS-OBSERVATION AS LITERACY PRACTICES

Central to the ethnographer's understanding, as we saw above, is sensitivity to the ways in which information is elicited, organised and circulated in the community being studied and how this might be different from the observer's own speech community. In order to understand these processes, the ethnographer must attain communicative competence in the culture under consideration and not simply impose her own preconceived academic models (cf., Bauman & Scherzer, 1974; Gumperz & Hymes, 1972); theoretical formulations must hover low over the interpretations and knowledge of the community itself. Mass-Observation in some ways fits these conceptions of the anthropological project better than it did the earlier formulations of the discipline by Firth and Malinowski and the critiques of Mass-Observation they led to. Observers in the Mass-Observation project can provide both knowledge of different communities and some reflection upon their interpretations: the writings of those who respond to Mass-Observation directives can provide "thick description", which can then be negotiated by both participants and detached researchers alike. In the tradition of the "ethnography of communication", the concept of "communicative competence" refers not only to language skills but to understanding of the rich nuances of a culture and the appropriateness of when and how to use specific linguistic forms. This is congruent with that reflective sensitivity to proximity and distance to which Todorov (1988) refers. Out of this tradition has come a range of detailed ethnographies of ways of speaking (and writing) and their connection to deep epistemological issues in cultural variation that provide the background for our current studies of Mass-Observation as ways of writing. Recently the ethnography of communication tradition has been extended by greater attention to power and ideology in what has come to be called the New Literacy Studies (Gee, 1990; Street, 1993, 1995). This involves, firstly, considering the written channel as well as the oral: "literacy" is seen as the "social practices of reading and/or writing" rather than from only a psycholinguistic or purely educational perspective, with their stress on individual skills; and secondly, recognising that literacy practices are always involved in wider social issues of ideology, identity and conflict. We use the phrase "literacy practices" (Street, 1988) as an extension of Heath's (1983) notion of "literacy events". By this she meant any activity or event that involved reading and/ or writing. While building on her work, we want to signal that we are not just talking about reading and writing as activities but we are also taking account of the fact that people doing them have brought to them conceptions, models, theories of reading and writing and that those conceptions, models and theories are culturally grounded (for a fuller discussion of this, see Barton & Ivanic, 1991; see also Baynham's 1995 book entitled *Literacy Practices*). People do not just do writing. They have ideas in their mind about what it means to do it. And that is rather harder to see. We can observe the external behaviour. Trying to get at the internal conceptualisation is rather harder. We are all conditioned to what appears to be natural, the common-sense naturalised views of everyday social phenomena, including those of reading and writing. The point is more obvious when looking at notions of literacy in different cultures. It becomes very apparent, when looking at different conceptions and practices of literacy, how particular the literacy practices in our own context are, how constructed and socially specific they are. Mass-Observation material, as Pocock suggests, can provide a way of exploring such practices—including people's own theories and models about them—within our own culture: viewing them as literacy practices extends the idea of an anthropology of ourselves to the medium through which such a study is conducted. We are using literacy practices, then, in a specific way in order to refer to the social uses and meanings of reading and/or writing (Barton & Ivanic, 1991). The dominant discourses on literacy tend to be either educational—which imply very often that people come from their home environments with some sort of literacy "deficit"—or national media representations of mass illiteracy, a literacy "crisis" and of social and intellectual decline. Trying to disentangle ourselves from those dominant discourses and talk about literacy practices as they are on the ground in real social conditions provides a way of interpreting Mass-Observation rather differently than through early dismissals of Mass-Observation by anthropologists and of understanding Mass-Observation writing rather differently than through dominant discourses on literacy in Britain today. Locating Mass-Observation in the context of concern with a cross-cultural conception of literacy practices, then, raises in a different way the question of what kind of evidence is Mass-Observation writing. One answer can be that the writing found in Mass-Observation is evidence of the nature of the literacy practices in our own culture.

As we suggest in the introduction, there are two senses in which the Mass-Observation material is evidence for writing. Firstly, it actually is writing; the archive is full of examples—the walls are lined with boxes of people's own writing, people writing on all kinds of scraps of paper in all kinds of different ways. In the recent Mass-Observation context that has been happening across Britain over the last decade or two. So we already have evidence of writing there. But interestingly, in relation to the subject we are researching, the Mass-Observation archive is providing evidence of writing at another level. In the directive on literacy issued in 1991, we asked the respondents to answer a number of questions about the writing process itself. This, then, is evidence of another kind, of people's ideas about writing. They are, of course, ideas elicited by us, but in many cases it is quite clear from the interviews which we also conducted that the respondents do already have very strong notions of what the writing process is. That is the issue that we want to try to address in this section: people's own models and theories of the literacy process. This perspective, we believe, is congruent with the view of Mass-Observation as "Personal Anthropology" which we suggest led to Pocock's interest in reviving the project. This perspective gives us two meanings to the notion of "invisible writing", which we first raised in the introduction: at one level, writing is invisible in society because a lot of this kind of everyday practice is not noticed. The dominant discourses represent illiteracy on the one hand or high literature and culture on the other. The real everyday practices that may make up most of the writing that goes on are invisible. But there is another sense in which writing is invisible, which is in the representations of the writing process itself. These, too, are invisible. There is very little attention paid to the notion that the people who do it themselves have ideas about it. This is familiar from the development literacy work, in aid and overseas development activities and literacy programmes. Often the assumption is that people are waiting, with empty minds as it were, to be filled up with literacy, for literacy to come and make them start thinking, as though they have not been for centuries already. The dominant model also assumes that, even if they do get literacy, they will simply do it as though it is a kind of behaviour. There is very little attention in any of these mass literacy programmes to questioning and exploring people's own views of literacy. What are the models of literacy that people hold? What do they think it is that they are doing? How are they "taking hold of literacy" rather than what is the "impact" of literacy on people (Kulick & Stroud, 1993): asking how people take hold of literacy puts people first rather than the technology. This seems to us a powerful concept and enables us to look through the Mass-Observation data from the perspective of the writers themselves, and so to focus on the ways in which they are taking hold of literacy.

In asking these questions of the data held in the Mass-Observation Archive we are treating it as ethnography in two senses: firstly, that it is data comparable to that which ethnographers encounter in face-to-face oral encounters during "field work". The accounts that Mass-Observation correspondents provide of writing in British society—

or their experience of it—is comparable to the accounts that New Guinean villagers provided to Kulick and Stroud (1993) or that Street (1984) elicited during fieldwork in Iran.

But the key point that comes from our research on Mass-Observation as literacy practices, is that the correspondents themselves are adopting an "ethnographic perspective", if not actually "doing ethnography"; in this case they are observers of and commentators on the literacy practices of members of contemporary British society. As Nick Stanley points out, there was an ambiguity in the original claim of Mass-Observation to be an "anthropology of ourselves". On the one hand, trained observers went to a town such as Bolton and effectively did traditional anthropological field work "on the natives". Those who did this were trained for the task or were already social scientists in their own right. On the other hand, the subjects themselves reported on their lives as though they were both objects of ethnography and the observers of it. These observers were not professionally trained—they were the "ordinary hard working folk" to whom Madge refers and whose amateur status perhaps sparked some of the professional critiques of Mass-Observation that persist to this day. While Firth and Malinowski both saw this ambivalence as a serious problem, N. Stanley suggests a more positive way of viewing it that is in keeping with contemporary anthropological thinking. The extension of Mass-Observation to such people, he suggests, requires also an extension of the phrase "anthropology of ourselves", which might thus be completed by the slogan "an anthropology of ourselves, by ourselves and for ourselves" (N. Stanley, 1981, p. 45), a sentiment that echoes the recent call for linguistic research that is not only "on" or "for" the subjects, but "with" them (Cameron et al., 1992) and Pocock's comment that whether Mass-Observation is "observation of the masses or by the masses (it is both) it is certainly for the masses" (in *May the Twelfth*, p. 416).

In this way, contemporary Mass-Observation might be considered as ethnography in both the senses noted above—as providing data for analysts and as itself providing analysis of the data. In the present case, we are particularly concerned with the latter—that is, the Mass-Observers' commentaries on their own writing practices. While this would have been problematic to an earlier generation of anthropologists, as we have seen, we would like to suggest that such commentary can be legitimately and fruitfully taken into account as part of an anthropology of ourselves. We consider the Mass-Observation correspondents' writing, then, as adopting an "ethnographic perspective" on literacy from which we have much to learn about how we in contemporary Britain "write ourselves". It is to their accounts that we now turn in Section 2.

SECTION II
Dialogues and Writing Practices

Introduction to Section II

The previous section provided a history of Mass-Observation that frames the intellectual and social climate within which Mass-Observation correspondents and others associated with Mass-Observation write. We now focus more directly on literacy practices, both those directly implicated in Mass-Observation and those taken up by the Mass-Observation correspondents in other aspects of their lives.

The attention to literacy practices and Mass-Observation is warranted in several ways. As we noted earlier, Mass-Observation consists of a great deal of writing. Our best guess is that the Mass-Observation Archive contains over a million pieces of paper. The Mass-Observation correspondents write in response to directives, researchers and university students read the writings in the Archive and write notes, papers and books, and the staff write directives, correspond with Mass-Observation correspondents, supporters, researchers, students and others, and maintain records that organize the Archive. Thus, understanding Mass-Observation writing practices lies at the heart of understanding Mass-Observation. We need to know:

What is this writing? Is it all of one kind? How is it done?

What meaning do these writing practices have for the Mass-Observation correspondents? For others?

Where do these writing practices fit with other writing practices, both those used by the Mass-Observation correspondents and those in the broader society?

The pursuit of the questions above is not just inquiry about Mass-Observation. We view the exploration of Mass-Observation and literacy practices as a "telling case" about the nature of literacy and society.

Section 2 begins with a discussion of our research project, "Literacy Practices and the Mass-Observation Project". Through that project, Mass-Observation correspondents described and reflected on the writing they did for the Mass-Observation Project and that they did at other times. We took that data and constructed "cases", which we have called "dialogues". We call them dialogues because the data came from two types of dialogues: interviews we had with a select group of Mass-Observation correspondents and the responses of 481 Mass-Observation correspondents to a directive on writing for the Mass-Observation. But they are dialogues in another sense as well. They are part of a broader, ongoing conversation about the nature of writing in society, a conversation including writing theorists, academics, educators, social commentators, politicians and ordinary people. Through their responses to the directive and through their interviews, the Mass-Observation correspondents become part of the dialogue. And, like any contribution to a dialogue, their comments both reflect and refract what has gone before (cf., Bakhtin, 1935/81) and provide part of the framing for what may come later in the dialogue.

Chapter 5 contains the dialogues of nine Mass-Observation correspondents. We have fashioned each dialogue using their words from their interviews and directive responses. It could be claimed that the dialogues reflect, at least in part, our views. We agree. We structured the directive and the interview protocol and selected what to present in each dialogue. Of course, on many occasions the Mass-Observation corespondents ignored the directions in the directive or reshaped the interview. They were not passive respondents but more like colleagues and co-researchers, using their observations and insights of their own life and the lives of those around them to explore questions about writing in society. Yet we agree that it is always the case that authors—whether anthropologists, historians, novelists or even auto-biographers—fashion the representation. There is no such thing as a transparent representation. But that does not negate the usefulness of the dialogues, nor does it negate the dialogues as hovering close to the lives of the people represented. We argue that we have fashioned emic (or close to emic) representations of writing practices in the dialogues. Indeed, to have merely presented the raw data from the directive responses and raw transcripts from the interviews would have been a more gross distortion and distancing from an emic perspective. It would hang with the pretense of transparency, while viewing all of the qualities of human character, interaction and life not reducible to text; it would present a flat picture of the conversations and of the people, with each word and topic taking on the same emphasis and foregrounded as the one before and the one after. It is the fashioning that allowed us the opportunity to create a textured picture of the Mass-Observation correspondents, capturing at least some of the social context and thematic connections that are needed to present an emic view.

We have presented the dialogues separately from the theoretical discussions that follow in Section 3 because we wanted readers to have the opportunity to reflect on the dialogues prior to our discussions. In this way, we hope to layer various interpretations and explanations of the writing practices described. One layer consists of the interpretations and explanations given by the Mass-Observation correspondents in their dialogues. A second layer involves the juxtaposition of the dialogues with the previous discussion in Section 1 about the history of Mass-Observation and the controversies in anthropology over Mass-Observation. Our comments in Section 3 provide other layers of interpretation and explanation. One might think of it as creating a painting on a canvas, built layer by layer. Although the layers build on each other, each layer also shows through.

4
Framing the Dialogues: Literacy Practices

A tape recorder, with microphone in hand, on the table or the arm of the chair or on the grass, can transform both the visitor and the host. On one occasion, during the play-back, my companion murmured in wonder, "I never realized I felt that way." and I was filled with wonder, too. It can be used to capture the voice of a celebrity whose answers are ever ready to flow through all the expected straits. I have yet to be astonished by one. It can be used to capture the thoughts of the non-celebrated—on the steps of a public housing project, in a frame bungalow, in a furnished apartment, in a parked car—and these "statistics" become persons, each one unique. I am constantly astonished. (Studs Terkel, 1972, pp. xxiii-xxiv)

One purpose of this chapter is to describe the processes we used in gathering, analysing and writing up the data in our research on literacy practices and the Mass-Observation Project. We describe the directive that we used, our analysis of responses to it, how we selected Mass-Observation correspondents for interviews, the interview process and how we analysed the data. We also discuss how we constructed the written text, with emphasis on how we constructed the dialogues that follow in Chapter 5.

Typically, the interpretation of data in a research study is framed by questions such as: What kind of knowledge is this? How does it fit with the knowledge we already have? Is it reliable? Generalisable? Valid? Such questions characterise knowledge as existing in and of itself. We hold a different view. We view knowledge as part of and inseparable from the contexts of its production and use; thus, some of the questions we use to frame the interpretation of data are: How was the knowledge produced? When? Where? By whom? For what uses? Who uses the knowledge? For what purposes? With what social consequence and meaning? And as importantly, how does the knowledge evolve and transform as it is used? Further, we view questions about knowledge as intimately tied to questions about power. In brief, we view knowledge as having multiple definitions grounded in the complex and multiple social events and practices of its production and use, and these multiple definitions have implications for power relations among people and social institutions. A third consideration is the representation of knowledge. In our view, the representation of knowledge is part of the construction of knowledge. How it is written, the genres in which it is displayed, the representation of authorship (who are defined as the authors, what relationships authors have to readers and others, and how authorship itself is defined [cf., Foucault, 1984]), and how the representation(s) is read, all are part of the construction of knowledge. In this book, we have provided several different kinds of representation: narratives (Chapter 5), historical accounts (Chapters 1, 2 and 3), ethnographic reports (Chapters 6, 7 and 8), statistical tabulations (see Appendices), argumentative essays (Chapters 3, 4, 6, 7 and 8), auto/biographical reports (see Chapter 5), among others. Authorship is also varied and problematised; the authors include the three of us (Sheridan, Street and Bloome), editors and publishers (Judith Green and Barbara Bernstein), the Mass-Observation correspondents,[1] all those scholars and others we have quoted, and more. At times, it is difficult to decide who the author is. For example, is the author of one of the dialogues in Chapter 5 the Mass-Observation correspondent (after all, the words are those uttered by her/him), or are the authors Sheridan, Bloome, Street and Hill[2] who fashioned the dialogues from the audiotaped interviews. To what degree and how do the authorship and genres of those dialogues influence how the dialogues are read and how the representation and nature of knowledge are read and then used? And we can ask similar questions about the other parts of the book. Although such questions have informed our thinking and our writing (e.g., we provide a variety of genres, multiple "locations" for framing the data, historical context, discuss the

---

[1] We have used pseudonyms for the Mass-Observation correspondents instead of their real names (see Appendix Biv). There are a few exceptions which are explained in the text. However, the numbers we have used are the actual numbers assigned to the Mass-Observation correspondents by the Mass-Observation Project. This decision is consistent with the policies of the Mass-Observation Archive and with the stated wishes of the Mass-Observation correspondents. As reported in Chapters 1 and 2, privacy is an important issue for many of the Mass-Observation correspondents; some-perhaps most-would not participate, or participate as freely, if their privacy was not respected.

[2] As noted in the Acknowledgements, Sara Hill helped edit several of the dialogues.

complexity of authorship and many of the processes involved in production of the text), we do not claim to have answers for the questions above, at least not answers that translate into simple algorithms or decontextualized social practices. Rather, writers and readers must struggle with these questions, holding stances that are at best temporary before moving on to other stances, creating coherence while acknowledging that it too is temporary.

READING MASS-OBSERVATION AND THE NATURE OF KNOWLEDGE[3]

The materials in the Mass-Observation Project are primarily written materials, and the primary activities of people using the Archive are reading and writing. Perhaps because the centrality of reading and writing is so obvious, the importance of reflecting on the nature of reading and writing may get overlooked. But it is important to do so, as these processes are not as transparent as they might first appear and recent research has raised many complex issues regarding the meaning and uses of reading and writing, many of which are relevant here (for example, see Bloome, 1993; Brodkey, 1987; Bruce, 1981; Heath, 1982; Street, 1995, 1996b, 1997). In this section we describe four different ways of reading the materials in the Mass-Observation Project, although there are many other ways of reading. It is likely that anyone using the Mass-Observation materials reads in several different ways, orchestrating these different ways of reading to accomplish particular social agendas.

Reading and Writing as Knowledge Transmission

One way of reading is to assume that the writer is sending us information he or she has gathered about the world. This is often called a transmission model of reading and writing because knowledge is transmitted from one place or person to another (see Figure 4-1).

Writer ⟶ Reader

Knowledge

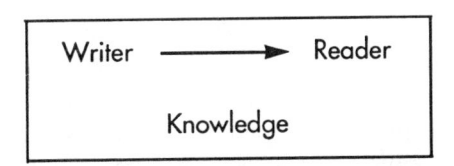

Figure 4-1. Transmission model of reading and writing

---

[3]Much of the text in this section is taken from Bloome, Sheridan and Street (1993) *Reading Mass-Observation Writing.*

To read the Archive materials as knowledge transmission fits at least some of the stated goals of the Mass-Observation Project. Ordinary people are transmitting knowledge about their daily lives and communities to scholars, students and others. The Mass-Observation correspondents can make available to people using the Archive knowledge about daily life in Britain that is otherwise unavailable or at the least very difficult to get. Further, they make available knowledge from one period of time that may be useful to people decades later. One implication of reading the Mass-Observation Project materials as knowledge transmission is that the Mass-Observation correspondents are defined as reporters or as field workers, gathering information and passing it on.

Although the Mass-Observation correspondents are directed in their information-gathering activities by the directives they receive from the Archive, they vary in how they respond. Some Mass-Observation correspondents follow the directives faithfully, responding to each question or task point by point. Others treat the directive as a whole and respond in general. Still others ignore the directive nearly entirely and instead transmit the information they think is useful. There is also variation in the styles of writing used by the Mass-Observation correspondents: some respond with exposition, others with narrative, some write as if writing a letter to a friend and occasionally a few may write a poem as part of their response to a directive. One way to view the variety of ways of responding is that they are transmitting different types of knowledge and different contexts of knowledge (e.g., personal context, community context, historical context).

There are limitations on reading the Archive materials as "knowledge transmission." First, we all have our biases and perspectives. What gets reported often reflects that. Who we are also affects what we report. Many Mass-Observation correspondents are very aware that they have biases, and they will often note in their writing that they are only describing things from their own perspective. Mass-Observation correspondents make special efforts to gather information from other people so that what they report is not limited to their own point of view. A second limitation in reading Mass-Observation writing as knowledge transmission is that sometimes Mass-Observation correspondents have other purposes than just knowledge transmission. They may be commenting on an event or giving a political opinion (indeed some directive tasks ask for that). Some Mass-Observation correspondents enjoy the intellectual stimulation and writing practice involved in responding to a directive, and so they are not just reporting. Writers may also be constructing personalities/identities as writers that are different from how they represent themselves in other contexts. For instance, they may present themselves as "researchers", as "social commentators", as "ordinary people", all of which affects the "knowledge" they are "transmitting."

Reading and Writing as Knowledge Construction

Whenever we read, we are affected by what we already know about the topic and by the experiences we have had. Thus, reading is not just a matter of getting knowledge from the written text, but is a process of knowledge construction (see Figure 4-2).

Similarly, when we write, both what we write and how we write are influenced by our previous knowledge and experiences, by our knowledge and experience writing and by our purposes for writing. Our writing is also affected by our reading. For example, consider the Spring 1991 Mass-Observation directive on literacy practices from the perspective of reading as knowledge construction. The Mass-Observation correspondents began by reading the directive. They interpreted the directive based on their own background experiences and knowledge, perhaps interpreting the directive differently from each other. Then, when they began writing their responses, they did more than just report information about literacy practices, they constructed knowledge as they wrote. They selected what to write about, they chose how to organize the information they presented and how to make it coherent, and they reconstructed events from memory and from their interpretations of what had occurred or was occurring.

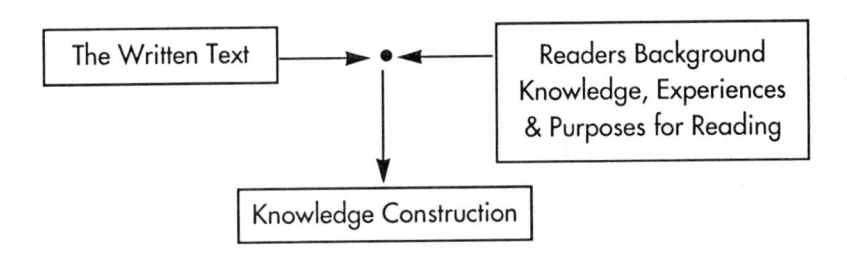

Figure 4-2. Knowledge construction model of reading and writing

One important implication derived from viewing reading as knowledge construction is that the responses of the Mass-Observation correspondents might be considered reports of their perceptions, memories and interpretations of events rather than just unmediated descriptions of events. For some researchers using the Mass-Observation Project, this is exactly what they hope to get. They are interested in what people in Britain think about a topic or how they perceive themselves, their family, their friends, their future, their past. From the viewpoint of reading as knowledge construction, the Mass-Observation Project is like a survey or a large-scale experimental task. The directive is like a survey questionnaire or an experimental prompt, and what the Mass-Observation correspondents write is like an answer to a survey question or a response to an experimental condition.

Acknowledging that background knowledge and experiences mediate what is written does not negate the importance of the writing collected by the Mass-Observation Archive project; rather it redefines the data as perceptions, views and interpretations. Similarly, researchers and others using the Mass-Observation Project are themselves readers constructing knowledge. Their background knowledge, experiences and purposes affect their understanding and interpretations of what they read and write no less than occurs for the Mass-Observation correspondents. The disciplinary background researchers and students bring to their reading also affects their understanding and interpretation. Given a view of reading as knowledge construction, researchers' reports—like the writings of the Mass-Observation correspondents—are also constructions of knowledge and not just factual reports.

Reading and Writing as Social and Cultural Practices

Writing and reading are activities for establishing and maintaining social relationships, too. For example, we may write letters to friends to keep a friendship going; we may write warnings, directions and other things to control or influence people's behavior. Sometimes we use writing to end social relationships (which is a kind of social relationship, too): redundancy notices, notes discharging a milkman or other service provider, letters ending a romance and so forth. But writing and reading are not social only through what is communicated, but also in the activity itself. Some writing and reading activities bring people together (e.g., writing a group report, bedtime story reading to children, creating a scrapbook), while other writing and reading activities separate and isolate us from others (e.g., writing a letter in private, writing a private diary, reading a book in a library carrel). In our terms, these activities are all social in the sense that these literacy practices and their meanings have been constructed in cultural and historical contexts.

Within a cultural group or society (or even within a sub-group), there are more or less shared ways of engaging in writing and reading activities in particular places at particular times. Furthermore, cultural institutions such as schools are often set up to promote those shared ways of writing and reading. Since the ways in which we engage in writing and reading activities are shared, they can be called writing and reading practices (or literacy practices). By viewing reading and writing as social practices rather than just events or activities, we can highlight how people "play" with literacy practices (vary the practice to create new social relationships and new social meanings) and how they adapt writing and reading practices to particular situations and to new situations.

One implication of reading the Mass-Observation Project as social and cultural practices is to highlight the social relationships being established between the Mass-Observation correspondents with both the Mass-Observation Project (as a social institution and with its staff) and with the researchers reading the materials in the Mass-Observation Project. Part of highlighting this social relationship involves highlighting social identities of the Mass-Observation correspondents and the various readers of the Mass-Observation materials. By how and what they write, the Mass-Observation correspondents are promoting a particular social identity for themselves, the social contexts of their lives, the Mass-Observation Project, the researchers and those they write about. These social identities have implications for the reader's social identity and may promote a particular kind of reading. For example, the Mass-Observation correspondent who presents an identity as an observer promotes the researcher as a reader of reports from field workers. The Mass-Observation correspondent who writes as a son about his family promotes the researcher perhaps as a voyeuristic reader. The Mass-Observation correspondent who presents herself as an "ordinary" person may be inviting the reader to be a co-conspirator in writing a history of "ordinary" people.

A second implication of reading the materials of the Mass-Observation Project as social and cultural practices is that it highlights various social purposes of writing for the Mass-Observation Project. Writers may be trying to establish or maintain a social relationship, albeit with a social institution and with an unknown audience (although many do write notes to the Archivist, Dorothy Sheridan, and so they do have a known person for at least part of their audience). As the writers establish and maintain a social relationship with the Mass-Observation Project, they involve themselves in a set of social and cultural activities they might not otherwise be involved in (the cultural practice of making history by recording it). Writers may also be trying to influence opinion of future generations, or they may be promoting an explicit or implicit political agenda (see Chapter 6 for a more detailed discussion of purposes for writing).

The writing and reading that researchers do also needs to be viewed as social and cultural practices. One implication for researchers is to be aware of the assumptions and limitations of various social and cultural practices with regard to knowledge, description, interpretation and narrative. Part of this awareness involves questioning the match between the researchers' assumptions about reading and writing practices and those of the Mass-Observation correspondents.

Reading and Writing as Contested Social Practices

It was suggested above that mismatches and incompatibility may occur between the writing and reading practices of Mass-Observation correspondents and those of researchers. Conflicts may occur over how the Mass-Observation correspondents and the researchers are defining each other. Conflicts may also occur in assumptions about the nature of knowledge. For example, a directive may be organised to elicit expository responses (following a "scientific" model of knowledge), while Mass-Observation correspondents may choose to write narratives instead, redefine the question or ignore the directive completely and write about something they feel the researcher should know about and be interested in. There may also be a conflict in how researchers present their findings. Some researchers may package their findings from the Mass-Observation project as scientific reports and coherent histories, although the collection itself is not a single coherent history.

The conflicts that may emerge from various writing and reading practices are not just between the Mass-Observation correspondents and researchers, they may also be part of what Mass-Observation correspondents are reporting. For example, one Mass-Observation correspondent described her experience going to court (discussed in Chapter 7). She not only describes what occurred, but her description also reveals conflicts in reading and writing practices between the Court and the Mass-Observation correspondent. The way the Court used written language limited the act of civil disobedience in which she was involved, and so she had to contest the reading and writing practices of the Court in order to highlight her act of civil disobedience.

Perhaps it should not be surprising that the reports of Mass-Observation correspondents often involve conflicts about writing and reading practices, either explicitly or implicitly. For at least the past four decades, reading and writing have been a topic of strong debate and conflict in contemporary society, and not just by academics. From discussions of the teaching of reading and writing in school, to teacher protests over testing, to calls for a written constitution, to the elimination of passports within the European Community and elsewhere, reading and writing are sites of turmoil. Further, a number of social and cultural theorists have suggested that language practices in general (including reading and writing) are the sites of much social conflict, as it is through language practices that social control is largely maintained in contemporary society, rather than through use of force (cf., Bourdieu, 1991; Fairclough, 1992; Lemke, 1995). Conflicts over reading and writing practices are not resolved by merely acknowledging all sides as valuable and ignoring what the conflicts reveal about the various enterprises that come under the rubric of writing and reading. Rather than view the conflicts as problems requiring resolution, the conflicts can be viewed as points of inquiry revealing yet more insight about everyday life in Britain, the nature of social life in general and the nature of inquiry on social life.

GATHERING, ANALYSING AND WRITING UP THE DATA

The Spring 1991 Directive

We began our inquiry with a research proposal by Sheridan and Street to the Economic and Social Research Council entitled, "Literacy Practices and the Mass-Observation Project". The research proposal focused on the nature of the writing submitted to the Mass-Observation Project. In 1991, we sent the Mass-Observation correspondents a directive about their writing for the Archive and in other contexts. The directive had three parts: Part 1: a request for an account of their experiences in education, a kind of education life history; Part 2: twelve questions about the uses of writing and reading; Part 3: a log of writing and reading activities that needed to be kept for a three-day period, 28 February-2 March 1991; and Part 4: some questions on risk-taking (see Appendix C for a copy of the directive).

We describe the content of the responses in Chapters 6 and 7. What we want to note in this chapter is that the nature of the responses varied greatly. Some correspondents answered each question at length, others gave one-word and very short answers. A few wrote sarcastic responses to questions they felt were repetitious, poorly worded or off the mark, and a few others just told us so. Many embedded stories or narratives within their responses, others gave lists, as appropriate to the question. As true of responses to other directives, many, if not most of the Mass-Observation correspondents, treat directive questions as both requests for information and as prompts for reflection. Further, the

Mass-Observation correspondents appear to feel that they can ignore questions, reframe them, and they let the Mass-Observation staff know when the questions are not insightful. Yet at the same time, most of the Mass-Observation correspondents have a great sense of commitment and loyalty to the Mass-Observation Project, and try to be as helpful as possible in their responses.

All three of us (Sheridan, Street and Bloome) read over the responses. We then discussed following up with interviews, as had been proposed in the ESRC proposal.

Based on our reading of the responses to the directive, the insights we gained from the interviews, and our discussions with others about issues in the field, we analysed the directive responses by reading through them and searching for examples of themes we believed were either recurrent or central. Later, we also used a computer software program, QSR NUD*IST, 1995. The computer-aided analysis requires coding the directive responses by predetermined topic or sub-topic, although additional topics can be added while the coding is in progress. While such a procedure allows researchers to identify within a corpus of data all comments on a particular topic or issue, and while it allows researchers to examine how many and what percentage of comments were made about a particular topic by which person, the results of the analysis give a static representation—as if the cultural knowledge people had about writing was a well-formed tree diagram.

Limitations aside, taxonomic analysis (such as that provided by Q.S.R. NUD*IST, see also Spradley, 1979) is helpful at gathering data to address a particular question or issue. Thus, all of the statements written by the Mass-Observation correspondents in their responses to the directive on a topic (e.g., where they write) can be culled and analysed. The strength of such analysis is that it raises issues across cases, and it was such an analysis that raised the issue of social space for writing (which we discuss in Chapter 6). But taxonomic analysis, within or across cases, loses the people. Gone is the sense of how a person defines and deals with an issue (like creating social space for writing) while dealing with a broad range of other issues, demands and conditions. Gone, too, is the tentativeness and ambiguity (sometimes purposeful) of their understanding of a set of cultural practices like writing. Cultural understandings of social practices are represented as shared cognitive schemata held by individuals, rather than socially constructed understandings. As we discuss later in this chapter, we viewed the interviews as opportunities to explore topics with the Mass-Observation correspondents, rather than "mining expeditions" in which we were trying to "dig out" their cultural knowledge. In order to highlight the complexity, tentativeness, ambiguity and socially constructed nature of the data we collected on writing practices, we created a series of cases which we call "dialogues." We created these dialogues from the responses to the directive and the interview. We discuss how we created the dialogues later; first we describe the interviews.

The Interviews

The original ESRC proposal called for only twenty interviews. However, when Bloome joined the research team there was the possibility of conducting a greater number of interviews. In the end, we interviewed 35 Mass-Observation correspondents (see Tables 7-4 and 7-5 on pp. 245-246). We began the process of deciding whom to interview by randomly reading through the responses to the 1991 Spring directive on literacy practices. We knew that the interviewees would be a subgroup of those that had responded to that directive. Since what we were looking for were "telling cases" and "representational cases", rather than "typical cases", we did not believe that there was a need for a random sample. We decided to combine practical and logistical issues with geographic diversity and representational diversity. Because Bloome did not have a car and would travel by train to interview people, it was decided that he would interview people easily reachable by train or bus and mostly within southern England, although he did interview Mass-Observation correspondents in Wales and Scotland when he took trips to those regions. The other interviews, especially those in more rural areas not accessible by train, were primarily conducted by Street. Sheridan conducted only two interviews. We believed, given her position as the Archivist, that she might complicate her position by conducting interviews. There needed to be someone at the Mass-Observation Project whom the interviewees could call about the interviews if they wanted to raise some issues.

Interviewees were chosen from various geographical regions including different parts of England, Scotland and Wales, and an attempt was made to include both men and women and people of a range of ages. We did not try to keep the distribution proportional to the overall distribution in the Mass-Observation Project, as we had no intention of aggregating data into normative conclusions and summaries.[4] After we identified a pool of people to interview, Sheridan wrote to each asking if they would consent to an interview. All but two did; one was too shy, she said. The other was unable to meet us because of practical problems in her own life at the time.

We developed an interview protocol before the first round of interviews, based on the Spring 1991 directive (see Appendix C). Our

---

[4]For further information about the interviewees, see Chapter 7.

intent was to follow up on the directive, seeking additional information and insight. Some of the responses to the directive were very insightful and generated for us a lot of additional questions. We were also interested in questions that reflected the "hot" topics in the field; the influence of gender, education, private and public domains of their lives, how reflective people were on their writing, formal grammar, definitions of good writing and of being a good writer, among others.

Our interviews were more like informal, open-ended discussions than highly structured interviews. We explored with the Mass-Observation correspondent their writing practices and together speculated about their meaning and the meaning of writing in general. Their responses to the directives could be viewed similarly, as exploratory and interactive. The interviewees were "ready for us" and already had expectations about the interviewers from their contact with Mass-Observation; we were not just outside researchers, but more like new members of the project—novices, asking for their expertise about the project. Thus, our corpus of data is also a record of how we and they together tried to document writing practices and their significance.

As part of the interviewing process, we decided to hold a series of meetings among ourselves to discuss how the interviews went, what we were learning from the interviews, and what might need to be revised in our interviewing techniques and in the interview protocol.

At the time of the first meeting, Bloome had conducted two interviews and Street one. All three of the people interviewed had asked why and how they were chosen, questions that subsequently many of the interviewees would ask. Although we had anticipated such a question, we reviewed how we addressed it. On one hand, we wanted to be truthful in stating that we did not especially choose people based on what they wrote or the quality of what they wrote, while on the other hand also showing that we were indeed interested in what they wrote and that we viewed it a having important value. In addition to stating the selection procedures at the beginning, we decided that bringing a copy of their response to the Spring 1991 directive with us to the interview and showing that we had carefully read it would be a good way of demonstrating that we were indeed interested in their writing. A second procedural item concerned the interview protocol (see Appendix D). We found that it was helpful and did not need much revising. The first set of interviews helped us clarify how the questions might be interpreted, but such variations were taken more as interesting bits of data rather than problems with the interviewing. We found it helpful to share a copy of the interview protocol with the people being interviewed so that it could be jointly reviewed during the interview and so that our agenda was out in the open.

Also at the first meeting, and then throughout the study, we found that Bloome and Street had different interviewing styles (Sheridan did not conduct her interviews until later in the study, and her interview style differed from both Street and Bloome). Street conducted his interviews more like a seminar among colleagues, jointly exploring topics and questions with the Mass-Observation correspondents. Bloome conducted his interviews as if soliciting stories and narratives from people about their lives.[5] While there were certainly aspects of seminar-style and narrative-soliciting interviewing in both Bloome and Street's interview styles, respectively, the differences in the style pointed to differences in their identities as well as differences in how they had implicitly conceptualized the interviews. As an American, Bloome's status as an outsider provided a natural social context for people to explain how things worked and what things were. People could explain how their lives fit into British history and into British culture. In many ways, his status as an outsider made him a safe person to whom to express and explain political and personal views and history. Street, on the other hand, because he was British, could use his shared experiences, history and knowledge to explore areas in depth with the Mass-Observation correspondents he interviewed and he could raise questions that only an "insider" would have the knowledge to be able to raise. Because we were not attempting to obtain normative data and because we were not especially interested in "typical" cases or in standardizing the knowledge we obtained, the differences in interview styles was not viewed as problematic, although we agreed that each could attempt, where appropriate, to employ some of the other's interviewing strategies. Nonetheless, differences in interviewing styles persevered throughout, and came to be thought of as a strength rather than as a limitation of the corpus of data.

The meetings to discuss our interviewing procedures were also helpful in dealing with various practical matters. The interviews took longer than we anticipated. We were all having difficulties with our tape recorders, and so we decided on several procedures to ensure that they were working during the interviews. We decided to carry back-up tape recorders; however, during one interview Bloome found that both tape recorders had "died" and he had to take notes during the second half of that interview.

Approximately every other week, we met to review the interviews. Funds from the ESRC grant to Sheridan and Street allowed us to hire someone to do initial transcription of the interview tapes; however, we did not have the funds to have all of the interviews

---

[5]Bloome's interviewing style has been analyzed by an outside researcher, see Baynham (in press).

transcribed and, as mentioned earlier, technical difficulties with a few of the early interviews made it impractical to have some transcribed. In addition, some of the interviews were transcribed by Bloome.

We each read over and corrected the transcripts, and listened to the interviews (including those not transcribed). We discussed how the responses informed our understanding of literacy practices in everyday life, the categories and labels people used, especially the term "ordinary;" and we discussed the nature of the knowledge we were gathering about literacy, ethnography, history, gender, economics, politics, nationality and geography (e.g., being Scottish, Welsh, living in northern England versus southern England) and social life in contemporary Britain. One of the things that impressed us was how deeply embedded and prevalent writing was both in the lives of the Mass-Observation correspondents and in the social contexts in which they lived, and how difficult it was to make summative statements about what literacy was or how writing was done. It was not just that how people engaged in writing varied—although that certainly was true—but rather that writing was bound up into the complexities of people's lives, and as their lives kept changing, both because people lead complex lives and because the social world in which we live keeps changing, writing is adapted to those changes. It does no good to talk about writing as if it is something separate from people's lives, their hopes, their dreams, their efforts to create and recreate the "worlds" in which they live. Thus, the more we read over the interviews and struggled with how to present the findings, the more we came to believe that it was important to provide multiple and overlapping representations and interpretative contexts. Thus, in addition to the more typical discussions of data found in Chapters 6 and 7, we decided to create a series of dialogues that would provide readers with an interpretative context that lay closer to the lives of at least some of the people we interviewed. These dialogues are presented in Chapter 5; their construction is discussed below.

CONSTRUCTING THE DIALOGUES

We constructed nine dialogues. These nine were chosen through a combination of reasons. We wanted a diverse group, not necessarily statistically representative of the Mass-Observation correspondents in general or of the group we interviewed, but diverse in terms of the issues they raised. We sought telling cases about literacy practices and the Mass-Observation project (cf., Mitchell, 1984).

We began fashioning the dialogues by constructing three dialogues. We cut and pasted what the Mass-Observation corespondents said during the interviews and what they had written in response to the directives. We eliminated many of our questions and comments, except when those were needed to make sense of what the Mass-Observation correspondent had said or written. We did not eliminate all of our comments and questions, as we did not want to pretend that the dialogues were monologues, but we eliminated much of our participation because we wanted to highlight what they said and wrote.

We are not pretending that somehow we are transparent vehicles merely transmitting what the Mass-Observation correspondents said and wrote, nor are we trying to present their "voice" as if providing a platform for those who do not have one. Any presentation of another's talk or writing is necessarily a ventriloquism (cf., Bakhtin, 1935/81). If nothing else, it is taken out of one context and placed in another. Rather, we have tried to create a context that highlights the complexities of people's lives and the writing they do.

The construction of the case studies was difficult in part because we had to translate an interview conversation and written responses to Mass-Observation directives into a written genre while still trying to capture its conversational tone. There are, of course, precedents for constructing case studies in this manner (e.g., Farrell, 1970; Terkel, 1972, 1988) and there are limitations and risks. But one of the unexpected difficulties was the tension between creating a coherent text and allowing the text to meander in much the same way that the conversations did. We do not view the "meandering" as a weakness in the text, although we recognize most readers look for explicit coherence. They expect that what follows underneath a heading will relate to the heading in an obvious manner. They also expect the text not to be self-contradictory. To some extent, we accommodated these expectations by reorganizing and weaving together comments from the interviews and the directives. But we also left many of the meanderings because they suggest a series of connections that are as much part of the findings as the explicitly stated descriptions of writing. We also debated among ourselves how much to standardize the style of the dialogues. For example, we debated whether to provide a floor diagram of each person's home and whether to include the same headings and sub-headings in each dialogue. Ultimately we decided against such standardization, as it seemed antithetical to the diversity we experienced while doing, discussing and writing up the interviews and dialogues, and it seemed antithetical to the variation in what we learned about literacy practices from each of the Mass-Observation correspondents.

After constructing the dialogues, we mailed a copy of each dialogue to each Mass-Observation correspondent. We asked them to read over the dialogue, to respond to any misrepresentations, and we asked if they would be happy to have the dialogue included in this book as it was written. We also asked them if they were comfortable with the pseudonyms we had chosen. Two people decided to choose their own pseudonyms. After some discussion with us, Mr. Reed preferred to have his real name used. None of the Mass-Observation correspondents asked for substantial changes, and only one person asked for a few minor changes.

FINAL COMMENTS ON CONSTRUCTING DIALOGUES

A recent letter from S481 that arose in a different context summarizes many of the issues that we have raised in this chapter about reading and analyzing the Mass-Observation writings.[6] The letter also provides evidence that the Mass-Observation correspondents struggle with many of the same issues about the nature of knowledge that researchers using the Mass-Observation Project do, and with many of the issues raised in Chapter 3 (on Anthropology and Mass-Observation). Although it is not clear how many of the Mass-Observation correspondents are as thoughtful or as eloquent as this one is about the nature of knowledge (few scholars are as thoughtful or as eloquent), the letter raises interesting questions. How does such awareness influence the construction of knowledge? And recognizing that such awareness exists, how should that influence its use?

[Letter from S481]

19.8.92

Thoughts on Writing for the MO Archive

The latest Directive has proved as provocative as ever and, as usual, it prompted as many questions as answers. This stimulation of thought and ideas is one of the attractions of writing for the Archive; another is the belief that it has public value. Yet I always feel I leave out so much, and so wonder how true the responses are, and thus how valuable or otherwise they can be.

Answers to Directives, in the sense of being correct, are of course understood to be both impossible and undesirable. What is required must be an individual's view on the particular topic, giving collectively a picture of the nation's thinking. But there must be many difficulties—those faced by the writer in covering the subject adequately, accurately, yet briefly, the problem of defining terms so that both writer and researcher comprehend,

---

[6]See Sheridan (1998) for a detailed discussion of the letter from S481.

and the degree to which M-O Archive writers form a cross-section of the public. One question or suggestion often begs another, and worded differently the item might elicit very different responses from the same person. The passage of time and experience reshapes one's opinions, so that what is recorded may differ as the writer ages. Sometimes a Directive, or a question within a Directive, may produce a response conflicting with views expressed in another—but perhaps this merely reflects human contradiction.

What becomes clear as one persists is that there can never be "right" or "wrong" personal responses, nor will those responses necessarily be clearly considered by the individual Archive writer. My own are mostly a mixture of "gut reaction" and attempts to think the subject through, tempered by constraints of time and space available. It's easier if the subject is of personal interest or one on which clear views are held, but even as I'm writing I'm aware of contradictions in my thinking caused by prejudices and preconceptions. Sometimes this leads to questioning whether what I'm writing is really what I believe, and this again may result in reconsideration of a subject at a deeper level—so that my response changes before it is sent!

I'm increasingly conscious that few topics can be considered in isolation, and views will be coloured by belief, experience, prejudice, ignorance, information, and even wishful thinking (ie what one likes to believe one believes!). It's difficult not to branch off to other issues in an effort to set one's thoughts into a truthful context. In general, I try to respond honestly to the subject in question. In regard to the "wishful thinking" element, however, I suspect that my response on an immediate level, if dealing with an actual situation, might sometimes be very different from the more considered recorded response. How complete, therefore, is the finished response?

Responses to the Directives must be subjective, just as, at least in part, the researcher's reaction must also be subjective, which raises the question of the relevance of this aspect to subsequent research? A picture of the writer, shaped by his style, must form in the researcher's mind. Does it affect his findings, and would these change if it was known that the writer had, for instance, a squeaky voice, was beautiful, or had a wart on his/her nose? The picture must necessarily be painted in shades of gray—how accurate, therefore, can the researchers' findings be? Do the responses and findings reflect all this or, having been recorded, are they henceforth to be regarded as "facts"?

Whatever the case, writing for M-O is great fun—long may it continue.

5
Dialogues about Literacy Practices and the Mass-Observation Project

> In the process of the construction of many kinds of texts, spoken or written, the memories of the past are in constant play, flashing beneath this still surface like gleaming fish in a still lake. . . . Narrative is about desire and seduction. And autobiography permeates the seductive strategies of ordinary people. They are always at it with their damned anecdotes and what an impatient nineteenth century judge once called their dangerous confabulations. . . . (Harold Rosen, 1993, p. 66)

The purpose of this chapter is to provide one description of the literacy practices of Mass-Observation correspondents. In subsequent chapters we provide other descriptions. This chapter contains nine dialogues. The dialogues are edited versions of the interviews we had with Mass-Observation correspondents. We have incorporated their written responses to the 1991 directive as well as other written documents they have sent to the Mass-Observation Archive (for example, Mr Reed [R450] sent a copy of a book of poems that contained poems he had written).

We have blurred the line between description and interpretation in the dialogues, a blurring that we believe is inherent in any description or representation. We have created them and thus they reflect our understandings of what was said and written (see Chapter 4 for a discussion of the method involved) and they reflect our attempts to portray in a few pages lengthy conversations and extensive written responses to directives in a way that maintains their texture and character, as best we could. The dialogues primarily consist of the words said and written by the Mass-Observation correspondents themselves. We have deliberately left in, on occasion, our questions or comments as interviewers, both to add clarity and as reminders that the dialogues were fashioned from interviews and responses to directives. Thus, although imperfectly so, as we discussed earlier, the dialogues do present an emic-like view of the Mass-Observation correspondents' understandings and activities of writing for the Mass-Observation Project and of writing more broadly considered in their lives.

We do not offer any commentary in this chapter on the dialogues. We do make use of the dialogues later in the book, bringing them together with other analyses we have conducted.

Before presenting the nine case studies, we want to raise a few themes that are informed by the case studies and that we pick up later. The first concerns access to writing. Finding the time, place and opportunity to write is not a simple matter but requires restructuring and negotiating environments—both physical and interpersonal environments. The second concerns writing positions. Whenever someone writes, they do so from a particular social position. Although the Mass-Observation correspondents have a wide range of backgrounds—geographically, occupationally, financially, and in terms of social class and generation—in our interviews and in their written responses to the directive, the phrase "ordinary" person came up again and again. We explored what the phrase meant in our interviews, arriving not at consensus in definition but at a "location" from which to view writing for the Mass-Observation Project and writing more broadly in society. The third set of issues we want to foreshadow is representation and knowledge. To the extent that knowledge needs to be understood in terms of its production and use, the dialogues help reveal the production of knowledge in the Mass-Observation Project. That production process (or more accurately stated, production processes, as there was no single production process that could characterise all of the writing) needs to be framed by a complex of representations. We talked to the Mass-Observation correspondents about who they were "writing for". As a group, they responded with multiple answers, but also each person gave multiple answers. To cite just a small selection of their responses, they wrote for other "ordinary" people, working-class people, anti-Thatcherites, themselves, but they also wrote for the Mass-Observation Project, for historians, for the future, for their grandchildren and for practise (as in practising to become a better writer).

The order of the dialogues is not especially important; they may be read in any order. We have organized the dialogues so that both the background of the Mass-Observation correspondent and the issues raised shift and vary. That is, we have tried to avoid an order in which all of Mass-Observation correspondents of a particular background, geographic location, or similar perspective are located together. We have done so because it is analogous to how we experienced the interviewing process and the process of trying to make sense of all of the various types of data we had collected. In brief, we wanted to highlight the particularities of the dialogues. Of course, there is some attention to commonalties and themes that run across the dialogues, but it is emphasized in Section 3 rather than here.

We have used a few conventions to assist in reading the dialogues. Words spoken by or written by the Mass-Observation correspondents are in regular print; words inserted by us to help a phrase or sentence make sense are in italics, as are our questions in the interviews and any comments of our own. Words that come from the *written* response to the Spring 1991 Directive are surrounded with UWR> and <UWR.[1] The text is reproduced as it is in the responses to the directive. With respect to spoken language from audiotapes of interviews, we have transcribed directly. Often the wording is informal and conversational as would be expected given the sources of the text. We have chosen as far as possible to be faithful to the original spoken text, rather than attempting to "tidy it up." Where words or sentences have been omitted, there are a series of dots (. . .), "xxx" is used where we believed confidentiality was required. Insertions by us to explain words or phrases are in square brackets. Pseudonyms have been used for all but two of the correspondents in line with the Archive policy of preserving anonymity. Mr Reed's real name has been used with his permission because he can be identified through the poetry he has already published. Mr Barrow's real name has been used because he can be identified through his work with the National Lesbian and Gay Survey. Since Mr Barrow very sadly died before the publication of this book, we conferred with his colleague at the NL&GS, Kerry Sutton Spence, who agreed with us that he would have liked his real name used. As we explained in Chapter 4, we sent the text of the dialogues to the correspondents to be checked by them and to ensure that they were happy to have their words included in this book. They suggested a few minor amendments and these have been incorporated.

MRS WRIGHT
(W632)

Mrs Wright lives in a working-class suburb of a major city, with her husband and son. It is a short walk from the railway station to their flat. She works for a public service company just outside London, taking the train to work daily. Her son was attending the local Polytechnic. Her husband was home full-time on a disability leave from his job.

---

[1]UWR stands for "Uses of Writing and Reading", the heading for Part II of the Spring 1991 Directive (see Appendix C).

140 CHAPTER FIVE

They had a one-floor flat which they bought on the second floor in a complex of council estates. They had a small kitchen, not big enough to eat in. Behind the kitchen was a small room with a small table and two chairs. This was where the interview took place, away from her husband and son, who were sitting in the living room watching television. Hallways lead to the bedrooms, the bathroom, and a storage area. The living room was set up around the television. David Bloome interviewed Mrs Wright in the evening, after work, at her home on 2 November 1992.

Beginning with the M-O Project

DB: How did you get interested originally in writing for the Mass-Observation project? It was in the Guardian . . . the numbers were dropping and they needed more writers and at the time I was on a course at the Polytechnic with the business studies and so the two combined and I decided to write. I must admit I was a bit lazy with the first ones [directives] that came through and it took me—it took about three or four of them to arrive before I did start actually writing. I'd finished with the Polytechnic by then. I had a full-time job, working for XXX; and I'm still working for them.

DB: Do you remember which directive got you motivated to write or did it just arrive at the right time? It just arrived at the right moment—I can't remember which the first one was, I can't remember most of them, but probably a day off sick and time to spare, you know, can't do the housework, so—not catch up on the chores, and I could sit and write instead.

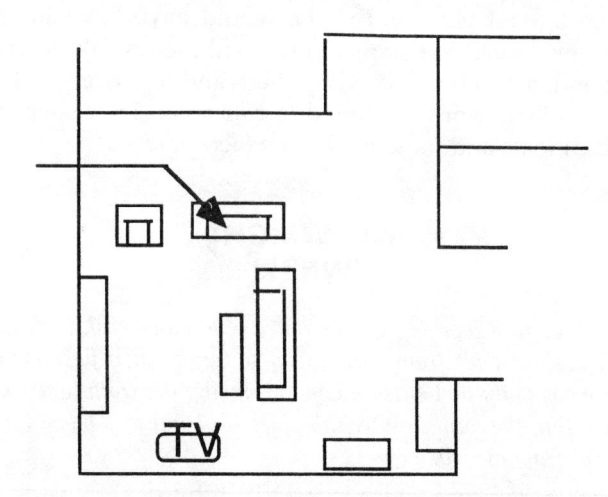

Mrs Wright's living room where she usually writes for M-O

How Mrs Wright Usually Responds to a Directive

When it arrives I read through it and I think about it—odd moments you know—like waiting for the train or on the train going up to work and sort of scribble bits down on bits of paper here there and everywhere. I scribble notes to myself—if I had this piece of paper in my bag I'd probably scribble all notes all over it and think, "That's along the lines of what they were talking about then"—I remember that and scribble a note down to myself and then I sort of—it's only on a day where I've got the time, then I sit down and sort of say, "Oh well there's that note there and there's this one here, and oh, there's another bit of paper there" and put them all together then. When I've got the time, which might not be for—nearly 'til the next directive is due,—I sit down and write it all out.

I'm usually sitting in the chair [in the living room] and there's probably football or something on the telly that I don't want to watch so I write it then. My husband and son are quite used to it now. I usually do my books in the chair, the finances and a crossword or something, you know—I'm not usually sitting watching television, I'm usually doing something else as well, knitting, or—anything.

I like to think about the directive especially exceptional points like [question] 12 in this directive [the Uses of Writing and Reading] struck me as unanswerable and I have given it a lot of attention. I answer as much as I have time for in each session but break off to talk, get refreshments or watch a TV programme. A session is flexible according to what else is going on, but I would wait until I felt I could give it at least an hour's attention. For diaries or the Gulf Crisis I would make notes first and then write up trying not to change things with hindsight. If I write on the train I would consider that a draft copy, as the writing would be illegible. Sometimes I make notes on the directive itself when reading through as ideas spring to mind.

I avoid questions that I don't want to answer and—it's the same with talking to you—I'd change the subject.

[The questions in a directive] strike you, as soon as you read them, you know. Some are busy ones—like collecting all the Christmas cards up and seeing which ones fall into what categories—that is a busy one, that is—a work one—one that you don't have to think about. It's an activity rather than a written . . . as such. And then there's other ones like—there's one I got quite cross about—about racial discrimination, because I know people do discriminate, and it annoys me that I'm being asked a question (laughs)—I meet and I mix with all sorts and I tend to judge people on how they react to me—rather than their colour or the clothes they're wearing, or what sort of posh accent, or London Cockney accent, or however they speak to me—it's how they respond to me, you know—if they've been helpful, if they've given me the information that I want, and it annoys me—it's one of the things that just irritates me about-talking about racial discrimination—it shouldn't be there. Why can't other people feel the same as I do about it? You know it doesn't matter—it's not something you can choose. So—I didn't want to answer that one—I did, but I felt uptight about it, I felt on the defensive. Why are you asking me this question?

I resented the question [on racial discrimination] but I felt that I had to answer it, whereas there's been other questions—I've tended to skate round—I'm trying to think of an example now—the ones you ignore are the ones you can't remember anyway (laughter)—that just didn't seem important enough—that seemed too trivial, you know, to— well nobody would be interested in that anyway, I've just remembered, ones that mainly strike me as trivial are the things that people are paying for—market research—like the BBC asking about soap and detergents and what not—soap and shampoo and things and—they're the ones that I find trivial and it's only that Mass Observation is earning money by writing for them that—I probably wouldn't bother otherwise.

Some [questions] seem to draw on unique experience and I think they are more interesting, the ones that call on your history—the uniqueness of your experience. And although you might feel as though it's unique to you—as unique as your first kiss—everybody else experiences it as well, so it's not. I don't mean that it's unique to you personally, but it draws on your history, your family, feelings, your emotions.

Questions about things that are happening in the world today, I feel as though I'm very much parroting my newspaper. You know I read the *Guardian* because I like their opinions on things and I feel as though when I'm writing about those type of subjects I'm really paraphrasing what they're saying. And then I begin to wonder if it—is it my opinion or whether I'm being brainwashed by the paper or whether I read the paper because they think the same as I do. So I—current affairs I'm not too sure about. When it's gone into history and I can look back on in and not be influenced by current events then I can think about it better.

UWR> I don't keep copies of what I send to you. I withhold sending the directive when it is finished so that I can read through your questions and my answers, to correct mistakes and to include any afterthoughts. <UWR

The Place of Writing for the M-O Project in Mrs Wright's Life

It's a pleasure because it's writing about my thoughts and feelings, rather than straight correspondence—you know, like business letters and so on. It's much more interesting writing what you feel about different things. I feel as though I'm writing to somebody that—it's flattering, really, to think that somebody's going to sit there and read it all, you know, and I think it's rubbish most of the time that I write—it can't possibly be that interesting to anybody else what I think about things, and it's flattering to know that somebody is interested. I feel as though nobody's interested in my opinions, really—I mean my husband doesn't ask what I think about all these things so why should somebody else be interested in what I think about them? My son might ask what [the directive] is about this time when it arrives, and give a bit of an opinion about something, but he doesn't ask whether I write or ask to see it or anything. He doesn't ask my opinion He'll give his. He'll give his opinion—hope it'll influence me perhaps. UWR> It is nice to think that someone wants to know what I think and I find I am now more interested in what other people think, less likely to want to change their view, more amenable to discussing it, more tolerant. <UWR

Other Writing Practices

I do my books—I know exactly what—how much I've got in the bank, every penny, and how much is going to come out over the next month, so—how much cash I've got to spare, and when the bank statements come through I check them, make sure there's no hidden options on there, additions.

I don't very often now, but I used to write letters to the newspaper and belong to other groups, or—and—yes I read all the mail that comes in and answer the letters and everything.

I've found that—I didn't know it, but a couple of friends are illiterate, you know, they can't read and write, and it takes me by surprise to find that something that I take for granted they can't do, and other people can't do very well. My nephew writes to me, to thank me for sending money for his birthday, and his letters look like my letters did when I was eight or nine, and he's 26—it surprises me, to see him—you just automatically think because you do it everybody else does it.

... I work in the planning department—and that's for customer accounts planning. And if there's any mandatory changes that come through by the Government then we have to update our billing system to be able to cater for these changes. And so that's my job—to be between the user and the systems—computer systems people, and to translate what each one's saying, so that the user says I want this, and the systems people are saying XYZ-formula, you know, and I'm saying will that produce this? And I test that out and make sure that this is what we want, the business is being met—the business requirements are being met.

At work it's taking away their ideas and testing them out and producing them for somebody else to read. Mostly very formal procedures. If you do this, this will happen. If you do that, you will expect this end result. And it must—every tiny little movement—or wrong movement—must be written down to say exactly what happened.

I wouldn't keep it up [the writing at home] if I didn't want to do it. I mean you only find time for the things you want to do when you're busy, don't you? So—alright it gives me an end result—I know how much is in the bank, but I could get that from the statement—I could believe the statement that came through without me writing down everything then saying—well, by the end of—by Christmas we're going away, we will have so much to—spending money. I don't need to go into that much detail. I know that there'll be money there, but I have to have every penny accounted for. So I must get pleasure from it.

Women and Writing

Whereas other people are just not comfortable with writing, [I am]—I know my dad never was—my mum always wrote the letters. If he did sit down to write a letter he was asking how to spell every other word, and she said to him "It's laziness with you." And he said, "I can't write and think at the same time" (laughter). And my husband leaves it to me to write all the letters—he'll sign them, but he leaves it to me to write the letters. And again it's laziness because he can do it. The women in the family, mother and sisters, do the writing. It's an expected duty, that you take over doing like—same as you take over the washing and the cooking.

Women are more methodical and think things through before they start writing, and I can see it with my sisters as well, you know that they enjoy—well I suppose it's a method of control, isn't it? If you're in charge of these things. You're actually running the household, aren't you—that is, beyond housewifely duties—if you're running the household and the finances and everything—it's your way of being in charge... unobtrusively.

Defining the M-O Project

The M-O Project had been keeping the—instead of being the history of kings and battles and so on—it was actually the living history of people that experienced and went through these times of change. UWR> Perhaps the government under Major will even release funds towards the Archive as it is the only place left where impartial evidence is collected. <UWR

DIALOGUES ABOUT LITERACY PROCESSES **145**

MRS FRIEND
(F1373)

Mrs Friend lives with her husband in a small terraced house in a city in southern England. They live in a working-class neighbourhood. When David Bloome interviewed her at her home on 4 November 1992, Mrs Friend was completing her last week before retiring from the store at which she worked. Mr Friend was already retired.

A Room For Writing

The front door of the house opens to a stairway to the second floor and a corridor to the kitchen, lined with a bookcase. To the left is their living room. Two stuffed, reclining chairs are positioned side-by-side, facing the television. A couch is against one wall and in the back of the room is a dining table, pushed against a wall, and partially folded. It is in this room that Mrs Friend does her writing.

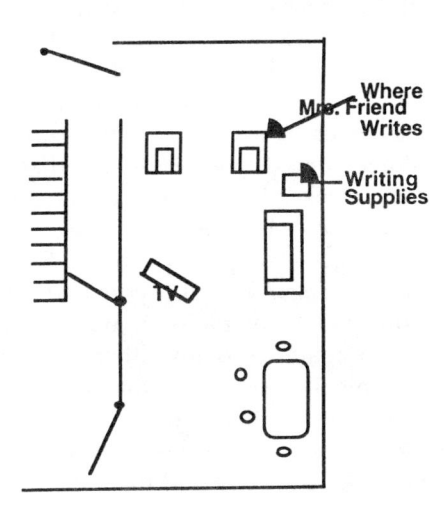

Mrs Friend sits in her chair, next to the end table which holds paper, pens and other materials needed for writing. She will often write in the evening while her husband is sitting in his chair watching the television or reading. At other times, she will sit at the dining table.

Letter Writing

DB: It sounds like you do other writing, other than for Mass-Observation? I do, yes, letters I write. I've got a friend in America, a friend in Portsmouth, a friend in Oxford. Those I write every week without fail, sometimes twice a week, so it's . . . it's a natural urge. The one in Portsmouth is a childhood friend, we've been friends since we were ten. The friend in America I met later on in life, and we worked together, and the friend in Oxford I also worked with her, and they moved away.

You can say more in a letter than you can on the phone, it's much easier. So we write, we all write. *DB: What do you write about?* Everything. What I've been doing, what's happened at work . . . building development and the footpaths, politics, religion—everything, we cover the whole lot, write the whole lot, just as it comes, just like sitting talking to someone really. And I also ask them questions, so they've got to answer you see, so I get answers to my questions back as well. So, it's nice. I always look forward to the postman coming. When I hear the postman in the morning, even if I'm intending to have a lay in I'll get up and come down and get the letters.

Letters to my friends are usually about fourteen pages, foolscap pages, so it's not just a little letter it's a big letter. Costs me a fortune sending it to America. £1.21 an average letter, one pound twenty-one pence. I can honestly say that since we've been corresponding like this they tend to follow my style. I write exactly as I talk. If I'm having a conversation, if I say, I said to him this, I will do it, you know, inverted commas and all. Just like a conversation. So I do find that now the letters come back from the other side on the same format, you know, the conversation! . . . "We went to Georgia State fair, that was on last week". And I had a letter this week. I had it all in detail, whereas when I first wrote to my friend over there she would have just said, "We went to the Georgia State Fair". You get a complete picture. *DB: If she stopped putting detail in . . . how would you react?* I would write and ask her, you told me about the garden, now, you haven't told me what plants you've got, so I would get it back then again. And my other friends now do tend to write the same way as me, it's something that's rubbed off. Strange isn't it? We also write jokes to each other as well, because there's nothing like an English joke is there, so I will write and tell her something, you know, in the way of a joke. And she said that, particularly her husband, he absolutely rolls on the floor with laughing at some of these jokes.

My husband's brother went to work in Saudi Arabia, and I said to him before he went, I'll write to you. When he got there he was very lonely, and so I wrote to him. And first of his letters started like everyone else's. Did this today, did that yesterday, tomorrow we're going to do this. And then I found that after about two or three months of having my letters, then his letters got more like mine and he would tell me in all this great detail. And he said that after a while he got to enjoy letter writing, but he did always look forward to getting a letter from me anyway, you know. And he said he particularly liked the jokey bits, you know, when I wrote.... Actually I can remember he was there, and it was winter here, it was December, and we had lovely weather like this, and I wrote and said to him, "G"—that's my husband—"G and I walked along the seafront with nothing on". And what I meant was, we didn't have an overcoat on, and I suddenly realised, when I re-read the letter what I had written, and then I said, "What I mean is that we only had cardigans on, we didn't need a big coat", you know, and he sort of . . . he could see the funny side of things like that.

It is the humour I think which makes it so nice. I mean, I've just had a particularly bad three weeks. My son's dog was run over and badly injured, my son broke his neck in a car accident, and I thought, I can't believe this, I was so depressed. And then my brother died, quite out of the blue, totally unexpectedly. And then I had a letter from my friend in Portsmouth, and it was such a jovial letter and it took it all away you know; it's nice like that isn't it? In actual fact she wrote and said that her and her husband have gone on a long train journey, and she's got multiple sclerosis so she has great difficulty in travelling. And for comfort on the journey—her husband always wears a suit, he never wears casual clothes, always wears a suit—for comfort on this journey he wore a dark suit, and instead of a shirt and tie he wore a white, lightweight polo-necked jumper underneath. And they were standing on the station at Preston, and a porter went by and he sneezed, and her husband said, "Bless you,' and the porter turned round and said, "Thank you Father!" And she said, "We were both convulsed with laughter". And, "Do you think Father Q"—because their surname is Q, "should now be defrocked?" And I thought, it so amused me that, you know, in all this gloom and doom, with all this that had happened, and I thought oh, isn't that nice, it's something you can pick up and read, and it's a laugh really. So it really did make me sort of happy, to think I had that sort of letter.

I'm an expert at rude letters to companies too, if something upsets me. It's rewarding if you've got the time. I was shopping once, and I picked up a tin of peaches, and on the outside of the tin was a picture of a glass bowl with all these lovely peaches in it. When I opened the tin they were all green, couldn't eat them. And I was so angry, I mean it was.... When my children were small money wasn't abundant, and I had wasted my money and I was furious. And I had to write to South Africa; these peaches had been canned in South Africa. So I wrote a letter and said, "Any similarity between the picture on the outside of the tin and the contents of the tin was pure imagination". And I didn't think about it, posted it surface mail, not air mail, to South Africa, just put it in a box, really furious, and I thought, I didn't care if nothing happened, I got it off my chest. And about eight months later, knock on the door one day, a parcel, a huge box, and I had got a tin like that of peaches, pineapples, and pears, all from South Africa from this canning company! And they apologised profusely, and I think I'd only . . . didn't pay that much for this tin of peaches, but it was worthwhile! So it does pay off. I mean and when we had all these problems, because we have footpaths all through there, and they sealed them off when they were doing the building. And I have written to the council, I've . . . oh, I've written so many letters, to the council, and a local planning engineer, and the building company, I've got reams of them like that, to get those paths back, and they haven't done it yet.

Writing to the M-O Project

My husband says people won't listen to me, they're all fed up with me talking. I'm an avid talker; they won't listen to me talking, so if someone's going to read what I write, then I write because someone's going to read it. And it's good writing practice for me. I mean they [the M-O Project] are prepared to accept something written in longhand, whereas if you're going to submit anything to publishers or anything like that it's got to be typewritten on A4, and there's lots of regulations to it. That is so easy, just sit down and write, and I do like writing, it just flows. *DB: Doing that kind of writing is different than writing for M-O?* Totally different. I think they want more. . . . I suppose it's going to be put by for future historians isn't it, and they really want to know the type of life that you have at this moment in time, so that is totally different. I try not only to put what I, my views down; I ask friends at work, I ask my husband, my family, how about your views on this, and then I try and write all the views down so that they've got sort of a wider version really than just my views.

    I saw [the M-O Project] in the local paper. They said they needed writers, and I wrote and said would they be interested, and they wrote back and said yes, and it's gone on from there. I think it's about 1989; it's only recent really.

    I love it. I just . . . well, you're leaving something for your grandchildren aren't you. I've got eight grandchildren and I mean, if they want to know . . . well not them, this would be in the next generation on after that won't it, if they want to know what at sort of a life we had they've only got to go there haven't they, and they can find out. I mean I'm lucky inasmuch as I could tell you probably how people's lives were prior to the First World War, because my mother used to tell me about it you know, so I know the sort of life she had. And I would like to think that some time someone could sort of say, well that's the sort of life she had you know. You've got to do it, haven't you? It's the only way. . . . I said this once before, made a broadcast about this.

Wouldn't you like to be able to say, I wonder how the cave men lived, and go and find something that they had written which said, I went out and caught a dinosaur today and we're going to have that for supper tonight. That would be nice, wouldn't it? I think we should . . . we should leave a whole . . . details about exactly how our lives are, like a diary really. I mean they said Queen Victoria wrote lots of diaries, so I would think that would be quite interesting to read, about life as it was then you know. So . . . no, I was thinking about my mother, 1898 she was born, so she would have been around about that time.

DB: When you get the Mass-Obs [directive] what happens then? I get the pad out and start right away. So I sit there on the settee and I can pick up the writing pad and just write away. I need to get my first thoughts down right away, so I do that and then I will put it to one side. And then perhaps, if I have sort of talked to people, or I've looked at something and thought, that's relevant, then I'll read it through again and think no, that's not right, I haven't got this right, and I'll probably . . . might rewrite it, might go over it again, you know. So it . . . it has to feel right; it's not just what comes off the top of your head, it has to feel right.

If I see something on television that is particularly interesting I write notes, and particularly if it appertains to what we are currently doing on the Mass-Ob, I will then sit down and write notes, so that I don't forget it, you know. So, I'll get up in the night and come down and write notes, if I wake up. Or if I . . . if I get a line of a poem or something like that I'll . . . if I think ah, that's a nice opening poem, a nice opening line, I'll come down and write it down. Because I'll likely wake up and will have forgotten it in the morning, so the writing pad is always there. I make notes all the time!

I make a terrible mess. I sit there and spread all my notes out on the next chair, and then I'll ponder over them and see where it all fits in with what I'm saying. And I might even get reference books out if . . . if I need to, if it's something that I'm not really sure. I more or less write it all in one go. I go over it all, and I . . . I've got to be happy with it before I send it. I would read it all through, and see if it feels right. I might censor it. Not often that happens, usually I am quite happy with it once it's done; I don't often . . . I think I did chop out something once before, but then it means rewriting the whole page both sides you know, but generally it goes right the first time. I think I would censor something if I felt it was too flippant, if I didn't think it was serious enough, you know. After all they don't send me a Mass-Observation for me to make jokes about it, do they? So I would, if I thought that I hadn't treated the subject reverently, then I would delete it and censor it. I think sometimes they might have problems with the writing, because I do tend to scribble if I'm going very quickly

It could take a long time. Perhaps two months depending upon how easy or how hard it is. If it's hard it tends to take me longer; if it's an easy one that is something that I'm familiar with, then it's much easier. If it's something I've got to think about, or perhaps ask other people about, then it takes me longer.

I found some of the topics absolutely fascinating. Some I haven't managed very well at all, I've had great difficulty with. This last one's been one of the worst ones. I haven't finished yet on the environment. This one, the one this time has been about the environment. You know, there was a big meeting, and I think it was George Bush said it would be too expensive to protect the ozone layer and things like that, you know, and they asked us to continue after the 17th of August. And I've continued a bit, and then I've got sort of stuck, so I've left it for a bit and I'll come back to it now. Actually the events here, there was all the business with Fergie and Di that followed, so all the papers dropped all the environmental bit you see, so there was nothing to read about what was happening, so it all sort of died a natural death, when I think it should have been continued. The media didn't cover it very well at all. They were more interested in this conference that was on about the environment and the huge Japanese delegation that was there, and how weird they were walking around with notebooks and pencils. Well it's nothing to do with it really. So I do think the media get it wrong sometimes.

I usually tend to like to write when I can do something off the top of my head. A lot of them I have had to think about. In fact some of them have been great fun, I've enjoyed a tremendous amount of them. I think sometimes you can be flippant, and make some jokes, and I've tended to like that, whereas others seem too serious you know. I suppose I'm a jovial sort of person really, and some of the serious ones, the one . . . we covered the Election one year, and, "Have you seen posters in neighbourhood?" and "Do you listen to convers . . .?" You listen to conversations on buses; I do, it's really strange, and you sort of think oh, that's . . . it does make you an eavesdropper really! Sometimes the questions on the directive are things that I don't know very much about, and I feel committed to writing a fair amount you know, not just a thing off the top of my head. And so I sort of . . . I have to fish around for what I'm going to say, and I always read it once I've written. I don't keep a copy of it, but I always read it once I've written it, and then look at it and make sure I'm happy with it before I send it off.

There have been directives when they've asked tremendously personal questions. I found that very difficult. I try to be as truthful as possible. They asked . . . they've asked you about your sex life and things like that you know, and I sort of think, I'll tell them what I'm prepared to say. If I find it difficult to write then I shouldn't say it, so I just was an honest as I could be. So . . . no, they ask you sometimes about . . . about your neighbours and things like that you know. It doesn't . . . they don't actually say, could you tell us what your neighbours are doing, but there are times when some of the questions would appertain to your neighbours, so of course you don't identify them, you just sort of give them a name you know, so . . . Morals and things like that they've asked you about, you know, so I think that's . . . it is a very personal thing isn't it, so it's . . . I try to be as honest as I possibly can.

It wouldn't worry me if I thought I'd say something that offended someone I don't think, because if it's . . . if it's necessary to say it then you should say it. It's like, perhaps when you get . . . when you see on a film you get a scene, perhaps a nude scene that would be offensive to some people, I sort of think, if that's the way it would go in life then they should leave it in, not just take it out because it's going to offend someone. But you know, there are times when it is necessary, and I think there are times when you can say things that offend people, but it is necessary.

Some of my friends know that I write for the Mass-Observation, and once or twice they've asked, can I read what you've written, when I've actually had some here you know. And I think, I can remember particularly we did one about holidays, and my friend sat and read it, and she said, "I thoroughly enjoyed it, it's like reading a book". But that was one of my better ones, you know. We are a holiday family, we like to, you know, just go off somewhere. But that one I found easy. It depends. If there's someone that wants to read it, OK, they can. If nobody asks then I'll read it myself and send it off. My husband [doesn't read them] . . . "No, I don't want to read it" he says. "I will only disagree with it anyway", because we're a bit . . . controversial the pair of us; we're chalk and cheese actually.

They [Mass-Observation] always acknowledge. That's the only thing I ask, that they acknowledge that they have received something. Now and then I get greatly encouraged. Because I wrote an article about, I think it was drugs or doctors, how did I feel about my GP. And next door, a terrible tragedy in there, a woman . . . we were the same age, we both moved in these houses at the same time. We had almost identical families; she had two boys and a daughter, except that hers . . . I had two boys and then a girl, she had a boy, girl, boy. She committed suicide in that house. From the time those children were small she had a mental problem, she was on Valium for years and years and years. And every time she went to the doctor he didn't talk to her, he didn't discuss anything, handed over the Valium. She had a social worker that came, he was brilliant. He really got her established. She seemed to want to have an identity, she didn't seem to have an identity, and he got, he really got her . . . fantastic, got her going. She was going out again, she was, you know . . . And then for some reason the council said they wanted him to work with someone else and they sent two young girls. Now these girls were about seventeen, no knowledge of life at all. And I tried to talk to her, I tried to say, basically I've always sort of felt that suicide, it's not for you to decide when you go, it's for someone else, it's you know, not your decision, and I used to try and talk to her along those lines. She made about three suicide attempts I suppose, possibly four. Each time I would call the ambulance. I walked up and down . . . I made her sick one day when she had taken aspirins, and I made her sick, and I walked her up and down to stop her from going unconscious till the ambulance got here. Ever such a lot of problems.

And then, my husband and I went away for the weekend, we went to Portsmouth to see the friend. And we came back on the Monday, and that teatime my husband came home from work, I said, "It's quiet next door". Her husband came home from work, and he went in and he rushed in here and he said, "I can't believe it". My husband rushed in there, and she had hung herself from the cupboard at the top of the stairs; she had put a rope round and round her neck. And my husband actually was the one that got her, and I rushed in and sort of said, you know, I'd done resuscitation at work, we had to do heart massage and resuscitation, and I sort of said cut her down and we'll try it. But she was too far gone, she was totally dead, there was no . . . And we didn't cut her down, which apparently would have been the wrong thing to do under the circumstances; you're supposed to leave them until the police get there and the fire brigade and the rest of it, which I was . . . it's not your reaction to do that, you know. And, the coroner—oh everything all went through. But in the evening the doctor came, and I was in there talking to her husband, and the doctor came and he said to him, "You're going to be naturally distressed. I think I'd better give you a prescription", and he wrote out a prescription for Valium and handed it to that man. And I was so angry, how I didn't hit that doctor I don't know, because, it was setting him on the same path as her!

She had been all these years on these drugs that . . . And they've now found out they are addictive; she couldn't get off of them. And that, I did write that, and when I wrote that I had a letter, a little note back to say that the writing had a tremendous vitality, and how much they had enjoyed reading it. That was rewarding, because I felt I had really done it well that time, you know. It's nice to know that you have done very well. I know they haven't got the time to . . . and they must have lots of reading and lots to do, and everyone's under pressure these days, but I do like the little note which says thank you, we have enjoyed your contribution; that's the only thing I really want.

DB: Does writing for Mass-Observation figure in your future? Oh yes definitely. I love it. It's . . . as I say I think it's for the future of our children. I mean, I loved history at school and it's . . . we wouldn't know . . . History repeats itself; you can often look at things and say, when you get say a political situation you can often look at it and say well, that's going to happen again. And if you've got it right that time, then it might be the same . . . I mean I can remember—well I can't remember it, I can remember someone telling me about it—that when New York was absolutely broke, and the President said right, we are going to invest money, we are going to put people to work, if it's building roads, during this. And it was the right thing to do, you know. And I sort of think that it could well come a time, the same thing could happen again, and if the answer was right then it would be right in future, wouldn't it? So I really think you've got to . . . history is very important.

Other Writing Practices

I've entered several competitions, the competitions were short stories that I wrote. I write poetry but I haven't entered that in competitions or even had any published, or even attempted to have it published. It's [for] my own satisfaction. I often find, particularly when I'm walking the dog over the downs, I get a poem and by the time I come back I just scribble it down and it's there. It's good isn't it? I'm lucky, I'm lucky, it happens. I find the poetry is a bit spiritual; it's usually if I am upset or sad, and I can write a poem and it's a comfort to me. A friend of mine's husband died recently, and I had written a poem when my cousin died and I sent it to her, and she said it was comforting to her as well, so that was nice wasn't it. But I don't think everyone would see it in that light, they'd sort of think oh, that's a bit morbid, to write poetry about people dying and things like that, but I don't think it is. It's a comfort to me, it's for me.

I want to write a novel, ultimately you know . . . I've got to have the time to do that. I retire from my job tomorrow. That is good news. The writing will take me over then; I shall sit and dedicate about an hour every day to some sort of writing . . . I've got to do it, it's an urge. There's always a pen and a paper handy over there and if anything, thoughts come into my head I write it down.

When I'm sitting here of an evening and I'm scribble scribble scribble, you know, and I say oh another pen I've used up, and I have to find another pen you know, and he can't understand it at all; he thinks . . . oh, it's just weird, because I sit and I write, and I might read at the same time, and I might watch television at the same time. But my husband's brother is very encouraging. He (for my birthday) paid for a subscription to a writers' magazine, so . . . and he said, "I am sure that you have got a novel in you that has got to come out at some time or other". . . .

If I write a novel it will be in the first instance my mother's life story, because she had a, oh, a fascinating life really, so that's the first thing I want to do in the way of a novel. So, I've got a lot of it written; I've drafted out the outline of it and given it to my daughter and she said, "Oh, go on and finish it. I sat in the garden and cried when I was reading it". She said, "You made me so emotional". But then I think that's possibly because it was her grandmother, and she had been involved with her you see, so if it's something that's happening to a total stranger you might not be emotionally involved

Time

It's hard to find the time to write at the moment, because of working. I work part-time, it's mostly afternoons, so . . . but to get to my job I have to leave here about eleven, mid-morning. I've got a lot of housework to do, the dog to sort out, walking, preparing the meal for the evening when I get home. And then I work . . . by the time I get home it's about half past six, so I've got an evening meal to do for my husband and I. And then I will sit down and write. I couldn't possibly contemplate doing a novel in bits and pieces like that; I'd have to really settle down to a set time each day. I've also got three children who are all grown-up and married, but they're always in and out; there might be one of them in one evening, and then it's . . . you know, something, a meal of some sort, and by the time they've talked . . . I can't really sit and write and ignore them, so . . . it is hard to find the times to write at the moment.

I don't go to bed early, I go to bed about one or two o'clock in the morning. So I usually read the paper: I love newspapers and magazines. Read the newspapers, might do the crosswords in the newspapers. All words isn't it? Do the crosswords, and then I'll sort of sit here and think about things, and then I will start to write. And if I haven't finished, if I've got a lot to say and I haven't finished it I might go on till two in the morning and writing and, oh, finish that tomorrow and go to bed, and then I might get up in the morning and do a little bit before I go to work.

Women and Writing

I do the housekeeping books . . . All down to me. I don't mind. As I said he [husband] hates writing, so it's something that just happened. I don't always keep a housekeeping book. In the past, when we were both younger and had a family of course, if my husband got a pay rise he would come home and say, "I've got a pay rise, how should we divide it up?" And then I would do the housekeeping; I would keep strict accounts for about three weeks, or a month, and we would run over the month and he would say, "Well I think you can do with an increase in your housekeeping money", because I could justify . . . But then, you can cook books anyway, can't you? I could have really sort of put everything, my own personal spending on the housekeeping, and . . . But no, I didn't. And he would then say well, you know, you've proved it to me, OK, you can have an increase in your housekeeping. That's . . . we're just doing this at the moment, because as from next week we both go on pension, so it's . . . because he's 65 and I'm 60 now, so . . .

My daughter works full-time and she doesn't really find the time to write a lot, but someone that she has written to has said to me what beautiful letters she writes, so I think she might have inherited it, because there's no way that I've written to her at any time, only when I went to America, not long letters, so it's some . . . I think she might have inherited it. She might have inherited something, or she might have seen me writing all the time, so I think it will probably . . . She reads a lot, so she sort of said, "When I read a novel", she said "I put it down and I think, well I could have written that". So, I think probably she will write as she gets older.

I couldn't imagine my husband coming home from work and writing, or any other men that I know come to that. I don't know any men that actually write. It's all the women that write the letters isn't it, when you think about it. Strange, very strange. Is it a need? Perhaps it's our husbands won't listen to us when we talk! Another way of writing . . . if you write it down you get your own back don't you, because someone's going to read it somewhere, aren't they?

Defining the M-O Project

. . . History is very important. *DB: Do you think the Mass-Observation Project is a kind of history?* Yes. I think, you read history books, and mostly they're full of wars aren't they? The Battle of the Roses, the Ten Year War, the Five Year War, the . . . you know, and I don't think that's what history's about, it's about people isn't it, everyday people. I'd have liked to, you know, known perhaps what it was like to be a housewife in Elizabethan days or something like that you know, it's . . . Ordinary, everyday people, they're the people that are important aren't they, not . . . I don't want to learn about wars and . . . what is mostly written in history, it's all battles isn't it? Henry V, and Agincourt and . . . all history, it's all the . . . Or even to the Romans, they don't really even give much . . . You don't really get much about medical history, or how people have developed over the years do you? I mean . . . I suppose years ago they weren't that educated, it was only the rich that was educated wasn't it, so if they didn't write nobody did, nobody got it. And I'd like to think, well I'm ... I'm putting it down for future generations to listen and read it.

When I die I want to leave things, I don't want to just pop my clogs and they'll say well there she goes, cheerio, good-bye. I want them to say well, she wrote a book, she did this writing for the Mass-Observation, she knitted me a lovely bedspread, things like that, you know. I won't be able to leave any cooking behind will I? I can't leave a cake for posterity! But you know, I'd like to think that there's going to be a lot left of me really.

MR BARROW
(B1106)

Ken Barrow joined Mass-Observation in 1984. He was born in Lancashire in 1945 and had a varied and artistic career which included teaching drama, acting and writing. Several of his books have been published. He was HIV positive and, despite being unwell, was an enthusiastic contributor to Mass-Observation.

Mr. Barrow was interviewed by Brian Street on 5 March 1993 in his flat in west London. The flat was at the top of a narrow flight of stairs and was surrounded by shelves of videos (he had 1,800 recordings, listed on index cards), a cuttings collection (also indexed), letters filed and classified by years, research files, papers, books, tapes and records, giving a somewhat bohemian and certainly literary feel. Mr. Barrow ran the National Lesbian and Gay Survey (NL&GS), modeled on Mass-Observation, and wrote books using the data from directive replies. He continued to write for the Mass-Observation Project as well, partly because he simply enjoyed the buzz of sitting at the typewriter and as part of a wider writing profile that included letters and bureaucratic activities like filing and indexing. He wanted to avoid the feel of writing as simply bureaucratic and preferred to write by hand and then type, keeping the pleasurable aspect to the fore. He dealt with an active post, from correspondents to the NL&GS, and kept blank cards on which to write messages to his many correspondents. Mr. Barrow died on 13 July 1993, not long after the interview; our use of his interview here is our tribute to the work he did for his contemporaries through the NL&GS and as an opportunity for his voice to continue to be heard. He used writing himself to give voice and support to many who felt marginalised and his work represents an historically and socially significant offshoot of the Mass-Observation Project as a whole.

The NL&GS continues under the direction of Kerry Sutton-Spence, and copies of the material are sent to the Mass-Observation Archive after care has been taken to ensure complete anonymity. In consultation with Ms Sutton

Spence, we decided it would be desirable to use Ken Barrow's real name because he is already identifiable through his connection with the NL&GS and because we felt that this would be in line with his own wishes.

Starting to Write for Mass-Observation

BS: Let's just start with a sense of how you got started. With M-O, I think I saw Dorothy [Sheridan] on a programme, it was an afternoon, you know, sort of TV programme, magazine programme, and it just seemed like the kind of thing that I would be interested in doing. Immediately I liked the idea of setting down history as it happens really, I guess. My first book was already out by then. I'm never really quite sure when it was; I think it was something like '81 that I joined M-O, it may have been later, but my first book came out in '81. UWR> I decided to write these reports straight off. In the past I let several stand for several months and dreaded having to sit down to do them. If I have free time and can answer them straight off I prefer to do this. I began my replies only an hour after opening the envelope today! I don't need to be in any special kind of mood as I love writing and always welcome the opportunity. Rather a lot of people know I'm a Mass-Observer. Running the National Lesbian and Gay Survey which is based on and complementary to M-O there's not a week passes without I have to give my speech on how it began! <UWR

The Process of Writing

I find generally speaking it does just flow. I can't sort of put it any differently to that. I don't . . . even when I'm writing my book, that I don't . . . I know what's got to go in a chapter, but I'm very often astonished when I get to the end of a particular paragraph [at] what I've just written. It's almost as though somebody else is . . . you know, what a lot of playwrights say about how they don't ever write their plays, they just write the characters' names down and then the characters tell them what to say. And I often feel like that myself, that there's someone, there's some entity beyond myself who is dictating to me things . . . Because I really have had many occasions when I just thought, where did that come from? If I read my books now, I think, did I write that? That's brilliant! How did I actually, you know, get myself into a position to write that? It's quite astonishing. And I think it's just, if you have an ability to allow flow, which I guess is what it is, that that can happen, and I suppose that's happened . . . that's why I enjoy doing the M-O things, is that I just sit down and let it happen, without thinking too much about it. In fact, the last one I did I didn't think enough about it and I felt so dissatisfied with it that I just shoved it to one side and unfortunately I haven't got back to it. That was about ecology.

Uses of Writing: Nostalgic Conversation

UWR>It isn't usually my practice to let anyone read my contribution. However, as I was writing Part One to this Directive, on Education, I decided I was going to photocopy it and send it to the one or two people I'm still in touch with who shared those days with me. We live, in one case three thousand miles apart, and it will be like a nostalgic conversation. I will also keep a copy for my own records. If ever I write my autobiography such reminders are useful . . . [No subject] is ever exhausted, but you have to put a full-stop to it somewhere. The benefit of writing for M-O is the occasional discipline of having to examine one's thoughts and memories and setting them down. It's the confessional box combined with the need for conversation and that instinct that underlines our every being, to leave something of our lives in perpetuity to the world. <UWR. There was one particular thing, I don't know how relevant it was to the Survey, but we had one respondent who I think through articulating to himself on to paper, reports, that he was able to come out for his father, which he hadn't been able to do before, and his father died very shortly afterwards, and he was really pleased that he had been able to do it. And I think . . . the implication was that it was a direct result of having to articulate on paper for the Survey that had brought him to that point.

On Being Ordinary

UWR>I don't think I need to write much about what I feel the value [of M-O] to be. Ordinary people writing about their lives. In fifty years time it will be fascinating. That's what history is all about, but the history of ordinary people has to be written while it's happening as there is no surviving source material otherwise. <UWR It's always subjective. Well I think that's the value of it; there's no point in writing down what you think everybody else is thinking about it, it's . . . I think the whole point of M-O is that it is the individual's own particular view. The ordinary voice.

And Being Lesbian/Gay

I've used it myself in relation to my own project, that we give a voice to the ordinary lesbian and gay, that it's . . . well it's the person who wouldn't have a voice otherwise, the ordinary lesbian or gay, I guess, as opposed to the ordinary general public, but yes, of course, but I feel that the reason lesbians and gays on the whole wouldn't have contributed to M-O, maybe it would be different now, but then, when I set the project up, is that they . . . I think that certainly in the case of women, they need to feel a security in who is going to be reading the material immediately

I guess, and how it is going to be treated; and with men, in many cases they could be compromising themselves in legal terms. And I think the thing is that why it has worked with a gay man running it, is that they are at least sending it to somebody who understands that whole area. For example in the mid-Eighties when we set it up there was a whole lot of paranoia about a very bad climate and people were very scared, and so we set the whole thing up on an anonymous basis, so that it's quite different from M-O. I know at M-O now everyone has a code number, but they do know which code number relates to which person, but we don't, our membership is made up entirely of people who have a code number and who are on our mailing list, and there's no correlation between the two. They get it in a . . . when I do a recruit we get . . . we do all the papers at once, and then shuffle them up and so we don't know which number goes out to which person.

BS: You are implying that various categories of people, including in this case gays and lesbians, may not respond to the questions in the M-O as fully as others? Yes, right. It's possible, I don't . . . I think the climate has changed. I don't know whether it has changed very much, because you get into different ways of thinking in London, but you know, as a national thing, but I think there are some people who are still very private about that particular area of their life anyway, and also there still are legal implications if the men are under 21, writing about his sex experiences. I mean he would be incriminating himself, you know, if it can be traced to him.

BS: Do you feel there's anything distinctive about the writing in your survey that needs a different kind of writing than what we get in the M-O? Well I don't know; I mean I'm always very frank in my replies to M-O, and I always say that I seem to look at everything through gay-coloured spectacles when I write for M-O because there's always something to do with my sexuality that comes up. I will always be very frank, and on the whole people are very frank in their replies to us. But I don't know whether the rest of the people who write for M-O are; I mean one has this image of these ladies that hero-worshipped David Pocock and you know, are a very specific kind of respondent [compared to the ones that write to] Dorothy. I felt very conscious of that when she took over. Apparently I was the only one at the time, in the early Eighties, as David Pocock kept writing to me and saying, keep this coming in, you're the only person, gay person writing, which is what got me to start the Survey in the first place, it was just that comment. So maybe the publicity could have been done through the gay papers anyway, which I don't think it ever has been, that maybe they didn't see anyone who came across who didn't feel secure enough. It [the climate of opinion] is more open now I think. Well yes, I think we're on the brink of change and I think everybody recognises that. I mean there was a lot of talk about the change in the age of consent, although since they've got in nobody seems to have made any moves on it at all, but it was in the air, and so that was . . . I think people are a little bit more optimistic at the moment. I think the whole scene is much more optimistic.

Writing Rather Than Speaking

There are other reasons I think why people contribute to my survey in that they feel that their experiences might be useful to other people, younger people who are coming to terms with their sexuality and coming to terms with coming out, and one gets a feeling of that a lot, in the frankness with which people relate their own stories. *BS: And do you think there's something about the fact that it's in writing, that allows a certain kind of frankness, that would be different in say a tape archive or face-to-face?* We have for some time offered the facility of sending in tapes, but fortunately only one person sent in one tape, which I still haven't transcribed, I've had it about three years now, and it still, you know, I can't be bothered with it, you know. We have to do a lot of transcription because part of our guarantee is that no one can be traced in any way, so anything that is hand-written we have transcribed into type, which is a bit of a . . . is a huge task. I think people are more concentrated about it when they write, and they think more about it. Speech is much more immediate. The thing is with . . . when you're typing something out you can sit for a moment, when you finish a particular sentence, and think how you're going to start the next one, whereas on tape in conversation you just drive on, you're not allowed the same consideration.

Writing at School

I was already writing, because I won a prize in my first year at school. I was a fairly average . . . I was at the top, in the top form at the grammar school, but I was fairly average within that, throughout my school career and at college. And I didn't really write much, but the writing thing is almost accidental and I'm astonished that I have a talent for it. I mean I was, I'm not any more because I have nowhere to do it, but I was astonished when people said that they liked what they read, you know, and I was a kind of writer who, they couldn't put the book down. *BS: But you discovered this after you had left school?* Oh yes.

Writing Letters

I was also always a great letter writer-I still am. I still write long letters to people rather than make a phone call. So I was always writing, you know, because I was a letter-writing child probably at that time. I don't know that the school did. I mean I guess I did write, but it was not . . . it's not anything that has stuck out. I mean I always got good marks for English and stuff that I had written, and I did write short stories. I would say that my school was very good at getting people to write, and it . . . well . . . you know, there was a kind of a literacy striven for at school I would say. But it's just that I didn't do anything that is memorable to me. I mean I did . . . even as a kid we . . . I had a proper theatre that we toured round at Christmas and stuff, and did shows, and I wrote all the plays, I mean I don't think anyone would have been allowed to write them but me, but that was because I wanted to be in the theatre.

Conditions of Writing

UWR> My typewriter is always here staring at me saying, "Use me." <UWR I love working at the typewriter. Well I love writing my book, and when I'm between books I miss it desperately, so that in fact doing M-O reports is an opportunity to get, you know, that kind of buzz which I really enjoy. I always have the TV on when I'm working. *BS: And the sound as well?* Yes, normally, unless I come to something that really needs, that really is tricky, that needs that bit of extra concentration and I would put the sound off, but I find that a bit distracting so I don't do it very often. And by the time that I write anyway I do know, I know virtually what I'm going to write; I don't actually know the words in advance of course, but I mean I research up to a point where I can just put a mental finger on anything. *BS: Or, if you're doing M-O writing because you've already had the experience.* Had the experience, yes. However, I often find when I'm doing M-O writing that I go off at a tangent because you follow a train of thought through. UWR> It is a strange phenomenon that writers seem not to be able to work without background noise. My television set is beyond and to the right of my typewriter. I can't work if the screen is blank. So it's on when I write. If I'm writing a particularly complex passage I may sometimes then turn off the sound, but very seldom. The movie "A Star Is Born" is just beginning at this moment. I paused to begin recording it and I keep glancing up to see what is happening. I remember Edmund White the major American gay novelist saying recently, "A writer needs background noise in order the better to concentrate in resisting it." <UWR When I write a letter, I mean letter writing is the only other thing, and I write long letters, you know, I mean I even have a continuation page, you know, because they do tend to go on. Occasionally I will hand write them, but I prefer not to.

Self-History

Self-history, or self-evaluation or whatever, that's what I mean, that's what M-O basically is. *BS: And you're saying that it's more the first self that is operative in M-O writing?* Not totally no, because a lot of it is opinion. A lot of my respondents to the Survey say that they find it very valuable, because they haven't been put in the position where they've had to have an opinion about some things before, and it's been valuable for them to work out what they actually feel on particular issues.

BS: Whose voice is being carried when you're here? It's not just your own, but that of other people like you somehow, or you feel are like you. No, I would say it's just my voice. *BS: Just your voice.* Yes. *BS: I thought I heard you say at some point that it helps particularly . . . now I'm switching to the Survey contributors, it helps other people at expressing their voice and coming out as you have done, it helps them to have you asking them questions and articulating them, because they feel, if you can do this I can do this sort of thing, and you're helping to articulate it for them. Is that part of the motivation?* No, I don't think I'm helping articulate it, but putting them in a position where they talk logically, that's slightly different. I mean like with M-O, we always make it clear with the directives that you don't have to answer every question, it's a springboard. I mean there are some people who, you know, slavishly go from one point to another, sometimes on separate lines as though, you know . . . which we hate, they're the least interesting of all; and it's those that do go off at a tangent, like I do myself when I'm doing my M-O reports, that are far more interesting.

Diversity

I found it very difficult to recruit people from ethnic minorities for our survey. So I'm sure it's equally difficult for . . . [M-O] *BS: Well what do you think is going on there?* I wouldn't like to speculate really, I don't . . . we really bent over backwards and targeted particular groups and didn't get anywhere with it. We did have a black man writing for us for a short period of time, and we had one Asian woman, again only for a short period of time, and I don't know why we didn't keep them either. I don't understand class at all. I mean I'm supposedly now a white, middle-class male; I come from a working-class family, possibly upper-working-class I guess because my father was an insurance agent. I suppose, but he did live on a council estate, you know, and I still live in a bedsit. Why does this make me middle-class? You know, I don't know where I am with that.

For the Future

That's the most important thing, that's the most important thing performing with it, is that there is something there in the future that has my opinion there; I mean I like the idea of that happening. And I suspect that's why a lot of people write for the Survey, is that they want the experience that they've had to be noted. In fact that's going to be our next slogan or whatever on our new leaflet. I can't think exactly the words really . . . , that say, who will know what it was like to grow up lesbian or gay, unless you tell them, something like that. Here's how! *BS: So what exactly then is the audience that you have in mind? When you're writing, have you got a reader in mind?* No. *BS: When writing for M-O?* No. Another me maybe. *BS: So it's not another researcher like us?* No, not at all. *BS: And yet, when you say, who will know, who is the who in there?* "Who will know unless you tell them?" Who is the them, the who? The who is everybody else really. The rest of the world. Right, yes. *BS: Not particularly academics or anything?* No. Interested parties.

Saving Letters

I never throw letters away, by the way, I've got every single letter I've been sent since 1964. Not bills and things, but letters that have actually got anything in them. *BS: Are they filed and classified?* Yes. Well, by year. And all of my research for my books is still in those shelves behind you. I never throw any . . . But I mean that was useful anyway, I remember Simon Cower did a book about Charles Laughton, and I was just able to pick out a handful of papers about Flora Robson and Charles Laughton that I was able to send him, which helped him a lot. And it's just good always to have it. I keep all this lot because you never know. And any writing that I have ever done I've got, I never throw any kind of creative writing away.

Stopping Writing . . .

BS: Is there any . . . what would stop you writing for M-O? Would there be anything about the directives, or the writing that we send you? No, I can't think . . . The only thing is my health, and so the reason that I am so behind.

MRS SAFRAN
(B2197)

Mrs Safran was interviewed by David Bloome on 11 February 1993 at her home in East London. Both her parents were born in East London and are of Eastern

European Jewish descent. Mrs Safran was born in 1954. She read Anthropology at Cambridge where she met her husband, who is a solicitor. They have four children.

Starting Writing for M-O

DB: What got you writing for the Mass-Observation? I can't really remember. I think I first saw an article on it in *The Guardian* newspaper, and it just sounded intriguing and my kind of thing, and I fancied doing it, so I wrote off for details. . . . My husband applied at the same time, but he just hasn't got around to doing it. He would like to, but he just hasn't had time. I think I wrote an initial inquiry asking for more information, and then they responded with details and asked you to give your life history, at which point we both wrote in, both sent one in. Then when the first directive came I did mine immediately, and my husband didn't.

Answering a Directive

It varies a lot. It depends on general pressure of life. I always have it in mind; I don't tend to forget about them, I'm always thinking, next time I've got a spare morning, or something, I'll do it. But that can vary from being a couple of weeks later to . . . as I say, I'm two directives behind, so that's some months behind. I have actually read the ones I haven't answered several times in between, and I can't remember when, probably . . . when I had the letter from Dorothy Sheridan about this interview I read back over the ones I hadn't done, and thought, I must do them! And I took one of them on holiday . . . thinking I might do it, and read it but didn't actually write or do it. I like to feel I've got enough time and steady energy to concentrate on it, and both of those are rare commodities, so it does have to wait its turn. I would like to have more spare time to do it, I always intend to do it quickly. I prefer daytime, so I usually wait till the kids have gone to school and there's some sort of peace and quiet—not that there's ever peace and quiet here, but something approaching peace and quiet. Otherwise I tend to do them in the evening, particularly if my husband is otherwise occupied, because I feel I've got a long span of being able to concentrate without other claims on my attention, that's the best way. Well, typically I'd go for an A4 lined pad which was put there for inspiration, and write the title and the date and number and references all ready. Then I usually read once . . . I only deal with one section at a time, and it will probably be true to say I would never do the whole thing in one go; it takes two sessions usually. So I read it, and usually I just dive straight in think at that point, having been mulling it over and not really sure what I'm going to say, then I just . . . it just takes off and I just write until I dry up. And usually stop part way through and read it back again. And then once I've finished it I read it through; I usually show it to my husband, partly because he has a photocopier in his office and I go in there to copy it. I'm not sure why I copy it, I have mixed feelings about copying it, but I do. It seems a bit silly really, just do it and send it back and forget about it. But when I re-read them, I'm quite surprised that I manage to get things down I think, I'm quite surprised that I manage to get cover the ground and say things. And when I've finished them he usually reads them. I wouldn't insist, I'm happy for him to read them; it's partly having . . . that's something about their selfishness basically, which I suppose, having given it that much of my time I feel it's not unreasonable to share it, and I don't mind him reading it. It seems like it's fair, if I've had all that time to myself, I can catch up with him. And also because I half feel . . . what do I feel? . . . I like to get his input on what I said. Most of the things I say I'm sure he knows already, but if there was anything different already then we talk about that, I'm interested in that. So, then I send it off. So it's really two sessions or three sessions . . . so that's how I go about doing it. I usually go down and copy it and say, "I'm just about to post this off, do you want to read it first?" And he says, "Yes please!" He reads it, and . . . I think . . . I feel partly, he feels I'm speaking for him. I don't feel I'm speaking for him, but I communicate our . . . to the extent that his and mine are the same, I communicate our joint ideas, and he enjoys the fact that I'm doing that on his behalf. I'm very pleased that he approves and like . . . I think he probably would want to do it and is pleased I put my attention towards it. I'm sure he doesn't resent it either, he feels he's pleased that . . . he thinks it's worth doing, he's glad I enjoy doing it, and he thinks I do it well-I don't know why he thinks that, but . . . he says nice things about it. I think it has quite a political element to it. It's very nice to be able to say things that you think and feel, particularly if you feel that the rest of the world isn't really interested and doesn't really listen, and you can't do anything about your views to occupy you, but you can actually put them down on paper, and I think that's a very valuable thing to be able to do actually, I like that. It makes you feel a bit less impotent!

Historical Reality

I mean it's part of the whole thing of M-O, that popular, or individuals' attitudes are not necessarily reflected by the historical reality, but is presented in retrospect, and I think to make your . . . you know, if you have a dissenting voice, if you actually write it down then yes, I have got these views; if I don't agree with people, I don't like what's happening; the fact that you actually have a way of vocalising it . . . I mean it's only on an individual, therapeutic level, I don't think it has any real influence on what goes on in the world. It's slightly reassuring somehow, to get it down. I often wonder what the other M-O people are like, how atypical they are, and I think of myself as being very atypical, and I think probably most people who write for the M-O think of themselves as being atypical, but maybe that's not true.

DB: *Do you feel that you're a dissenting voice?* Definitely. Just that I don't feel I subscribe to most people's values or most people's ambitions, or . . . I just, you know, basically feel out of step with the rest of, most of the rest of my kind, not all of it. It's a big question. I don't know what to say really. I mean at the moment in one level I've been very unhappy with what's happening here politically, but that's only one element of it really. So it's just nice to feel there's some kind of channel for this feeling, that you can write down what we think and feel, and that there's a little space for what you think of it, even if it doesn't actually have any tangible effect. And I think we do have an effect because like everything else I do, interact with society. It's quite a pure thing to do. It often occurred to me that writing for M-O could be very . . . and people who write could actually manipulate obviously if they wanted to, could write what . . . I mean if you take it as a . . . for me it's very truthful, I write what I really think and feel and believe, but you could actually, as an exercise, do it in a very different way. You could pretend you're somebody else. There was a question in the M-O, in the education one, do you think it's changed you. I don't think it's changed me but I think it has enabled me, it's helped me be myself more, if you see what I mean It gives a public voice to your own self, so that makes you almost more yourself. It's quite interesting really. DB: *You said it helps you be more your own self. One way somebody might interpret that is to say, given all the things that you do in your day, it's very hard for you to find time, place or ways to be your own self, and that Mass-Observation is one of those times.* Yes, I think that's right really. I mean I try and make everything I do a part of myself, but you can only do it to a certain extent obviously, whereas this is undiluted, which is good. I don't know if I write to anybody else or not. Maybe it's just to myself, I'm not sure. I mean it's very nice to know that it will be useful to somebody, or may be useful to somebody, that's a big plus as far as I'm concerned, but I don't specifically think, I don't really think of the audience when I write at all. It's mostly the things you would like to say and you don't really have a chance to say.

Finding Time

I make conscious efforts to make some space for myself, but it's very hard to find it because there is a never-ending series of demands, I've actually quite recently begun to say, no not now, I'll stop now, I don't want to take that on, I'm too tired tonight, which I never used to do; I used to do everything, and there's just too much really, so I've been putting out stops. If you're involved in any kind of support work, there are endless things, so you're just in it really and you've got to prioritise the family, and the extended family. I've got my sister and her children, and then a brother I mean there are just . . . and the ramifications there are always plenty of things to do, but I'm not as ready to take them on now as I used to be, I just stop when it gets too much. I actually look on my "M-Os" as very much my own time just time to indulge.

M-O as Indulgence

UWR> I feel M-O is almost a self-indulgent exercise, but its good to think that others also find it useful. It is partly for me, a way of keeping my hand in at writing, also a way of clarifying thoughts. It has often occurred to me that it would be a useful way of passing something on that one finds difficult to articulate publicly. I also enjoy the opportunity to indulge in introspection. Also I have always felt myself to be quite unlike most people and therefore it is good to feel that my voice gets on record a weeny bit, even if in a limited way. <UWR It is quite a selfish activity, but it's very nice to have such activity, because other people like to read it, so you get all the benefit without the self-sacrifices. And it's nice to sit down, and I think all the time, I never stop thinking, but it's nice to actually push everything else out the way and concentrate on thinking about things. It feels quite selfish in a way. And also because in a way it seems quite an arrogant thing to do, to say what you think about. But because of the context that you're doing it in . . . it's quite private as well . . . it's pretending making a political issue and stand up on a soap-box or that sort of thing . . . Well I really enjoy doing it, it's always a treat to do it. And a lot of things I like doing I feel guilty about doing, because there are other more worthy things to do, so for example I always feel guilty about the garden, because it's so way down on the list, it never gets the attention it deserves. M-O is a bit like that, it feels like an indulgence to do it, so it tends to be put to one side a bit more. But when I actually do it I very much enjoy it, it's a treat. It's quite a soothing thing to do, really actually write up what you're thinking and feeling about something. Therapeutic sort of exercise, it's good. *DB: Is it an indulgence because it's mostly for you?* Yeah. That's definitely true, but because it's sought after by somebody else, it's possible, whereas normally I don't ever make space for that sort of thing. *DB: So, you don't keep a diary, or . . . ?* Not now, no, not since I was young.

Other Writing

Mostly letters, a lot of letters to friends and family, quite long letters. And I do report things, and articles to do with the [a national charity for which she works] and certain functional things, letters to school about the children and bits and pieces like that. Not much, I don't do any sort of creative writing really. Again I used to when I was younger, an adolescent, but I don't think I've done it for a long time. Long letters are specifically to people like my sister who is abroad, or a friend who used to live here and is living a long way away, where I consciously want to keep the relationship going. It's like talking to them, and those are quite long letters, and they respond, and not everybody writes; some people do and I think as an activity and some people don't, and I don't tend to write to anybody who doesn't respond, for a long time. So, letters are important. I was just thinking the other day, they actually played quite an important part in our courting relationship, because we were at university together and then during the holidays we both used to write, and there was a large quantity of the relationship tied up in letters, which is quite interesting. I saw something in the *Guardian* today, there's apparently an exhibition in London to do with the forces during the war, and correspondence, and mementos and things, and you know, it just made me realise there is actually a whole exhibition of written documentation, of letters. It's nice.

DB: Other than the letters that were between you and your husband, these long letters which you write, you mentioned to your sister. Are they mostly to women? Yes, pretty exclusively Yes, they are. My sister, several friends who have moved away. I don't know, my husband also writes letters. As a family we always did, and when our children go away, everybody, the extended family, writes to them, so that my kids get twenty letters and the others kids get one or two if they're lucky. And my childhood was like that, if ever we went away all my brothers and sisters, everyone used to write. So a certain circle of us letter writing was basic to us; when he's away we communicate by letter.

My daughter actually has just come back from five months away, and I think she had about . . . I don't know how many letters, but a huge pile of letters. She went to Israel with a school trip, and had a wonderful time. But letters were absolutely vital. And it's interesting, because she has always resisted writing letters, not been very interested in it, and when she was away she found them very useful. And she wrote wonderful letters, really wonderful letters, wrote to us what she was doing and how she was. So she really appreciated the value of them. And she used to write to [her brothers] individually, because it's nice to get letters. Actually I thought that was very impressive, because it took quite an effort for her write to us, let alone to each of them, but she did, which was very good. [My husband] sometimes put a few sentences at the end of my letters, and he wrote to her himself about three times, and she was away for five months, so it's not that good. I used to write every week. But then he knew I was writing; if I hadn't been writing he would have made sure he wrote, so I'm sure . . . you know, the need was for communication, and one of us had to do it or the other, it was likely to be me. But that didn't feel self-indulgent, again because I had an obligation to do it, to keep the relationship alive. And it's not just keep it alive, it's actually keeping her in touch with where everybody is up to, so when she came back the gulf wouldn't be too great, because five months is quite a long time for her to be away, and it seems to work very well . . . So the whole family use letters as a real tool. *DB: Would I be right in guessing that it's mostly the women who do the letter writing?* Not always. When I was at university, I discovered this again the other day, I'd completely forgotten, my brother, who's older than me, used to send me postcards from all over the place regularly, just a fraternal kind of way, and I have an enormous collection of them. Not just, "Hi, how are you?", but long, detailed communications, bits of advice and jokes. And I had actually forgotten he had done that, but there's a big collection of them. It is really nice. *DB: Do you remember your mother writing lots of letters, or your father or relatives or others when you were growing up?* Some, not an enormous number. The main memory is, on the odd occasion if I was away, then everyone would write to me, or if any of us went away we would write to each other. It's hard to remember. My father used to write letters which was . . . Not all the time, but he saw letters as a tool to be used. He used to draw pictures on them.

Themes

I prefer the [M-O directives] that are more personal and more to do with intuition, or emotional, or . . . I don't like the more practical ones, I find they're . . . well I do, I do like them, I like them all I don't dislike any of them. You mentioned the environment one, which is the one I'm stuck on, I haven't been back to it for a while, because I don't really feel like I'm coming up with too much on that topic for the moment for various reasons, but I sort of can't really be bothered to make the time to do it, although I will do it, I want to do it and I think it will be a useful thing to do, but that feels like more a chore and less of a thing I really want to do, for myself anyway. But I really enjoyed the education one and the one about close relationships, and, well most of them really. And maybe this will focus on something and it will justify doing it.

    I don't deliberately try and relay other people's views, because that's not a thing I particularly see as part of it. If other people's views have influenced my thinking about it, I would probably put that in. And actually that's probably a shortcoming, because I think M-O would quite like you to write what you feel I mean I do . . . sometimes I put that in, if there were . . . my sister was over here from Israel during the Gulf War, there were things she said about it that I wrote about the war in the Gulf War diary, but I wouldn't go out of my way to sort of question other people about other topics, and make sure that their voices were heard as well.

DB: One of the things I wanted to follow up on is, you're being very honest in your writing, and I think you mentioned being honest in terms of your emotions and thoughts and feelings, honestly getting them down. As far as I can tell. I think I am an honest person anyway, but it's certainly the fact that you are actually committing down yourself on paper, and you feel there's a strong obligation to get it right. So writing does in fact does influence you. In a conversation you only cover, unless it goes on for hours with somebody you know really well, you're only likely to cover some of the things that you think, and if anything weren't well received you won't necessarily cover the whole ground, whereas for M-O you cover something as completely as you want to, which is a rare opportunity, and that's nice. But honesty comes in there, because you feel you want to cover all the things you think about, or all the . . . it obviously isn't possible to get everything down, but it's a much rounder opportunity than really you have in close conversation. So, a bit like a conversation but a much more in-depth conversation.

DB: Would it be fair to say, well this is the thoughts of a college-educated, Jewish woman living in a northern London . . . in northern London, at the time, early 1990s? Yes, that would do I think. I don't know how representative I am of the population at large. It's quite rare. I suppose it's probably rare for most people, but it's rare to find people who really understand and really agree with the way you think and feel about things. So if you're putting yourself as a mass speaker, I wouldn't like to think I was speaking for very many people! I'm sure I'm not speaking for very many people.

DB: Do you think about, in being a woman, that you are conscious of writing for the Mass-Observation as a woman? I don't really think about it for myself, from the point of view of actually being a woman except writing about my experience as a woman. But I think it is a very sexless activity actually, or potentially, and I think the spectrum of the ways in which people can write is enormous, and I'm sure there are men who would write, who could potentially write and who have written. I think men . . . I don't know, I think men might tend to be more matter of fact, but I'm sure there are men who are more intuitive like women and who write on that level as well. *DB: What about being Jewish?* That's much more of an influence. I'm sure that influences a lot of how I think and feel. Many of my personal, private aspects, or things that I'm trying to do in my life are very tied up with that. Your general religious awareness affects everything you do; there's no way to separate it out really. Again it's quite hard to talk about, I think quite an intangible thing.

Being an Observer

I'm an observer by nature, and in contact with a lot of different kinds of people, so I think I could. I mean obviously it will be subjective, but I think most people would have a fair idea of their environment, wouldn't they? I don't know, maybe not. *DB: You mention that you are an observer by nature. What does that mean?* Well, I like people and am interested in people. I watch them, listen to them, see things about how they go about their lives. So I did anthropology at university, which probably says as much about me as anything else! I think anthropologists like to think of themselves as people who can empathise with experiences that are not directly their own, and I mean that's how I feel about life really, a lot of life, and I go round doing that in every sphere in which I work, and play. So, I think that . . . you know, that's the anthropologist in me, definitely. I mean maybe most anthropologists may not be like that, or not any more, but that would be my approach.

On Being Jewish

DB: I want to return to the question of how being Jewish affects your . . . might affect, or might be part of, or reflect in the writing that you do, if not directly perhaps indirectly? Well, on a direct level a lot of the specific experiences will relate to Jewish practice, or festivities or whatever, so on that level there's obvious connections. Oh it's just part of . . . being Jewish affects my entire world view, the way I interact with people, and so . . . you know, it's not something that I put on on Saturdays, if you know what I mean, it doesn't have a religious time, it's all the time, so . . . And a lot of my basic values I'm sure come from that, things like the way families . . . the role families play for each other, and a fundamental duty of helping people and seeking to understand people. I mean to me it's all very tied up with religious belief, but I don't preach, I mean I don't go on talking about it, but it effects everything I do. Is that anything like an answer? I don't know, it's very hard. I mean I've always been an outsider; even in my own community I'm an outsider, even within the Jewish community I feel like an outsider in a way . . . maybe it's the anthropologist again. I'm not sure. Although I feel part of the community, I also feel outside it in a way, so it's not like belonging to a club that separates you off from the rest of society, it's not like that at all. We go to services, and we keep a kosher home, and keep Sabbath, and are sort of seen socially to be in rather than out, so from that point of view they would say we were mainstream, but I think really . . . our world view is probably not like most mainstream Jewish members. Part of the struggle is reconciling to being the two But it's very hard to talk about, and not because I'm shy, it's just hard to find words to convey it, it's a difficult subject.

Do You Think of Yourself as a Writer?

Not really, no. I always thought as a child that I would be a writer when I grew up; I used to write a lot as a child, but I'm too busy living now, coping with life. I suppose at the back of my mind there's a thought that maybe one day I would actually write something more permanent, but I'll have to wait till my old age if I get there, I think. I don't actually know any personally any artists or writers. In art, I think maybe I would apply the same kind of assessment. It's like somebody who actually has the courage to decide they're going to do it. I mean, if I think of a writer I think automatically of sort of Gnostic or someone like that, but I also think that if you're a real writer then you can't help but be a writer, you have to do it. That's partly why I haven't pursued it, because I don't feel that driven to do it. I'm not a real writer, and therefore that's not really necessary. And also because I have enough little bits of outlet to use up that drive; if there were no scope for writing letters, no scope for this kind of thing, then maybe I would write something else. I like the process of writing, of physically writing.

DB: *What would stop you writing for Mass-Observation, not only in you own circumstances but what about the Archive and the way it operates, [what] might discourage you?* If it was being used as a political tool. I mean you get the impression that it's an apolitical institution, but I don't really know much about it but I assume that's what it is. If they were directed by outside political influences, if it influenced the way they were going about getting information. And I suppose, I was thinking today actually that in a sense you're quite vulnerable, if anybody actually wanted to keep tabs on a person, there's an awful lot about that person there; I don't know how easy it would be to get, but . . . So I think if you felt your anonymity was not protected you would be much less enthusiastic. What else? it's because you now feel that you can write anything, that anything you have to say is wanted and it's appreciated. I think if you didn't have that feeling about the Archive, then I wouldn't be interested in doing it, if it had to be selected, or I had to say what I felt they wanted me to say rather than what I wanted to say, then I would do something different. But I can't actually change in that way. I hope it keeps going, it would be a great shame if it had to fold up.

MRS MARTIN
(M1498)

Mrs Martin was born in 1954 in a small town in the south of England. She married when she was 20 years old and moved with her husband to the north where his family lived. In 1986, the family returned to her home town where she lives with her husband and two young sons, and works as a care-assistant in a local nursing home. She joined Mass-Observation in 1986 after reading about it in the local paper. She was interviewed by David Bloome on 14 January 1993 at her home.

Answering M-O Directives

Well, I generally know that it's [a letter from the] Mass-Observation; I think it has "The University of [Sussex]" on it, or something to identify it. And I open it usually straight away, and I just have a quick look at what it is. If there's a directive in there, the topic will interest me, I think . . . I may think, oh this is a good one for me, or I may think, it's not very interesting but I'll have a go. And usually I then put it away in a drawer or something like that, and it's usually quite a few weeks before I'll get down to it, and I'm usually thinking, I'd better hurry up and start it. And often I don't get time, and then I'll eventually begin. And once I begin I generally do sort of blocks of writing; I'll perhaps spend an evening where I'll just sit here on the couch; the television's on, the family's here, but I'll just write, and then when I get tired usually I think that's enough. Because once I'm mentally tired I don't like to carry on. And often I'm physically very tired, for instance if I've been working hard, and when I'm physically very tired I find I can't write the same, so I don't attempt it. So, I've got sort of about a third of the way through of the current directive, and it's put away at the moment, but I'll get it out and have another sort of block. And that happens about three times, and there may be weeks in between, but I do sort of think about it in the interim. I don't write in at all an organised way; I don't sit down and organise my thoughts, as I should, if I'm, say, taking an exam. There's no time-scale, there's no real organisation, I just sort of read it, and write, and it just sort of flows. And often I'll look back and think, oh, I should have written that there in that paragraph, and that doesn't really connect the way it should. But I just don't get the time to really do it properly, as I think, so I do it and then when it's finished I'll read it through and correct mistakes, but I'm usually not very satisfied with it. Occasionally I'll think, mm, that was all right, but usually I send it off and I'll think, I don't think that was very good, or that was a bit of a mess, you know. But as long as it's done I think well, I want to carry on writing it, so you know, I wouldn't like to let it lapse. That's happened on an occasion or two, where I've sort of let one lapse and have thought, oh dear, they'll be thinking, oh she's not bothering any more, but I always sort of pick up on it and start again.

Being Ordinary and Writing to Express an Opinion

I don't think ordinary people get the same chance as many perhaps academics, or so-called educated people, and people in the media, to have their say. *DB: How would you define an ordinary person?* It's very difficult really. I don't think anybody's really ordinary, but when I started writing for the Project, David Pocock (who was then in charge of it) put in a newspaper that he wanted people who were as ordinary as possible! (laughs). And I thought well I'm fairly ordinary. I think ordinary really, you think of yourself as someone who hasn't perhaps achieved fame, or great success; just live a sort of normal, everyday life, going to work and with your family.

DB: Do you feel that when you write for the Mass-Observation for your directive that you're consciously aware of writing as an ordinary person? I think so, yes. I think it's nice to know that my thoughts will be stored rather than just writing something which will be thrown away or discarded, that there is a record, which I think is wonderful really. If after you're dead for instance you know that other people may read what you've written, and might even find it interesting or informative, then you feel that it's worthwhile really. *DB: How would you describe the opposite of ordinary?* Well, the way I tend to think of it is, perhaps that there are some people who have more power in society to change things, in government for instance, and often I think you feel you're ordinary because you don't have this power, and so you have very little influence sometimes over the big decisions, like ecological decisions and world decisions. Therefore you would probably write differently to the way, for instance, somebody in power might write; they would have reasons why they could or could not achieve certain things. So it's a bit easy really to criticise them, as an ordinary person, to say well, why did they not stop chopping the rain forest down, or why didn't they do something about pollution earlier. And at least you can have a view on it, even if you don't actually change it.

I think particularly in Britain, because we have a history of a class system, where we've had two different educational systems, there is also a feeling that people who are wealthy, from my point of view, and who have had, say, a private school education and material wealth, possibly they have more chance of getting their work published, if that's what they want. So somebody who, for instance, may come from a powerful family, or a well-known family, their diary might be of interest, and just because simply of who they are they might have it

DIALOGUES ABOUT LITERACY PROCESSES **175**

published, or their memoirs, or even their opinions sought, and maybe interviewed on the television for instance. Whereas I would say that so-called ordinary people may never get that kind of attention if you like, so there's another difference I think.

UWR>I have strong opinions and I value the chance to express them. I think ordinary people have few chances to express their opinions in the media generally. Letters pages in newspapers are very selective and limited. When I lived in the North I had several long letters published in the [local newspaper] which had an excellent letters page but here in the Eastbourne area the letters from readers are edited and have to be very short. Programmes like "Right to Reply" use very little viewers' material and BBC's "Points of View" is patronising, condescending and basically a waste of time. I think Mass Observation is an excellent idea as it reflects such personal views and experiences. <UWR

Preferences For Directive Themes

The good one for me was the education one, because I'm interested in education. Not for any particular reason, but I just have always been. I think it's very very important; I place a lot of [store] on my children's education. And I think the more money I had the better their education would have been, because I do think it's very important. Most social issues I find interesting, and I want to write about them, and I'm particularly interested in the current one because that's caring for the elderly, and that's what I do, so for me that was an excellent one because I've got a lot of material really, anecdotal things that have happened, the way the elderly are treated generally. I think anything that's social; I'm quite interested in political ones. I can't really think of the ones I really don't like, but there have been one or two things that I've thought, oh I'm not very interested in that.

Letters

Letters I would definitely write in the same way. Occasionally I prefer to write when I'm on my own, you know, if it's something I've really got to think about. For instance if I was trying to write a poem or something, not that I write many poems, but that's something I would probably do when everyone else is out of the house. *DB: Could you give me an example of a time when you did write a poem, and what motivated you to write the poem?* Well, I once wrote a poem when I was at work! (laughs) This was before my present job. As I say, I very rarely write, like I used to write a lot when I was a teenager, but I think a lot of people go through a phase of that; you sort of seem to say a lot, and then . . . I don't know, you get older and you're busy with other things, and it sort of drops off you know. But once when I was in a job where it was very quiet and I was on my own, and I sat and had a piece of scrap paper and I wrote a poem, which was about my sister who died, and I was just alone and thinking about her. But I don't often write poems. I did write one a few months ago which I entered for a competition with my son, and the date for the competition was almost upon us, and I suddenly remembered I had picked up this form in the library, and he said, "Oh I've got a poem", and I said, "Oh I think I've got one", and we just sent them off quickly. But neither of them got anywhere.

DB: It sounds to me that within your family people kind of see you as a writer? I think they do; the boys would know, you know, that I'm interested. I don't know about my family as a whole; certainly when I was younger my whole family, my parents, brothers and sisters were aware of it, and my friends, because I was quite busy then. But I'm not so sure so much now; I don't think they would think of me as a writer now. *DB: What about your husband?* My husband thinks that it is perhaps a thing I do best, if you like. If I said to my husband, what should I do, he would probably say—you know, as a past-time, should I paint, or draw, whatever—he would probably pick writing. Because it was my husband who encouraged me to go to college, and I said I think I would like to go to college just to do something different. It was when the children had just started school. And he was the one who said to me, "Do your English A-Level, because you were good at English and you would be good at that". But I personally at the time didn't think I could accomplish that at all. I thought there's no way I could pass an advanced level, I thought that was for people who went to what was a grammar school when I was young. There was a test and you passed the 11-plus and you went to grammar school. I didn't pass my 11-plus, so I always felt that, you know, I wouldn't be clever enough.

I was 29 when I went to college, and I was living in the north of England then, and I had been married since I was 21 and the children were then, as I say, they were both at school during the day. And they ran day-time classes for four hours a week, which was very good, because I wouldn't have been able to go perhaps to an evening class, it would have been more difficult.

But I went, and for the first two or three lessons I felt I could hardly put a sentence together properly, but I decided that I was going to persevere, whatever, and it gradually sort of came back. Because I hadn't really written much for a long time, it was just . . . the only things I had been writing were letters to my family, and I remember one essay, about the second essay I did, I wrote one sentence and it was grammatically appalling, it just wasn't right at all, and the tutor ringed it and put on it, "Avoid this". And I thought, oh yes, that's terrible. But I never did that again, it gradually just came back.

I got an A, which was the top. But even though the tutor implied that I was capable of that, there were two other women that she said the same thing to, and I still thought, is she talking about me? I wasn't that confident, but as it happened the exam went very well. The questions were exactly what I had been concentrating on, and everything just sort of gelled on the day, so I was lucky.

I didn't start writing for the Mass-Observation until I moved back to [the South], which is where I come from originally. And that was around 1986, I'm not quite sure how old I was then. It's 1992 and I'm 39 now, so it's . . . about six years ago, something like that, yes. So there was quite a gap between doing the A-Level and starting the Mass-Observation.

DB: Do you think of yourself as a writer? No, I think of myself as a hopeful, would-be writer. I don't know any other Mass-Observers, but I think I would be very dishonest if I didn't say I wasn't a frustrated writer if you like. There's a very strange dichotomy in that I think in some ways I like to be very private about writing, and I don't mention it to many people, particularly outside the family. And if I was lucky enough to ever have anything published, I wouldn't want my own name on it, I would . . . I don't like . . . I like the thought of people reading what I write, but I don't like the thought of them knowing me personally. I don't know why that is, but it . . . *DB: Writing for the Mass-Observation, you write under a number?* Yes. *DB: That's a kind of pseudonym?* Yes. *DB: That appeals to you?* It does, very much. I wouldn't be so comfortable about writing, and I probably wouldn't write so frankly, if I knew that people would be able to identify me, at any time, even in the future, even after I was dead, I wouldn't particularly want people to know who they were reading. *DB: And you do write frankly?* I think so. I try to be as honest as I can; I think that's important.

I think if somebody has had something published, other people would tend to say . . . I think you can then say, yes, I'm a writer, and other people would . . . well I think the first question people would ask was, what have you written? Was it a novel, or . . . And then if you said yes, it's published by such and such, then I think I would feel sort of I could legitimately describe myself as a writer. But although I write, as I say I don't write for Mass-Observation the same way as I would write if somebody said I want you to write a story about this, with a view to publication, because what I'm writing for Mass-Observation I hope is more informal, because that's what I feel they want. I feel that for the Mass-Observers, the people who run the Archive, they want opinions, experiences; they don't concern themselves too much, I should imagine, with the way you write, as long as they can understand what you write. I think it's the content that's very important, it's not flowery language, or good grammar, or . . . as long as it's legible. I feel it would be wrong to sort of use the Mass-Observation writing as a sort of vehicle to think, whoopee, people are going to read this, I'm a writer. That's not why I do it. I do it because it gives me satisfaction, and because I'm hoping to give a different view of events to people in the future. *DB: A different view than the . . . ?* Than the media for instance, and the sort of official establishment view. *DB: Would it be fair to say that you are anti-Establishment?* I think so, yes. I think I always have been a little bit non-conformist. I think on a personal level it means to me that I have never liked the idea of people being stereotyped, pigeon-holed, made to dress in a certain way, act in a certain way, simply because their company image requires it, or the school wants it to be so. I hated wearing a school uniform, and I myself was very surprised when we were asked at school who would rather not wear a uniform, and I was the only person in my class who said I wouldn't. And I was really surprised by that; I thought, surely you others must hate it as much as I did, but nobody seemed to bother. And they were all very practical about it, saying oh well, if we have a uniform we won't compete about the kind of clothes we wear, and what we can afford, and I thought well, that's silly, because if you can't afford many clothes your uniform may be a little bit tatty anyway, it's not going to make a difference. But I just resented being told what I had to wear, and I'm afraid I've always been a bit that way inclined.

The Desk

DB: Does anybody write at the desk [in the living room where the interview took place]? Nobody writes at the desk. It's my husband's. Somebody gave us that desk, and immediately he said, "That is mine". And he keeps all his personal papers and forms in there, so it's not actually used for writing. *DB: So it's more storage?* Yes. But there is some writing paper down there which I use, in the cupboard. *DB: Can I ask you where you keep your pens?* In my handbag strangely enough! (laughs) So that I can use them at other times, you know. *DB: Do you have a desk in the bedroom?* No. I just bring them back in here when I want them. I tend to keep them there so that they're separate and they don't get mixed up with anything, or thrown away. But the drawers in this piece of furniture I have all my own papers and bits in there.

Education, School, Writing

I think I would have written regardless of my education. It just began when I was about eight years old I think. I think one influence was, I actually visited a beautiful old house with my parents who were considering buying it, but they didn't in the end, and it was almost a . . . well it's a folly, a very unusual building. It still exists, it's called the Clock House, and it's in a place called St. Leonards-on-Sea, and it's a sort of Victorian house with this clock tower. And as a child to visit it, it was so fascinating to me that I wrote about it, I wrote a little verse afterwards, which I just sort of composed in the car going home, because this house was so sort of inspiring and it had this beautiful garden. And that was the first time I had written anything, I was eight then, and it just went on from there. And my aunt was quite interested, and she encouraged me; she got me to enter competitions, which I never got any prizes, but she did say, you know, come on, send this one to that, you know. And I did get quite a good report, I remember, in my primary school, which said I had a vivid imagination, and that used to crop up every now and then on my report, and that I was . . . one actually said a gifted writer, but as a child, I would have been about nine then, or ten I suppose, and that, reading my own report and seeing that written by a teacher was quite, you know, a feather in my cap if you like. I remember thinking, wow, you know! And then I went on to the secondary school, which as I say was the school where you went if you didn't pass the 11-plus, and I had a very good English teacher there, and she was very encouraging. And I learnt a lot outside school hours, and really it became a sort of . . . I don't know how you would put it, but it was my own little thing, my own little world if you like; I could sit on my own and write, and it was . . . I don't know, I just think it's kind of solitary, but it's nice. And I remember one of my friends at the time, as we got older during our teenage years, she wasn't having a very good time, and it had always stuck in my mind that she said to me, "It's all right for you, you've got your writing". And I thought that was a very strange comment, because I thought to myself, well, my writing as far as I was concerned wasn't something that somebody had just suddenly given me out of thin air and said, oh you do that; it was something I had to make an effort to do, because I wanted to do it. But her view seems strange; it was almost as if she couldn't do it, and I thought that was very very odd, because to me, everyone can write, once they've learnt to actually . . . the technique of writing, everyone can do it. And you know, I would never think of myself as having any real gift for it.

Work

Well, I'm on a rota, and I work 25 hours one week and I now work 32 hours the following week, that's just been increased. But what happens is, roughly once a fortnight I get four days off together. And I work at various times of the day. My shifts are normally 2 in the afternoon till 9 at night, but I do one morning a week, which is 8.30 to 12.30. So of course, when I am at home I'm doing my housework a lot of the time, and going shopping and doing meals and things like that, so I find I don't get a lot of free time now. *DB: You are primarily responsible for the upkeep of the house, and the family.* Yes, definitely. Washing and ironing and things. In fact they don't do much at all! (laughs). When I'm here I tend to cook, but my husband I must say does a lot of cooking. He's better at it than I am, and fortunately he's a good cook, because with my hours, if he wasn't, he wouldn't do very well, you know. But I mean I still, as I say I still have the cleaning and that kind of thing to do. Plus I tend to visit my own relatives as well, which takes up a bit of time, chatting and so forth. *DB: You spend time helping them as well?* Yes, I do on occasion, so for instance this week we've had a funeral, which was a distant relative, but I helped to provide the tea, and so I went to my mother's while she was at the funeral and prepared all that with my aunt. And so I do, things like that come up in the family and I do help out when I can. *DB: You did tell me that you had been taking a course as well.* Oh that's right, yes. I finished my course last June, and that was a ten-week course in the evenings, one evening a week. Fortunately as I say I've finished that now, but at the time that took quite a lot of time up as well, because I had to do a project connected with my work as well in my own time, and so I was quite relieved when I came to the end of it. I've done two courses since I've been working; the first was an Open University course which was only a short course, that was called "Working with Older People", which I did because of my work: it wasn't compulsory, but I do find that if I do something else as well like that, it's quite demanding really to fit it all in. *DB: So, when you do have time to write, either for Mass-Observation, or poetry, or any things like that, it's difficult to find that time?* Yes, it's not that easy. I mean I can, you know, if I really want to; I think I could probably find more time if I made more effort to, but you know, you get a bit lazy sometimes.

MR RICHARDS
(M1593)

Mr Richards works for an oil company in a professional capacity and spends a good deal of time away from his home in Scotland where he lives with his wife. The interview by Dorothy Sheridan took place at the flat which is his base in London on 22 May 1993. The flat, though perfectly comfortable and well-appointed, seemed rather impersonal and it was clear that he did not think of it as "home" but only as a convenient place from which to travel for his work. He was born in 1946. He joined Mass-Observation in 1986.

Starting to Write For the M-O Project

I think I first heard of it, oh, it must be twenty odd years ago, I think it was . . . was it Humphrey Jennings, the documentarist? I think it was either on television or in books. I mean I like modern history, you know, 1900 onwards, up to about 1950 fascinates me, including the 1950s. So, you know, I read all sorts of books about modern history, and I've come across it several times. And I think it was quite by chance that I saw your advertisement, and I can't even remember what paper it was in, but I was in Great Yarmouth at the time, so I don't know if it was the local paper . . . it could be the *Sunday Times* because . . . well it probably was . . . when I say Yarmouth it was probably on the rig, and they probably had a *Sunday Times* on the rig, papers and that, because people read newspapers all the time, it doesn't matter if they're old or not.

I happen to be very good at everyday diaries, because I'm never usually able to produce something or record things on the day that you're interested in; but I can record, I mean in particular during the Second World War there were all sorts of continuous mass observation recording going on, and it was interesting reading them, the personal histories, personal viewpoints. So, I thought, yes, I wouldn't mind contributing to that.

Answering the Directives

UWR> I would like to say that I always mull the directive over before starting; unfortunately I lead such a hectic life that I tend to treat work—and life—as a series of hurdles to leap over. So do I treat M.O. It is rare that I achieve the writing in one session though and frequently reread—the better to align my thoughts. I never make notes or a draft copy—I had understood that spontaneity—even if rather inchoate!—was important . . . I never discuss my ideas with anyone else before I sit down and start on my Directive. No particular mood—it's simply a matter of availability of time. Usually in the evening or at night though. <UWR

I was just thinking the other day, I wonder how long ago it was, because, I mean time goes so quickly now, and I'm always busy, I'm never not busy. I mean that you say, when you send these things out you say, oh take your time to do them, but I don't look at things like that. Everything that I'm given to do, be it socially or at work is a challenge, and I have to do it there and then, or very soon after, you know. I'm like that all the time, so that's why I get things done. But I never relax and do it, I always have to go at it hammer and tongs.

UWR> I have tended to believe that it is one's personal feelings/views/perceptions that are sought—irrespective on any value placed upon them personally—and I may well be wrong in my interpretation of M.O.'s requirements <UWR . . . I think it's a fairly intensely personal thing that you're doing, and you know, I'm assured of no interruptions at all when I'm in a hotel, or on a ship . . . Actually it's odd you know, my wife knows that I do this; I think she was sort of mildly amused at it, that was I doing it, but we have talked about it briefly, but not a lot I must admit, and she says that, or she believes I probably am more open and honest in this document than anywhere else, and she's probably right. It's quite cathartic actually in some ways. It's like an outpouring of thoughts and things on various topics, so . . . I just quite enjoy doing it. It's quite releasing if you like.

Place of Writing and Materials for Writing

UWR> Almost invariably I complete my M.O. submission when I am away at sea—or in an hotel, so I have some peace and quiet. <UWR In the hotel, especially, there's not a lot to do, so that makes life easier. And I've done loads of directives in hotels. And of course at sea, especially in the U.K., you get a lot of bad weather, and you just sit there waiting on the weather, just going up and down, so you've got all the time in the world. I mean sometimes we can be out there, and I've done two hours' work in a month in winter time. So I mean that occupies some time quite happily.

Contributing to History

UWR> I like to think that I am contributing to a worth-while project. I have always been fascinated by modern (twentieth century) history and social history in particular. So contemporary views do have an historical relevance and if my contributions can form a small part of an historical record or archive for future use then I will be well satisfied. Maybe it's just a longing for immortality in print! Looking back at some of the programmes and books I have enjoyed the view of the contemporary witness has helped to place a perspective on events. The whole M.O. response or record to a particular subject must form a fascinating overview of a national response to a topic/subject <UWR

Other Writing

UWR> The only other writing that I do is at work and I always use a Word Processor and electronic mail systems. I write reports and memos and technical arguments etc. When I am offshore I use the telex a lot so—in all my professional scribblings the key words are brevity and lucidity—unlike my M-O. ramblings! If you are trying to get across a point to a senior manager it has to be done in one page—otherwise a busy reader will get bored and discard your paper. Hence the need for setting out: the problem, possible solutions, optimum solution or recommendation and the cost. Similarly, when writing in "telexese" (which I can do from my desk) one learns to be very lucid and clarity, even to the point of pedantry is sometimes essential. Ambiguity or hesitation are "no-nos"! <UWR

Yes, I like writing. [He writes regular reports for work from his postings abroad.] Oh you're expected to communicate. I probably do far more than most people, because I like to get across the nuances rather than just the bald facts; I want to give the whole picture with the various influences. I finish by about 8 usually. In fact I do it that day so it's still immediate, and I send it away about 7 in the morning

When I was a kid I kept a diary, but not religiously, and I don't really use a diary at work either. I've got a very good memory for numbers, not names though, but numbers, yes. I used to be known as the talking directory, because people just used to shout out, "What's the number of that one?" and I could tell them, you know, telephone numbers, fax and everything. But I use them all the time you see, so they're always in the front part of my brain. I don't really write many personal letters these days; most of my writing is done for business reasons I suppose you could say.

DS: *Do you write to your wife when you're away?* Well that's an interesting one, I wondered if you were going to ask that. I used to. I do, sometimes; that sounds as though I don't bother communicating, but normally, if you're out in the ocean you can't post it anyway, so you can't get a letter back. And normally I have one phone call a week, wherever I am, for three or four minutes, and if I'm in Singapore, I mean it's great if it's just like here you know, just pick up the mobile phone and just dial straight through. And then of course you get the bill at the end of the day, which is quite steep. But, yes, I mean if I'm in the U.K. I will phone every night, always. DS: *But you talk rather than write?* Yes that's right, it's more convenient. DS: *Do you ever write to [your mother]?* No, but I phone her once a week. DS: *Sounds like the phone is a way that you use for keeping in touch with people more than writing now, generally?* Yes, I think that's just . . . that's just the technical evolution if you like, because I certainly used to do a lot of posting letters to quite a few people. Those days, say you know, twenty years ago, not everybody had phones, and it was always difficult to get a phone. And I mean my mother is still the same; I mean elderly people are I think, they tend to regard the phone as an instrument for emergency, and they never normally use the phone. They don't normally phone you, they always wait for you to phone them, and I don't think it's out of meanness or anything, it's just that you know, the phone is something only to be used on special occasions. Whereas now it's just an everyday thing. I mean, I can't remember what my phone bill was in the office, because I spend all my life on the phone, you know, shouting down the phone arguing with people, when things are going . . . Phones, and fax and telexes all the time.

Themes of Directives

DS: Do you find that you have preferences with the directives? Are there some subjects you prefer to others? Do you ever recall not writing, or thinking, oh, I can't be bothered with that one? Well I've never done that, but there are some subjects, but I can't honestly recall them, that . . . or some elements of the subjects, I occasionally find that I really have nothing to say about it, you know. I maybe just don't have an opinion on it, or it's not relevant to me. *DS: Have you thought, you know, why don't they ask a question like this, or that? I mean have you got any recommendations for us?* No. I should have really; I know it sounds dreadful but I don't, because as soon as it's done it's forgotten, because I'm busy doing something else. Because I don't have enough hours in the day. The workload has just got heavier and heavier and heavier, as it has for most people in the U.K. There's been a tremendous difference you know, with the workload. And so, as soon as I've done it, it's in the past, and I get on with something else. I mean in the office here, I mean I usually go to work at half-past six in the morning, I don't stop for lunch, and I will leave at about half-past six at night. And a lot of people do that, you know, it's a long day. I was in the office at one o'clock this morning and somebody was still working there. I was quite enthusiastic about [the Directive on] books. Very enthusiastic, I get enthusiastic about all of them. I mean the pace of life, and growing old and things like that, which is all highly relevant, sure. The day ones I usually find difficult, because that actually intrudes into a working day, and I've got to remember it, and . . . I'm usually so busy; I know it sounds very exaggerated, but we do work at a furious pace.

Being Ordinary

DS: Some of the people we've interviewed say that they do it because they're "ordinary". Does that ring any bells with you? Do you think you're "ordinary"? Yes, reasonably ordinary. Depends what you tend to find ordinary, I mean, I'm extremely lucky in many ways. Because I've a good relationship with my wife, a generous relationship with my wife in so far as you know, she lets me go off and do these things, and is able to cope on her own without any aggro. It's also a terrifically interesting job, and we get treated very very well, and I am well aware of it. OK, maybe

I'm not ordinary in some ways because . . . I move very fast, I run everywhere, and I speak very fast, and people can never understand what the hell I say. I think I'm fairly mainstream, and perhaps very conservative with a small c as well, partly because of age and upbringing. I don't like a lot of things that are happening today, with education, crime and what have you. And you know, there's a lot of this modern jargon, and bizarre theories that are floating around, I don't have much patience with some of those things. It's jargon that really upsets me, all these buzz words. People can't, you know, express themselves clearly, they've got to talk in acronyms all the time. Crazy.

Men and Writing

DS: Do you think that being . . . maybe you find this question a bit odd, but you can tell me. Do you think that being a man affects the way you write? Yes, probably. A typical male outlook on life I suppose. *DS: You think you have a typical male attitude?* Yes, probably; I've been told I do. *DS: What would you say if I told you that most of the people that write for the Archive, like two-thirds, are women?* That wouldn't surprise me. *DS: Can you say why it doesn't surprise you?* Well one of the reasons I suppose is because women have more time, and that may be a bit offensive. *DS: It might not be true.* Yes, it might not be true, you're quite right actually. Maybe women look at things more subjectively I suppose, [men] more objectively. I don't know why; I mean, I'm not surprised, but . . . there again I guess my interests are fairly narrow. Not many people I know are very much interested in social history. *DS: You mean men that you know, yes?* Yes. I mean there must be . . . must be employed women and they have even less time than I would. *DS: You may be right when you said you thought women were more subjective. Would you say that that was something that was important for this kind of project?* Yes, I think so. Look upon life with a certain sympathetic slant I think, and be interested . . . Actually I suppose women are more interested in other people. *DS: Is that your experience of men and women around you?* No, I think that was a bit of a generalisation really. *DS: I mean would you recommend to any of your male colleagues or friends, doing this?* No. *DS: Is that because you don't think they would be at all interested, or because you don't want to particularly talk to them about the fact that you do it?* I think it's probably the latter. I don't think that many of them would want to do it. Most of my friends are from . . . most of them are from the same industry naturally, which is basically the oil industry so they're all very down to earth, and I wouldn't say—well some of them are aggressive, but they're fairly hard-working people, and wouldn't have a lot of time for . . . Yes, it's the latter really isn't it; we said that earlier on, you can always make time if you want to do something. They may regard it as introspective. *DS: Are you saying that a lot of men wouldn't want to be introspective?* I can't answer it, because I've never put it to them. I mean it's a sort of, I wouldn't say a secret but it's an inner part of themselves that you don't normally communicate with. I just think that some of the people I work with or know tend to be fairly cynical, so I wouldn't be . . . it's not the sort of thing which one would volunteer. *DS: How do you decide what you think we want? How do you decide to write the way you do?* I don't even think about it really; as I say it's just really in some ways an outpouring. I actually was wrong earlier on. I do it straight away, but sometimes I think of additions. I don't change things, but sometimes I'll think of additions, and where I notice things are a bit cramped up in places. *DS: So you add them on at the end.* Yes, something that occurs to me. So I don't . . . once I start writing I have no . . . I don't really think about it. I look briefly at your, and refer back to your subject headings, and your topics, and I generally follow those. Yes, I don't normally deviate too much in my own sort of . . . my own sort of interpretation of what I think you want, I just generally head off and start writing and just carry on. *DS: Have you ever thought of just writing about something that we haven't asked you about, you know, and just sending in something?* No. I prefer you to choose the subjects really.

Grammar and Spelling

I can usually check on the spelling of a word. I write fast, so I don't really have much of a chance to change the grammar at all. I like to be grammatically correct, sure. Because a comma here, a comma there can change the whole context. The standards of grammar are getting worse and worse generally, and you see this; I mean you see it in written reports, it's amazing. You see some really bad English from fairly young, well-educated people, very senior people, it is amazing.

I do proof-read. Sometimes I don't get it right, because you filter [your own] mistakes out. Oh yes I always try and get the grammar correct, for sure. I mean it's the art of communication. I mean you're changing the inference of what you're saying by having incorrect grammar, or you're losing the inference, you're losing your thrust of your reasoned argument by having incorrect punctuation, incorrect grammar. I just think it's bad practice. I don't hold this policy of, oh, they know what you mean anyway and . . . this very modern thing where punctuation doesn't matter at all, you can always get the meaning across. I don't think you do get the meaning across unless you use correct punctuation. I mean I was working with a lawyer yesterday actually, because we were just preparing some sort of protocol . . . I really wasn't too interested in it, because it was just another delaying tactic, so I couldn't be bothered. We changed a few things to reduce our commitment, and then this lawyer got hold of it, and he went to town on it in a big way, especially on the grammar, and so we re-wrote the whole thing again. And that was an interesting and enlightening exercise. I mean, there is a classic case whereby incorrect punctuation, grammar as well actually, can land you up in a hell of a lot of trouble and cost you a lot of money.

Stopping Writing

DS: Can you imagine what would stop you writing? Well let's say the Archive released my identity or something like that, without my permission, or . . . that would stop me for sure I would think, I would be somewhat annoyed to say the least. Otherwise I can't think of anything that would stop me. I mean I quite enjoy it.

MS MCPHAIL
(M2493)

Ms McPhail lives in Edinburgh in a house that she is "doing up", having previously done the same in other places which she then sold before moving on. She joined Mass-Observation in 1990. She partly does her Mass-Observation writing "for her daughter" so that she will have a record across her life, which is in keeping with her interest in genealogies—to save details that would otherwise be lost. Her daughter also keeps a diary and is entering into the spirit of writing, record-keeping and story-writing on the computer. Ms McPhail works for a television company and thinks of herself as a visual story teller: she feels that she has to make a special effort to do the writing required for Mass-Observation—her motivation is precisely to ensure that Mass-Observation records are not only those of keen writers but also "represent" people like her. Indeed, when she learned that excerpts from her interview were to be used in this book, she saw it as one up for the non-professional writers: "I'm absolutely knocked out that you're going to publish some of my scribblings and ramblings! It's one up on the journalists I work with whose professional writing for TV bulletins is mere ephemera". But the joy is tempered with the continuing feeling that writing is difficult: "I'm writing this as painfully as ever on the same computer". Indeed, she had stopped writing for a while to do up the house, but now that this is finished, "I now have no excuse for not starting to write again for Mass-Observation".

She was interviewed on 21st April 1993 by Brian Street in the large kitchen of her home, at a good-sized pine kitchen table where papers could be spread out and a comfortable atmosphere created. Her daughter, who was 7-years-old at the time of the interview, worked on the computer and did some "scribbling" at her own writing desk in the same room. Other writing paraphernalia included a regular desk calendar, post-its and scraps of paper to list tasks which she ticked off. Books were also evident, and she said in the interview that she always liked to have unread books around; it would be unthinkable to go to bed without having read one of these. Despite her anxieties about writing as opposed to other media of expression, then, her room was well set up for doing writing, which was evidently part of the family environment and activity.

Getting Involved With M-O

I read Naomi Mitchison's autobiography,[2] and it mentioned there that she worked for [Mass-Observation], and this was something that intrigued me, I had never sort of been aware that there were any sort of archives like this, and I thought well, I could do something like that too, you know. And I wanted to find out more about [it]. And I thought well, what they want is more people maybe who would write, not journalists and so on, but people, ordinary people doing ordinary things, the sort of things that are fascinating. They want to know the sort of nuts and bolts of people's lives, rather than perhaps, you know, the battles and all the rest of it that are well documented anyway.

On Not Being a Writer

I'm not a literary person. Well, I read a lot but I'm not a writer. I find it very hard to write, it's a big struggle. Every time a Mass-Observation directive comes in I find it very daunting. I force myself to sit down; I really do have to struggle actually, because I'll do anything rather than sit down. It's amazing that I ever write anything at all. The most I normally write is you know, a shopping list or something like that. My job I don't have to do any writing you know, and I'm a very poor correspondent to friends and things. It really is a struggle, yes.

    I mean in my work it's very much a visual thing. I go out and tell stories with pictures. I work very closely with journalists, and our newsroom is a very small newsroom, there's only ten of us, but there's a big divide in the newsroom between the journalists, who pride themselves on being wordsmiths and they are the masters of the word, whereas you know, we have the . . . we don't have the same literary skills that they have. Sometimes there's a great deal of banter in the office. They will tease us because it takes us all our time to write a very basic letter and on the other hand you know, we can tease them because they don't have the same grasp of technicality as we do.

---

[2]Naomi Mitchison kept a diary for the war years for Mass-Observation. An edited version was published entitled *Among You Taking Notes* (Sheridan, 1985).

Diary

I write a diary, and I've been doing it now for about eight years. I started one day, when I was on a train and I thought, well why not? And, I don't write it every day, I don't write it at an appointed time; it's just whenever I maybe have a moment and I feel I have something I want to write down. It's very . . . in a way talking to myself, or sometimes I think maybe I'm writing it for my daughter when she's older. She's also funnily started writing a diary; she sits down every day; I mean it's very basic, she's only seven, And, I find it interesting for myself, just being able to look back over things and you know, maybe something that seemed traumatic at the time, in retrospect isn't so. I have the diary with me all the time. [If] I'm out and about or if I go away for the weekend or something, holiday, or working away, or anything like that. I mean it's with me.

Purpose of Writing for M-O

UWR> I enjoy the creativity of it & the thought that in some small way I am writing history. I don't think it has changed me but I have only been writing for M-O for a short time . . . I think the project is useful in giving future historians an idea of what ordinary people thought of today's events and about the trivia of everyday life not always recorded formally in history. <UWR

BS: Can you say a bit more though about this notion about speaking to your daughter across the years? Yes, uh-huh. Just, I mean it's only because I . . . because of the M-O thing I suddenly felt, well why am I writing this diary, you know? Gathering all these notebooks. Are they for anyone? And it was coincidence that at the time I started it was when I was pregnant with her, so I don't know whether, you know, there was a kind of germ of an idea there, that I was going to be writing it so that she would understand how I felt throughout all her life, you know, so that she would have a better understanding of her life too, as much as mine. I think when I'm writing for M-O I don't think I'm specifically thinking of my daughter, . . . although it's not specifically for her, the M-O. Why I was interested in starting to write for M-O, I do a bit of genealogy research, and I find it very interesting to find out any little snippet about any of the people who I . . . my ancestors I found out about, and it's fascinating you know. And my father came out with some snippet about his grandmother, and he said, oh that was granny, she used to tramp clothes. I said, "What do you mean?" He said, "Well, she tramped clothes." Now it turned out later that I discovered she was a laundress. That's how she did the washing. She got you know, hoisted up her skirt and got into the big basin and . . . This was just [a] little detail, and I thought well, things like that will be lost unless they're recorded. And people's birth dates and death dates and marriage dates, they're all faithfully recorded, but none of the sort of, the colour of their life is recorded.

Themes

The different directives in M-O, some of them I find easier to write than others. Some of them are topics that I have thought about and I have ideas; others are some things, you know, I think well you know, what do I think about this? And I've got to sort of, you know, wonder about for a few days or a few weeks. And even then, sometimes I sit down to write pages and pages and pages and . . . pour out. Other times you know, I'm sort of paragraphs come painfully from my pen. Even the ones that are relatively easy to write are still a struggle, I force myself to sit down, and get a pen. I mean I would rather do anything, I would rather you know, paint the old ceiling than sit down and write.

A Place to Write

I have obviously just recently moved here, but my past house, and eventually in this one I have a little, a study, somewhere where I have my own desk, and I can . . . you know, when I'm writing something, if I do get called away I don't necessarily have to tidy it all up, it's still there to go back to. Though the most recent M-O thing I wrote, I cleared a corner of the table there, and did it there. But you know, I don't do notes; I think it out and then just start writing.

Filing Systems

I have a file, a basket in my bedroom, and things that have to be dealt with, maybe not immediately but at some point soon, go into that. Things like my tax form for this year is in there waiting to be filled in, and every two or three weeks I will take . . . you know, I've know that I've got a couple of hours free and I'll take those and I think right, I've got to tackle it, it's getting . . . you know, critical. I've got to sit down and I've just got to wade through this lot, you know, reluctantly, and I'll do that, I'll work my way through it until it's empty.

    I mean once I've dealt with things I do have a number of other files you know; I've a file for solicitor's letters, another file for anything to do with tax. So once they're dealt with they go in there, so I mean they don't just disappear. So, I suppose I do keep lots of files on things. I think I've got to the stage that I am fairly organised out of necessity I think, I've had to become organised.

Daughter

She does like writing, she's got her desk and she'll spend hours sitting there, just scribbling away something, she'll write a little story, or . . . she does a lot of drawing and things like that, she's more, maybe visual too, rather than dealing with words. We have a computer which [is still] in boxes, which is frustrating both of us. And she'll sit for hours with that, and maybe, you know, write a story or something, not just play games on it all the time, which is quite nice.

They started computing very early at her school, and then she came home one day, and I said you know, how are you dealing with computers? And she said, "Oh well, it's just for boys isn't it, computing". And I thought, aha! I thought, oh, here we go, right, let's buy a computer now, it's time I became literate, computer-literate too. So the two of us, we learn together, and we're now, you know, reasonably au fait with the computer. Although I mean she always has more to learn. But I was horrified that she can [pick up the stereotype] at that early age. I feel she has a wonderful role model, this mother who's doing what is traditionally a man's job, and yet she comes away with amazing stereotypes sometimes.

BS: Do you read her stories aloud? Yes, uh-huh, I do nights. *BS: And then does she read?* She will read stories to herself. I will read to her, either a story or a chapter of a kind of book or whatever at night, and then after I've tucked her up and said goodnight she will pick up one of her books and read a little bit to herself. But we both have a pile of books by our beds; neither of us would think of going to bed without a book or two handy. In fact, I begin to get panicky sometimes if I don't have two or three books in the house unread; the idea of not having something to read almost frightens me.

Being Scottish

I think I'm aware that perhaps many or most of your other contributors to M-O would be English, and my Scottishness is a very important part of my . . . I'm very proud to be Scottish, and I want people to know that there are things that are different in Scotland, and Scottish people think differently about things, and very often will do things differently. I spent a couple of periods of my life living in England, when I became aware of my difference from other people sometimes. *BS: Where do you think that comes in the writing? I mean does it make you respond differently to some of the questions?* Well it might do, simply . . . I can't think of any specific examples, but certainly . . . if there was something that I felt it was important to make a point, where there perhaps might be a difference, I would make surely the point. *BS: Does that apply both to content and to language?* Yes. Speaking to you I'm speaking a sort of formal English. I wouldn't perhaps always speak the same way to my daughter and my mother; I would use different language and be a slightly different form. I'm not always aware that I'm doing that; sometimes people will hear me on the phone to my mother and they'll say, "Oh you sound quite different"; my accent also changes, becomes very much more Highland, which is where I'm from originally. I was reading funnily enough a part of my diary just the other night, and I thought that it was strange. I noticed I used the word "trauchle", which is not a word I would use for example if I was thinking of my writing as in any way formal, because it's a sort of language I would use just to, you know, close family or friends.

So, you know, I . . . perhaps because you were coming this had sort of stuck in my mind, that this was something that perhaps, you know, is a little bit different, and this is my own personal value. *BS: In your writing for M-O, are you saying that you write in the way you're now speaking to me?* Yes. *BS: Now what is it about the way we've asked questions, or the way the whole thing is set up that forces that?* I wonder if, it's not so much the M-O and the way you ask questions, it's the education system. Particularly when I was at school, I don't know if it's changing now, but when we were writing and when we were speaking at school it was expected to be standard English; any colloquial or dialect forms were frowned upon. The only time, when I got to my sixth form I did a bit of Scottish literature, and then obviously you know, you had . . . But it was like studying a foreign language, you were still using standard English to write your essays but talking about use of language.

BS: So what . . . what might stimulate your writing for M-O in a more direct form? I don't know if I could. *BS: That's interesting. You feel it's too personal maybe?* Not necessarily too personal. I think . . . just in order to be understood. I'm not sure, you know . . . well, for example the word "Trauchle", it was meaningless to you, so [it's a question] of communication. It's not so much personal, I mean I will speak to colleagues and to friends and use words that I wouldn't use to you. I think it's just the fact that I've had instilled into me that you know, when you're writing you do sort of formally, you don't write in dialect.

I do try and explain words to my daughter; you know, I'll say to her, you know, we say such-and-such, but you know . . . We had trouble with the drains the other day by the side of the road, and I said well, and we used to call them branders, and you know . . . So, I think it's important that, you know, different dialects don't completely die out. Although you know, television and mass media are doing their best. *BS: I presume then, that what you had in mind, an audience for this stuff, is in a sense English?* Yes, yes, uh-huh . . . But then that's a thing that we come across all the time up here. The ideas coming from London and the South of England, things are interpreted in a way that we may not interpret them ourselves up here. And so you know, a lot of our thinking is sort of . . . you know, dominated by this, the news, the media is centralised in London, the big newspapers and so on. So we have this kind of thinking forced on us really. *BS: Yes. But then, there's a sort of internalisation which we all do, so in a way you've internalised the notion that Mass-Observation is essentially an English thing; you're writing for the English audience. Which it doesn't have to be. And supposing it were based in Edinburgh, or even better, up in the Highlands, do you think you would write differently to there?* I might do, yes, uh-huh. Yes I think you know, if something was going to a chiefly Scottish archive I might change the way I said things. *BS: You think of it as an English archive?* Oh yes, uh-huh.

BS: So would there be questions that you might want M-O to ask, that would allow Scottishness to come through to history as it were? Yes, I think that there are things to explore there, you know. Our cultural identity is in danger of being swamped from London and the South. And yet, if you don't embrace the ideas from there, you're in danger of being thought of as belligerent.

BS: Are you saying in fact, I'm putting words in your mouth but are you saying that in a way you exclude your Scottishness from your M-O activity, or would that be going too far? I think perhaps partly I do. I think . . . I don't know how to put it, perhaps in order to be taken seriously people have to be less Scottish, or maybe more sort of British or international or whatever. But then, one of the reasons that maybe I started writing was because I thought well, I am Scottish and I have something different to offer; I'm not down in, you know, the South of England, where I for some reason imagine people, lots of the people might . . . well, there's a big population down there, so why shouldn't a lot more people do this than the others. I felt well no, you know, maybe I am slightly different from your average writer.

I mean if I was to start writing in dialect, would I then have to put a glossary at the end of the piece, or would it be just . . . You know, sort of . . . remain in blissful ignorance, and never know what various words or phrases meant. *BS: Well, who's the "you"? I mean people reading in a hundred years' time may have trouble with some of the south-eastern terms.* Of course, yes . . . Well I think I would assume that the way everything's developing, what is likely to last is what, you know, the majority of people are embracing, which is you know, the culture from England and from the south-east, and that is more likely to survive. *BS: You are sort of assuming that a historian who is reading this stuff is also going to be from the south-east.* Well, the probability is that, it's likely. *BS: So we're not making much of a contribution here to Scottish history.* No. *BS: You didn't come to it in the way that, you had a sort of sense of Scottishness in the back of your mind, and of ordinariness as well, but you didn't have a sense of genderness at the point of writing, that stimulated you to write.* No I don't think so.

Making Lists

I'm a great list maker. People laugh at me at work; every day I go into work and I have a list of, it's either things to do, or lists of shopping I have to get, or I have to remember to phone, or . . . anything. And I'll have a list for that day and I'll maybe have written on another piece of paper somewhere a list of things to do, you know, especially at the end of the week, and another piece of paper tucked away in my diary, there might be a list or two, of maybe measurements of different rooms or numbers of rows of wallpaper. I'm continually jotting things down on odd scraps of paper. I'm very often losing these scraps of paper. I sometimes think, why don't I just get a notebook and put them all in this little notebook. I get great satisfaction from, as I accomplish each thing, or buy a pound of apples, or whatever . . . Then when I've actually got through a list at the end of the day—I don't always, you know, there's usually a few things to carry on the next day [talking from other part of room] . . . there's a couple over there, there's another one here for tomorrow. That's the one for Friday already. Here, this paper here. Usually it's the backs of envelopes, or . . . you know, anything that is handy for writing a list on. A receipt from a shop, or . . . It's got to be a little piece of paper so that, if it's any bigger I wouldn't be able to stuff it in my pocket or my purse or whatever so easily, and have them with me all the time.

I may use a different colour ink if I want something to stand out, something that's important, or you know, maybe put it in a box or something you know, so . . . or a different script, maybe capitals.

I have a calendar on the wall through there, and I also have, you know, a Filofax in which I will write appointments and so on. I'll make a conscious effort to ensure it's on everything, because if it's only on one thing and I forget to look at that, and just look at something else and I forget . . .

You know, I was quite bemused, I thought I wonder why you want to come and speak to me, because I don't find writing easy, and I don't do much of it, and I thought well . . . *BS: Yes, I'm delighted we found you, because that's exactly what makes you interesting.* So you know, I thought well, you know, once I've explained that to you, you will probably be away, you know!

MR RUSSELL
(R1671)

Mr Russell was born in what he describes as a "pebble dash semi" near Watford in 1940. He became a mature student at the University of Sussex in the late 1960s after having had a series of manual jobs. He lives in a Lancashire town with his partner, having recently given up his post teaching Media Studies in order to write full-time. He was interviewed by Brian Street at Mr Russell's home on 5 December 1992.

Why I Write For M-O

UWR> I have every reason in the world for writing for M-O. I first came across it as an ignorant but curious teenager haunting second-hand bookshops. I suppose I paid threepence or sixpence for those Penguin and Gollancz collections on the thirties and the war. One was called *Puzzled People* (I still have it). It attracted me because I was a puzzled person—stone puzzled. Those books started to make real for me a recent past which had formed me but which I knew very little about. I also discovered that ordinary people are not blind slaves but can project a knowledge of the world in "good sense" terms, hence possess the potential to change it, so I have never been able to believe that "history is a process without an agent". I was delighted when I had the chance to contribute, especially as—for once—my motives weren't mixed but complementary. <UWR

I found it amusing, partly because there was something winningly daft about the original project, and partly because I felt I always have been a mass observer . . . I've always been an observer rather than a participant, a people watcher, almost a permanent eavesdropper on situations. When you're writing you're testing skills, I mean you have technical problems to solve in writing that you don't when you just hang in, or spying on people.

UWR> Objectively, I see the work of the archive as vital, and if it's starved to death for the lack of a cash sum that wouldn't buy a bomb to murder Iraqis with, it won't be the least disgrace of the last twelve years. At the same time it provides an expressive channel for my vanity, egomania and self-obsession and for the erotic-aesthetic satisfactions of writing. In short, I'm writing my autobiography, and it will gain value and significance precisely because it won't stand alone as the record of a single, ignominious 20th-century life but will enjoy a collective, historically-based context. <UWR

Its Value

UWR> The Owl of Minerva flies at dusk, and there may be uses for the archive's material that can't be imagined now. Historians will have their own checklist, that of a specialised discipline. My own belief, or hope, is that M-O may help form the basis of a counter-history some day, when the rainbow dazzles away the misery and terror of the modern dark age. The words of the peasants of the Middle Ages are lost to us, swallowed up in the silence of an enforced illiteracy. What did they think, when they trooped in for Mass under the censorious eyes of a fat priest or burned a greedy lord's castle? The experience of the French Revolution comes to us mainly via the rhetoric of lawyers in the Assembly. How did a landless worker from the provinces feel as he or she listened to Camille Desmoulins calling for justice in the gardens of the Palais-Royal? There have been some illuminating re-inventions, but we always need more clues, more worm's-eye ideograms. M-O has a record of commitment to something more than formal scholarship or record-keeping. I remember that the faintly opprobrious label "history from below" was placed on the kind of work Sussex was instrumental in making happen. Fucking right on, I say. I'd rather have that sort of history than history written by eminent ass-lickers, honours-junkies and apologists for state crimes. <UWR

Sense of Audience

UWR> The most difficult aspect of writing for me—its heart of darkness—is the sense of an audience. I tend to take an "I write as I please" approach. No harm in that, I suppose, as long as it doesn't lead you into the self-indulgence and obscurity of a purely internal address—yet since I am hoping to sell a popular novel, it's crucial that my frame of reference coincides with a lot of other people's. But, though I claim no special integrity as an author and certainly have no message for the world, I would find it impossible to write in sheer bad faith to an external formula. It would bore me, and boredom would stop me writing. Mexican stand-off, right? You just have to hope that you're somehow in tune with the zeitgeist. It can be done. George V. Higgins, for instance, does technically innovative things with the novel, but he's found a big market. OK, I'm dodging the question. I've no distinct image at all of the appearance or personalities of the workers at M-O, and no common stereotype to draw on. Probably they're not as tiresome as their infatuation with the word "directive" suggests. I sort of take it for granted they'll get my jokes. I think of my responses as being delivered to a building that I remember well, on the steps of which I learned that Robert Kennedy was dead. Summer of 68. I'd had a coupla bevies in Falmer House [student union building]. You know. Other than that-very well, I'll confess. Don't hit me again. M-O is gendered for me. Since I made a private contract not to exercise self-censorship when writing for M-O, and since I have never given my confidences to men, at some poeticised level what I imagine myself doing is writing to a woman. <UWR

One of the great benefits is that I'm speaking to a stranger all the time, to this anonymous outfit on the Falmer campus, and I feel a lot less inhibited than I would do in conversation. I mean I would say one of the reasons I write is that I always find that I have much greater control over language when I'm writing; when I'm speaking I'm tongue-tied. The point I was making about addressing a stranger was, in fact in a sense you can please yourself, you don't have to adopt your address and vocabulary and behaviour and so on, in the way that you do under the usual everyday social pressures. I think what I said in my written reply to that directive was that I can do it best by imagining that I'm talking to a woman, so it becomes a kind of ideal woman reader. *BS: Does that mean that you craft a style then that is in some way male in order to respond to this woman as the reader? Is there some kind of symbiosis going on there?* I think there probably is, I don't think that can be avoided. But I mean if I were to incarnate the reader it would certainly be G [partner]. I think what I'm probably doing is creating a mythical self in the act of writing. You know, face to face you have many fewer defences than you do when you address people via written language at a distance, and it enables you to try out identities and adopt poses, and play around a lot. I mean a big element of writing for me is playing.

I think I've come to be a writer, and M-O is one facet of that.

The Process of Getting Started

I usually start by making lots of scornful jokes about Mass-Observation, and then I read through the directive, and in fact that has to happen, because the sort of pre-production part of it is intuitive and it relies I think upon letting your subconscious ferment away for a while, and finally you tap the subconscious at the moment when you're ready to write. And a lot of things in it of course surprise you. I also am inclined to pick books off shelves and read around the topic as well. *BS: You've got a notion at the moment of being ready to write. How do you know when that point has come? Is it sort of something welling up, some sort of hydraulic sort of pressure somehow?* No it's more like going to the lavatory (laughing). You know, and if I'm ready for a dump then I find my fingers moving over the keys. But if I sit there for ten minutes and I haven't got anything on the screen I forget it and go away and start again later.

Where I Write

UWR> I write in the upstairs study, formerly just the "spare bedroom", but since I unchained myself from employment primarily where I work I've redesigned it specifically to suit my needs. These include (in no special order):

1. At least two sources of indirect lighting.
2. Radio & cassette player.
3. Plenty of ashtrays.
4. Ample shelf space for books and files.
5. A wallboard for ephemera.
6. Ornaments, pictures, flowers (dried), familiar objects.
7. Pens, stationery, etc. in neurotically excessive amounts.

I write at a white Habitat workstation, and keep on a matching low trolley my tobacco, reading glasses, ashtray, tapes and whatever documents I need to refer to when word-processing. My chair is a throw-out from G's college, a typist's chair on castors with a swivel seat and adjustable backrest. It suits me fine though apparently it doesn't conform with some lumbar health regulation. I did have it recovered in a silver-grey Dralon to blend with the rest of the furnishings. The PC is a Mac Plus. It totally blows me away because, though I actually use very few of its manifold functions, it has made a world of difference to my relationship with writing. At the technical level, this rests above all on the editing fluency I can achieve. But to me, a word-processor isn't a high-tech machine. It's a piece of primitive magic and a love-object. I'm not even slightly interested in how it works, and I have read almost nothing of the absurd, heavy-duty, user hostile manuals that came with it. My pet name for it is Garbo, because the only analogue for its fascination in my cultural experience is the greatest, most incandescent and most mysterious of all Hollywood stars. I hate writing in longhand, and almost never write (except in my head) when I'm away from Garbo. But we're never parted for long. <UWR

The Feeling of Writing

I guess it's just the best thing aside from sex, drugs and rock and roll. I mean in terms of its feel-good factor. I tend to work in two-hour stretches. I find that two hours is about as long as my concentration on any given task usually lasts. *BS: Do you review it and change it?* Yes, I mean that has to be done because of the way I work, and using a word processor has made a lot of difference to that; it's much easier to try something out that may not work. I mean you don't lose a lot of time and energy doing that on a word processor, you're not filling a wastebasket or rejecting scraps of paper. It's a production process

Well when it's finished, as far as M-O is concerned, it goes straight in the mail. And then I send a copy to a chum in Yorkshire. *BS: Do you think about them later, and think about what revisions you might have done?* I do, but I have to keep that to a minimum because it interferes, and that's why I don't keep copies of it.

BS: If M-O weren't there, would there be a hole? No, I always think that there would be a hole in M-O without me actually! (laughs). I think [I write for M-O] partly, just for a second not to be flippant, but partly a genuine commitment to the M-O project. I like it, I always liked reading the books, and it seems to me that it's a kind of unique institution that ought to be kept going. *BS: What kind of role do you think it's played so far in that?* Well it's got to be a people databank. I mean a specialised area right outside my own kind of limited sphere of knowledge. I mean it's [up to] guys like you to, and women, to do the scholarly thing with it. It's got to be a kind of fun factory it seems to me, with all that stuff coming in. I think I'm just an old soft Leftie, and I believe in letting the people's voice be heard, and there is a kind of history that is far too reliant I think on, you know, documents that simply retell the discourse of big cheeses.

I think one of the big topics to be aired in the last probably twenty years or so is the notion of subjectivity; I think it's sometimes been aired in a pretty unhelpful way, but I think you've got to look at that received notion of the individual as some kind of completely separate and atomised entity. And try and understand what kind of social values, and prescriptions, and also what kind of social defiance are involved in what's seen to be individual identities and choices. I mean you know, it opens up one of the big big topics of all time.

Past Life and Influences

I mean I think a lot of the way I am now is probably due to the fact that I was out of formal education for ten years, and therefore when I came to it, which was largely because I failed at everything else (laughing), it had a different meaning for me. I mean my Sussex days stand out very, very vividly in my mind, but I didn't experience Sussex as an eighteen- or nineteen-year-old straight from school, I experienced it initially as a 27-year-old, and spent quite a few years in unskilled manual occupations. And I think it was a huge advantage to me, to be in that situation, both because I was sort of more clued up and discriminating about how I could use it, and also because there was a lot of it I just couldn't take seriously.

I think primarily that between 1957 when I was chucked out of school, and 1967 when I went to Sussex, I piled up a lot of experience, but I had very limited channels of expression for it. I mean in a sense what I am doing now, although not literally or exactly so, is sort of recalling that experience and transforming it in language. Because the only kind of novel I want to write is a thriller, and in particular a sort of low-life thriller, so I've still got a kind of memory bank of the kind of London demi-monde of the late Fifties and early Sixties, about which I have no nostalgia, they're just a kind of texture in my mind, that I feel I can reproduce and give a contemporary dressing to.

I had nowhere to go with it at the time. I was pretty disempowered as far as language and self-expression were concerned. And I had always sneered at formal education as ghastly memories of school, but at Sussex, in effect I was being paid to write. I turned up twice a week to tutorials, with an essay, you know, that I would read and have discussed, and you know, bit by bit I began to see that I was actually writing quite good essays, that I shouldn't think of myself as someone who was blocked. One lecture and I think we had . . . as a rule two tutorials a week, and I was writing regularly, and I had no problems about that, I loved it. Two 3,000-word essays a week. You took nine finals papers then, and you did an additional kind of own-time long essay. I think it was the year before they moved more towards some kind of continuous assessment, and relied less on exams or whatever. I felt I was lucky, because exam conditions, which are I think insanely unfair, benefited me because I was a quick thinker, and I had learnt to put words together fast, and I was quite a good bullshitter. I could write exam papers that seemed to imply I knew a lot of stuff that was just off the page.

BS: *Was there anything more on that one that you felt you wanted to say, how a person's past life has influenced their writing processes?* Well, in a general sense, you know, I think I'm one of those people who has extreme difficulty in separating their fantasy and their real lives, and a lot of that's got to do with the fact that a lot . . . my mid-teenage years I was a kind of obsessive reader. Books are the great salvation if, as was the case with me, you felt like a real cuckoo in the family nest. I was always a chronic, although fairly indiscriminate reader. I certainly wasn't the dedicated self-improver.

Arrangement of Books

There's a loose pattern of organisation. The books in this room are American or America-related books, because in this particular fantasy space, I am a fantasy American, so to speak! And it was reading American literature that first gave me some idea of what writing could be. The next room is G's study, and has her books, which are mainly work-related, she's head of English at XXX. The bedroom has a shelf beside the bed, which is all thrillers, and mainly American thrillers, and they are alphabetic every so often when I get around to putting all the loose ones back and arranging them. The books in the spare room are . . . well they're spare room books, spare books, books that, you know, are somehow miscellaneous, or an overflow from somewhere else, so they are as it were in a class of all unclassifiable objects.

Ground floor. One bookcase devoted to books on media and film. Some shelves with larger books on them, including some vital reference books. And more shelves that contain things like biographies of media stars and books that contain things I've done. And in the large bookcase are a collection of Modern Library books that I used to collect, but again are surplus from elsewhere.

[The arrangement] certainly has to do with the physical character of the objects, like some books won't fit on certain shelves and have to be put on others . . . But that could apply across the categories. When we moved here for the first time in my life I just took a whole load of books to the Oxfam shop. I was building up a kind of anal nostalgia about books, and Christ, the number of books in there, a nightmare. So, I did some weeding and got rid of a lot. I had accumulated books for years, because I used to haunt second-hand bookshops. I've still got plenty of books that occasionally when I reopen them have the Sussex University Bookshop stamp in them. In general . . . I don't think of books as commodities that have an emotional meaning for me. Some of them do acquire an emotional meaning, I mean I've got a two-volume dictionary there, published in 1927, and it's quite a beautiful object, and it's still a thoroughly useful dictionary.

MR REED
(R450)

Mr Reed is from the East End of London. He left school in 1940 when he was fourteen years old and had no formal education beyond that. He worked as a builder until he took an early retirement at 57. At the time he was interviewed, he was living with his wife, brother-in-law, daughter and granddaughter in a small council housing flat. David Bloome interviewed Mr Reed at his home in London on 10 March 1993. Mr Reed was a member of a writing group, the Plaistow Poets, which produced a poetry anthology. One of his poems, "How Can Poppies Bloom in Plaistow?" follows:

HOW CAN POPPIES BLOOM IN PLAISTOW?
How can poppies bloom in Plaistow,
Glowing red among the grain,
Caressed by salty marshland breezes
And gently falling rain?
How can woodlands rise in meadows green
And bankside ferns drift down
To linger by the waterside
In some dockland Canning Town?
How can skylarks sing and serenade
The hedgerows damp and still
In early morning summer haze
By some old water mill?
How can craggy rocks and lonely pines
Invigorate my soul,
A soul of insignificance
That knows no other goal?
How can we reach this freer world
And touch its vibrant self
Where shallow streams and darkened pools
Add to nature's wealth?
How can we feel the urge of spring
And watch the leaves unfold
And shelter us through summer skies
Until they turn to gold?
After a while we close our eyes
And lock our thoughts away.
Our hearts are too encumbered
With some promise yet to be.
We turn instead to the friendly smile
We'll find by the firelight glow,
The smile on the face of someone we love
Can compensate where poppies can't grow.

Writing Poetry and Letters

Writers are solitary people, they're not mixers, they're loners, really, aren't they, writers, they don't like to be with the crowd all the time. People, that's why I left the building game . . . they're very brutal. We were renovating a building near the *Mirror* [newspaper] offices and I went in a pub on Fleet Street coming home from work and asked for a pint of beer and they said, "Sorry, no service". And I couldn't believe it. And I wrote to my MP and he wrote back saying, "In some cases if the governor doesn't want you in the pub he can [refuse you]". So I thought in the end it must have been because I was a building worker. Cause building workers look different. Building workers stand out in the city, I don't know why, you look different.

I write to newspapers—never get accepted. I used to write letters, they were never printed. They'd write back an acknowledgement saying we can't print this. I used to put it straight . . . on the nub of what it was. I wouldn't mince words, you know, I used to get annoyed and I'd write. But they wouldn't never print my letters.

Once my daughter was on her bike and a man knocked her off when he opened his car door. I wrote a letter to my MP but I didn't post it . . . to ask could in future all drivers get off, out of their cars on the inside, because every time I go on that main road on my bike I'm dead scared.

I was working in the town centre and I started getting songs coming through, so I thought I'd put them down. First one I wrote was "The old are not only the lonely". I've been listening to songs all my life and love music. I like songs that have some meaning . . . they don't come at once, the whole thing, and I start getting them late at night when everything is quiet. I wrote them all down, and I've got music with them. The melody came as with the words. I can't write music, and if I could I'd submit [them]. I should go to Tin Pan Alley and get a man who does manuscripts for ten pound or twenty quid and I'd put one on recording and he'd give me the manuscript at the end of it. I once got a record made in America. I saw an ad for it in one of those books, like "True Crime" or something—I used to buy a lot of them—I sent away to America, Boston, Four Star Music Company or something. They wanted thirty quid for just a manuscript. And this one, Four Star, I got the record back. It was to Grieg's music, the "Loneliness of Autumn", and I gave it to a man in Tin Pan Alley, who was an agent, and I never seen him again. I lost that record (laughs).

I write short stories, silly stories, you know, poetry, I was with a poetry group. They've got my book [*The Plaistow Poets*] in the [M-O] archive. See, when I was on the building site at Trafalgar Square . . . every morning I'd come out Charing Cross Station and there were all the derelicts under the arches . . . down and outs . . . so I used to give them cigarettes, because they liked cigarettes, and I took one boy into a shop, a newspaper shop opposite the station, and the lady said, "Get him out of here". And I said, "Ten cigarettes", and I gave him two. And then I wrote "Avenues of Hope and Glory by the Streets of Sad Despair" because we were out on Northumberland Avenue . . . It's such a paradox of life, I couldn't believe it, that it got so close. You know, you used to think of derelicts as being out in the suburbs, but now they were encroaching the very top notch areas. So I wrote this poem, it came to me, and I wrote it right through, straight away. It flowed.

AVENUES OF HOPE AND GLORY
Avenues of hope and glory
By the streets of sad despair
We passed in whispered dignity,
Pretending they're not there, not there.
Their eyes cry silent charity
To strangers who don't care
And the shadows whisper softly,
'Are you hungry? are you bare?'
Will there be a bright tomorrow?
Had I a mother yesterday?
Hell hath not haunted features
Like broken-bottle alleyway.
Did I meet them in some foreign field
When they were young and free?
Did I share their uniform to fight
Forgotten enemy?
I close my eyes and pity
A land that doesn't care,
With avenues of hope and glory
By the streets of sad despair.
Did we plan their world of sorrow
Where I pass them every day?
Was that the broken brother
Whose wife they stole away?
Am I making some amendments
Placing statues in the park?
Close my eyes and I don't see them when
It's cold and midnight dark.
The city lights are gleaming,
Laughing lovers everywhere
On avenues of hope and glory
By the streets of sad despair.
Avenues of hope and glory,
The streets of sad despair—
I could write a similar story
Of nations everywhere
Where progress and compassion
Go their separate ways-
Cold hearts and stony statues
Proud hearts and lonely shadows
In ragged streets of yesteryear.

Writing for the M-O Project

DB: When did you begin writing for M-O? In 1981, I saw the advertisement on television. And I thought, "I like writing". *DB: What do you do when the directive from M-O arrives?* I put it away in my drawer next to my desk. *DB: Does anyone else see it?* Nobody else sees it, the directive is personal to my thoughts and leanings. I take it up to the bedroom because I like the privacy of reading it slowly. Once I've read it I know what I must do. My mind will fill up with the directive, and as I start on it my mind will whirl around with all the ideas that they're asking questions about. My ideas are formulated, every time I see anything, so all I've to do is write it down. I don't even have to think about it. I want to get it right. I want to get right on to the nub of it, grasp it properly, what they're asking, and work it all out. It'd take awhile, I'd keep thinking about it. It'd go for days. And then once I'd got writing, it all flows through.

I have to give my version of things, I couldn't otherwise, although I knew it was going to the wrong, like the directive [suggested by] the BBC, I knew it was going to the wrong people to read it. Cause I know when my mind's made up, we're all made up, aren't we, we're all indoctrinated. I know my ideas are way out, way over the top, really, I know I'm out on a limb, cause I can't I don't think like the majority. See, I'm an oddball, really. I'm going to be taken down to the Tower of London for my subversive feelings.

DB: You mentioned something about not being able to be totally truthful [in response to the directive sent by the BBC], because you knew it was coming from the establishment. Well, I know what the makeup is, what they'd expect of people. I know what they'd expect to hear. They only want to hear what they want to hear. So, it's not good for me voicing an opposing opinion, because they'd scrap around it. They'd say, "Right we won't read the one, it's too subversive". See, you can't get through to established people. *DB: In response to the directive from the BBC?* I wrote back shortly, quickly. I didn't give a lot of depth to it. I didn't like to give a lot of depth to it because it just wasn't worth the while. *DB: Before you start writing for the M-O, do you discuss your ideas with anyone else?* Never do I discuss my ideas with anyone—I am living in a desert! I have mentioned that I write for M-O with absolutely no feedback whatsoever from anyone. People are definitely more wrapped up in themselves than ever before. I never show my writing to anyone. I would be ostracised by their jealousy that I could put two words together. People read me as an illiterate. I wait until I get a terrible urgency for writing that builds up over a period when frustrations at the sick world we live in get too much-I am probably a world changer! It has given me a marvellous confidence writing for M-O and I feel I have an audience for all my petty qualms . . . It is a platform that a working man would never have in his everyday life, exhilarating—like my songs which nobody ever hears, but which are wonderful tonic to me. When writing for the M-O I'm getting myself across in a way to an audience, although it's archives, you're speaking to a group.

I used to try to open people up, like a journalist might want to know what they think about something. Cause you have to when you write a directive, you keep your ears open, to know what the general feeling is, of the populace at that time on certain subjects. Nobody wants to tell you, closed books, aren't they, people here.

DB: *What if a directive didn't come on a topic you're interested in?* I would write a personal letter in front of (my writing) to Dorothy. A covering letter, a general topic at that time, about how I feel about certain things.

DB: *In your opinion, what is the value of writing and of the M-O project?* The value is of the utmost importance—if only the proletariat had had a voice in Rome—our world might have come right sooner. If only people were more open and simply honest as Jesus seems to have been instead of aping the monetarists throughout history. We must be heard to know we didn't all condone cardboard city with the queen making a million interest every week on her capital investments—some of us did cry for Whom the Bells Toll. Some of us were genuine humanists who decried fox hunting and animal experiments and third world or any world poverty.

Writing in the East End

I marvel at people who write books, how they can set them out into different characters and follow the characters through . . . to get that intricate thing about people that makes a certain person tick. It's marvellous.

DB: *Do you think of yourself as a writer?* No. DB: *Who do you think of as a writer?* Thomas Hardy. Marvellous . . . I can write anywhere, preferably in bed. I cannot write unless absolutely isolated. I write all at once, once the mood arrives. I never keep copies, never look back—always tomorrow. I do feel taken over by a more literate being and don't quite understand it—it is probably my large alter-ego trying to break out. I like to write . . . suddenly, after you've put it all into your mind, what questions are asked, suddenly, once you get going writing, it all comes flowing. And the words come through, words I wouldn't normally use in conversation. I express myself better in writing than I could ever do in conversation . . . talking to people I'm not so good as I am with writing, see, it builds up, it comes through . . . all different phrases comes through I never use normally . . . it doesn't sound like me.

I've got a little dictionary. I've written so many words in it I've found, and it's lovely, it's very precious to me, it's got every little word I come across I write across the top of the page. Full of it. It's such a lovely little collection.

DB: Do you speak the truth as lots of people see it? The ordinary people. The working man. I don't relate to the world out there. See, I'm isolated really. When I used to go to work every day and meet all [the] obstacles, you know, brick walls. I was like a sore thumb, really, because I couldn't relate to the general public's thinking. The mass thinking, I couldn't do that. I used to think things out all the time, I'm too analytical. Yesterday I stood in a queue for butter, we get butter once a month with our books. So I was in this queue and they're all people who have retired. And I heard some terrible conversations, I couldn't join in because I was anti to what I was hearing. They were talking about those children, the Sudanese, on telly night before last. Old woman says to this other lady, "Did you see all those flies on that child", she says, "made me feel sick". And I thought, "What did that child feel?" You know people are for their own, something's missing in people, I don't know what it is. There's so little compassion about, especially the East End, it's a hard place, East End.

SECTION III
Ordinary People Writing

Introduction to Section III

So far, we have provided an historical context for Mass-Observation writing and a series of "dialogues". The discussion of the historical context highlighted the institutional history, its interdisciplinary effort to create an anthropology and history of ourselves, and later a personal anthropology and collective life history, and it highlighted the intellectual debate that, simply put, asked what kind of knowledge was Mass-Observation and of what use. The historical context was not, of course, specific to Mass-Observation but reflects struggles and debates at the time. Thus, to some extent, the history of Mass-Observation is a mirror that brings into focus the controversies defining writing in society at a particular time. The dialogues in Chapter 5 showed the diverse ways in which people write for Mass-Observation, how such writing fits into their lives, and what meanings and social consequences it has for them. The cases provide a way to view Mass-Observation and writing as a peopled process, full of the broad range of human activities, dilemmas, goals, emotions, contradictions, loyalties, ambiguities and complexities that make up people's lives. At the same time, the dialogues reveal social group dynamics—the need expressed by several of the women to find or create a social and physical space for writing, the desire to create a "voice" and a history for ordinary people, to highlight their lives and not just the lives of kings and their battles.

In this Section (Chapters 6, 7 and 8), we build on the dialogues presented in Section 2 as well as on other data we collected, to discuss what we believe are key issues in the study of writing and literacy in contemporary British society (and elsewhere). Although we may discuss these issues in the jargon of our academic disciplines, in most cases these are issues that the Mass-Observation correspondents have identified themselves. These issues are: the uses of writing in everyday life (Chapter 6), and personhood, power and the creation of social space for writing (what we call "Crossings", see Chapter 7). In Chapter 8 we bring together many of the issues discussed throughout the book.

Each of the issues in this section cuts two ways. First, as we have noted earlier, it cuts against what we take to be dominant views of writing and literacy. The dominant discourses in education, business, government and elsewhere present illiteracy and aliteracy on the one hand or high literature and culture on the other. The real everyday practices that may make up most of the writing that goes on are invisible. But there is another sense in which writing is invisible, which is in the representations of the writing process itself. These, too, are invisible. There is very little attention paid to the notion that the people who do it themselves have ideas about it. Our discussion of the uses of writing cuts against the invisibility of everyday writing practices and against the dominant discourse that views writing and literacy as a continuum from illiteracy to "high literature". Similarly, the dominant discourse simplifies the relationship of writing to power and negates a relationship between writing and identity. The simple equation is a technical one: writing well provides access to power; in writing one can express oneself. Not only are these equations oversimplified, they are deceptive. They promote a stance that all we need to do to remove inequity and improve our material and social conditions is learn how to write well. But what does writing "well" mean? Who gets to decide? Could everyone actually be viewed as writing well? If everyone did write well, would inequity disappear? Would we all have access to power? And what power is it that we would have access to? Power to do what? Who would decide? Deceptive also is the relationship of writing and knowledge promoted by dominant discourses in most of our major social institutions. They imply and make seem natural that knowledge exists, waiting to be discovered or learned, and that writing is a "transparent" vehicle for communicating that knowledge. Thus, the first cut is against the conceptions of writing promulgated by dominant discourses.

The second cut is a creative one—not creative in the sense of artistic or talented, although these characteristics may be involved, but creative in the sense of creating and transforming "worlds". The writing people do both for Mass-Observation and elsewhere in their lives is not just resistance to a dominant discourse, such as the omission of ordinary people in official histories. It is also the creation and the transformation of the worlds in which people live. Through their writing they are creating social contexts—webs of meaning, affect and social relationships—which they and others inhabit, not in isolation of other "worlds", but in addition.

6
The Uses of Writing

> It will no longer do to think of writing as a mechanical manipulation of grammatical codes and formal structures leading to the production of perfect or perfectible texts. Reading and writing are not unitary skills nor are they reducible to sets of component skills falling neatly under discrete categories (linguistic, cognitive); rather, they are complex human activities taking place in complex human relationships. (Jay Robinson, 1987, p. 329)

We begin this chapter with a brief discussion of ordinary people writing. When asked, many of the Mass-Observation correspondents defined themselves and those who wrote for the Mass-Observation Project as "ordinary people". It is not easy to define what an ordinary person is, but at least one implication of the discussions we had with the Mass-Observation correspondents around the issue of ordinary people writing is that they believe that the voice and contribution of ordinary people is often missing from official histories and characterisations of Britain. We follow that discussion with a description of the broad range of uses of writing listed by the Mass-Observation correspondents we interviewed. That description establishes the social fact of ordinary people who are thoughtful about their writing, reflect on both what they write and how they write, and write in a broad range of genres for a broad range of purposes. Then, we describe uses and genres of writing associated with the Mass-Observation Project.

Our purpose is to show how the Mass-Observation Project creates a particular social context for writing that, on one hand, provides a forum and set of uses for writing that are otherwise unavailable to ordinary people, yet on the other it creates a context that is both sufficiently ambiguous and indeterminate to allow participants (including the Mass-Observation correspondents, the staff of the

Archive, researchers, the general public) to co-define the Mass-Observation Project. The argument we make here is not that the Mass-Observation Project is unique because it is a people's history or a people's ethnography-since there are other social and life history projects and other people's ethnography projects. But rather the social context for writing that the Mass-Observation Project has established, and that continues to evolve, is important because of how its uses and genres of writing, including who writes to whom for what purposes with what kinds of legitimacy, are positioned against uses of and genres of writing promoted by other social institutions, both those of the establishment (e.g., government, business, schooling) and those more associated with the private sphere (e.g., family).

The data on which we base our arguments in this chapter come from the full range of responses to the directive on Uses of Writing and Reading [UWR] (where applicable, we note the question on the directive using a Q and the number of the question), the Education Directive of Spring 1991 and other directives, unsolicited materials sent to the Mass-Observation Project by Mass-Observation correspondents, the interviews, histories and descriptions of the Mass-Observation Project (including the history and description presented in Chapters 1, 2 and 3) and the dialogues presented in Chapter 5.

Ordinary People Writing

We found that nearly all of the people we interviewed said that they wrote as an "ordinary" person. An "ordinary" person was primarily defined by what it was *not*, as the excerpts below illustrate.

> I think that media coverage is very poor especially the press which is very right wing. Historians in the future would, I think, get very inaccurate opinions by looking back at today's press. Similarly TV coverage of news events is very sensational/biased—from personal experience I just don't trust what they say. Radio is rather better but leaves much to be desired. Thus, something like the Mass-Observation is valuable in giving an accurate view of what ordinary people rather than the professional media think about events. (P2250, UWR Q10)

> And I thought well I'm fairly ordinary. I think ordinary really, you think of yourself as someone who hasn't perhaps achieved fame, or great success; just live a sort of normal, everyday life, going to work and with your family. . . . Well, the way I tend to think of it is, perhaps that there are some people who have more power in society to change things, in government for instance, and often I think you feel you're ordinary because you don't have this power, and so you have very little influence sometimes over the big decisions, like ecological decisions and world decisions. (M1498, interview)

The definitions given by Mrs Purcell (P2250) and Mrs Martin (M1498) are definitions by exclusion: "ordinary" means not someone with power, fame, success, influence; not the television, radio or professional media.

Many Mass-Observation correspondents see their efforts as a corrective to the professional media and some see their writing as an antidote to the privileges of the rich and powerful who more easily have their voices heard.

> [what] ordinary people rather than the professional media think about events. (P2250, UWR)
>
> The ordinary voice . . . the person who wouldn't have a voice otherwise. (B1106, interview)
>
> We form an antidote to published work, so much of which is propaganda. It seems to me that journalists will write anything that they think will catch people's eye, and politicians etc. always have axes to grind. (C1990, interview)
>
> I don't think ordinary people get the same chance as many perhaps academics, or so-called educated people, and people in the media, to have their say. (M1498, interview)
>
> . . . I think particularly in Britain, because we have a history of a class system, where we've had two different educational systems, there is also a feeling that people who are wealthy, from my point of view, and who have had say a private school education, and material wealth, possibly they have more chance of getting their work published, if that's what they want. So somebody who for instance may come from a powerful family, or a well-known family, their diary might be of interest, and just because simply of who they are they might have it published, or their memoirs, or even their opinions sought, and maybe interviewed on the television for instance. Whereas I would say that so-called ordinary people may never get that kind of attention if you like. (M1498, UWR)

The archival function of the Mass-Observation project and its affiliation with a university provide a way, according to some of the Mass-Observation correspondents, for the writing of ordinary people to be valued. It may also help redress the imbalance between those who are deemed *able* to write, whose writing is worthy of reading and those who are not.

> the value [of writing for the Mass-Observation Project] is for posterity; a living record, as it happens, seen from the eyes of a cross section (hopefully) of ordinary people, with all our prejudices, people of our own time & culture, seen from our own point of view, perhaps revealing how we, at our particular age, see what is

> happening now, or what has happened to us & to others, from our own individual point of view. The very stuff of real history. And, of course, to have it filed & located where researchers can get at it is of vital importance. (E174, UWR Q10)
>
> Up till now, the writings of "ordinary" people have possibly not been valued & certainly not accumulated & stored securely in one place. (B1215, UWR Q10)
>
> Ordinary people writing about their lives. In fifty years time it will be fascinating. That's what history is all about, but the history of ordinary people has to be written while it's happening as there is no surviving source material otherwise. (B1106, interview)

Mrs Burgess (B1215) and Mr Barrow (B1106) link the writing of ordinary people to the provision of source material for future historians. In our interviews with the Mass-Observation correspondents we came to realise how important it was to probe this issue, to better understand how viewing one's writing as "source" materials for future historians might influence both what was written and how it was written. As a result we recorded many views on writing for posterity, including some negative views about "experts", as Mrs Burgess (B1215) below expresses.

> "History" features a few major characters who have the power to change events. I am more interested in the lives of "the masses" over the centuries & their reactions to their situation and major events. The actual writings of our ancestors, in the form of letters and diaries, and interviews with the "man in the street" today are often far more telling or poignant than the learned views of the historian or so-called expert. History is all about flesh & blood people & their emotions, not just a studied evaluation of events. (B1215, UWR)

Mrs Burgess's comments above suggest that she believes that people will be reading the writings of the Mass-Observation correspondents directly, not filtered by historians. Perhaps she has in mind such books as *Wartime Women* (Sheridan, 1990) that included a lot of original, unfiltered writings by ordinary people. Although these books were edited by academics, the large amount of source writing may give the impression of being mostly by ordinary people and, of course, they can be read that way, ignoring the role and commentary of the academic who compiled, selected and ordered the material. However, Mrs Burgess may also have had in mind people going to the Mass-Observation Archive and directly reading the materials there, as school groups do. Also, people can access information about the Mass-Observation Archive and Project—though not the materials themselves—through the Internet. Again, whether through new technology or as part of a course, there is likely to have been an historian or some other academic who has had a hand in shaping what is available and how. Nonetheless, the impression is that one may be able to directly access the writing of ordinary people from past generations. The issue here is intimately although subtly linked with power in a transformative manner. As definitions of writing change and as changes occur in what writing is valued, such changes will be inseparable from changing power relations (see Bloome & Kinzer, 1998; Lankshear & McLaren, 1993).

It may be the case that many Mass-Observation correspondents take a dual or ambiguous stance, viewing their writing as source material while also seeing it as directly addressing a future audience; for example, Mrs Burgess below:

> I believe the Mass Observation Archive will be of great use to students & future historians, providing them with a rich source of material which in previous generations has been scarce. . . . Indeed, its only in recent years that the majority of the population has had the ability to express its views and details of everyday life. (B1215, UWR)

For some Mass-Observation correspondents, the inclusion of ordinary people in the writing of history is not just about having a different point of view on historical events, it is about redefining what is important. For example, as Mrs Friend (F1373) said in Chapter 5:

> I think, you read history books, and mostly they're full of wars aren't they? The Battle of the Roses, the Ten Year War, the Five Year War, the . . . you know, and I don't think that's what history's about, it's about people isn't it, everyday people. I'd have liked to, you know, known perhaps what it was like to be a housewife in Elizabethan days or something like that you know, it's . . . Ordinary, everyday people, they're the people that are important aren't they, not . . . I don't want to learn about wars and . . . what is mostly written in history, it's all battles isn't it? Henry V, and Agincourt and . . . all history, it's all the . . . Or even to the Romans, they don't really even give much . . . You don't really get much about medical history, or how people have developed over the years do you? I mean . . . I suppose years ago they weren't that educated, it was only the rich that was educated wasn't it, so if they didn't write nobody did, nobody got it. And I'd like to think, well I'm . . . I'm putting it down for future generations to listen and read it. (F1373, interview)

Generally speaking, when people describe themselves as "ordinary" they do not mean that they see themselves as representative in a statistical way of the whole population, but they do see themselves as standing for (or representing) a particular voice, or set of voices, which do not as rule get the opportunity to be heard on a public platform.

> I don't say we are representative since there don't seem to be that many people left who can put pen to paper, but certainly several varieties of ordinariness. (C1990, interview)

Yet, there is a sense in which being defined as "ordinary" is vague, more of a place holder waiting on how each writer will define it, rather than a given definition.

> It's very difficult really; I don't think anybody's really ordinary . . . (M1498, interview)

The notion of writing as an ordinary person dichotomises the positions associated with writing—either one is writing as an ordinary person or one is writing from privilege; the privilege of the professional media, class, wealth, fame, political office, and so forth. Writing as an ordinary person for Mass-Observation can be viewed as attempting a reconstitution of a hierarchy of authority; the professional media cannot write about the lives of ordinary people with authority because they are not ordinary people themselves. Of course, there are some who write for the Mass-Observation Project who hold privilege in other spheres of their lives; including professional writers (e.g., novelists, journalists, academics) and people who hold positions of power (e.g., high-ranking executives in major corporations). But when they write for Mass-Observation they do not write from these positions of privilege; indeed, in our interviews it was clear that the writing done for Mass-Observation by people who wrote professionally (i.e., academics, fiction writers) was done differently from their professional writing. Writing for Mass-Observation enabled them to express something different about themselves, more personal, more experimental, more candid.

There may be more to this business of writing as an ordinary person than just shifting from a focus on kings and battles and the writing of academics to everyday events and the writing of non-academics, and more than just acquiring the authority to be heard. There is a sense in which writing about and by ordinary people gives value to ordinary people, makes lives count that are usually lost in aggregations of statistical data for marketing and political purposes.

Viewed from this perspective of giving and claiming value for the lives of themselves and other ordinary people, it makes sense to claim at one and the same time that while people are ordinary, as M1498 stated (quoted earlier), no one is really ordinary. And, as Mrs Wright (W632) points out, whereas each person's experiences are unique, in another sense they are not:

—as unique as your first kiss—everybody else experiences it as well so it's not. I don't mean that it's unique to you personally, but it draws on your history, your family, feelings, your emotions. (W632, interview)

A Broad Range Of Uses And Genres Of Writing

The dialogues in Chapter 5 and in the data we have collected demonstrate the prevalence of a broad range of uses and genres of writing: poetry, short stories, shopping lists, letters to friends, family, and newspapers, genealogies, lists of things to do, diaries, reports, among others. We view the broad range of genres and uses of writing as a social fact about life in contemporary Britain worth noting, among other reasons, to counter prevailing popular and mass media images of an aliterate and illiterate society.

The Mass-Observation correspondents write for the Mass-Observation Project, but also some write as part of their jobs, some write for themselves (for example, to clarify their thinking), and some write for others (for example, to create a record for their children or grandchildren). They write in protest (to newspapers, government officials, businesses) and to maintain social relationships with friends and family. Some belong to poetry writing groups, like Mr Reed (R450), and book groups, some take writing classes and others are involved in clubs and other activities that involve writing (such as local history clubs and letter writing clubs); for example, consider Mrs Smith (S2207, interview):

> [I am engaged in] literacy activities [with Woodcraft folk and I was involved in a writing class] in doing autobiography and fiction class and I've started writing my life story. . . . I read actually more than I write, . . . I belong to a book group, we meet once a month . . . we choose a book to read and then talk about it. [I also read a newspaper every day] I mean not necessarily cover to cover but I try to skim it at least; and I've always got a book on the go so I try and spend about half an hour a day or so reading it . . . I write the occasional letter; diaries—sometimes I try to keep a regular diary but usually it's just on holidays now, because I find you lose momentum after a while—you start and then it just stops . . . ; occasional letters; and as I say I've been trying to write my life story on and off . . . I just want to get all the basic facts down. (S2207, interview)

The Mass-Observation correspondents not only "do" writing-they are conscious of and reflect on the writing processes they employ. For example, consider Mrs Friend (F1373):

> I make a terrible mess. I sit there and spread all my notes out on the next chair, and then I'll ponder over them and see where it all fits in with what I'm saying. And I might even get reference books out if ... if I need to, if it's something that I'm not really sure. I more or less write it all in one go. I go over it all, and I ... I've got to be happy with it before I send it. I would read it all through, and see if it feels right. I might censor it. Not often that happens, usually I am quite happy with it once it's done; I don't often ... I think I did chop out something once before, but then it means rewriting the whole page both sides you know, but generally it goes right the first time. I think I would censor something if I felt it was too flippant, if I didn't think it was serious enough, you know. After all they don't send me a Mass-Observation for me to make jokes about it, do they? So I would, if I thought that I hadn't treated the subject reverently, then I would delete it and censor it. (F1373, interview)

Although explicit reflections on the writing process were to some extent prompted by our questions, in some cases the Mass-Observation correspondents appear so comfortable with the discussion that it is reasonable to infer they have reflected on the writing process before, and often with great sophistication and sensitivity. For example, Miss Early (E174) from her written response to the Spring 1991 directive on the Uses of Writing and Reading:

> I write to my eldest sister. Of late she has written a lot about our mother and of how she felt they could never understand each other. It seems she felt "left out" whereas I felt she, as the eldest and the next eldest sister were our parents' and grandparents' "real" family and I and my other sister, post 1918 war, were afterthoughts. But it is being revealed that this eldest sister was not treated honestly by my mother. Some family matters were kept from her and we are at this late stage in the process going over these. She obviously needs to write about this and I am trying to help with sensitivity. My other sister, 8 years my senior, I write to in answer to the scrappy little notes she sends me infrequently. My replies are bland, . . . but I try not to mention our eldest sister as the two don't get on even though they live in the same village. (UWR)

Writing has enabled Miss Early to continue to develop and extend her understanding of family relations, and even of events that occurred half a century earlier that she had not understood before. She understands the therapeutic value of writing for her eldest sister. She has insight here into the uses and meanings of literacy in contemporary society that extend well beyond the dominant stereotypes of what writing is for, who does it and how it is done.

The Mass-Observation correspondents often have strong views on what reading and writing should be for. Some, like Mrs Wright (W632), view the reading of literature as a form of escapism, acceptable for pupils but not adults:

> I know I buried myself in books a lot—perhaps I didn't do so much writing then [when I was a pupil learning to write] . . . Escaped into the books instead of thinking my own thoughts . . . I feel as though I've been through that phase and it puzzles me that people are still reading short stories and books, novels—. . . on the trains, and in the smoking room . . . I want to tell them you're escape—you're trying to escape from life (laughs) these short stories are irrelevant you know (W632, interview)

Similar opinions were expressed by Mrs Smith (S2207) when she was interviewed:

> I used to escape into books as a child, very much . . . it was a reassuring other world that I could escape into where I wasn't threatened, and you know when I was shy and found it difficult to talk to people I'd hide behind a book instead, because that was easy. I think probably I relied upon books too much at one stage, you know, being the be-all rather than an accessory (laughs). Well they were more than an accessory, but I think I probably depended on them too much. (S2207, interview)

While only a few of the Mass-Observation correspondents we interviewed expressed opinions about fiction reading similar to Mrs Wright and Mrs Smith, many told us of social practices organised around writing rather than reading. This does not mean that reading and writing activities were not embedded in each other—for example, reading books to get information for writing or writing notes as part of reading—but rather that the interactional scheme for the activity was organised around a particular set of writing or reading practices, and named as such. Thus, Mrs Smith (S2207) described differences between her reading group and her writing group:

> that last book we we've been reading, well, we don't always stick to the subject—we got onto the miners (laughter) . . . it's amazing how discussions can get round, you know, . . . like with Dickens . . . nothing has changed since, you know.
>
> DB: *Do you find that happens with the—in the writing group that you're a part of?*
>
> S: Well, in the writing group you're not into so much sort of discussion

In addition to differences between reading practices and writing practices, the Mass-Observation correspondents are conscious of different genres and of the differences among them. They distinguish between "professional" writing and what they do (e.g., "odd letters to newspapers" and perhaps occasional articles); they talk about "free" writing as opposed to constrained and structured often "work" writing; some describe analytically the different principles underlying work writing and home writing; a number feel they are better on paper than orally; some see writing as a way of "letting off steam", of releasing things that have got bottled up; some (like Mrs Smith below) express views about how certain genres of writing and writing activities provide structure and discipline for themselves:

> I usually prefer to have something to work towards like the life story, or writing something definite or something that we've been set to write for next week in the class. But occasionally something particularly strikes me I'll try to set it down-if I've watched a TV program that's particularly set me off or we've done something unusual I try and get it down. (S2207, interview)

Some of the Mass-Observation correspondents have theories of literacy, about what literacy is:

> I mean literacy is literally the ability to read and write, isn't it? It doesn't have to mean that it's particularly good reading or writing, it's just what you do, whether it's reading the labels on the tins of soup, or writing a shopping list, or whatever. (S2207, Interview)

—and they have theories about the processes involved in writing. For example, Ms Cleer (C2295) in her written response to the Spring 1991 directive gives a quantum theory of writing—if the energy for writing is taken up in one activity, then it cannot be expended on another:

> ... by the time I have completed other necessary writing such as minutes for the committee of which I am secretary or letters, my writing capability is exhausted. (C2295, interview)

Ms Cleer (C2295) also theorised in her response to the Spring 1991 directive:

> I do enjoy writing and Mass-Observation balances out the day. Indeed expressing myself in written form is so necessary to me that if I did not have Mass-Observation to do in this circumstance, I would probably be keeping my intermittent diary or writing a letter to a friend. (C2295, UWR)

To summarise, little attention is typically paid by academia and other dominant institutions to writing in everyday life, it is frequently not even considered to be writing, and the people who produce such writing are not usually considered "writers." The interviews with the Mass-Observation correspondents and their responses to the directive on Uses of Writing and Reading and other data make writing in everyday life "visible" and worthy of note. The data provide evidence for kinds of writing in contemporary society that debunks the view of an aliterate and illiterate society and, at a theoretical level, undercuts the legitimacy of previously dominant assumptions of literacy as a monolithic phenomenon contrasted only with illiteracy. While our data do not let us claim that the uses and genres of writing we found can be generalised to the broader population, our study, when added to previous studies of writing in society (e.g., Barton & Hamilton, 1998; Barton & Ivanic, 1991; Conquergood, 1997; Graff, 1979; Hamilton, Barton & Ivanic, 1994; Heath, 1983; Mace 1995; Maguire et al., 1982), emphasises the variety and complexity of writing practices, both within and across social and cultural groups. Our data also emphasise that people are reflective in the reading and writing they do and how various uses of writing can influence their social life. Returning to the discussion in Chapter 3, the data provide ethnographic insights that are both "subjective" in Malinowski's sense and analytic in a way comparable to the reflexive commentary of contemporary anthropology.

Uses and Genres of Writing Associated with the Mass-Observation Project

In this section, we discuss both the writing done by the Mass-Observation correspondents and the writing practices employed by the staff of the Mass-Observation Project at the University of Sussex. Some of these writing practices were described in Chapters 1 and 2.

The Mass-Observation correspondents write for the Mass-Observation Project for a variety of reasons; and these reasons are part of the context for understanding what the writing is. Among the personal rewards people get from writing for the Mass-Observation Project are (see Sheridan, 1993c, for a more detailed discussion):

1. enjoyment of the reading and writing itself;
2. practice for other writing;
3. a reason and structure to organise or develop their thinking, to help "sort out ideas";
4. refreshing their memories about the past, or to "keep their minds active" (mentioned frequently by older people);

5. communicating with other people (some send copies to friends or let their families read their replies);
6. creating space and privacy for themselves for a "legitimate" goal ("legitimate" in the sense of being publicly acknowledged as allowing one to claim a priority);
7. linking up and identifying with educational activities and ideas;
8. adding to their own status and sense of self-esteem;
9. creating an emotional outlet, or for therapeutic or confessional purposes;
10. finding a safe outlet for political or social views that can't always be expressed in their immediate life;
11. ensuring that their ideas, thoughts and experience can live after their death.

The last reason noted above (11) is mentioned by many people. They speak of writing for posterity, for the future, for their grandchildren, or for people like themselves in future generations. For example, in her interview Mrs Friend (F1373) said:

> When I die, I want to leave things. I don't want to just pop my clogs and they'll say, well, there she goes, cheerio, goodbye. I want them to say, well she wrote a book, she did this writing for Mass-Observation, she knitted me a lovely bedspread, things like that you know. I won't be able to leave any cooking behind will I? I can't leave a cake for posterity! But you know, I'd like to think that there's going to be a lot left of me really . . .

Below, we discuss three issues related to writing for the Mass-Observation Project: (1) how the directives influence what is written and how; (2) Mass-Observation as audience; and (3) how the Mass-Observation correspondents go about responding to a directive. The Mass-Observation correspondents are themselves reflective and insightful on these issues.

How the Directives Influence Writing

At the beginning of each directive, and often at the beginning of each section of each directive, there is an introductory paragraph explaining and contextualising the questions or tasks that follow it. Following Halliday's (1978) heuristic for explicating the context of situation, namely, field, tenor and mode, these introductory paragraphs can be viewed as contextualising the directive tasks in three important ways. First, they locate the content asked for in a broader field or set of experiences. Second, they establish and maintain an interpersonal relationship (or tenor) between the Mass-Observation correspondents and the Mass-Observation Project staff, and in particular Dorothy Sheridan, the present Archivist (and before her David Pocock, when he was director of the Mass-Observation Project). As part of establishing the interpersonal context, the introductory paragraphs help to "identify" the Mass-Observation correspondents. They suggest a "subject position" with regard to the knowledge asked for and with regard to the Mass-Observation Project. The third way in which the introductory paragraphs contextualise responses to the directive is by establishing qualities of the *mode* of communication; namely, a register, tone and style of writing.

After the introductory paragraph, there are usually a series of questions, topics or tasks. The directives vary in what they require of the Mass-Observation correspondents and within a directive there may be various types of tasks. Some require reflection, others observation and recording, or diary writing, among other writing genres.

It is important to note that the Mass-Observation correspondents do not always follow directions and may contest the demands implied in the structure and content of a directive. Some, like Mr Purcell (P2250), use the directive as an opportunity to write as they see fit and tend to ignore many of the implied demands of the directive.

> I just write what I think I'm going to write, and I wouldn't take any notice of . . . I mean I follow, I try to follow the little guidelines that you know . . . but there are certain things which don't appeal. I mean there was one of the assignments didn't interest me at all, and I mean I just said that in the assignment. But I wouldn't say that . . . you know, if you told me, you know, oh you haven't done this, or you haven't done that, I feel well, you know, hard luck, you get it; you take what you find I'm afraid. (P2250, interview)

What Mr Purcell's statements reveal is a sense of shared ownership that many of the Mass-Observation correspondents feel about the Mass-Observation Project as well as a sense of independence. It is not a subversion of the Mass-Observation Project or of any particular directive so much as an assumption of the right to co-define what the Mass-Observation Project is and what will be collected for history.

We have taken one directive, the Education directive (the first part of the Spring 1991 directive, the full text of which can be found in Appendix C) and describe in detail the interaction between the structure of one of the tasks given in the directive and the different stances that the Mass-Observation correspondents take toward such demands. To foreshadow our discussion, although the structure of the directive did have an influence, its influence varied across people, with some Mass-Observation correspondents subverting the influence of its structure (which is not to claim that they subverted the intent of the directive; indeed, in the example we use it could be argued that subverting the influence of the structure of the directive enriched the information and insight provided).

The first item in the Education directive asked for a list of schools attended, qualifications achieved, and list of experiences as a teacher or educator, if any.

> Please start by listing your own schools and colleges with dates and your age. This is NOT another request for a Self Portrait! We just want the bare bones. You don't have to provide the full names of places but it would be useful if you could indicate what kinds of institutions they were. Please include a note of any qualifications you received. Don't forget to start right at the beginning (nurseries? playgroups?) and bring it right up to date with evening classes and adult education if it applies to you. Please include apprenticeships and day release and any other training schemes you can think of. The rule is—if in doubt, include it. (Spring Directive, 1991)

Of the 39 responses closely examined, 33 provided a list that looked much like a table or curriculum vita, such as the one below.

The lists provide one definition of the person and one definition of the educational road taken. For example, the list below defines the person as a successful pupil and student who moved through school eventually becoming a teacher. The person is wholly defined by the school list. Part of the power of the list is the slots that need filling: a list of schools from infant/junior school through secondary and higher

---

Education
Retired SCHOOL TEACHER
Born in 1923
Full-time education
Small private prep school in private house for one term, aged 5
St. Anne's College, Sanderstead (Convent) 1929-1937
Croyden High School (GPDST) 1937-1940 General schools with Matric. exemption
Pitman's College, Croydon 1940-1941 Licentiate of Institute of Private Secretaries
Borthwick Teacher Training College (Emergency) 1946-1947 Teacher Training Certificate

education, with slots for qualifications and certificates achieved. Although the types of schools (e.g., grammar school versus regular school) and which schools (e.g., schools that are known to be prestigious) that fill the list vary, the list also communicates important information about the person. An incomplete list may define the person as aberrant requiring an explanation. For example, at the beginning of his response Mr Fisher (F1701) writes:

> Here we have a "minority" situation.
>
> For I never went to school!
>
> Although the Directive states another Self Portrait is not required, *some sort of explanation for this situation is advisable perhaps.* (our emphasis)

Thus the list can be viewed at a gross level as dividing people up into those who have been "successfully" educated and those who have not, with "successfully" being defined from within the social institution and referring to following an available and legitimised route through schooling. Progressing from one school to another until one achieves a recognised and achieved exit is "success". The list provides no consideration of whether the person defines the journey as successful. Stated in other terms, listing schools and qualifications achieved is not just a technical task but an ideological one with consequences for personhood and inclusion/exclusion.

Mrs Williams (W2151) undercuts the power of the list with humour. Instead of writing a list of schools and qualifications, she lists a one-sentence story by each age.

> At 5 yrs I remember the Dentist coming, I refused to open my mouth.
> At 6 yrs, a teacher tried to make me write right-handed and failed
> At 7 yrs the H.M. (Miss G . . .) told us that unless we stopped talking she would cut off a piece of our tongues. She drew it on the board /\ !
> At 7 yrs I stole a penny and bought sweets.
> At 8 yrs on a rainy day, I was running to an outside toilet & bumped into another child and got a huge bruise on my forehead.
> I remember I couldn't write a j satisfactorily and had to write a page of jj's.
> We had to learn tables.
> I didn't pass the scholarship, but was borderline.
> I was entered, <u>I think</u>, for a private payment & failed by a short margin & parents said: "It is God's will you don't go to the Grammar School."
> I wanted to go to wear school uniform.
>   [original underlining]

Her stories are presented in a list, each age and story on its own line, just as others listed their schools and qualifications. Her list can be viewed as contesting being placed in the type of resume-like list illustrated earlier. While it is impossible to know Mrs Williams' (W2151) intentions, her list not only contests who gets to define whom, but also the implicit taxonomy involved in the resume-like list. The first line of Mrs Williams's list establishes herself as a person who acts and who resists: "I refused . . .". The first line also locates the struggle between herself and the school as a bodily one: "my mouth", "right-handed", "cut off our tongues", "sweets", "running . . . bumped . . . bruises" and "school uniform". Her list refuses to allow education to be defined solely in ethereal intellectual, academic, religious or aesthetic terms. It is corporal, material and economic. Part of the rhetorical strength of her list comes from the narratives encapsulated in each line. Her narratives include the agency missing from the resume-like lists: the "H.M. told us", "she drew it on the board", "a teacher tried". But Mrs Williams also uses a phrase found in nearly all of the responses to the Education directive—"had to". She was forced to ("had to") "write a page of jj's" presumably by a teacher. The repetition of "had to" in the next line emphasises a characteristic of her schooling. One way to view the absence of the agent—who made her write her jj's and learn her tables and who made other school children do numerous other things they did not want to do—is that it is not a specific agent that creates a "had to" but the nature of the institution. "Had to" does not take an agent in that discourse of education (similarly in contemporary education policy documents for England and Wales; see Street, 1998).

Later in her response Mrs Williams describes her time at Hillcroft Adult Education College. Her description raises another issue about the definition of a resume-like list of schools attended. Although it may seem unremarkable, a list of schools belongs to the domain of education, as if that were the natural and only category to which education (as opposed to schooling) might belong. Mrs Williams writes:

> 1956/7 I was a resident at Hillcroft Adult Educ. College (started for women by the Labour party).
>
> THIS WAS MY EDUCATION !!! [original uppercase]

Mrs Williams's parenthetical comment—"(started for women by the Labour party)"—is accompanied by other comments that also suggest that schooling can be located in the political domain rather than solely in the education or school domain. Or perhaps more accurately, education is not the superordinate category, but rather politics.

Where schooling is located, in the education domain or the political domain, has implications for how people in education get defined as well as how education itself is defined. Mr Thwaite (T2222) also locates education in the political domain by how he describes and comments on schools in his list.

> 1930 JOHN RUSKIN GRAMMAR SCHOOL specialised in turning out clerks for the London workforce. [Original uppercase]

"Turning out clerks" characterises the school as a factory and in combination with "London workforce" locates schooling as an economic institution. Part of what is at stake in where schooling is located is the range of options for interpretation and action that people view as available to them. What Mrs Williams and Mr Thwaite have done is to place themselves in a discourse where a particular set of issues, definitions and actions are highlighted that differs from what issues get highlighted when schooling is located solely in the institutional discourse of education

What we have illustrated in the brief analysis of the responses to the first task in the Education directive are: (1) how the structure of a task demanded by a directive may influence what the Mass-Observation correspondents write, how they get defined (e.g., the subject positions they are offered), the institutional discourse domains promoted and the stance toward agency promoted; (2) the limitations of influence exerted by the structure of the directives; and (3) a series of rhetorical strategies employed by Mass-Observation correspondents in response to directives, operating beneath the broad and general level of "genre", that provide ways for them to articulate meanings and experiences that would otherwise be hidden.

Mass-Observation as Audience

The directives provide an opportunity and audience for writing. As Mrs Friend writes: ". . . if someone's going to read what I write, then I write because someone's going to read it". The audience provided by the Mass-Observation Project is multi-layered.

Members of staff at the Mass-Observation Archive are the first and most immediate audience once a response to a directive has been mailed. As discussed in Chapter 2, Pocock and Sheridan often wrote notes to the Mass-Observation correspondents. When the number of Mass-Observation correspondents was manageable, a note would be written to each person after they had submitted a response to a directive. As the number of Mass-Observation correspondents grew and the activities of the Mass-Observation Project increased, personal notes were written to a subgroup, whereas others were sent an official but not personalised acknowledgment. However, efforts are still made to respond personally to as many of the Mass-Observation correspondents as possible As described in Chapter 2, at least some of the Mass-Observation correspondents highly value the personal notes from Mass-Observation staff. Part of what is interesting about the Mass-Observation staff as audience is that their primary role is one of *facilitating* communication between the Mass-Observation correspondents, researchers and "people in the future". They themselves are not a formally designated audience. Their role as audience is not as consumers of information but rather in roles more associated with a meta-function: commenting on the quality of insights or efforts made, responding with sympathy and care to personal crises or difficult topics described, and noting particular ethical issues (or potential ethical issues) that occasionally arise. In one sense, the Mass-Observation staff acts as audience in the role of friend, colleague and collaborator.

But there is another dimension to the Mass-Observation staff as audience that is also important to note; and this dimension has more to do with their institutional role than with personal relations. The Mass-Observation Project is viewed as willing to accept a broad range of writing; writing for the Mass-Observation Project is freer than writing for (or in) most other social institutions. The Mass-Observation correspondents can feel free to write (and not to worry too much about keeping to the point, grammar, spelling, being relevant, being discreet and so on). They can feel that they have greater choice over what they write (within certain limits) and that this is appreciated; they feel more in control. For example, in her interview, Mrs Friend (F1373) said:

> I mean they [the Mass-Observation Project] are prepared to accept something written in longhand, whereas if you're going to submit anything to publishers or anything like that it's got to be typewritten on A4, and there's lots of regulations to it. That is so easy, just sit down and write, and I do like writing, it just flows.

A second audience of the Mass-Observation correspondents is the researchers and historians who will use the Mass-Observation Project later.

> I believe that the Mass-Observation Archive will be of great use to students and future historians, providing them with a rich source of material which in previous generations have been scarce . . . (B1215, UWR)

Nor are researchers and historians themselves the "end" audience, but part of a vehicle for communicating with and informing people in the future.

> The whole project has a value in itself as a record for this and future generations about what the world was like during the period which is being written about . . . the project is a link in the chain binding generations together-real people from one age writing about their age brings it to life. (C2295, UWR)

One consequence of these two sets of audiences, "people in the future" and the Mass-Observation staff, is that at one and the same time writing for the Mass-Observation Project is both personal (a known audience) and abstract. Of course, some Mass-Observation correspondents ignore the Mass-Observation staff as an audience, and this may be true whether or not they have met any of the staff members or have received a personal note. When they sit down to write, they do not think about the Mass-Observation staff. Some have hardly given a thought to who the staff are, and in response to a question on the Spring 1991 directive about their conception of the Mass-Observation facility and staff (see question 12 in Appendix C), some confessed that they had not thought of it until asked. Others have developed a personal relationship with the Mass-Observation staff, perhaps first with Pocock and then later with Sheridan. As we reported in Chapter 2, when the leadership of the Mass-Observation Project shifted from Pocock to Sheridan, some Mass-Observation correspondents wrote that they would miss Pocock and some openly worried about what the change would mean and if it would affect their writing. But beyond the variation in how much the Mass-Observation correspondents consciously consider the Mass-Observation staff as audience, the multi-layered audiences have other implications, including the assumptions the Mass-Observation correspondents use with regard to time, knowledge, safety and identity.

In brief, if the Mass-Observation staff is considered an important audience, then the observations, insights and commentary are framed in and by the present tense and assumptions can be reasonably made that the audience shares knowledge of a contemporaneous world. For instance with respect to the Mass-Observation correspondents' reference to their own past experience, they are often extremely sensitive to the needs of a contemporary audience. When describing schooling during the 1940s, a Mass-Observation writer will often explain aspects of schooling no longer current (such as particular instructional practices, tests, policies and kinds of schools). However, writing to a future audience seems to be more difficult. It requires authors to provide knowledge that readers might not have and address issues assumed to be of interest and significance to a them. It is, of course, difficult to anticipate what knowledge a future audience might need and what items might need explicit explanation. For example, in Chapter 7 where we include W632's writing about going to court to protest against the Poll Tax, we have had to explain what the Poll Tax was, as W632 did not do so. The nature of Mass-Observation writing therefore involves a different relationship to audience than do other genres of writing. Reading Mass-Observation writing thus requires recognition of the issue of explicitness and reference as we have described here.

In addition to these linguistic and literary features of Mass-Observation writing, the fact that Mass-Observation correspondents are writing for future audiences also warrants a broader social, political and philosophic commentary, one less tied to the issue of the moment. Thus, Mrs Friend writes in her response to the Spring 1991 directive:

> History repeats itself; you can often look at things and say, when you get say a political situation you can often look at it and say well, that's going to happen again. And if you've got it right that time, then it might be the same . . . I mean I can remember—well I can't remember it, I can remember someone telling me about it—that when New York was absolutely broke, and the President said right, we are going to invest money, we are going to put people to work, if it's building roads, during this. And it was the right thing to do, you know. And I sort of think that it could well come a time, the same thing could happen again, and if the answer was right then it would be right in future, wouldn't it? (F1373)

As we discuss later in this chapter, the opportunity to write and the audience provided by the Mass-Observation Project need to be viewed against the other obligations and priorities that the Mass-Observation correspondents have. For example, some women state that they view writing for themselves as an indulgence they cannot afford given obligations to children, spouses, family, friends, work, community, and so forth. However, the explicit audience and purpose of the Mass-Observation Project—providing a history for scholars and future generations—legitimises their participation. Thus, the opportunity for writing is not simply a technical matter, but one of creating a social space that allows Mass-Observation correspondents to claim that their writing is a socially legitimate use of their time and effort.

How Mass-Observation Correspondents Write a Response to a Directive

Mrs Martin's (M1498) description in Chapter 5 of how she writes a response to a directive is typical of many of the Mass-Observation correspondents (see pages 173 to 180). What is typical about Mrs Martin's description of writing a response to a directive is that the process starts when the envelope is received. The directive will be looked over, the topic(s) judged as interesting or difficult, and so forth, and even if a response is not written right away, it will be thought about. Yet, as Mrs Safran (B2197) said:

> I always have [the directive] in mind; I don't tend to forget about them, I'm always thinking, next time I've got a spare morning, or something, I'll do it. But that can vary from being a couple of weeks later to . . . as I say, I'm two directives behind, so that's some months behind.

Many of the Mass-Observation correspondents stated that they needed uninterrupted time. That might mean peace and quiet (as Mrs Safran [B2197] describes in Chapter 5) or it might mean writing while others are occupied with the television even if there is noise in the same room where they are writing. While some Mass-Observation correspondents mull over the directives and wait before they write—either because they want to think about it or because it is difficult to find the time, others respond either right away or they respond quickly. For example, consider Mr Barrow's (B1106) and Mr Richards's (M1593) statements below. From Mr Barrow (B1106, UWR):

> I decided to write these reports straight off. In the past I let several stand for several months and dreaded having to sit down to do them. If I have free time and can answer them straight off I prefer to do this. I began my replies only an hour after opening the envelope today!

From Mr Richards [M1593 interview]:

> I would like to say that I always mull the directive over before starting; unfortunately I lead such a hectic life that I tend to treat work—and life—as a series of hurdles to leap over. So do I treat M.O. It is rare that I achieve the writing in one session though and frequently reread—the better to align my thoughts . . .

Some, like Mr Richards and Mr Reed respond to the directives on their own and by themselves. Depending on the task, others like Mrs Friend, as she said in her interview, make a special effort to find out information from others, so as to write from a wider perspective.

> Writing to the Mass-Observation Project is different than writing letters. I think they want more . . . I suppose it's going to be put by for future historians isn't it, and they really want to know the type of life that you have at this moment in time, so that is totally different. I try not only to put what I, my views down; I ask friends at work, I ask my husband, my family, how about your views on this, and then I try and write all the views down so that they've got sort of a wider version really than just my views.

Mr Russell (R1671) gave us an unusual description of how he begins his responses to directives.

> I usually start by making lots of scornful jokes about Mass Observation, and then I read through the directive, and in fact that has to happen, because the sort of pre-production part of it is intuitive and it relies I think upon letting your subconscious ferment away for a while, and finally you tap the subconscious at the moment when you're ready to write. And a lot of things in it of course surprise you.

Mr Russell's jokes can be viewed as a way of distancing the directive and undercutting its and the Mass-Observation Project's authority.

After finishing their response, most of the Mass-Observation correspondents reported that they re-read what they had written. As Mrs Wright wrote:

> I withhold sending the directive when it is finished so that I can read through your questions and my answers, to correct mistakes and to include any afterthoughts. (W632, UWR)

A few stated that they just sent it off. Only a few, like Mrs Safran below, stated that they kept copies, but that may reveal more about the accessibility of photocopiers and use of computers than a desire for copies itself.

> I have mixed feelings about copying it, but I do. It seems a bit silly really, just do it and send it back and forget about it. But when I re-read them, I'm quite surprised that I manage to get things down I think, I'm quite surprised that I manage to get cover the ground and say things. (B2197, interview)

Few people stated that they showed what they wrote to others. Although they might talk to others about it before they wrote or while they were writing, once it was done most sent it off to the Mass-Observation Project without having others read it or give feedback. It may be the Mass-Observation correspondents do not believe that others around them are interested in what they have to say. For example, Mrs Wright (W632) told us that although her son and husband offer their ideas on directive topics, they do not ask her what she thinks about those topics. Not asking others to read their responses to a directive may be a way to protect their ownership and ideas.

Summary Comments on Ordinary People Writing and the Uses and Genres of Writing

Our data on the uses and genres of writing can also be viewed as taking up the calls that Szwed made in 1981 and Basso in 1974 for ethnographies of literacy and writing. They argued that little was then really known about the writing and literacy activities of ordinary people in everyday life. Since the late 1970s there have been numerous ethnographic studies of literacy. Szwed's and Basso's calls for ethnographies of writing and literacy assumed an accumulation of data that would lead to taxonomies and models of writing and literacy in everyday life that would, on one hand, show diversity while on the other locate who was doing what with written language, when, where and how. Our study and ethnographic studies of literacy since Basso's and Szwed's classic articles have validated their assumption about diversity of writing and literacy practices. And, while some studies have suggested that particular writing and literacy practices can be aligned with particular cultures and particular social and institutional settings, our data—like the data from more recent studies of writing in the community—show a more complex and dynamic picture (cf., Street, 1993b).

It is not just that writing and literacy practices evolve and change, and it is not just that cultural groups are internally complex and diverse rather than monolithic. The difficulty of fitting the findings from ethnographic studies of literacy into taxonomies is that people have different conceptions of what counts as literacy, so an outsider's comparison is not always comparing like with like. Further, people "take up" various writing and literacy practices, adapting them and transforming them to their own social and cultural lives, using writing and literacy to create social spaces and social relationships. At the same time they are caught up in and responding to the promulgation of dominant writing and literacy practices in our society. Taxonomies either background or make invisible the dynamic relationships and complexities between domains (such as settings, discourses, social institutions), and seem to fix structural relations between domains. What needs highlighting is exactly those dynamic, changing and sometimes contentious relationships—the complexity, transformation and indeterminacy of social life and social practices.

In this chapter we have described a broad range of uses of writing by Mass-Observation correspondents both in their writing for the Mass-Observation Project and otherwise. We have shown how the Mass-Observation Project creates particular spaces, time, audiences and opportunities for writing that do not exist for most people, including for most of the Mass-Observation correspondents. The particular opportunities and audiences created by the Mass-Observation Project are not the same for everyone, as people take up and define what Mass-Observation is differently. But we have also shown how the nature of the Mass-Observation Project may influence what and how people write in response to directives. This influence is mitigated by a "feisty" attitude that is held by many Mass-Observation correspondents, who often override the questions, format or topic of a directive. And, although they describe themselves as ordinary, such a description more reflects a system of social relationships that provide some with more access to audiences, time, space and recognition for writing and authorship, while making it difficult for others. In the next chapter we take up these issues of access more directly by discussing personhood, power and what we call "crossings". We define crossings as the ways people use writing practices to create social relationships and social spaces and to the interpenetration of uses and genres of writing from one social setting to another.

7
Power, Personhood and Crossings

> The texts of everyday life are not innocuous, neutral texts requiring simple decoding and response. They are key moments where social identity and power relations are established and negotiated. (Allan Luke, Jennifer O'Brien & Barbara Comber, 1994, p. 140)

In the previous chapter, we described the Mass-Observation correspondents' uses of writing, both for the Mass-Observation Project and beyond it. In this chapter, we build on the data and discussion in Chapter 6, focussing on how writing is implicated in the exercise of power, definitions of personhood and the creation and transformation of social space. Some of the issues we raise here were signaled in Chapter 6, especially the discussion of ordinary people writing.

We begin by discussing concepts of power, especially as they relate to writing. Then we take up the question of who are the Mass-Observation correspondents? We do so in two ways. First, we analyse the social "positions" from which they write. That is, social institutions provide positions for writing to which only a few have access. While people can attempt to transform those positions, create new positions and gain access, doing so is often difficult. We examine how the Mass-Observation, on the other hand, creates positions for writing outside of the dominant institutions in which writing is usually treated, and how people use and transform the positions made available. But we also look at the role that education has played in "positioning" many of the Mass-Observation correspondents. Finally, at the end of this chapter we focus on "crossings"—the creation and transformation of social space for writing that "crosses" those conventionally available.

Power

As we discussed in the introduction to this book, power is often seen as a quantity, a property to be possessed, an object (Street, 1996b). Following this model, if someone has a quantity of power, then others need to take it away from him in order to become "empowered" themselves. This is a theory of power that lies beneath many debates on empowerment and is probably the dominant and "common-sense" view. However, viewing power as a quantity is problematic, especially in relation to writing and literacy. The quantity theory of power, for instance, is often thought of in terms of technical control, competence, skill: if someone achieves a particular competence, for instance in writing, then according to the theory they increase their "power" in the world—they become "empowered".

However, writing is more than just a skill. The last two decades of research and practice in writing and literacy has made it apparent that writing and literacy are social practices that vary from one context to another and are part of cultural knowledge and behaviour, not simply technical competencies to be added on to people as though they were machines being upgraded (Barton & Hamilton, 1998; Heath, 1983; Street, 1984). Writing and literacy are social and cultural processes related to people's cultural identity, their sense of self, their knowledge and world view, their epistemology.

As with literacy, so power can be viewed as a process. The process model considers power as always contested and in negotiation; power is also always being changed and transformed. This model assumes that power varies between sites and contexts rather than remaining the same. Power in this sense is thought of as being exercised in a number of different ways; for instance, it may be thought of as exercised through force—the use of military power or individual strength, or through discourse, the use of language, social institutions, words to control others.

The exercise of power is often treated by people as though it were a given and inherent, rather than being always socially and culturally created in different contexts. For instance, those exercising power may claim that what they are doing—for example, through bureaucratic institutions, aid agencies, schools, and so forth—is simply technical, neutral and "functional", where a closer analysis would indicate how they have created and are maintaining their power over others through those practices. Power, then, is not simply something to be acquired, as an outcome of learning to write, for example, but is already involved in particular processes of learning and writing themselves.

Many who adopt the power as process model argue for the revolutionary transformation of subjects and of institutions. Foucault (1965; see also Poster, 1984), for instance, describes power in terms of "disciplinary" procedures, or "regimes of truth". Within institutions, such as those of the academic world, disciplines operate through their language, social authority and institutional force to establish what kind of person we can be and what truths we should adhere to. Social institutions, such as psychiatric asylums, for example, police the distinction between the sane from the insane by restricting the latter to buildings where they are under continual close surveillance. One of Foucault's most devastating critiques of modern society has been to argue that the buildings and disciplines of the educational world are in fact very similar to the buildings and disciplines of the asylum—both involve close and powerful surveillance over dominant truths and over people who may diverge from them (Foucault, 1965). Foucault also argues that all forms of discipline are associated with resistance: activists, creative thinkers, radical academics and revolutionaries work to oppose dominant disciplines and the ideas that legitimate them. Resistance to dominant assumptions about social position and about literacy constitutes one of the primary foci of our research on "everyday" uses and meanings of writing.

The problem with Foucault's model of power is that it appears mainly negative, as though power was always a bad thing, a coercive force exercised by some human beings on others who then struggle to resist it. Bourdieu (1977) has also tended to see power as mainly negative and oppressive, though he links it more to the nature of the dominant modern economic system of capitalism. According to Bourdieu, just as there is economic capital, which its holders can use to acquire material resources and political power for themselves, so there is cultural capital: forms of language, dress, social manners, institutions such as museums and schools, and so forth. Some members of society have access to this cultural capital, while others lack access. The most powerful form of capital, however, is neither economic capital nor cultural capital in themselves, but symbolic capital—the means to convert or transform these kinds of capital into real, material resources and social authority. If you have cultural capital without symbolic capital, then you may still find yourself excluded from the material resources of society. For Bourdieu, power is intimately bound up with the forms of capital.

Power, especially that connected with writing, can be thought of in a way that has the potential also to be positive in contrast to the apparently negative view of power given in either Foucault's or Bourdieu's discussions, while retaining the process model of power that they put forward. One such view of power and writing has been made by Smith (1987) in her outline of a feminist sociology. She argues that a fundamental role of sociology—and by extension one could include all of the social sciences—has been to put into text the experiences of people in a manner that reveals the nature of society. The experiences of women have been largely ignored both because they have not been part of the written record and because those written records of women's experiences which do exist have either been created by men, or if created by women, have been necessarily within a predominantly male discourse. Thus, the division of public and private, the location of work, definitions of labour, class, sexuality and violence have all been conceptualised from the viewpoint(s) of men, overlooking women's labour in the home and in childrearing, the conditions in which women participate in the workplace, as well as women's writing (both in its academic forms and in its everyday forms such as diaries, poems, stories, crafts). Although Smith argues that it is important to keep concepts such as work and alienation in mind, she suggests that a feminist sociology would need to begin with women's everyday world experiences rather than with grand sociological theory. The task is to write about the everyday world in which women and men live in a way that captures the realities of their lives as they experience them, while at the same time acknowledging insights about social life and the economic system generated by social research. The writing itself, however, is not enough; it needs to be part of actions taken on and in the world—not an isolated intellectual exercise stuck on a shelf.

The connection, then, between writing and power is not just a question of putting women and others who have been excluded back into writing and history, nor is it just in capturing the realities of the everyday world in which people live, although that is crucial in ways that this book is attempting to demonstrate. According to Smith, a key issue involves addressing the alienation that is a seemingly inherent part of the social science disciplines and in taking action on those realities and conditions that promote suffering and pain and that limit possibilities for fulfilling lives. This notion of writing, framed in Bourdieu's terms, reveals and redefines the habitus in a manner that realigns symbolic capital, so that cultural and economic capital may also be realigned. In Foucault's terms, it is a writing that contests the ways that the discourses of the social science disciplines and the professions position people and constrain their bodies. (Later in this chapter, we discuss Mrs Wright's [W632] experience of challenging the judicial system. Her account written for the Mass-Observation Project is a good illustration of the way the legal system positions people as writers and speakers and at the same time constrains the body).

For writing and literacy researchers concerned with "productive" power (cf., Barton & Hamilton, 1998; Kress, 1994; Luke et al., 1994; Street, 1996b), the question is not "how can a few gain access to existing power", nor "how can existing power structures be resisted", but rather how can power itself be transformed. Such a question involves a transformation from the disciplinary and coercive forms power has taken on in modern society, so that power works instead in a positive way to bring out human potential and to harness creative energy. The model of power we employ in our research on literacy practices and the Mass-Observation Project is a "process" model that focusses on transformation. This view of power enables us to see the apparently mundane, "everyday" writing and literacy practices of the Mass-Observation correspondents in a new and more illuminating light, particularly with regard to how writing opens up and transforms the social positions occupied and available to be occupied.

Position(ing)

The social positions from which people write provide warrants and constraints for what they may and may not do (including what and how they write), as well as constitute part of the interpretative context for both the texts created and for the writing event itself. Being able to exercise symbolic power is not simply a matter of engaging in a particular writing practice or assuming a particular social position within a particular writing practice. Although a particular writing practice may imply particular social positions, not just anyone can assume those positions. As Bourdieu points out, one must have the symbolic capital to assume a particular position. Thus, being able to exercise symbolic power from within a particular writing practice and from a particular social position within that writing practice depends on more than the practice itself. For example, an ordinary person might write a history of education in Britain and might include documentation, citation and other accoutrements associated with academic history texts. But if the person lacks the symbolic capital to claim the social position of historian, then the history written will lack symbolic power. It is, of course, not just a matter of whether the writer has the symbolic capital but rather of whether others assign it to him or her.

Of particular importance to our use of the idea of social position and writing in this chapter is Bourdieu's conception of "delegation." Delegation is one way to acquire symbolic capital—being authorised to speak and act on behalf of a group. Although Bourdieu focused primarily on delegation within political parties and religion, his discussion is also useful here. At times, the Mass-Observation correspondents are delegates of the Mass-Observation Project; they are asked to act on behalf of the Mass-Observation Project in gathering information about life in Britain. At other times, they are delegates of ordinary, everyday people in Britain, speaking for them. As Bourdieu points out, the relationship between a delegate and the group being represented is complex, involving a series of dialectics over symbolic capital and symbolic power. Simultaneously, a delegate speaks from the group to others while speaking to the group, in both cases exerting symbolic power (although in neither case, totalising symbolic power). The Mass-Observation correspondents are variously positioned (and self-positioned) as delegates for—as writing for—ordinary people, working-class people, middle-class people, women, older people, Scottish people, marginalised groups, and so forth, but also as delegates for the Mass-Observation Project and the academic scholars who make use of the Mass-Observation collection or who sponsor directives. What we claim is that understanding the delegation relationship is not a technical matter of nailing down the various influences on the writing and claims to authority, but is more an ideological matter concerned with power, its transformative potential, and its contestation.

Personhood

We view the concept of social positioning and the related concept of delegation as part of the broader concept of personhood. The concept of personhood is taken from recent anthropological (e.g., Besnier, 1993) and educational studies (e.g., Egan-Robertson, 1999) that have argued that definitions of "person" are socially constructed, and may vary both across and within cultures. In Britain, no less or more so than anywhere, there are particular definitions of what a person is and what inherent rights and qualities "people" are assumed to have and not have, including definitions of who can do what in what situations. Definitions of personhood vary over time and across situations. It is frequently the case that definitions of personhood are taken for granted, and thus questions about what a person is and what rights a person has are viewed as common sense or simply given. Thus, in Britain as in most Western societies, we take it for granted that people are endowed with a series of inherent traits such that some people are smarter than others, more athletic than others, more creative than others, and so forth. This definition of personhood permeates most of our social institutions, including business, government and schooling, and feeds into a conception of writing. That is, such a definition of personhood suggests that it is only "natural" that some people are writers because only some people have the inherent trait of being a writer (just as only some people have the inherent trait of musical talent) and that given the opportunity (e.g., appropriate schooling) this talent will come out. To question such a view of writing is to question the common-sense view of personhood. Rather than accept a view of personhood as given, inherent or natural, we view personhood as situated and as contestable.

The discussion of social position, power and personhood in writing for the Mass-Observation Project that follows in the rest of this chapter focusses on how group social positions are constituted and used as ways to acquire symbolic capital and assert symbolic power. What we present here is a case of the adaptation of the social positions inscribed in writing for the Mass-Observation Project using evidence from different people and texts. In our research, we have found that just as people may adapt and transform literacy practices to their own needs and agendas, so, too, they adapt, transform and contest the social positions inscribed in written language practices.

Who Are the Mass-Observation Correspondents?

We could describe the Mass-Observation correspondents by reference to traditional demographic and sociological measures—so many middle-class versus working-class, men versus women, young versus old, rural versus urban, southern England versus northern England or Wales or Scotland, Afro-Caribbeans and Asians versus whites—and we have done so in Tables 7-1, 7-2, 7-3, 7-4 and 7-5.

Table 7-1. Demographic Characteristics of the Mass-Observation Correspondents 1981-1998.

Gender	Regional Location*	
	Scotland	3.4%
Total—2478	Northern Ireland	0.56%
	North England	18.0%
Women—1701 (68.7%)	Wales	3.8%
	Midlands	18.7%
Men - 777 (31.3%)	South England (inc. London)	55.0%
	Abroad	0.52%

*The regional groups are based on the areas used in producing Social Trends. "Abroad" category refers to people who began writing while living in the United Kingdom but have moved to other countries, yet still wished to keep writing. The distribution of the Mass-Observation panel mirrors the national distribution of the population in the United Kingdom.

Table 7-2. Age Distribution for all Mass-Observation Correspondents 1981-1998.

Date of Birth

	Born 1973 or after		Born between 1972 and 1948		Born between 1923 and 1947		Born before 1923	
	Total	%	Total	%	Total	%	Total	%
Men	26	1.04	261	10.53	278	11.21	178	7.18
Women	42	1.69	539	21.75	802	32.36	258	10.41
All	68	2.74	800	32.28	1080	43.58	436	17.59

Note: 94 (3.79%) people have not supplied their date of birth

Table 7-3. Age and Gender Distribution of Correspondents Responding to the Spring 1991 Directive.

Age group	Men	%	Women	%	Total	%
Under 20	1	0.75	1	0.28	2	0.41
21-30	1	0.75	15	4.29	16	3.32
31-40	10	7.57	33	9.45	43	8.93
41-50	14	10.60	56	16.23	70	14.55
51-60	18	13.63	77	22.06	95	19.75
61-70	45	34.09	105	30.08	150	31.81
71-80	38	28.78	56	16.04	93	19.33
81-90	4	3.03	6	1.71	10	2.07
91 +	1	0.75	0	0	1	0.20
Totals	132	100	349	100	481	100

Table 7-4. Number of Mass-Observation Correspondents Interviewed, by Demographic Characteristics (Age, Gender, etc.).

Gender	
Male	7
Female	28
Total	35

Age When Interviewed	
20 or under	1
21-25	0
26-30	0
31-35	1
36-40	6
41-45	4
46-50	4
51-55	3
56-60	1
61-65	4
66-70	5
71-75	2
76-80	4
81+	0

Occupation (Before Retiring)	
Clerical	5
Educator	12*
At home	2
Health, non-prof	2
Prof. tech field	2
Administrator	1
Civil Service	2
Accountant	1
Crafts	1
Nature warden	1
Builder	1
Writer	1
Shop keeper	1
Student	1
Farmer	1

Ethnicity	
English, white	26
Scottish, white	3
Welsh, white	2
Jewish	2
German, white	2
Asian	0
Afro-Carribean	0
Other	0

Age Started Writing for M-O	
20 or under	1
21-25	0
26-30	2
31-35	3
36-40	9
41-45	2
46-50	2
51-55	5
56-60	4
61-65	2
66-70	3
71-75	1
76-80	1
81+	0

*Includes teacher, educational administrator, educational psychologist, or other professional educator at all levels-primary, secondary, further education and university. Also includes librarians.

Table 7-5. List, by M-O Number, of the Correspondents Interviewed, Showing Demographic Characteristics.

M-O Number	Gender	D.O.B./Age When Interviewed	Occupation p = part-time r = retired	Ethnicity	Year/Age Began M-O	Location
A1706	Female	1946/47	Art Teacher (p)	English, white	1986/40	Shoreham-by-Sea
B1106	Male	1945/48	Writer/actor	English, white	1984/39	London
B1215	Female	1953/40	Supervisor	English, white	1984/31	Plymouth
B2197	Female	1954/39	Librarian	English, Jewish	1990/36	London
C1990	Female	1946/47	Civil servant	English, white	1987/41	Cardiff
C2079	Female	1948/45	Swimming Instructor	Scottish, white	1988/40	Edinburgh
C2091	Female	1930/63	Librarian (r)	English, white	1989/59	Eastbourne
C2295	Female	1954/39	Adult Ed Teacher	English, white	1990/36	Manchester
D2092	Female	1919/74	Secretary (r)	English, white	1989/70	Eastbourne
E174	Female	1924/69	Teacher (r)	English, white	1981/57	Manchester
F1373	Female	1932/61	Shop worker (r)	English, white	1986/54	Brighton
G1483	Female	1914/79	Postal Clk (r)	English, white	1986/72	Brighton
G2524	Male	1975/18	Student	English, white	1990/15	Brighton
H1709	Female	1925/68	Farmer	Welsh, white	1987/62	Oswestry, Wales
M381	Male	1917/76	Insurance clerk	English, white	1981/64	London
M645	Female	1916/77	Nurse, Health educator (r)	English, white	1982/66	Seaford
M1368	Female	1936/57	Housewife	English, white	1986/50	Tavistock, Devon
M1498	Female	1954/39	Non-prof. nursing home worker	English, white	1986/32	Polegate

Table 7-5. List, by M-O Number, of the Correspondents Interviewed, Showing Demographic Characteristics (con't.).

M-O #	Sex	Birth/Age	Occupation	Ethnicity	Year/Age	Location
M1593	Male	1946/47	Hydrographic surveyor	English, white	1987/41	Aberdeen, Scotland
M1879	Female	1958/35	Dressmaker & jeweller	English, white	1987/29	Welshpool Powys, Wales
M2446	Female	1914/79	Doctors' clinical asst.	Welsh, white	1990/76	Cardiff, Wales
M2493	Female	1955/38	Sound engineer	Scottish, white	1990/35	Edinburgh
N2208	Female	1938/55	Educational psychologist	South African, Jewish	1990/52	London
P2250	Male	1950/43	Nature Reserve warden	English, white	1990/40	Devon
R446	Female	1930/63	Polytechnic lecturer	English, white	1981/51	Llanbrynmair Wales
R450	Male	1926/67	Builder (r)	English, white	1981/55	London
R1671	Male	1940/53	Writer	English, white	1986.46	Lancaster
S496	Female	1926/67	Drapery clerk	English, white	1981/55	Devon
S1570	Female	1928/69	Accountant	German, white	1987/59	Penarth, Wales
S2207	Female	1952/41	Housewife	English, white	1990/38	Brighton
S2220	Female	1922/71	Head teacher (r)	German, white	1990/68	Kennoway, Scotland
S2271	Female	1930/63	Clerical, various (r)	English, white	1990/60	Edinburgh, Scotland
T1961	Female	1948/45	Teacher's asst (p)	English, white	1986/38	Burgess Hill, Sussex
W632	Female	1941/52	Clerk, senior	English, white	1981/40	Fishergate
W729	Female	1957/36	teacher librarian (r)	Scottish, white	1987/30	Dundee, Scotland

We could also describe the Mass-Observation correspondents in terms of their socio-political identity (conservative, liberal, left-wing) and whether they supported the status quo or were a critic of it. For example, some, such as S496, clearly state their identity as a member of the "working-class":

> Our family would say there must be millions of people like us yet when we watched TV and read the papers people like us seemed to be extinct. Working class people do not seem able to stand up for themselves very well. I have always thought we are a great crowd and have always been proud to be working class. When I hear politicians say we have the politics of envy I get very hurt. We do not envy, in fact the majority of us are very happy with our lot although life can be very hard at times, and very unfair. (S496, UWR Q1)

and some clearly state their identity as part of the opposition to the government and the status quo:

> I feel as if I'm a silent minority in terms of media coverage. When I joined I felt it was vital to have an anti-Thatcher voice in the Archive—history should know that less than 40% of the electorate supported her policies. . . . Mass-Observation is valuable in giving an accurate view of what ordinary people rather than the professional media think about events. (P2250, UWR Q1&2)

> I remember the fairly opprobrious label "history from below" was placed on the kind of work Sussex [the Mass-Observation Project] was instrumental in making happen. Fucking right on, I say. I'd rather have that sort of history than history written by eminent ass-lickers, honours-junkies and apologists for state crimes. (R1671, UWR)

Others support the government and express conservative political views.

But descriptions of "who" the Mass-Observation correspondents are using traditional demographic and sociological measures or according to their political views hardly do justice to their complex and shifting identities or to the ways they define themselves, never mind the difficulties we have in trying to define and apply terms like "middle-class" or "working-class". Part of the difficulty with traditional sociological labels is that they give no indication of the social dynamics involved in defining "who" somebody is, and they give no sense of how "who" they are depends on what they are doing, with whom, when and where. Traditional sociological measures index a particular frame of reference for defining social life at a broad, macro level rather than how people define and live through and in their everyday lives (cf., Heath &

McLaughlin, 1993; Smith, 1987). And, in some traditional sociological formulations, the descriptors suggest a kind of determinism and stasis that is at odds with a view of people as agents acting upon the worlds in which they live. Our concern with traditional descriptors is not a rejection of issues of class, gender, race and so forth, but recognition that such labels are more problematic than some have taken them to be, and that figuring out "who" people are requires understanding how they "position" themselves and are "positioned" by others in various social scenes which they have at least some part in creating.

The Mass-Observation Project and Writing from Positions

In one sense, "who" the Mass-Observation correspondents are and "who" they are studying depends on what happens in the Mass-Observation Project itself. As we described earlier in Chapter 6, the directives inscribe (that is, are written in a way that defines) the Mass-Observation correspondents as ethnographers, observers of everyday life, interviewees, survey respondents, social historians or autobiographers, and so forth. However, most of the Mass-Observation correspondents do not passively accept the social identities they are given through the directive. For example, one Mass-Observation correspondent wrote to Dorothy Sheridan objecting to a directive that asked them to write about their birthdays. He stated that he was willing to be an observer of others and life around him, but he was not willing to write about his private life. He would not be inscribed as an autobiographer.

The Mass-Observation correspondents use writing for the Mass-Observation Project as an opportunity to create a range of social identities that are complementary to (or parallel to) the social identities inscribed in the directive. For example, Mr Muse (M381) wrote in his response to the 1991 Spring directive that writing for the Mass-Observation Project

> gives me a certain amount of kudos when I modestly admit to acquaintances that I am doing some research work on behalf of Sussex University! (M381, UWR)

Similarly, **Mrs** Smith (S2207):

> I told my parents about it and they were very impressed . . . my mother only you know just thought "Oh, what a clever, girl," I think (laughter) . . . doing something sort of clever . . . they thought it was something clever to do, really. That's the way they thought . . . prestigious occupation, you know, sort of, well a hobby but a sort of academic style, probably, you know—well yes, I suppose as a family

they've always sort of valued sort of academic, intellectual achievements more than practical ones because we're not that practical a family really, you know, sort of more brain than muscle I suppose. (M2207, interview)

And Mrs Douglas (D2092) as well:

I feel their [family and friends] reaction [to being told she was a Mass-Observation correspondent] for the most part was amazement. Perhaps grandmothers do not do this kind of thing, but I love it. (D2092, interview)

These Mass-Observation correspondents (M381, M2207 and D2092) use their affiliation with the Mass-Observation Project or with the University of Sussex to define themselves (or be defined) within a local context, the network of family, friends, and people they know. Other Mass-Observation correspondents, like Mrs Wright (W632), do not inform friends and family of their affiliation with the Mass-Observation Project or with the University of Sussex (although they do not hide it either), but nonetheless the affiliation has importance in how they define themselves to themselves.

Participation in the Mass-Observation Project allows Mrs Wright to define herself as someone with opinions, and opinions that someone is interested in, despite the fact that, as she sees it, the people in her local situation are not especially interested in her opinion on the issues in the directives. Her identity as far as her husband, son and friends are concerned does not change because of her participation in the Mass-Observation Project, but it nonetheless changes for her, as she is able to place herself in a context that is outside of and broader than the context of family, friends and the day-to-day activities of work and family.

The writings sent to the Mass-Observation Project are kept in boxes, with all responses to a directive separated by gender and then filed together. Within a box, the contributions are arranged in alphanumeric order by the identification number of the Mass-Observation correspondent. Although it is possible to read the collection of writings sent to the Archive by an individual Mass-Observation correspondent, the nature of the filing system and the nature of use in the Archive makes it more likely that people using the Archive do so by reading through the contributions of many people on a particular directive rather than following a particular person's writings. From the perspective of readers in the Archive, the social position of a Mass-Observation correspondent is bounded by the immediate piece of writing they are reading. To read successively the contributions of a particular Mass-Observation correspondent would require a great deal of work. The Mass-Observation staff do record which directives are responded to by each Mass-Observation correspondent. From that information, the particular papers would need to be pulled from each of the many boxes in which they had been filed. The organisation of the storage system makes it difficult to read the collection as individual autobiographies. It promulgates a view of a collective response, separated by gender.

The view of the Mass-Observation correspondents, promoted by the ways in which the collection is stored, is primarily an issue for users of the collection, and less so for the Mass-Observation correspondents themselves. Many Mass-Observation correspondents do not know how their papers are organised at the Mass-Observation Archive. Through our interviews we found that at least a few of the Mass-Observation correspondents assumed that the papers were organised by person. The occasional written comments on previous contributions made by some Mass-Observation correspondents in a current piece of writing suggest similar impressions, as the Mass-Observation correspondents would refer readers to their previous writings. However, at least for some of the Mass-Observation correspondents, the identity they build up through their writing to the Mass-Observation Project over time is not readily available to readers at the Archive.

Issues of identity, social positioning and power are highlighted and are illustrative in an unsolicited contribution from Mrs Wright (W632). She sent a description of what happened to her and her husband when they went to court because of their refusal to pay the Poll Tax.[1] The full text of her description is shown below.

Mrs Wright's Poll Tax Report

My husband and I went to court today to answer the summons for non-payment of the community charge. We arrived 15 mins before the court was due to start at 10 A.M. The entrance was crowded with people waiting in line to see the clerk, about fifty answering the same summons that we received. The clerk advised everyone to go and talk to the counsellors about payment arrangements, they had a room set up at the courts for that purpose, I said I would see them after I had seen the Magistrates, and my name was entered on a list and I was given [next page] a raffle ticket. There was several people there that we knew but gradually the crowd thinned out and there was only about sixteen people left. We had a cigarette and coffee when names started to be called. I was seventh, my husband wasn't called. I

---

[1] The Poll Tax was a highly unpopular tax introduced by the conservative government during the 1980s.

was the only woman. There were eight altogether and all the others were young Jack the Lads' under 30. We were given a page of instruction saying what we couldn't dispute and what we could, these were six items like not living at the address stated, already paid & having proof of payment, the forms not properly served etc.

Each person was called to the stand and asked if they had paid in full, to which the answer was no in every case, and whether they had a defence as specified in the instructions. Several brought in points such as can't afford to pay—they were advised to see a counsellor, disagreed with the Law—they were advised to contact their MP and one contested the amount of the court costs—ours was L20 whereas another area charged L10.60 to which the Magistrate's clerk said they could set a charge of any amount that the court decided was reasonable. All these points had been listed in the instructions as matters not in the jurisdiction of the Court.

When it was my turn I took an Affirmation, rather than an oath on the Bible, and was asked the first two questions, had I paid in full—no and did I have a defence as listed in the instructions to which I said "No, I am here as an Act of Civil Disobedience in protest at this regressive tax and it will be recorded for History to judge"

The magistrate laughed and said "So you are going down in history," I said "yes my grandchildren will read about this." He said "I have no alternative but to grant the liability order, unfortunately the reporter has just left so you won't be in the newspapers." I said "Thank you, perhaps next year."

I joined my husband in the entrance foyer and waited for him to be called. A court clerk was asking everyone if they had been seen to access how things were going. I said I had been in court and was waiting til my husband was called, she was perplexed, they hadn't put him on the list as he hadn't made clear his intention of going before the Magistrate. apparently all the other people who turned up at court had gone to talk to the counsellors and didn't go into court, so there had only been the one sitting that I attended. My husband said not to bother them, we would just go and make an arrangement with the council advisors. A chap with the court clerk said well he would attend to us now. So we stayed where we were and he joined us. He turned out to be the manager of the District Council's Recovery Department. Although I had put money aside each month to pay the Poll Tax once we had been to court, it seemed that wasn't expected so we agreed to pay it in five monthly installments so it was cleared in this financial year. He asked if we would like to make an arrangement for next year and we said no we will go through the same procedure again. We sat chatting to him for half an hour, talking about the unfairness of the system and he [top of next page] seemed to think that the social services would be adjusting benefits to pay the 20% liability of benefit recipients' Poll Tax direct in future. He told us that he recommends people to pay their mortgage first as it would cause the Council more problems if their property was repossessed than if the Poll Tax wasn't paid. He said he has agreed payments as low as £2 per week, which would take years to clear, because he lives in the real world and knows the hardship some residents suffer.

I had a lovely morning altogether, the atmosphere of the people at Court was friendly and helpful. The attitude of the other defendants was jocular or amiably defiant & there were no banner-waving, angry militants to be seen so my husband was relaxed. I will be there again next year unless the whole system is scrapped.

Altogether 47 non-domestic and 200 domestic liability orders were made in that one court on that one morning, the media have given us no clue as to how prevalent the discontent has been but these figures must be published some day. I believe it was the cause of the Tories losing the safe seat at E_____ in the byelection but again the media didn't mention this aspect as a reason at all. (W632, 16-11-90)

We provide a detailed analysis of Mrs Wright's description below. In brief, her description has importance for our purposes as researchers of literacy practices because it highlights (a) how dominant social institutions, like Courts, use written language to control and define people, (b) how the Mass-Observation Project is located in relation to dominant institutions through the literacy practices it employs, and (c) how literacy practices are implicated in power relations and processes including transformations of dominant power relations.

Mrs Wright and her husband received a summons to appear in court in conjunction with her refusal to pay a Poll Tax. At court they were given various documents. Mrs Wright, along with some others, testified. By the time Mrs Wright testified, the newspaper reporters who had covered earlier cases had left. In her description of events at the Court, although apparently not an explicit intent, Mrs Wright described how written language was used to control what people could and could not say, and how written language was used to define the people at Court. Further, in her writing, Mrs Wright describes the Court as only recognising the existence of newspaper reporters and Court recorders as writers, as the only ones empowered to record the event and locate it among other recorded events. Not only did they have the "right" to create a text out of the event, they also had the "right" to establish or impose an intertextual world on that event-text, creating its social significance and location in history. Both in her contribution to the Mass-Observation Project and in her actions in Court, Mrs Wright contested the intertextual world they created and their right to do so.[2] In the following paragraphs, we provide a detailed analysis of what Mrs Wright wrote.

There are at least four institutional contexts that are either implied or mentioned explicitly in the beginning of her account:

1. Mrs Wright's family (she and her husband);
2. the Court, legal and governmental system;
3. the media; and
4. the Mass-Observation Project.

The last, of course, is not mentioned explicitly, but is implied because the text was written for and sent to the Mass-Observation Project. Indeed, it is our knowledge that this is so that later undercuts the magistrate's comments about being too late to be recorded for history and that allows us to understand a meaning of Mrs Wright's statement, "it will be recorded for history" that is not known by the magistrate.

Before beginning analysis of Mrs Wright's description, it is important to note that Mrs Wright's account of events at court on that day is only one of many different descriptions possible. Presumably, official court records give another description, as would those written by the court clerk, the magistrate, the counsellor, a newspaper reporter, and so forth, in large part because of the different social positions from which they would be writing. Part of what is important about Mrs Wright's narrative of events at court is that it describes how ordinary people may not be provided a social position from which to write. Mrs Wright writes about the event from the social position of a Mass-Observation correspondent. Yet, that social position is not a well-known public social position. There was no mention of it at court and many Mass-Observation correspondents (Mrs Wright included) do not tell people other than close family that they are Mass-Observation correspondents. Further, there is no established genre for writing as a Mass-Observation correspondent and thus no established social position to take up.

Mrs Wright begins by locating herself as family ("My husband and I") being brought into the court. As an institution, and as shown throughout the text, the court deals with individuals not with families. Each person is given a number (a raffle ticket), and there are continual references to the number of people there (e.g., "fifty [people]",

---

[2] A detailed discussion of this event and Mrs Wright's description can be found in Bloome, Sheridan and Street (1998).

"everyone", "sixteen people", "I was seventh"). Within the first few words then, Mrs Wright has set up a tension between definitions of personhood—personhood as defined in the family context versus personhood in the court context.

The first mention of writing is the "summons" which is located in the court context. Indeed, almost all of the types and uses of writing are relocated in the court context (list, raffle ticket, page of instructions, Bible). The Court's uses of writing are to control people (e.g., the summons is used to bring people before the court), to constrain what they can and cannot say, and to define them as individuals. The Magistrate recognised only the media context as an institutionally available writing position outside of the Court, a position not available to Mrs Wright.

The tension between the Court and how it was controlling and positioning Mrs Wright through writing climaxed immediately after Mrs Wright said, "I am here as an act of Civil Disobedience in protest at this regressive tax and it will be recorded for History to judge". Mrs Wright's statement is in defiance of what the list of instructions provided as allowable statements. The authority of the written instructions derives in part from the court—it is a court document and presumably the court can enforce the content of the instructions; but its authority also derives from the status often attributed to particular genres of written language in British and other Westernised societies. Information and directives in a textbook, a written contract, a legal document, a newspaper, and so forth, are often treated as more valid and true than information given in spoken form (Clanchy, 1979). Mrs Wright is not only defying the court's authority to constrain what may be spoken in court, but is also violating a widely shared cultural significance for certain genres of written language.

Mrs Wright may have several intended meanings when she said, "recorded for History to judge": recorded in the court records, as well as in newspapers, in her writing at home and in her writing for the Mass-Observation Project. The Magistrate recognises only one available space for Mrs Wright's protest to be recorded in history and that was in the media, in the newspapers. There is no institutionally recognised position from which she can write, from which she can put her protest in written history (other than the Mass-Observation Project, but that is not a publicly acknowledged presence). It is not just that the reporter has left, but that the Magistrate does not assign to Mrs Wright a personhood associated with writing. Stating an alternative case makes this point clearer. If Mrs Wright had been a newspaper reporter herself, a university-based historian, or held a position of power, she would have been viewed as having available to her various writing positions. However, Mrs Wright is only an ordinary person, without any available writing positions for having her protest recorded in history. From the Magistrate's perspective, Mrs Wright is powerless to get her protest in history and powerless to change her personhood (as an individual protest and as an individual who did not pay the poll tax), because there are no writing positions available to her to do so.

Although Mrs Wright does not have available to her institutionally recognised positions in the media, the court or in other dominant institutions, besides the Mass-Observation Project she does have writing positions open to her within the family context (signalled by her reference to "my grandchildren"—line 38).

In the second half of her description she describes the conversations ("chatting") she and her husband had with "a chap with the court clerk". Her husband is not called to the magistrate, as his name was not entered on the list. Within that paragraph, the tension reappears between the family context and the court context that only recognises individuals: Mrs Wright "joined her husband" versus the "court clerk asking everyone if they had been seen ..."; "My husband ... we ... us" versus "he hadn't made clear his intention". The references then to Mrs Wright are to the family unit (she and her husband, together). The one exception ("I had put money aside" is also a reference to the family context, as Mrs Wright handled all of the financial matters in her family).

The last paragraph in Mrs Wright's description is important with regard to the construction of a social position from which to write. Mrs Wright is no longer telling an autobiographical story but has assumed a writing position, perhaps that of a historian or political observer. Her use of details, technical jargon, the repetition of "that" and the distancing of the first person singular in the first part of the sentence—"Altogether 47 non-domestic and 200 domestic liability orders were made in that one court on that one morning, ..." reposition her as an observer and reporter for the Mass-Observation Project. She is no longer invoking the family context as social identity, but the writing position of ordinary people ("us") who live in the "real world", in opposition to the authorised writing position of the media who are described as aligned with the court and the Tories and who attempt to construct reality by what they do not publish. The writing position of "ordinary people" that Mrs Wright takes up is one aligned with the Mass-Observation Project as a social institution that is both part of and yet separate from the dominant institutions of society (as we have discussed in earlier chapters). Thus, although she takes up the position of ordinary person, she writes in a conventionalised genre and style associated with an establishment institution.

By writing up the event and sending it to the Mass-Observation Project, Mrs Wright not only recorded her protest for history, but she also redefined personhood and repositioned various people who participated in the events that day. Where personhood had been defined in terms of individuals with positions assigned by Court roles—Magistrate, recorder, newspaper reporter, clerk, defendant—with a particular distribution of qualities and rights, including who could write and who was subject to what was written, Mrs Wright redefined personhood along the lines of those who live in the real world (e.g., herself as a member of a family, the Court clerk, others suffering because of the Poll Tax) and those who don't (e.g., the Magistrate, the newspaper reporters), with ordinary people like herself delegated to write on behalf of other ordinary people, with claims to record/make history.[3]

Simply stated, the patronising attitude and remarks of the magistrate described by Mrs Wright (W632) did not just marginalise her and deny her the status of a writer, but trivialised her protest and her life; and in so doing, trivialised that of other ordinary people. She uses her writing to give her protest, her life and the lives of others at court, a value denied by the magistrate. She uses the other writing she does for the Mass-Observation Project similarly; not just as a source for future historians, but as a means for claiming that the lives of people like her have value and need to be valued.

Education, Writing and Identity

As we have described in Chapter 4, the Spring Directive of 1991 contained several parts. In this section we use the responses to Part 1 of the Directive (which requested an educational history) to seek connections between the educational history of the Mass-Observation correspondents and the writing they do. In brief, was there something in their educational history that predisposed them to be Mass-Observation correspondents? Did they have a special love for writing assignments and English classes? Did they have a teacher who encouraged them to write or taught them to love writing?

Following the first question in the education directive, which asked the Mass-Observation correspondents to list the schools they attended, degrees achieved, and so forth, the questions in the education directive asked them to recount and reflect on their educational history and provide opinions on current educational practices. The responses, of course, are primarily constructed from memories and are not documented, dispassionate descriptions. Thus, it is reasonable to argue that the data we have do not really point out historical antecedents to

---

[3]We are not unaware that by incorporating Mrs Wright's narrative into our chapter that we have added yet another level of defining Mrs Wright as a writer (and of disseminating Mrs Wright's description of events at court that day). We do not have space in this chapter to discuss this additional layer of defining writing positions.

any person's writing or to any group's writing, but may more accurately be described as people's interpretations of their educational history. One's educational history may be reconstructed in order to create a coherent "story". We are not suggesting that people deliberately distort, lie or fabricate their educational history but rather that what gets highlighted and what gets left out, what events get connected to what other events, and how they all get interpreted are filtered through how they currently view themselves and the world in which they live. We argue that such data are all the more important and useful because they are reconstructed history. It gives us insight into what happened during people's educational history (although not everything that may have happened) and what meaning those past events hold for them now-and it is the latter that, we would argue, that is key to understanding the role of education in defining people as writers.

Often the descriptions of schooling are very moving as people described how circumstances or someone's ill-will denied them educational opportunities and chances for a better life. Many of the women described what we have come to call "de-railed education"; reasonable aspirations for pursuing education were obstructed or redirected in ways that were both disappointing and that made life difficult.[4] We have come to view their educational history, especially that concerned with writing, as part of "who" they are, because that educational history played a major role in positioning them within various institutions. And this is so whether their education was "de-railed" or not.

One example of a de-railed education is that the person was doing well in school academically (even if she disliked it) when something happened that would disrupt the education trajectory. For example:

Mrs A616: failed university examinations.
Mrs A1733: won a scholarship to grammar school, but father had died when she was seven and with her mother working it was impossible to go.
Mr B1442: mother died very young, father deserted them. He missed grammar school exam because his mother was injured and couldn't take him.
Mrs C108: could not go to higher education because she became sick.
Mrs C1883: parents thought school was unnecessary and forced her to leave.

---

[4]The "de-railed education" narrative structure was not as frequent among the men Mass-Observation correspondents as among the women.

Mrs H260: mother would not let her sit for scholarship examination as they didn't have the money for uniform or bus fare.
Mrs W569: teachers thought she was a bright student but she failed her 11+ examinations.
Mrs W571: was not allowed by the headmaster of her school to sit for the examination to be admitted to a School of Art.
Mrs Y1514: had to drop out at fourteen as her father could not afford to pay for her schooling.

Several of the women, including those who were de-railed, described having to overcome a father who did not believe in education for women. Often, they were able to overcome their father's prejudice with the help of their mother. For example, W640's mother was able to prevail against her father in large part because she saw that other girls were going on to further schooling. W1835's mother faked her father's signature so she could go to Nurse's Training School instead of staying home and marrying a farmer.

For those women who were denied the academic credentials they had hoped for, education—as a social institution—defined them in relation to others, located them in a particular set of career and job opportunities and overlaid a series of skills and abilities that they were and were not assumed able to do. Although many wrote in ways that either stated or suggested that they were treated unfairly—that they should have been allowed to go on to Grammar School or treated better by teachers, peers and parents—few questioned the right of schools to structure the dimensions upon which people—children—were judged. If you did well in school, if you learned what was being taught, if you wrote well, you should have been given the opportunities you deserved.

We argue that part of what schooling does is define important aspects of personhood, and we are especially concerned with those aspects related to writing and being a "writer." First, schooling plays a role in what counts as "writing" (cf., Street & Street, 1991). Essays, reports, stories and poems done for the teacher or similar legitimated authority are "writing". Writing notes to schoolmates, graffiti and other forms of vernacular writing do not count as "writing." How well one does on school literacy tasks predisposes one to be viewed as a writer. But what does it mean to do well on such tasks? In part it means doing it better than others (cf., McDermott, 1977).

Schools define doing well on writing tasks as a matter of ability and morality (e.g., hard work, listening to the teacher, having the right attitude; see Gilmore, 1987), and these qualities constitute fundamental measures of how schooling defines personhood. People have various abilities that allow some to excel at writing and others write less well, but ability must be combined with hard work and following directions (morality), and sorting people out according to ability and morality is viewed by the schools as a technical task, not an ideological one.

Yet doing well on officially defined school "writing" tasks does not in itself define one as a "writer", it only places one in the position to be eligible to compete for those social positions that grant the status of "writer." Those students who do not go on to Grammar School, for example, are not in a position to compete for University or for jobs as newspaper reporters or other jobs that carry the identity "writer." And, for those people interested in writing a novel or other form of creative composition, the label "writer" is only assigned to those who get published—and getting published requires access to those social practices and those writing practices that allow one to be recognised as available for the identity of "writer". People whose education was "derailed" find themselves greatly distanced from being considered "writers", because even if they had obtained the technical skills associated with writing (in Bourdieu's terms, the cultural capital), they lacked the social connections and recognition (in Bourdieu's terms, the symbolic capital) to use their writing skills in a way that would acknowledge them as "writers". And this is not only so with regard to how others view them, but also how they view themselves.

Not everyone buys into the power of schooling to define people or personhood. For example, Mrs Friend's (F1373) experience at work questions the legitimacy of the credentialling done by schools.

> The only time I could have done with qualifications was when I first started work at Marks + Spencer. I was put on a men's pajama counter and a qualified school teacher was on the next counter which was a men's Shetland sweater counter. Every sweater on her counter was £2-10s shillings and it was Christmas and every time she sold two sweaters together she would get a slip of paper and write down a little sum
>
> £2-10s
> £2-10s
> £5-00s
>
> —if the next person had two sweaters still the same written down sum. [In the old monetary terms used by Mrs Friend, two lots of 10s shillings made £1]. Now my pajamas were £2 9s 11d. £2 19 11d and all various prices. One day the personnel manageress sent for me + said they were going to swap us over as the Shetland counter was much faster and this school teacher couldn't cope. I didn't mind until I found out she was earning 6d an hour more than me so off I went to the manageress who took great delight in belittling me and telling me this school teacher had qualifications, little bits of paper.

So I said they didn't give little bits of paper for what I had. What's that? says she. Common Sense says I and if you don't mind I'll stick with the pajamas. Needless to say they then levelled everyone off with the same rate of pay and put us on whatever counter they liked. (F1373, education directive)

Mrs Wright (W632) tells a similar story:

The Department I work in has just been advised that in order to progress to higher grades, senior officer, posts etc. we will need the relevant paper qualifications and the B/TEC CMS was specifically mentioned in my case. So I produced it and said it was ridiculous to ask for these qualifications at my age and with my experience. The bits of paper were only important when leaving school. They were trying to move the goal posts and thought we wouldn't be able to come up with the right results, as most of the others in the department could not and had felt dismayed at the thought of having to sit more exams. (W632, interview)

Having proven themselves as capable and worthy workers, both Mrs Wright and Mrs Friend had to confront definitions of personhood located in the social institution of education, with its hierarchy of certified achievement. It is not just that schooling serves the elite at the expense of others, but that the future is thrown back into the past (having to sit more exams) after believing the past was over.

With regard to writing, although some of the Mass-Observation correspondents mentioned that during school they had a special interest in writing or a special teacher who motivated them to write, there were not enough remarks of this nature to confirm a general trend, although there were enough such remarks to make us suspect such a trend. It may be that some Mass-Observation correspondents overlooked noting such an interest in writing in their educational histories. Regardless of whether they had a special interest in writing or wanted to become writers, what seems likely is that their experiences in education positioned them as people who were not writers, a quality many came to believe about themselves and that was reinforced later, perhaps, by rejection notices for stories or other works submitted to publishers or by a society that reserves the label "writer" for a select few.

It is difficult to say how widespread the phenomenon of derailed education is. Although it is pervasive within the responses of the women Mass-Observation correspondents to the Education directive, it is not clear if it is pervasive in the general population of women, or to what extent it is prevalent among men. It may be the case that a derailed education motivates people later in life to find outlets for their denied writing, and Mass-Observation provides one opportunity that some people find rewarding. In that sense Mass-Observation provides a telling case of such processes without necessarily being typical in numerical terms (see discussion of telling cases in Chapter 4).

Crossings

Although it is not our purpose in this chapter or in this book to devise a new schematic for embedding social contexts, nonetheless we have had to rethink social context to better understand the significance of how people use writing.

Social contexts exist in time, with what went before and what will, or might, come later influencing the present context. But there is also a dynamic play of social contexts; they infringe upon, incorporate, oppose and redefine each other. To the extent that a particular social context tends to impose itself—and its ideological and power trappings—upon other social contexts, defining them in terms of itself, the dynamic play of social contexts can be viewed as hegemonic. Such hegemony has been described by numerous social theorists (e.g., Althusser 1971; Fairclough, 1992; Giddens, 1984; Gramsci, 1971). Particularly in the United States, social theorists have characterized the dynamic play and structures of social contexts and ideologies as the setting up of social borders (Anzadula, 1987; Giroux, 1992; Guiterrez & Larson, 1994). These social borders are socio-political (for example, a state, a business institution, a classroom, a profession, a community, a church), but may also have physical and material realizations (such as walls, police patrols, identification cards, membership requirements and dues). Further, these social borders exist at both micro and macro levels, such as the boundaries between advanced, average and low reading groups in a classroom, between non-Anglophone neighborhood communities and Anglophone neighborhoods and institutions (such as schools), as well as national borders.

Yet despite the power and seemingly totalising effect of the hegemony of social and cultural institutions, social processes and social contexts which may appear seamless and orderly may only be so on the surface. Lying just under the surface may exist a set of messy, contested or even anarchistic social dynamics. Part of the complexity of social contexts is that people are continually pulling contexts into each other, borrowing a bit here for use there, tearing them apart and tearing them down, rebuilding and recreating, using the "what was" and "what is."

De Certeau (1984) has argued that despite the penetration of the discourse of market economy and mass media (with its social institutional ideology) into people's daily lives and homes, people adapt and transform much of that penetrating discourse and adapt it to the social contexts they have otherwise created. Similarly, studies in a volume edited by Street (1993) show how people in a wide range of locations and situations have adapted and transformed the literacy practices imposed upon them by a dominant group; as he summarizes, we need to focus on how people "take hold" of literacy rather than, as in dominant discourse, what is the "impact" of literacy. As Guerra (1997), Gilyard (1997) and Mangelsdorf (1997) have argued, people can and do cross over, back and forth, between dominant discourses and the local social contexts in which they create their daily lives. Mangelsdorf (1997) describes the efforts of students from minority communities (and their teachers) to learn how to use the textual practices of dominant institutions without losing their relationship with, or identification with, their minority community as "crossing textual borders" (p. 302). Although not giving it the same label, Gilyard (1997), Guerra (1997), Giroux (1992) and others describe similar processes, whereas Guiterrez and Larson (1994), although not building on de Certeau, suggest a similar notion in the creation of space where teachers and students can engage each other in an educational discourse beyond that of the dominant ideology. We have borrowed the construct of "crossing" from the discussions of those cited above, adapting it to the particulars of the social contexts we have encountered in our research on literacy practices and the Mass-Observation Project.

We use "crossings" to refer to both the movement back and forth between dominant institutional contexts of writing and local non-dominant ones, and to the use of writing to cross the social separation, alienations and marginalisations (which may have physical and geographical manifestations) created by the dynamics of contemporary social structures and institutions. In the rest of this chapter, we discuss some of the messy, contested and anarchistic social dynamics involved in some of writing practices used by Mass-Observation correspondents—their crossings.

Creating Space For Writing in Everyday Life

Writing requires space and time. For some Mass-Observation correspondents, space and time for writing compete with space and time for other activities and needs. For some, spouses and children make it difficult to obtain the space and time required for writing. One woman reported that she had to go to her daughter's house to escape the demands of her family in order to write. Another, Mrs Caldwell (C2079), told us that she left the house to write and think in a caravan parked in the garden.

> I do the thinking these days in the caravan in the garden which I use as a sort of office, and which is the only place I can have peace at

home. Even then I usually just get sorted out when they [family members] put my switch [supply of electricity from the house] off as a signal that they want something like dinner money or whatever. (C2079, interview)

Most cases of needing to find time and space were not so dramatic. Mrs Friend (F1373), who did a great deal of letter writing, sought additional time for other writing, including the writing of a book. Her job, rather than spouse or family, constrained the time she had for writing. To create physical space for writing, she organised her living room so that its use as a writing workshop was hidden. When Mrs Friend was ready to write, for example in the evenings when she and her husband would sit down in front of the television, she took out supplies—a lap desk and files camouflaged behind end tables and other furniture. Similarly, Mrs Wright (W632) did not have a dedicated space for writing but often wrote sitting with her husband while he watched the television. Of course, women who lived alone and many others did not have the same issues with finding space—either physical space or social space. They often had a dedicated space for writing, often a table area or shelf area if not a room or alcove.

Finding space for writing was not just an issue for women. For example, Mr Richards (M1593) saved his writing for the Mass-Observation Project for those times when he was away on business and had nothing to do. He often worked on oil rigs in the sea, and bad weather could stop work for days at a time. Mr Richards would write during such times, as he would then have the stretch of time he needed for writing and the writing would help fill the time.

Few people had a room dedicated to writing, although some were able to create a space in a room that they could dedicate to writing. The comment below is typical of many statements people wrote in their response to the Spring 1991 directive.

I've got a sort of work top in our bed-room (which is also studio and office!) so I always write there, so I can leave it lying about. (A1706)

However, having a physical space dedicated to writing in one's home did not always mean that one had the social space that allowed one to write there, as Mrs Caldwell's (C2079) quotation earlier illustrated. People tended to write in whatever space and time were available—on the train, on holiday. Sometimes notes will be made in the odd moment and then later written up at home when a stretch of time could be found.

The difficulties in finding space for writing—both physical space and social space—give another perspective on why it is that many of the Mass-Observation correspondents are retired or older (their children having grown up and left home). The following statements by Mr Muse (M381) and Mr Russell (R1671) show that at least some people are aware of how retirement freed up space and time for writing.

> I have a small bedroom converted to a study and sit in a very comfortable executive chair at my desk. I have been retired since I started with Mass-Obs. and have always completed my efforts in the same place. (Mr Muse, M381, from response to the Spring 1991 directive)

> I write in the upstairs study, formerly just the "spare bedroom", but since I unchained myself from employment primarily where I work I've redesigned it specifically to suit my needs. These include (in no special order):
> 1. At least two sources of indirect lighting.
> 2. Radio & cassette player.
> 3. Plenty of ashtrays.
> 4. Ample shelf space for books and files.
> 5. A wallboard for ephemera.
> 6. Ornaments, pictures, flowers (dried), familiar objects.
> 7. Pens, stationery, etc. in neurotically excessive amounts.
>
> (Mr Russell, R1671, from response to the Spring 1991 directive)

Given that space and time are needed for writing, it is reasonable to ask how the social institutions in which we live—work, family, church, community, and so forth—provide the needed time and space. The answer for many people, including many Mass-Observation correspondents, is that these institutions do not provide space or time for writing (except for work settings that provide space and time for writing directly related to work). What people must do is find space and time in odd moments such as riding on the train, take themselves out of ongoing events by writing (for example, while others watch television they write—see Mrs. Wright's description in Chapter 5), or they transform the space and time they have by converting a room, taking a writing course, retiring or waiting until the children leave home, and so forth. Seen from this perspective, writing for the Mass-Observation Project, and similar writing, is not just a technical issue of skill or of finding space and time, but of countering and transforming the social institutions in which people live, at least for oneself if not for others. Such countering and transformation requires prioritising particular kinds of writing, and for many people that is difficult to do, since writing—as an activity that requires space and time—competes with demands to engage in other activities.

But the competition is not just a matter of one activity versus another. The activities that constitute any social institution are related, such that one activity implies or requires another, and the activities implicate people in taking up particular roles within the institution. Further, the discourse within a social institution tends to support one set of activities over others, in part by linking them together and in part by making one set of activities seem "natural" and other activities seem either weird, selfish or otherwise socially negative. Thus, to supplant one activity with another activity, with an activity that involves different roles and that may not necessarily relate in the same way to the other activities and social practices that occur within that social institution, is to contest and transform that social institution. The difficulty of doing so may explain how it is that much of the writing for the Mass-Observation Project occurs in the odd moments of people's lives, when they can easily take themselves out of ongoing activities without interpersonal conflict, or at times when changes in their lives have placed them on the boundaries of usual work, home and social categories (such as retirement or redundancy).

Of course, some people come to place a high value on writing for the Mass-Observation Project or for similar writing and thus do create the space and time for writing in ways that do contest and transform the social institutions in which they live. In some cases they engage in such contesting and transformations alone (such as Mrs Caldwell, C1709), while in other cases, spouses, family, and friends are supportive of the change (such as Mrs Friend, F1373).

Mrs Safran's (B2197) comments reveal yet another dimension of social institutions and finding time for particular writing activities.

> I make conscious efforts to make some space for myself, but it's very hard to find it because there is a never ending series of demands, I've actually quite recently begun to say, no not now, I'll stop now, I don't want to take that on, I'm too tired tonight, which I never used to do; I used to do everything, and there's just too much really, so I've been putting out stops. If you're involved in any kind of support work, there are endless things, so you're just in it really and you've got to prioritise the family, and the extended family. . . . I actually look on my "Mass-Observations" as very much my own time just time to indulge. . . . Well I really enjoy doing it, it's always a treat to do it. And a lot of things I like doing I feel guilty about doing, because there are other more worthy things to do, so for example I always feel guilty about the garden, because it's so way down on the list, it never gets the attention it deserves. Mass-Observation is a bit like that, it feels like an indulgence to do it, so it tends to be put to one side a bit more.

DB: Is it an indulgence because it's mostly for you?

Mrs Safran (B2197): Yeah. That's definitely true, but because it's sought after by somebody else, it's possible, whereas normally I don't ever make space for that sort of thing.

Although she and her family highly value her role as mother and wife, both she and her husband (and presumably many others in their lives as well) also highly value academic and intellectual pursuits (both she and her husband studied anthropology at university), as well as other activities that they also view as contributing to a better society (Mrs Safran volunteers a significant amount of time to a local organisation that helps women and children experiencing various economic, health, and social problems). In part their values are at odds with dominant social institutions, especially those institutions that create inequity and poverty. However, they also view many of the values they hold as consistent with other dominant social institutions in their lives, including their religious and ethnic heritage (Judaism), and education. As her comments in Chapter 5 show, writing for the Mass-Observation is an activity that can be justified because it has importance in countering dominant institutions (e.g., the mass media accounts of life in Britain), but also because it has value within other dominant social institutions (e.g., religion and education). Thus, when Mrs Safran finds time and space for writing, it is not a simple matter of supplanting an activity associated with a dominant institution (family) with an act of resistance or with an attempt to transform family. Rather, one needs to examine how she orchestrates the broad range of activities in which she is engaged; then, a more complex picture emerges. In examining her case, it is difficult to determine where one social institution ends and another begins, what is an act of resistance and what is an expression of a dominant social institution. Is writing for the Mass-Observation supplanting a family activity with an academic activity or social activism? Is it indeed a selfish activity, an indulgence, as Mrs Safran suggests it might be and thus worries about taking time away from her family? Is justifying the time writing for the Mass-Observation Project in terms of various dominant social institutions "creative" interdiscoursivity (i.e., adapting the language and values of other social institutions to redefine the relationship of one activity to another)? Or, given her family's support for the activity and that doing such writing is consistent with the values of other dominant social institutions, is writing for the Mass-Observation Project an activity consistent with how Mrs Safran and her family have balanced and orchestrated their relationships within the various social institutions that constitute their lives? Is the orchestration itself, rather than any activity per se, an act of contesting one or more dominant social institutions?

We do not believe that it is necessarily important for us, as researchers, to answer the questions above with regard to Mrs Safran or with regard to any other particular writer for the Mass-Observation Project. Rather, the importance of the questions is that they prevent a simplistic view of social life as constituted by social institutions with well-defined boundaries and domains or as structured around activities that are either acts that support dominant social institutions or acts of resistance and contesting. People continuously move across social institutions, embed them within each other, adopt and adapt the values, practices and activities of one for use in another, and "creatively" orchestrate their lives across multiple social institutions and domains of social life—and they do so both as individuals and as various collectives. The power of people to orchestrate their lives (either as an individual or as a collective) depends on many factors which we would not claim are equally or equitably distributed. Without underestimating the importance of resources (or in Bourdieu's [1977] terms—economic, cultural and symbolic capital), it is also important to highlight the "creative" ways in which people orchestrate their relationship with various social institutions as they individually and collectively create lives for themselves; and this is no less so for Mrs Wright (W632) or Mr Richards (M1593) or Mr Reed (R450) or Mrs Safran (B2197), whose economic situations vary greatly.

Using Writing to Create Social Relationships Across Physical and Social Boundaries

As described in Chapter 5, Mrs Friend (F1373) writes letters.

> I do letters. I've got a friend in America, a friend in Portsmouth, a friend in Oxford. Other people that I write to. Those I write every week without fail, sometimes twice a week, so it's . . . it's a natural urge. The one in Portsmouth is a childhood friend, we've been friends since we were ten. The friend in America I met later on in life, and we worked together, and the friend in Oxford I also worked with her, and they moved away . . . letters to my friends are usually about fourteen pages, foolscap pages, so it's not just a little letter it's a big letter. Costs me a fortune sending it to America. £1.21 an average letter, one pound twenty-one pence. I can honestly say that since [my friends and I] have been corresponding like this they tend to follow my style. I write exactly as I talk. If I'm having a conversation, if I say, 'I said to him this', I will do it, you know, inverted commas and all . . . just like a conversation. So I do find that now the letters come back from the other side on the same format, you know, the conversation! . . . it's not just, oh, we went . . . 'We went to Georgia State Fair, that was on last week'. And I had a letter this week and it wasn't, 'We went to the State Fair; the State

Fair was on and we saw the chopping of the logs, and all the other, the popcorn eating contest', and things like that. And I had it all in detail, whereas when I first wrote to my friend over there she would have just said, 'We went to the Georgia State Fair'; now I get it all in detail, so that's nice isn't it? . . . You get a complete picture; . . . I have been to the Georgia State Fair, I did go when I was there, so I do know what it's like, but it's much nicer to have complete details like she now writes you know. And she tells me about her garden; she's got a little garden there, and she took over a lot of English flowers, so I get all the details of, 'The pansies are out now, and it's so nice', whereas not, 'The garden's looking nice'. All the plants are listed. So it's great detail, I like a lot of detail. [If she stopped putting detail] I would write and ask her, you told me about the garden, now, you haven't told me what plants you've got, so I would get it back then again. And my other friends now do tend to write the same way as me, it's something that's rubbed off. . . . I do now get all the little details, so it's lovely. All about the family, and where they're going and what they're doing, and I mean . . . my friend in America's got a married son, and he and his wife have just bought a house, and she's described all the house in detail as well as sending me photographs of it, so. . . . We also write jokes to each other as well, because there's nothing like an English joke is there, so I will write and tell her something, you know, in the way of a joke. And she said that, particularly her husband, he absolutely rolls on the floor with laughing at some of these jokes, you know. . . . She said, because you know in America you have a postbox outside don't you, and she said in the morning he races down to the postbox and she says if there's a letter from you, he comes racing back in and says, 'There's a letter from Betty', and she says he tears it open and he sits and reads it and laughs and then passes it over to her! And . . . he's a man that I know how to make him respond; it makes me laugh, because he is steeped in British tradition. He's very rigid in his views, he doesn't expand either way. And just to absolutely stir him up, I always go on about the Labour Party and things like that. And I said something once about Arthur Scargill, and I had a letter back from him then, 'Don't you ever mention that man again', and it amused me so much that I have to now. And you know there's recently been a threat, about the mines being closed? Well just as a wind-up really, I wrote and said that they requested that as a mark of your support for the miners, you turned your lights off for one minute at nine o'clock on Sunday evening. And I said, 'You couldn't believe it, but when I looked out the whole of B_____ was in darkness!' It wasn't, but—only the lights were on at the hospital—and I said it's even reported that motorists in Western Road stopped and turned their lights off. And he's written back and said, 'You're all insane!' I had another letter from him! 'You're all insane! You know, they should have closed the mines years ago, they're all radicals, and all reds, and communists, and everything, you know.' That sort of correspondence is great fun really.

270 CHAPTER SEVEN

Mrs Friend's (F1373) letters connect friends and family across space. The movement of friends and family away from her was necessitated by economic conditions, as people look for jobs and for places to retire that are affordable and enjoyable. The point to make about such movement is that it is part of the social and economic conditions in which we all live. It is no longer unusual for grown children to move far away from their parents' home, or for friends to do the same, making extended families and local communities of long-lasting relationships less likely. Although Mrs Friend has not moved herself, she is as much caught in this broad economic and social process as those who have moved, with the same effects—loss of friends and family. What Mrs Friend does is maintain and build social relationships. Notice how important detail is to her. Letters are more than a matter of keeping connected, they are ways to keep involved in each other's lives. Thus, the joke and the teasing take on importance far beyond the value of their humour or entertainment. One argument that can be made about Mrs Friends' letters is that they are one way that people contest current social and economic conditions that pull friends, family and community apart. In this sense, community can be rebuilt through literacy practices.

Mr Reed (R450) also uses writing to contest social conditions in which he and others are caught:

> We've had some bad knocks, but that wakes you up, really, bad knocks, More than the other way . . . it makes you want to express yourself . . . people, that's why I left the building game, I thought I can't work with them. They're very brutal . . . I was walking through an alley and I say hello to a [person] in a office, you know, Fleet Street? I was working Fetcher Lane, we were renovating a building near the Mirror offices, and I walked past one lunch, and I said, "Hello girls" in an office, they were about the windows on the lower level down this little alley way. A man poked his head out about three floors up and said, "If you don't get away," he said, "I'll call the police immediately". And I was walking further on, and in five minutes there were two police grabbed me and it was weird. I couldn't believe it. And then, I went in a pub coming home from work, and I walked down Fleet Street to a pub called "The Old Londoner" and I walked in there and asked for a pint of beer, five o'clock in the evening, no, it was lunch time, I booked up the holiday, and it was packed and I asked for a pint and they said, "Sorry, no service". . . . And I thought, that [the] beer was off. So I said, "I'll have a pint of . . ." He said, "I told you, no service now get out". I couldn't believe it. [I contacted my MP and] he said, "Let me have it in writing". And I wrote to him, . . . and he says, he wrote back saying, "In some of the cases, where, you're still, if the governor doesn't want you in the pub he can . . ." So I thought in the end it must have been because I was a building worker. Cause

building workers look different. They've [office workers] got good complexion . . . building workers stand out in the city, I don't know why. You look different. My mate says, "No, a lot of pubs around here we're not allowed in, the building workers". (R450, interview)

But it is not just the social injustice he faces himself that motivates Mr Reed to write. He writes about the social and economic injustice that he sees as he traveled to and from work and that he sees in the East End of London. In Chapter 5 he describes how he came to write one of his poems, "Avenues of Hope and Glory by the Streets of Sad Despair" after seeing a boy who looked to be homeless and outcast thrown out of a newspaper shop.

Although Mr Reed, like anyone else, can write poems about social conditions, he has no access to audiences who might read his poems (other than those he might hand a copy to) and he has no access to the time and support (both social and economic) that would allow him to refine his poetry, if he so chose. Before job-related health problems forced him to retire, he spent most of his day as a construction worker on building sites and the rest of his time taking care of his family and neighbors. In order to acquire both the opportunities to write (e.g., time and support) and an audience, Mr Reed (R450) joined a group of writers similar to himself called the Plaistow Poets and in so doing they contested the lack of opportunities for writing and, through the substance of what they wrote, transformed the meaning of the East London community in which they live (at least to the extent of providing an alternative meaning to that of dominant institutions and representations).

The lack of opportunities and audiences for writing that Mr Reed (R450) confronts is something he shares with other East Londoners, other working-class people, and many others across class borders—although class issues do present different kinds of constraints and different degrees of constraint. The point is twofold. First, the social institutions that constitute much of Mr Reed's life provide no opportunity for writing and do not leave room even for consideration of him as a writer. In order to get consideration, to create space and audience, he has to join with others with similar motivation and interest in creating a community writing group, and even so space and audience for writing are limited. Nonetheless, and this is the second point, he does so and in so doing inserts into the set of dominant social institutions that constitute social life in East London an anomalous set of writing practices that do not really belong to any of the dominant institutions there. He, and the other members of the Plaistow Poets, have taken a set of writing practices that belong to other institutions, ones associated with power and privilege—academia, publishing firms and their legitimised authors, newspapers, and so forth—and adopted them without adopting the class values and meanings with which they are associated.

Mrs Wright (W632), who might also be described as working-class, provides another perspective on creating social relationships through writing. Unlike Mr Reed (R450) or Mrs Friend (F11373), whose jobs did not involve writing, Mrs Wright's does. She works for a major utility company. Although Mrs Wright (W632) does write in her job, those writing practices require that, metaphorically speaking, she make herself invisible.

> My job [is] to be between the user and the systems—computer systems—people, and to translate what each one's saying, so that the user says, "I want this," and the systems people are saying "XYZ formula," you know, and I'm saying, "Will that produce this?" And I test that out and make sure that this is what we want, the business is being met—the business requirements are being met. There is a lot of reading and writing involved in the job much of it involving other people, making sure that what is written is accurate and works. (W632, interview)

Her job is to make other people's ideas clear to audiences they designate and for purposes circumscribed by the company's goals. Her experiences and knowledge, other than as a company employee, have no place in the writing.

The claim might be made that since she has been hired by the company to do the kind of writing she does that being invisible in this way is not unreasonable (although interestingly, similar arguments would not even be considered for university academics or newspaper reporters). However, the point here is not about her job per se. Merely because people write on their job, and even if their job is to be a writer (as is the case with Mrs Wright), that does not mean that they have opportunity to engage in those writing practices that allow them to define and describe the worlds in which they live. As described earlier and in Chapter 5, even at home there are no official spaces for writing; Mrs Wright must transform the living room into a writing space and most often do so in a way that does not interfere with the typical activities that occur in those spaces (e.g., watching television). The Mass-Observation Project, while not inherently providing space and time for Mrs Wright, does provide an audience.

> It's flattering, really, to think that somebody's going to sit there and read it all (laughs) you know and I think it's rubbish most of the time I write. . . . I feel as though nobody's interested in my opinions, really (laughs)—I mean my husband doesn't ask what I think about

all these things (laughs) so why should somebody else be interested in what I think about them? (W632, interview)

Writing for the Mass-Observation Project provides a reason for writing that is viewed both by dominant institutions and by the individual Mass-Observation correspondents as sufficiently important to justify transforming social space and taking away time from other activities and obligations.

In addition to time, space and audience, in her interview Mrs Wright (W632) raised another constraint on the writing of ordinary people. She was not confident that the opinions she held about broad, national and international issues were indeed her own or if she had been brainwashed.

> I feel as though I'm very much parroting my newspaper [in response to directives on national political issues]. You know I read the *Guardian* because I like their opinions on things and I feel as though when I'm writing about those type of subjects I'm really paraphrasing what they're saying. And then I begin to wonder if it—is it my opinion or whether I'm being brainwashed by the paper or whether I read the paper because they think the same as I do (laughs). (W632, interview)

Thus, those directives that focus on personal and local issues have more appeal to Mrs Wright, in part because she is not constrained by the opinions of the national media. She sees those issues as a "space" that is hers, that belongs to ordinary people in their lives.

Of course, other Mass-Observation correspondents may view the situation differently. For them, the Mass-Observation Project provides a rare space for them to express their opinions; for example, Mrs Smith's (S2207) and Mr Purcell's (P2250) statements below.

> The social issues are also ones where you can let off steam. (S2207, interview)

> I suspect a lot of the work I have to write is deliberately non-political, it has to be non-political. I mean in the Archive, maybe I saw a way of getting out some of the feelings which had been bottled up, particularly at that time of the Thatcher Government, I had all these sort of feelings within me that I wasn't allowed always to express in my work. And so maybe that, you know, that was certainly I think a motive, somewhere, I think. (P2250, interview)

Yet even those Mass-Observation correspondents who have strong opinions about national political issues and who want and do express them in their writing for the Mass-Observation Project, nonetheless may accommodate what they see to be the views of dominant social institutions. For example, Mrs McPhail (M2493), who says that one reason she writes is to express a Scottish view, nonetheless accommodates her writing to what she views as expected in an English-based institution.

> Our cultural identity is in danger of being swamped from London and the South. And yet, if you don't embrace the ideas from there, you're in danger of being thought of as belligerent. (M2493, interview).

Similarly, Mr Reed (R450), who is angered by the establishment view of the world, its politics and actions, nonetheless worries about the acceptance of his views when he writes for the Mass-Observation Project. It has been his experience that failure to accommodate what he writes to the dominant view, at least in part, may mean that he is denied access to forums for writing. As noted in Chapter 5, he says,

> I write to newspapers—never get accepted. I used to write letters, they were never printed. They'd write back an acknowledgement saying we can't print this. I used to put it straight . . . on the nub of what it was. I wouldn't mince words, you know, I used to get annoyed and I'd write. But they wouldn't never print my letters. (R450, interview)

While he does write, the writing is denied an audience, which we argue is equivalent to being denied a forum for writing. Perhaps it is his experience with newspapers, or his experience as a writer (although he does not claim to be a writer) that influences him to accommodate his writing to the views of the audience he expects at the Mass-Observation Project, at least occasionally.

> *DB: You mentioned something about not being able to be totally truthful* [in response to the Spring 1992 directive sent by the BBC on personal hygiene], *because you knew it was coming from the establishment.* Well, I know what the makeup is, what they'd expect of people. I know what they'd expect to hear. They only want to hear what they want to hear. So, it's not good for me voicing an opposing opinion, because they'd scrap around it. They'd say, "Right we won't read the one, it's too subversive." See, you can't get through to established people. *DB: In response to the directive from the BBC?* I wrote back shortly, quickly. I didn't give a lot of depth to it. I didn't like to give a lot of depth to it because it just wasn't worth the while.

Mr Reed's occasional accommodation does not call into question the frankness of his writing, but rather reveals how precarious his writing position is. Of course, it is not just Mr Reed whose writing position is precarious, but also many of the Mass-Observation correspondents (see comments by Mrs Wright, Mrs Martin and Mr Barrow in Chapter 5).

Proper Writing: Grammar, Spelling

Within the overall self-consciousness about the writing process, a key issue about which many Mass-Observation correspondents expressed concern is that of "correctness" with grammar and spelling. This is often linked with their sense of the seriousness of their mission. Writing for Mass-Observation and for posterity imposes an obligation of credibility, which they see as associated with not only content but form. The very techniques of writing affect how they will be read; it is necessary to write "properly" to be taken seriously.

Proper writing is connected with schooling. Some Mass-Observation correspondents still have unpleasant memories of the way "English" was taught at school, but nevertheless believe that it is important to get it right in order to get on and express themselves.

> I've always been interested in, I mean, English essays at school—I was keen on writing, when I didn't have the spelling or the language, sentence—the power to be able to—put sentences together, I still had ideas that I wanted to get down, and it was frustrating not being able to write—properly (laughs)—to write as I could read. Reading books was another thing that I always enjoyed doing, and I could—wanted to write like that, you know, without going through the learning stage . . . It was a long time ago, but I remember I used to get annoyed when the papers came back from marking and there was all these big S's through the spelling mistakes and so on, and I'd say, "But what did you think of it?" and never got much of a satisfactory answer to that. "What did you think of what I'd written?" you know, "not all right, it's wrong, you know, but (laughter)—and I can see—I know the English is wrong, but what about what I've written," and I don't feel as though that was taken into consideration enough. So I had to get the spelling and the grammar right in order for people to listen or want to read what I was writing. . . . I think if I can't spell and write correctly then—people stop at that point and think there's something wrong here. Like reading the *Guardian* I finish up proof-reading it you know (laughs). I'm not reading what it's saying. I'm proof-reading the spelling mistakes. It stops me getting this sense of the paragraph when there are mistakes in it, and I think other people must find the same if my writing isn't correct. (W632, interview)

Ms Cleer (C2295) in her interview expressed similar concern about whether she was a good observer; she wanted to learn to do it better and worried that she would not be taken so seriously by history if she spelt badly. Future researchers would judge the whole person by her or his spelling.

Getting the spelling and grammar "right", the educational practice of emphasising the "correct" form and ignoring content, creates on the one hand a large category of people who are labeled as not qualified to write (and consequently largely excluded from writing), and on the other, creates a category of people skilled at getting the spelling and grammar right who serve to frame meanings and communicative functions consistent with and constrained by the social positions they occupy in their jobs. We are not arguing that members of this latter group are empty vessels merely putting form on meanings somehow hovering on the shoulder of the occupational positions they hold. But rather, on the job, their creative efforts with written language are circumscribed by the social and economic location of that job and by the dominant image of writing being about "correctness". For example, the secretary who writes letters on behalf of the boss may indeed do so creatively and insightfully, but that creativity and insight are circumscribed by the social and economic function the secretary is taking up and by the secretary's social and economic relationship to the boss. In brief, the educational emphasis on getting the spelling and grammar "correct" while ignoring and discounting content appears to be consistent with the writing practices that are required on the job. However, the data suggest that it is not the skill of "correct" spelling and grammar per se that is at issue, but rather the relationship of the writer to the writing and to the social and economic institution in which the person works.

The location of the Mass-Observation Project in southern England is not viewed by all Mass-Observation correspondents as a neutral location. For some Mass-Observation correspondents, the location represents both a language style and a viewpoint. For example, Ms McPhail, who is Scottish, states that she changes her writing to a style that she believes is more acceptable and respected by those from southern England.

> perhaps in order to be taken seriously people have to be less Scottish, or maybe more sort of British or international or whatever.
> (M2493, interview)

Note that her accommodation to a "southern" style is not something demanded by the Mass-Observation Project, but is something initiated by Ms McPhail herself. Such accommodations are common whenever people interact with others whose language is dominant; power involves not just imposition of dominant norms but internalization of them.[5] At the same time, it is also clear that Ms McPhail is extremely proud of her Scottish background and culture, and that indeed she writes in part to provide a Scottish viewpoint.

In this chapter we also explored ways in which people were not only passive subjects of dominant power but also transformed for their social and economic situations through writing, including through writing for the Mass-Observation Project. We described how people created and maintained social relationships with others and how they created time and social spaces for writing and attended to audience. But, it was not always easy to do so and there were many constraints and issues that, on the one hand may facilitate what and how Mass-Observation correspondents write, while on the other hand they limit the conditions for such writing.

As we noted earlier, Mrs Wright stated that she needed to first learn spelling and grammar before she could expect people to respond to her ideas. Her conclusion may be a pragmatic response or one that reflects the "folk" wisdom of school and people around her. But her conclusion and comment also point to the establishment of a hierarchy—those whose ideas are worthy to read and those whose ideas get no attention—based on the use of standardised spelling and grammar. It is the establishment of this hierarchy and the location of people within it that may help explain the emphasis on grammar and spelling in schools and dominant institutions in contemporary society. But learning to spell and write in "correct" grammar did not give people access to opportunities to write.

> DB: *And once you did [learn how to spell and use grammar] then they listened, or—not, or?* Mrs Wright: Oh, I don't know—I suppose once I could do it then perhaps the interest waned . . . perhaps I didn't do so much writing then—once I knew I could do it. (W632, interview)

There may be many reasons for why Mrs Wright did not engage in writing once she could get the spelling and grammar "right". Her explanation puts the blame on herself—she was not motivated to write. But motivation for writing, the kinds of writing associated with school—essays, stories, reports and related genres—does not exist separate from the social and institutional contexts one is in and the opportunities for engaging in those genres of writing as part of a meaningful and productive participation (productive in the sense of producing oneself and the world in which one lives).

---

[5]We are using the term "accommodation" in a specialized way, associated with sociolinguistic studies of face-to-face interaction (cf., Giles, Coupland & Coupland, 1991).

What would those opportunities look like? At the very least they would include available social positions that a person could take up that would give what they wrote authority, legitimacy and a sense of needing to be attended to. It would also include an audience and a relationship to that audience (as a journalist has a relationship with a newspaper's audience). Even so, these social positions and social relationships are based on expression of sets of meaning consistent with the meaning of the social positions and social relationships and consistent with the sets of meaning legitimated by the institutional discourses and social ideologies in which they are embedded.

These opportunities were not made available to Mrs Wright, who was directed in her education to courses on shorthand and other clerical skills. In her job, she writes memoranda, reports, letters and other documents, but the content of those texts belongs only in part to her; the greater part belonging to the social and occupational position she occupies within the company she works for. We want to be clear; it is not that the writing that Mrs Wright does in her job is not the result of her efforts and insight, and we are not claiming that what she writes does not require creativity and her particular talents, but rather (and obviously so) that her creativity and talents are in the service of the company she works for and that the writing she does serves the company and, more specifically, its forms and content are constrained by the particular tasks the writing fulfills. Regardless of her insights or eloquence, it would not be appropriate, to say the least, if in the writing she does in her job she presents her thoughts on the Poll Tax, describes what happened to her in Court, expresses her emotions, or writes in verse, and so forth. If she wants to do so, she must create other opportunities and audiences for writing in which such content and forms are acceptable and desired, which may mean creating "new" social practices (either by adapting old ones or creating new ones) which will necessitate changes in the organisation of her everyday social life.

By "new" social practices, we do not mean "new" in the sense of never having existed before—although that may be the case—but rather "new" in the sense of providing opportunities for types of writing, with incumbent audiences and social consequences, for people who may not have access to the limited set of writing practices in society that do provide opportunities for such writing. Stated in Bourdieu's terms, it is not just a matter of obtaining the cultural capital needed for particular types of writing, nor is it a matter of acquiring the symbolic capital to transform cultural capital into economic capital, but rather of transforming the habitus with regard to how symbolic capital and cultural capital are defined. This is what we referred to above as a transformation model of power rather than a quantitative model of power.

Mrs Friend is a good example of someone who adapted an extant social practice, letter writing, to create writing practices both for herself and others. In so doing, she was required to change the social organisation of her everyday life, although these changes may be invisible to others and do not necessarily cause disruption to others or to other domains of her life. Her living room becomes a writer's workshop in the evening as she sits with her husband while he watches television. She creates long-term relationships with family and friends through the letter writing and by pestering them to write frequent and long letters, too.

What is at issue is not whether creating an opportunity for particular kinds of writing flows easily with one's everyday social life or whether it causes disruption, but rather that such opportunities are not readily available for ordinary people in their everyday lives. They must be created, and in creating those opportunities, people create themselves and transform the social institutions of which they are a part. It is important not to overly emphasize the role of the Mass-Observation project in helping to create such opportunities. Many of the Mass-Observation correspondents reported that had the Mass-Observation Project not been created, they would have engaged in some other form of writing. Some stated that they would have even engaged in similar kinds of writing as the Mass-Observation writing, as it was a part of their personality. It is also important not to romanticize or overstate the power of the Mass-Observation Project to transform extant social institutions and the writing positions made available to ordinary people in contemporary society. The invisibility of both the Mass-Observation correspondents and their writing activity suggests how fragile such writing positions and social spaces may be for many of the people involved. Nevertheless, Mass-Observation does provide a space, a time and an audience for many whose writing might otherwise be "invisible". We hope that by writing about Mass-Observation in this way, we have contributed to making such writing more visible and helped provide a framework for understanding the significance of such everyday writing of ordinary people in contemporary society. In the next chapter we explore the significance of this writing and this framework for "Writing Britain".

8
Writing Ourselves and Writing Britain

In previous chapters we have documented the history of the Mass-Observation Project, both in its early years and in its revitalisation since 1981. We have focussed attention on the literacy practices involved in the Mass-Observation Project as well as the literacy practices employed by the Mass-Observation correspondents in their daily lives. In this chapter, we bring together the variety of issues we raised through our study of literacy practices and the Mass-Observation Project—in particular concepts of ordinariness, reflexivity and the awareness that knowledge is messy. The theme of power—who has the right to write, who can represent the views of others and of themselves—runs throughout not only our account but those of the original founders. Mass-Observation itself emerged out of a perceived need to challenge the dominant channels available in pre-war Britain for representing how people felt and thought about their society. Tom Harrisson, Charles Madge and Humphrey Jennings, in their different ways, were sceptical about what they saw as Establishment "propaganda" and wanted to provide a forum for "ordinary" people to express their ideas. As we noted in Chapter 1, they were

> continually impressed by the discrepancy between what is supposed to happen and what does happen, between law and fact, the institution and the individual, what people say they do and what they actually do, what leaders think people want and what people do want. (Charles Madge & Tom Harrisson, *First Year's Work*, 1938, p. 32)

Our account is particularly interested in what ordinary people *write* and again, the Mass-Observation founders had views on this:

> Much lip service is paid to the Man in the Street (sic)—politicians and newspapers claim to represent him, scientists and artists want to interest him in their work. Much of what they say is sincere, but it must remain ineffective while the Man in the Street has no medium through which he can express with equal publicity what he thinks of them. The present position of the Intellectual Few is a relic of the times when the mass of the population consisted of serfs who could neither read or write. Then a few people at the top could impose their beliefs and rule on the multitude. The whole tendency of history has been away from this state of things. (Harrisson & Madge, 1939, p. 11)

Mass-Observation, then, was seen from the outset as part of the tendency of history to move away from élite control of literacy. And yet, there are contradictions here as in other accounts of literacy and power—history does not move in such linear, one-directional ways. For instance, these three young critical men who founded Mass-Observation were themselves already a part of the British "Establishment" and the project that they founded to challenge dominant discourses has itself taken a place amongst the classic institutions of public life in Britain. As we have demonstrated throughout this book, such a project is fraught with such contradictions. But that need not undermine its value, and indeed we would argue that it is precisely this location at the cusp of so many established ways of thinking and its tendency therefore to slide across boundaries—in post-modern terms, to provide a somewhat messy view of knowledge—that is the strength of Mass-Observation. Although some have argued that it can be seen as a "movement" (Summerfield, 1985), and as we described in Chapter 3, others argue that it is simply poor social science (Firth, 1939), the reality when we survey the material left to us and indeed still being produced by Mass-Observation, is less certain on either side. Mass-Observation was never coherent enough, and its founders were never really sufficiently in tune with each other, for it to emerge as a quasi-political "movement", such as the "people's movements" of the nineteenth century—for example, Chartism and the Dissenters.

But nor can it simply be dismissed as a failed attempt at social documentary, as professional anthropologists and sociologists at the time argued: as we have shown (see Chapter 3), the idea of "an anthropology of our own people" has indeed in some ways been realised, and the "reflexive turn" in contemporary social anthropology makes Mass-Observation look more legitimate as social science now than perhaps it did at the time it was founded.

Crossing these academic and political goals, the attempt by Mass-Observation to represent "voices" that were otherwise silenced by the uniquely British configuration of public ways of speaking and writing has also been fulfilled, again in ways that might not always have been recognised at the time. One of the strengths of the Project has been that its participants themselves have held firmly to this belief, from the early accounts of ordinary people's everyday lives and habits, through their endurance and fears in the war period, to the responses to directives in the new project in the 1980s and 1990s: people write to Mass-Observation precisely because they want posterity to hear the voices of ordinary people that they fear are being drowned out by media and political noise. If the aim of the founders was, as we noted in Chapter 1, to challenge the assumption that the press could genuinely represent public opinion and, above all, to bridge a gulf of ignorance between the establishment and the ordinary working people of Britain, then that aim still informs the attachment of many people to the continuing Project.

Our interest in writing this book, however, is not simply to document these processes in ways that earlier accounts of Mass-Observation have not yet done, or have done in less accessible places. Rather, we have written this book in order to focus attention on the writing processes and literacy practices involved in Mass-Observation as a case study for understanding the role of writing in particular and literacy in general in British society. While dominant discourses rail against "falling standards" of literacy and suggest that people no longer write as they used to (Street, 1998), we see Mass-Observation as evidence for an alternative view of literacy in which writing continues to play a significant role in everyday life, but a role that is sometimes hidden from view. Making visible the literacy practices of contemporary Britain is a larger project than Mass-Observation can capture, and indeed there have been other attempts recently at documenting everyday writing in society, notably *Local Literacies* (Barton & Hamilton, 1998) and Michelle Knobel's *Everyday Literacies* (1999). We see this book as part of that larger project: just as the founders of Mass-Observation saw their challenge as helping to make visible the ideas and feelings of ordinary people, so we see the challenge of the research on which this book is based as helping to make visible the literate ways in which people express such ideas and feelings—their everyday writing practices.

Moreover, in keeping with the shift in "literacy studies" documented in Chapter 6, we see such writing practices as not simply transparent conduits for thoughts and feelings, but as themselves helping to construct—indeed constitute—them. The *ways* in which people write and the ideas they have about writing affect deeply the meanings and knowledge that their writing conveys. To understand their thoughts and feelings we have to understand their writing. This book, then, offers a way of interpreting such writing in order to get to underlying meanings. In some ways we, as authors of this secondary account of Mass-Observation writing, are attempting to mediate what is present in the texts and materials stored in the Mass-Observation Archive. We are suggesting a way of reading that material. In doing so, we are also trying to make a broader point: that this may be a way of reading literacy practices more generally. Rather than seeing literacy only in terms of dominant accounts of skills and their decline and as simply an issue for educationalists, we would like to reclaim literacy as the founders of Mass-Observation wished to reclaim "ordinary voices"—to recognise how literacy is an integral part of meaning making for everyone, not only for those whose trade is writing and publishing. And we are looking to Mass-Observation because it is a major source of information on such everyday literacy practices. The correspondents can tell us about the ways in which "ordinary" people, in writing about their lives for future generations, are in a sense actively "Writing Britain", bringing the country, the people, the society and ideas about them into being through their literacy practices. Thus, there are two meanings to "Writing Britain": one meaning refers to people who write but whose writing is often invisible; the other meaning refers to the use of writing to assert a place in history that is often invisible. The correspondents for Mass-Observation indicate what such writing may be like in contemporary Britain by the evidence their writing for Mass-Observation provides; but they also comment themselves on their other writing practices—the everyday uses of literacy for recording, listing, framing, marking the flow of life, from making lists and tables to writing diaries—and in this way, too, they provide evidence for "Writing Britain".

We suggested earlier that the location of Mass-Observation at the cusp of established ways of thinking and its tendency therefore to slide across boundaries means that it provides "a somewhat messy view of knowledge". We would like now to elaborate on this view, as it is central to the questions that have been asked since its inception regarding the legitimacy and claim to knowledge of the Mass-Observation Project. From the outset, anthropologists and sociologists have questioned the validity of its methods for collecting data, and newspapers have questioned, often through parody and sceptical articles, the value of such knowledge of "ordinary" people's lives. Even today, when we have given talks about our research on the writing by contemporary correspondents, questions are still asked about the significance of the project as a whole and the representativeness of such data in particular. In Chapter 4 we addressed the methodological issues this raises by arguing that the data can be treated as "case studies"—a particular example need not be statistically representative for it to provide a telling case of some principle, to enable us to elaborate and develop theoretical propositions. For us, Mass-Observation as a whole, and the examples we have drawn out in particular, represent telling cases for the significance of writing in people's lives and for the propositions regarding "Writing Britain" we have outlined. Here we would like to address the question of what kind of knowledge this is.

Themes that are central to contemporary debates about knowledge in scientific and philosophical circles emerge here in the account of Mass-Observation: the importance of the "ordinary", which emerged in the early chapters as we described the genesis of Mass-Observation (Chapters 1 and 2); reflexivity as it has developed within academic disciplines, notably that of social anthropology—a discipline or view of knowledge which had informed the early research and whose recent attention to reflexivity has enabled us to re-view many of the features that were criticised at the time (Chapter 3); and messiness or "serendipity", which suggests a view of knowledge as more partial and less certain than post-Enlightenment science liked to believe. Mass-Observation, both in its often quirky history of individual participants and relations to the state and in the biases and peculiarities of its self-selected correspondents, illustrates strikingly how messy knowledge of our own worlds can be and yet how important it is to retain some of that messiness in our accounts lest they become simply imposed straightjackets that fracture the integrity of the reality they purport to "represent".

The theme of "ordinariness" runs through the accounts of the early founders and of the participants themselves both then and now, and also recently through the debates in academic circles. The theme was struck in the Foreword to this book by Shirley Brice Heath, who cites William Carlos Williams' concern that the very attempt to direct and control the ordinary may run counter to true knowledge. As Heath states, "In the end, Williams . . . leaves us in no doubt that all of us are ordinary and the ordinary is history. The irony is that when historians write history, they often try to dispose of the ordinary while also recognising that any proposal for the future lies very much with what lies in the ordinary". For Heath, were Williams to know of Mass-Observation, he would see it as "a combination of the dilemmas surrounding disposal/proposal." As Heath writes in the Foreword:

> The materials of Mass-Observation, though part of a *proposal*, that is, written in response to public requests as well as directives regarding content, resulted from a *disposal* of will and time from correspondents: hence women and retirees have contributed a large proportion of the archived records. Furthermore, many of the

writings over the years show how certain proposals that individuals made for relationships, life courses, or organisational changes aborted or went astray (see Chapter 6). More often than not, what became available to one's disposal determined the course of individual *proposals*. Furthermore, particular historical and economical conditions disposed individual correspondents to choose one or another slant on a topic at one point in time, while several years later, they themselves found their earlier responses quite curious and even inexplicable. The pinch between extreme contingency and planned consistent pattern catches all of us, and in our reflections about ourselves, we are forced to take note of both. The focus of this volume on writing by individuals who both create and derive social meaning from their literacy enables us to see clearly just how important the "taking of note" is to the complex process of self-knowledge. We come here face-to-face again with William's lament that we cannot know the "whither" of our direction. We can, however, know much about the *how*—those ways in which as writers, we find a measure of temporary control over direction, and we move closer to accepting our ability to be "watchers" of ourselves.

The knowledge represented by the writing of Mass-Observation correspondents, then, is not simply empirical knowledge of everyday writing in Britain, or "representative" knowledge by selected samples of the population: nor is it knowledge of the "direction" in which the writers are going; rather it is knowledge about how we know, including the ways in which we take "temporary control over direction". It is for this reason that we have focussed so closely on the writing processes rather than simply the "products". Mass-Observation has been treated, by the popular press and some scholars, mainly as such a "product"—a source of factual knowledge about Britain, about its views on the Royal Family, for instance, or its understanding of the Gulf War or, for the early phase, how people lived through the Blitz. We would like to argue, in keeping with Heath's interpretation of Williams, that it is more appropriate to focus on the *how* rather than the what of Mass-Observation knowledge. Certainly Mass-Observation attunes us to the importance of the "ordinary"—but more importantly perhaps it reminds us that knowledge of the ordinary is contingent and changing and to try and pin it down in consistent ways distorts the truth: "The pinch between extreme contingency and planned consistent patterns catches all of us, and in our reflections about ourselves we are forced to take note of both". This, in fact, is what the writers themselves frequently do, reflecting on their own earlier comments and lives in the light of their present circumstances and, in one case that we described in Chapter 7, asking that an earlier record be expunged, since the truth of her life was now represented in her current account. Whatever the archival solution to such a dilemma, it points up the contested and shifting nature of knowledge. It is this view of knowledge that informs the writing of this book and which, we argue, the focus on the ordinary sources of history and of social knowledge put forward by Mass-Observation forces us to acknowledge. There is a crucial link here, in the history of intellectual endeavour, between focus on the ordinary and focus on a messy view of knowledge.

The theme of reflexivity is closely connected to the above discussion. How we can be "watchers of ourselves" is the central focus of Heath's use of Williams and of her interest in Mass-Observation. In keeping with our account of earlier anthropologists' criticisms of the Project, she points out that what is valuable about Mass-Observation is precisely the feature they found problematic—its self-selection. As Heath writes in the Foreword:

> Literacy (and several other topics) turn in on themselves here to give us a view of particular phenomena from the inside out: participants use their own writing to reflect on their uses of reading and writing. In keeping with this focus on participants' own voices, practically half of the present volume is given over to the writing of Mass-Observation correspondents (see especially Section 2). Autobiography, case study, memoir, and ethnography all come together to make up the corpus of Mass-Observation writing.

As we noted in Chapter 3, it is precisely this attention to reflexivity in the writing process that has enabled contemporary anthropology to come to terms with its own role in the neo-colonial world and in turn to come to terms with the writing represented in Mass-Observation. Whereas Firth and Malinowski worried that early Mass-Observation would bring their discipline of anthropology into disrepute by failing to provide representative samples, present day anthropologists like Heath, Street and others value Mass-Observation because it is writing. Such writing, they believe, can tell us about not only the ideas and thoughts of the writers, but also about the processes through which such ideas and thoughts are represented—"from the inside out". The above account of "Writing Britain" depends, then, upon a reflexive view of knowledge, just as it depends on the attention to the "ordinary" also privileged in Mass-Observation. The attention in Chapter 6 to the uses of writing provides the knowledge base for what we know about Mass-Observation; it is that kind of knowledge, reflexive knowledge in process by ordinary people. On the basis of this kind of knowledge, we are able to pursue our own interest in "personhood and power" explored in Chapter 7, and, we would argue, this approach opens up the space for other scholars to explore their interests, using the Mass-Observation material as process knowledge rather than product knowledge.

Finally, we turn to the theme of power that has run throughout this book and that figured from the very inception of the Mass-Observation Project. In this context we see power as closely linked to the kinds of literacy practices exemplified by the Mass-Observation correspondents. As we discussed in Chapter 7, elaborating on Foucault's notion of power, we view power as process and as transformative; all of those engaged in networks of social relations along which power flows, in different directions not just from top to bottom, are able to define and change what counts as power in specific circumstances. And consideration of literacy practices and power is no different. That is, although a set of literacy practices may make demands upon people's lives and influence how they act toward each other and how the world they live in is defined, at the very same time, people act on, adapt and transform literacy practices to pursue social, cultural, economic and personal agendas reflecting how they define the worlds in which they live (Street, 1993).

De Certeau (1984) makes a similar point, and we have found his formulation helpful in thinking about literacy practices and the Mass-Observation Project. De Certeau was interested in opening up the study of everyday practices that took seriously the notion that ordinary people act upon the worlds in which they live. He writes, "Everyday life invents itself by *poaching* in countless ways on the property of others" (de Certeau, 1984, pp. xi-xii, original emphasis). De Certeau argues that even though at one level the society is structured so that production of meaning and activity appears to be given by dominant institutions to people, who are defined both explicitly and implicitly as consumers, nevertheless, at other levels people make meaning and do things with the materials provided by dominant institutions. People in their everyday lives are not necessarily bounded by those dominant institutions in what meanings they make, how they make them or in the actions they take. This level of activity is often "invisible" as, we have argued, are the writing practices that the Mass-Observation Project is bringing into view.

> The "making" [by ordinary people in their everyday lives] in question is a production, a *poiesis*—but a hidden one, because it is scattered over areas defined and occupied by systems of "production" (television, urban development, commerce, etc.), and because the steadily increasing expansion of these systems no longer leaves "consumers" any *place* in which they can indicate what they *make* or *do* with the products of these systems. (de Certeau, 1984, p. xii)

We would like to suggest that Mass-Observation does indeed provide a space in which ordinary people *can* make and do with the literacy practices available in this society. Earlier, in Chapter 7, we noted the tendency of dominant institutions to expand into the social institutions and domains that "ordinary" people occupy, although we did not discuss that tendency in depth (see Bloome, 1997; Fairclough 1992; Gee, 1991). The account we provided there of Mrs Wright's (W632) description of going to court over non-payment of the poll tax might appear to lend support to de Certeau's observation, in that Mrs Wright seemed to have no place to record her protest for history, and the magistrate mocked her attempt to do so. Mass-Observation, however, did provide such a *place* and a set of social practices (literacy practices) where, if nothing else, Mrs Wright could make clear what she made of the event.

Space is both physical and social. As we described in Chapter 6, some Mass-Observation correspondents must work very hard to create spaces to write. For some, creating space is a matter of justifying the time to write and time away from family and children. Some Mass-Observation correspondents cannot write in their homes and must leave to find space and place to write. Mrs Caldwell (C2079) leaves her house to write in a trailer caravan in her garden to create both a physical space and a social space to write. Nonetheless, she has to suffer the occasional encroachment on that space by family members who will pull the electric plug that serves the caravan to bring her back out of that space. Some who write in their homes create a dedicated space for writing, and others must use their creativity in making spaces easily transformable into places to write or places that can simultaneously serve multiple functions. Thus, as we described in Chapter 5, Mrs Friend's living room hardly looks like a writer's workshop until she pulls out her writing materials and files from the cabinets.

Mrs Friend is not just transforming a physical space, she is also transforming social relationships. Economic pressures often require family and friends to move, and there is a potential for such movement to lead to the diminution or even disintegration of family and friendship relationships. Mrs Friend's letter-writing activities, with all of her cajoling of friends and family to write more frequent, longer, and more detailed letters counters, to at least some degree, the potential loss of intimacy. That is, just as Mrs Friend, Mrs Wright and the other Mass-Observation correspondents transform spaces into writing spaces, so too, at least to some degree, they transform themselves, others and the places in which they live, using writing to reduce distance and to compress time.

Mass-Observation writing can be seen as a telling case of such transformative aspects of power; transforming space, identity, literacy practices and other social practices. The Mass-Observation correspondents respond to the directives sent them by the Archivist and her team by redefining what counts for them as writing for Mass-Observation. In so doing they also challenge and redefine relations of authority over knowledge between dominant institutions on one hand and "ordinary" people on the other.

The Mass-Observation Project is located at The University of Sussex and part of its purpose is to contribute to the academic mission of the University, including the education of students and the accumulation of academic and disciplinary knowledge. In that sense, it is located in dominant institutions. However, as the Mass-Observation correspondents made clear to us in their interviews and in their responses to the directive sent out as part of our research, many of the Mass-Observation correspondents feel a strong sense of ownership of the Mass-Observation Project. In that sense, Mass-Observation is located in the world of ordinary people. Dorothy Sheridan as the archivist is careful to direct the Mass-Observation Project in a way that reflects such "dual" ownership as well as a sense of responsibility to Mass-Observation's history, as we described in Chapter 2. Further, although not with the explicit purpose of challenging the boundaries of academic practices of inquiry, the Mass-Observation Project has nonetheless done so by raising questions about (problematising) the location, nature and generation of knowledge in the social sciences. Directives, for instance, are crafted in ways that often reflect questions about knowledge and knowing raised by feminist social theory and other contemporary social theories, and continue to highlight the importance of what ordinary people do in their daily lives, what they think about the worlds in which they live and how they act on (and are acted upon by) those worlds. The Mass-Observation Project, then, provides a telling case about the nature of literacy practices in contemporary Britain that involves tensions and transformations of what counts as knowledge, power relations and the relationships of dominant social institutions and ordinary people in their everyday lives.

The issues we have discussed in this book can be viewed from the perspective of global politics, making the particular accounts with which we have been dealing much more telling than simply the local struggles of British interests. The "story" we have told may be indicative of the broader shift in world social and political relations to which many of the authors we cite and the Mass-Observation correspondents themselves frequently allude. It is a world in which the hearing of manifold voices and the acceptance of broad distributions of knowledge provide the basis for political decision making and institutional arrangements rather than the narrow restrictions of elite knowledge that have characterised the nation-states of the recent past. It is, of course, too early to know whether such a transformation will flourish or will be repressed.

Who, then, has the power to define and control the kind of knowledge represented by Mass-Observation? Our own intervention has certainly involved some attempt at defining, if not controlling, the knowledge base. But we recognise that such definitions are open to contestation, as indeed our engagement with the views of early anthropologists on the one hand and the correspondents' own engagement with the directives sent out by the Archive on the other, demonstrate. But ultimately, the material in the Archive speaks with multiple voices, just as the views of knowledge we have been outlining are multiple. In that sense there is a congruence between the Mass-Observation correspondents and ourselves as writers of the present volume: both parties recognise the centrality of the concepts of "ordinariness", "reflexivity" and "serendipity" to understanding the nature of the Project. Both in various ways recognise the power dimension of the Project, as contests over knowledge, representativeness, ordinariness flow back and forth between the correspondents, the Project team and the commentators upon it. And both parties value the Mass-Observation Project for precisely the features for which some early scholars and many journalists have derided it: its particularity and ability to represent experience from the inside out. If we seem to end on a confrontational note—arguing that previous readings and uses of Mass-Observation need to be revised—that seems to us congruent with the spirit of the founders and with the theory of knowledge that we have propounded here. We hope that this book will make a contribution to that debate and we will judge our success by the degree of contestation and argument it generates.

Bibliography

Abrams, M. (1951). *Social surveys and social action*. London: Heinemann.
Addison, P. (1975). *The road to 1945*. London: Cape.
Agar, M. (1980). *The professional stranger: An informal introduction to ethnography*. New York: Academic Press.
Althusser, L. (1971). *Lenin and philosophy and other essays*. London: Unwin.
Anzadula, G. (1987). *Borderlands/La Frontera: The new Mestiza*. San Francisco: Spinsters-Aunt Lute Books.
Asad, T. (1979). Anthropology and ideology. *Man* (n.s.), *14*(4) 607-627.
Asad, T., & Dixon, J. (1985). Translating Europe's others. In F. Barker (Ed.), *Europe and its others* (pp. 83-93). Colchester: University of Essex.
Bakhtin, M. (1935/1981 trans.). Discourse in the novel. In M. Holquist (Ed.), *The dialogic imagination*. Austin: University of Texas Press.
Barton, D., Bloome, D., Sheridan, D., & Street, B. (1993). *Ordinary people writing: The Lancaster & Sussex research projects*. Centre for Language in Social Life Working Paper Series #51. Lancaster, UK: University of Lancaster.
Barton, D., & Hamilton, M. (1998). *Local literacies*. London: Routledge.
Barton, D., & Ivanic, R. (Eds.). (1991). *Writing in the community*. London: Sage.
Basso, K. (1974). The ethnography of writing. In R. Bauman & J. Sherzer (Eds.), *Explorations in the ethnography of speaking* (pp. 425-432). Cambridge, UK: Cambridge University Press.
Bauman, R., & Sherzer, J. (Eds.). (1974). *Explorations in the ethnography of speaking*. Cambridge, UK: Cambridge University Press.
Baynham, M. (1995). *Literacy practices: Investigating literacy in social contexts*. London: Longman.

Baynham, M. (in press). Narrative as evidence in literacy research. *Linguistics and Education.*
Bell, S.G., & Yallom, M. (Eds.). (1990). *Revealing lives: Autobiography, biography and gender.* Albany: State University of New York Press.
Benjamin, W. (1969). *Illuminations.* New York: Schocken Books.
Bertaux, D. (Ed.). (1981). *Biography and society: The life history approach in the social sciences.* Beverly Hills, CA: Sage.
Besnier, N. (1993). Literacy and feelings: The encoding of affect in Nukulaelae letters. In B. Street (Ed.), *Cross-cultural approaches to literacy* (pp. 62-86). Cambridge, UK: Cambridge University Press.
Besnier, N. (1995). *Literacy, emotion and authority.* Cambridge, UK: Cambridge University Press.
Bloome, D. (1987). Reading as a social process in a middle school classroom. In D. Bloome (Ed.), *Literacy and schooling* (pp. 123-149). Norwood, NJ: Ablex.
Bloome, D. (1991). Anthropology and research on teaching the English language arts. In J. Flood, J. Jensen, D. Lapp, & J. Squires (Eds.), *Handbook of research on teaching the English language arts* (pp. 46-56). New York: Macmillan.
Bloome, D. (1993). Necessary indeterminacy: Issues in the microethnographic study of reading as a social process. *Journal of Reading Research, 16*(2) 98-111.
Bloome, D. (1997). This is literacy: Three challenges for teachers of reading and writing. *Australian Journal of Language and Literacy, 20*(2) 107-115.
Bloome, D., & Kinzer, C. (1998). Hard times and cosmetics: Changes in literacy instruction? *Peabody Journal of Education, 73*(3&4) 341-375.
Bloome, D., Sheridan, D., & Street, B. (1993). *Reading Mass-Observation writing: Theoretical and methodological issues in researching the Mass-Observation Archive* (Mass-Observation Archive Occasional Paper No. 1). Brighton, UK: University of Sussex.
Bloome, D., Sheridan, D., & Street, B. (1995). *Literacy, personhood, power and the everyday lives of "ordinary" people: Research with the Mass-Observation Archive.* Paper presented at the American Education Research Association Conference, San Francisco.
Bohman, S. (1986). *The people's story: On the collection and analysis of autobiographical materials.* Methodological Questions No. 3. Stockholm: Nordiska Museet.
Bourdieu, P. (1977). *Outline of a theory of practice.* Cambridge, UK: Cambridge University Press.
Bourdieu, P. (1991). *Language and symbolic power.* Cambridge, MA: Harvard University Press.

Brodkey, L. (1987). *Academic writing as a social process*. Philadelphia: Temple University Press.
Bruce, B. (1981). A social interaction model of reading. *Discourse Processes, 4*, 273-311.
Calder, A. (1969). *The people's war: Britain, 1939-1945*. London: Cape.
Calder, A. (1985). Mass-Observation. In M. Bulmer (Ed.), *Essays in the history of British sociological research*. Cambridge, UK: Cambridge University Press.
Calder, A., & Sheridan, D. (1984). *Speak for yourself: A Mass-Observation anthology 1937-49*. London: Cape.
Cameron, D. (1992). "Respect, please": Investigating race, power and language. In D. Cameron, E. Frazer, P. Harvey, M.B.H. Rampton, & K. Richardson (Eds.), *Researching language: Issues of power and method*. London: Routledge.
Cameron, D., Frazer, E., Harvey, P., Rampton, M.B.H, & Richardson, K. (1992). *Researching language: Issues of power and method*. London: Routledge.
de Certeau, M. (1984). *The practice of everyday life*. Berkeley: University of California Press.
Clanchy, M.T. (1979). *From memory to written record: England 1066-1307*. London: Edward Arnold.
Clark, R., & Ivanic, R. (1997). *The politics of writing*. London: Routledge.
Clifford, J. (1988). *The predicament of culture: Twentieth-century ethnography, literature, and art*. Cambridge, MA: Harvard University Press.
Clifford, J., & Marcus, G. (Eds.). (1986). *Writing culture: The poetics and politics of ethnography*. Berkeley: University of California Press.
Collins, J. (1991). Hegemonic practice: Literacy and standard language in public education. In C. Mitchell & K. Lueiles (Eds.), *Rewriting literacy: Culture and the discourse of the other* (pp. 229-254). New York: Bergin & Garvey.
Conquergood, D. (1997). Street literacy. In J. Flood, S. Heath, & D. Lapp (Eds.), *Handbook of research on teaching literacy through the communicative and visual arts* (pp. 354-375). New York: Simon & Schuster Macmillan.
Dumont, L. (1975). Preface to the French edition of The Nuer. In J. Beattie & R.G. Lienhardt (Eds.), *Studies in social anthropology-Essays in memory of E.E. Evans-Pritchart*. Oxford: Clarendon Press.
Easthope, G. (1974). *A history of social research methods*. London: Longman.
Egan-Robertson, A. (1994). Literacy practices, personhood, and students as researchers in their own communities. Unpublished doctoral dissertation, University of Massachusetts, Amherst.

Egan-Robertson, A. (1999). Learning about culture, language and power: Understanding relationships of personhood, literacy practices and intertextuality. *Journal of Literacy Research, 30*(4) 449-489.

England, L. (1949-50) Progress in Mass-Observation: An internal view. *International Journal of Opinion and Attitude Research, 3*(4) 592-595.

Fairclough, N. (1989). *Language and power.* London: Longman.

Fairclough, N. (1992). *Discourse and social change.* Cambridge, UK: Polity.

Fairclough, N. (1995). *Critical discourse analysis: The critical study of language.* London: Longman.

Fardon, R. (Ed.). (1990). *Localising strategies: Regional traditions in ethnographic writing.* Edinburgh: Scottish Academic Press.

Farrell, E. W. (1990). *Hanging in and dropping out: Voices of at-risk high school students.* New York: Teachers College Press.

Ferraby, J. (1945). Planning a Mass-Observation investigation. *American Journal of Sociology, 51*(1) 166-193.

Finch, J. (1986). *Research and policy: The uses of qualitative methods in social and educational research.* London: Falmer Press.

Firth, R. (1939). An anthropologist's view of Mass-Observation. *Sociological Review, 31*, 166-193.

Fleck, L. (1979). *The genesis and development of a scientific fact.* Chicago: University of Chicago Press.

Fleming, S., & Broad, R. (Eds.). (1981). *Nella Last's war.* Bristol: Falling Wall Press.

Foucault, M. (1965). *Madness and civilization: A history of insanity in the age of reason* (R. Howard, Trans.). New York: Vintage Books.

Foucault, M. (1980). *Power/knowledge: Selected interviews and other writings, 1972-1977.* [Edited by C. Gordon]. New York: Pantheon.

Foucault, M. (1981). *History of sexuality* (Vol. 1). Harmondsworth: Penguin.

Foucault, M. (1984). What is an author? In P. Rabinow (Ed.), *The Foucault reader.* New York: Pantheon.

Gee, J. P. (1990). *Social linguistics: Ideology and discourses.* London: Falmer Press.

Gee, J. P. (1996). *Social linguistics and literacies: Ideology in discourses.* London: Taylor & Francis.

Geertz, C. (1975). *The interpretation of cultures.* London: Hutchinson

Geertz, C. (1983). *Local knowledge: Further essays in interpretive anthropology.* New York: Basic Books.

Giddens, A. (1979). *Central problems in social theory: Action, structure, and contradiction in social analysis.* Berkeley: University of California Press.

Giddens, A. (1984). *The constitution of society: Introduction to the theory of structuration.* Berkeley: University of California Press.

Giles, H., Coupland, J., & Coupland, N. (Eds.). (1991). *Contexts of accommodation: Developments in applied linguistics*. Cambridge, UK: Cambridge University Press.

Gilmore, P. (1987). Sulking, stepping, and tracking: The effects of attitude assessment on access to literacy. In D. Bloome (Ed.), *Literacy and schooling*. Norwood, NJ: Ablex.

Gilyard, K. (1997). Cross-talk: Towards transcultural writing classrooms. In C. Severino, J. Guerra, & J. Butler (Eds.), *Writing in multicultural settings* (pp. 325-332). New York: Modern Language Association.

Giroux, H. (1992). *Border crossings: Cultural workers and the politics of education*. New York: Routledge.

Goffman, E. (1963). *Behavior in public places: Notes on the social organization of gatherings*. New York: Free Press.

Goffman, E. (1981). *Forms of talk*. Philadelphia: University of Pennsylvania Press.

Graff, H. (1979). *The literacy myth: Literacy and social structure in the 19th century city*. New York: Academic Press.

Gramsci, A. (1971). *Prison notebooks* (Q. Hoare and G. Nowell-Smith, Trans.). London: Lawrence & Wishart.

Grillo, R., Pratt, J., & Street, B. (1987). Anthropology, linguistics and language. In J. Lyons, R. Coates, M. Deuchar, & G. Gazdar (Eds.), *New horizons in linguistics* (pp. 268-295). London: Penguin.

Green, J., & Bloome, D. (1997). Ethnography and ethnographers of and in education: A situated perspective. In J. Flood, S. Heath, & D. Lapp (Eds.), *A handbook of research on teaching literacy through the communicative and visual arts* (pp. 181-202). New York: Simon & Shuster Macmillan.

Guerra, J. (1997). The place of intercultural literacy in the writing classroom. In C. Severino, J. Guerra, & J. Butler (Eds.), *Writing in multicultural settings* (pp. 248-260). New York: Modern Language Association.

Guiterrez, K., & Larson, J. (1994). Language borders: Recitation as hegemonic discourse. *International Journal of Educational Reform*, 3(1) 22-36.

Gullestad, M. (1995). The intimacy of anonymity: Reflections on a Norwegian life story competition. *Oral History*, 23(2) 51-64.

Gumperz, J., & Hymes, D. (Eds.). (1972). *Directions in sociolinguistics: The ethnography of communication*. New York: Holt, Rinehart & Winston.

Gurney, P. (1997). "Intersex" and "dirty girls": Mass-Observation and working class sexuality in England in the 1930s. *Journal of the History of Sexuality*, 8(2) 256-290.

Halliday, M. (1978). *Language as social semiotic*. London: Edward Arnold.

Hamilton, M., Barton, D., & Ivanic, R. (1994). *Worlds of literacy*. Clevedon, UK: Multilingual Matters.

Harris, L. (1966). *Long to reign over us*. London: William Kimber.
Harrisson, T. (1937). *Savage civilisation*. London: Gollancz.
Harrisson, T. (1947). The future of sociology. *Pilot Papers*, 2(1) 10-25.
Harrisson, T. (1959). *World within: A Borneo story*. London: Cressett Press.
Harrisson, T (1976). *Living through the blitz*. London: Collins.
Harrisson, T., Jennings, J., & Madge, C. (1937). Anthropology at home [letter to the editor]. *New Statesman and Nation*, 30 January, p. 12.
Heath, S. (1982). Protean shapes in literacy events: Ever shifting oral and literate traditions. In D. Tannen (Ed.), *Spoken and written language: Exploring orality and literacy* (pp. 91-117). Norwood, NJ: Ablex.
Heath, S. (1983). *Ways with words*. New York: Cambridge University Press.
Heath, S., & McLaughlin, M. (1993). Ethnicity and gender in theory and practice: The youth perspective. In S. Heath & M. McLaughlin (Eds.), *Identity and inner-city youth: Beyond ethnicity and gender* (pp. 13-35). New York: Teachers College Press.
History Workshop Collective. (1976). Editorial. *History Workshop*, 1, 1-3.
Howard, U. (1991). Self, education, and writing in nineteenth-century English communities. In D. Barton & R. Ivanic (Eds.), *Writing in the community* (pp. 78-108). Newbury Park, CA: Sage.
Huxley, J. (1937). Foreword. In C. Madge & T. Harrisson, *Mass-Observation*. London: Muller.
Hynes, S. (1976). *The Auden generation: Literature and politics in England in the 1930s*. London: Bodley Head.
Ivanic, R. (1994). I is for interpersonal: Discoursal construction of writer identities and the teaching of writing. *Linguistics and Education*, 6(1) 3-17.
Ivanic, R. (1998). *Writing and identity: The discoursal construction of identity in academic writing*. Amsterdam: John Benjamins.
Jahoda, M. (1938). Review of *May the Twelfth*. *Sociological Review*, 30, 208-209.
Jeffery, T. (1978/1999). *Mass-Observation: A short history*. Mass-Observation Archive Occasional Paper, 10. Brighton: University of Sussex.
Jennings, H., & Madge, C. (1937). Introduction. In H. Jennings & C. Madge (Eds.), *May 12th. Mass-Observation day surveys, an account of coronation day*. London: Faber & Faber. (Republished by Faber with a new afterword by David Pocock, 1987)
Jennings, H., & Madge, C. (1937). *May 12th. Mass-Observation day surveys, an account of coronation day*. London: Faber & Faber. (Republished by Faber with a new afterword by David Pocock, 1987)
Kent, R. (1981). *A history of British empirical research*. London: Gower.
Kertesz, M. (1993). To speak for themselves: Mass-Observation's women wartime diaries. *Feminist Praxis*, 37-8, 50-80.

Knobel, M. (1999). *Everyday literacies: Students, discourse and social practice.* New York: Peter Lang.
Kress, G. (1994). *Learning to write* (2nd ed.). London: Routledge.
Kress, G. (1997). *Before writing: Rethinking the paths to literacy.* London: Routledge
Kulick, D., & Stroud, C. (1993). Conceptions and uses of literacy in a Papua New Guinean village. In B. Street (Ed.), *Cross-cultural approaches to literacy* (pp. 30-61). Cambridge, UK: Cambridge University Press.
Kuper, A. (1973). *Anthropology and anthropologist: The British School 1922-72.* London: Allen Lane.
Laing, S. (1980). Presenting "things as they are": John Summerfield's *May Day* and Mass-Observation. In F. Gloversmith (Ed.), *Class culture and social change.* Brighton, UK: Harvester Press.
Lankshear, C., & McLaren, P. (Eds.). (1993). *Critical literacy: Politics, praxis, and the postmodern.* Albany: State University of New York Press.
Lemke, J. (1995). *Textual politics: Discourses and social dynamics.* London: Taylor & Francis.
Luke, A. (1988). The non-neutrality of literacy instruction: A critical introduction. *Australian Journal of Reading, 11*(2) 79-84.
Luke, A., O'Brien, J., & Comber, B. (1994). Making community texts objects of study. *Australian Journal of Language and Literacy, 17*(2) 139-149.
Lyons, J. (Ed.). (1981). *New horizons in linguistics.* London: Penguin.
Mace, J. (Ed.). (1995). *Literacy, language and community publishing: Essays in adult education.* Clevedon: Multilingual Matters.
Madge, C. (1937). They speak for themselves. *Life and Letters, 17*(9) 37-42.
Madge, C. (1976). The birth of Mass-Observation. *The Times Literary Supplement,* 5 November, p. 1356.
Madge, C., & Harrisson, T. (1938). *First year's work by Mass-Observation.* London: Lindsay Drummond.
Madge, C., & Harrisson, T. (1939a). *Britain by Mass-Observation.* London: Penguin.
Madge, C., & Harrisson, T. (1939b). "They speak for themselves". BBC Radio script broadcast, 1 June, BBC Home Services (available through the Mass Observation Archive, File Report A26).
Maguire, P., Morley, D., & Worpole, K. (1982). *The republic of letters: Working class writing and local publishing.* London: Comedia.
Malinowski, B. (1922). *Argonauts of the Western Pacific.* London: Routledge.
Malinowski, B. (1938a). A nation-wide intelligence service. In C. Madge & T. Harrisson, *First year's work 1937-1938* (pp. 81-121). London: Lindsay Drumond.

Malinowski, B. (1938b). Afterword. In C. Madge & T. Harrisson, *First Year's Work, 1937-1938* (pp. 83-121). London: Linsday Drummond.

Mangelsdorf, K. (1997). Students on the border. In C. Severino, J. Guerra, & J. Butler (Eds.), *Writing in multicultural settings* (pp. 298-306). New York: Modern Language Association.

Marshall, T.H. (1937). Is Mass-Observation moonshine? *The Highway, 30,* 48-50.

Mass-Observation (1939). *Britain.* London: Penguin.

McDermott, R. (1977). Social relations as contexts for learning in school. *Harvard Educational Review,* 47(2) 198-213.

Mitchell, J.C. (1984). Typicality and the case study. In R. Ellen (Ed.), *Ethnographic research: A guide to general conduct* (pp. 238-241). New York: Academic Press.

Morley, D., & Worpole, K. (Eds.). (1982). *The republic of letters: Working class writing and local publishing.* London: Comedia.

OECD (1995). *Literacy, economy and society: Results of the First International Adult Literacy Survey (IALS).* Ottawa, Canada: OECD/Statistics Canada.

Olson, D. (1977). From utterance to text: The bias of language in speech and writing. *Harvard Educational Review, 47,* 257-281.

Olson, D. (1994). *The world on paper: The conceptual and cognitive implications of writing and reading.* New York: Cambridge University Press.

Parkin, D. (1987). *Contested sources of identity: Nation, class and gender in the second world war.* Ph.D. Thesis, London School of Economics.

Plummer, K. (1983). *Documents of life: An introduction to the problems and literature of a humanistic method.* London: George, Allen & Unwin.

Pocock, D. (1961). *Social anthropology.* London: Sheed & Ward.

Pocock, D. (1975). *Understanding social anthropology.* London: Hodder & Stoughton.

Pocock, D. (1987). Afterword to second edition of *May the Twelfth* by *Mass-Observation.* London: Faber.

Poster, M. (1984). *Foucault, Marxism, and history: Mode of production versus mode of information.* Cambridge, UK: Polity.

Pyke, G. (1936). King and country (letter to the editor). *New Statesman and Nation,* 12 December.

Qualitative Solutions and Research Pty. Ltd. (1995). *QSR NUD*IST 4.* Melbourne: Author.

Richards, J., & Sheridan, D. (Eds.). (1987). *Mass-Observation at the movies.* London: Routledge.

Robinson, J. L. (1987). Literacy in society: Readers and writers in the worlds of discourse. In D. Bloome (Ed.), *Literacy and schooling* (pp. 327-353). Norwood, NJ: Ablex.

Rockhill, K. (1993). Gender, language, and the politics of literacy. In B. Street (Ed.), *Cross-cultural approaches to literacy*. Cambridge, UK: Cambridge University Press.

Rosen, H. (1988). The autobiographical impulse. In D. Tannen (Ed.), *Linguistics in context* (pp. 69-89). Norwood, NJ: Ablex.

Rosen, H. (1993). *Troublesome boy*. London: English and Media Centre.

Rowbotham, S. (1973). *Hidden from history: 300 years of women's oppression and the fight against it*. London: Pluto Press.

Shaw, J. (1994). Transference and countertransference in the Mass-Observation Archive: An underexploited research resource. *Human Relations, 47*(11) 1391-1409.

Sheridan, D. (1984). Mass-Observing the British. *History Today, 34*, 42-46.

Sheridan, D. (Ed.). (1985). *Among you taking notes: The wartime diary of Naomi Mitchison*. London: Gollancz.

Sheridan, D. (Ed.). (1990). *Wartime women: A Mass-Observation anthology*. London: Heinemann.

Sheridan, D. (1993a). "Ordinary hardworking folk": Volunteer writers in Mass-Observation 1937-50 and 1981-91. *Feminist Praxis, 37/38*, 1-34

Sheridan, D. (1993b). Writing for . . . Questions of representation/representativeness, authorship and audience. In D. Barton, D. Bloome, D. Sheridan, & B. Street, *Ordinary people writing: The Lancaster and Sussex writing projects*. Lancaster, UK: Centre for Language in Social Life Working Papers Series No. 51, Lancaster University.

Sheridan, D. (1993c) Writing to the Archive: Mass-Observation as autobiography. *Sociology, 27*(1) 27-40.

Sheridan, D. (1996). *Damned anecdotes and dangerous confabulations: Mass-Observation as life history*. Mass-Observation Archive Occasional Paper, 7. Brighton: University of Sussex.

Sheridan, D. (1998). Getting on with Nella Last: Romanticism and ambivalence in working with women's stories. *Women's History Notebooks, 5*(1) 2-10.

Silvey, R. (1974). *Who's listening?* London: Allen & Unwin.

Smith, D. (1987). *Everyday world as problematic: A feminist sociology*. Boston: Northeastern University Press.

Spender, H. (1982). *Worktown people: Photographs from Northern England 1937-8* [Edited by Jeremy Mulford]. Bristol: Falling Wall Press.

Spradley, J. (1979). *The ethnographic interview*. Fort Worth, TX: Harcourt Brace Jovanovich.

Stanley, L. (1989). Historical sources for studying work and leisure in women's lives. In E. Wimbush & M. Talbot (Eds.), *Relative freedoms: Work and leisure* (pp. 18-32). Milton Keynes, UK: Open University Press.

Stanley, L. (1990). *The archaeology of a 1930s Mass-Observation project.* Occasional paper no. 27, Department of Sociology, University of Manchester.

Stanley, L. (1995). Women have servants and men never eat: Issues in reading gender using the case study of Mass-Observation's 1937 day diaries. *Women's History Review,* 4(1) 85-102.

Stanley, N. (1981). *The extra dimension: A study and assessment of the methods employed by Mass-Observation in its first period 1937-40,* Ph.D. Thesis, CNAA.

Steedman, C. (1986). *Landscape for a good woman: A study of two lives.* London: Virago.

Stocking, G. (1968). *Race, culture and evolution.* New York: Free Press.

Stocking, G. (1983). *Observers observed: Essays on ethnographic fieldwork.* Madison: University of Wisconsin Press.

Street, B. (1984). *Literacy in theory and practice.* Cambridge, UK: Cambridge University Press.

Street, B. (1988). Literacy practices and literacy myths. In R. Saljo (Ed.), *The written word: Studies in literate thought and action* (pp. 59-72). Vol. 23 of Language and Communication Series. Heidelberg: Springer-Verlag.

Street, B. (1992). Literacy and nationalism. *History of European Ideas,* 16, 1-3, 225-228.

Street, B. (1993a). Culture is a verb. In D. Graddol (Ed.), *Language and culture.* Clevedon: Multilingual Matters/British Association of Applied Linguists.

Street, B. (Ed.). (1993b). *Cross-cultural approaches to literacy.* Cambridge, UK: Cambridge University Press.

Street, B. (1995). *Social literacies: Critical perspectives on literacy in development, ethnography and education.* London: Longman.

Street, B. (1996a). Academic literacies. In D. Baker, J. Clay, & C. Fox (Eds.), *Alternative ways of knowing: Literacies, numeracies, science* (pp. 101-134). London: Falmer Press.

Street, B. (1996b). Literacy and power: Open letter. *Australian Journal for Adult Literacy Research and Practice,* 6(2) 7-16.

Street, B. (1997). The implications of the New Literacy Studies for literacy education. *English in Education,* 31(3) 26-39.

Street, B. (1998). Literacies in theory and practice: What are the implications for language in education? *Linguistics in Education,* 10(1) 1-24.

Street, J., & Street, B. (1991). The schooling of literacy. In D. Barton & R. Ivanic (Eds.), *Writing in the community* (pp. 143-166). Newbury Park, CA: Sage.

Summerfield, P. (1985). Mass-Observation: Social research or social movement? *Journal of Contemporary History, 20,* 429-452.

Swindells, J. (Ed.). (1995). *The uses of autobiography.* London: Taylor & Francis.

Szwed, J. (1981). The ethnography of literacy. In M. Farr (Ed.), *Writing: The nature, development, and teaching of written composition.* Hillsdale, NJ: Erlbaum.

Terkel, S. (1972). *Working: People talk about what they do all day and how they feel about what they do.* New York: Ballantine Books.

Terkel, S. (1988). *The great divide: Second thoughts on the American dream.* New York: Avon.

Thornton, R. (1983). Narrative ethnography in Africa, 1850-1920. *Man* (n.s.), *18,* 502-520.

Todorov, T. (1988). Knowledge in social anthropology: Distancing and universality. *Anthropology Today, 4,* 2-5.

Willcock, H. D. (1943). Mass-Observation. *American Journal of Sociology, 48*(4) 445-456.

Williams, R. (1976). *Keywords: A vocabulary of culture and society.* Oxford, UK: Oxford University Press.

Williams, W.C. (1948). *Patterson.* New York: New Directions.

Wray, D. (1997). Research into the teaching of reading: A 25-year debate. In K. Watson, C. Modgill, & S. Modgill (Eds.), *Education dilemmas: Debate and diversity.* Vol. 4, *Quality in education.* London: Cassell.

Ziegler, P. (1977). *The crown and the people.* London: Collins.

ARCHIVAL/UNPUBLISHED SOURCES

Madge, C., & Harrisson, T. (1939). "They speak for themselves". BBC Radio script broadcast on 1 June on the BBC Home Service, Mass-Observation Archive, File Report A26.

Mass-Observation Bulletins for 1937: Mass-Observation Archive: University of Sussex, File Report A4.

Pocock, D. (1985). Application to the Nuffield Foundation. Unpublished paper at the Mass-Observation Archive, University of Sussex.

Pocock, D. (1998). Personal communication with authors.

Appendix Ai
Bibliography of Original Mass-Observation Books

Twenty-five books appeared during Mass-Observation's original phase of activity. Many other manuscripts were prepared but for various reasons were never actually published (for example, three companion volumes to *The Pub and the People* about Bolton and Blackpool). The books have been listed by date of the first edition, but titles which have been re-published since 1981 are marked with an asterisk*.

1937	*Mass-Observation* by Charles Madge and Tom Harrisson with a cover designed by Humphrey Jennings (Frederick Muller, Ltd). Introduction by Julian Huxley.
1937*	*May 12th: Mass-Observation Day Surveys*, an account of Coronation Day edited by Humphrey Jennings and Charles Madge with T. O. Beachcroft, Julian Blackburn, William Empson, Stuart Legg and Kathleen Raine (Faber & Faber). Re-published by Faber with a new afterword by David Pocock in 1987.
1938	*First Year's Work* by Charles Madge and Tom Harrisson (Lindsay Drummond). Postscript by Bronislaw Malinowski.
1939*	*Britain by Mass-Observation* by Charles Madge and Tom Harrisson (Penguin Special). Republished by Century Hutchinson, the Cresset Library, with a new introduction by Angus Calder in 1986.
1940	*War Begins at Home* (Chatto & Windus).
1941	*Clothes Rationing* (Advertising Service Guild Bulletin, Change No 1).
1941	*Home Propaganda* (ASG Bulletin, Change No 2).
1941	*A Savings Survey* (ASG).
1942	*People in Production* (Penguin Special, also ASG Bulletin, Change No 3).

1943*   *War Factory* (Gollancz). Re-published by Century Hutchinson, the Cresset Library, with a new introduction by Dorothy Sheridan in 1987.
1943   *People's Homes* (ASG Bulletin, Change No 4).
1943*   *The Pub and the People* (Gollancz). Re-published in 1971 (Seven Dials Press) with a new introduction by Tom Harrisson and including photographs taken by Humphrey Spender which had not been included in the original edition. Re-published by Century Hutchinson, the Cresset Library, with a new introduction by Godfrey Smith and a new afterword by Dorothy Sheridan in 1987.
1944   *The Journey Home* (ASG).
1945   *Britain and her Birthrate* (ASG).
1947   *Puzzled People* (Gollancz).
1947   *Browns of Chester* (Lindsay Drummond).
1947   *Exmoor Village* by W. J. Turner with colour photographs by John Hinde (George Harrap & Co).
1947   *Peace and the Public* (Longmans).
1948   *Juvenile Delinquency* (Falcon Press).
1949   *The Press and its Readers* (Art & Technics, Ltd).
1949   *Meet Yourself on Sunday* (Naldrett Press) with illustrations by Ronald Searle.
1949   *Meet Yourself at the Doctor's* (Naldrett Press) with illustrations by Ronald Searle.
1949   *People and Paint* (ICI Publications).
1950   *Voters' Choice*, a pamphlet (Art & Technics, Ltd).

Microfilming of all the original Mass-Observation books is being undertaken during 2000 for future publication by Adam Matthew Publishers.

Mass-Observation Publications 1950-70

Two books appeared between the formation of Mass-Observation (UK) Ltd in 1949 and the establishment of the Archive at the University of Sussex in 1970. These were:

1961   *Britain Revisited* by Tom Harrisson with Leonard England, Celia Fremlin, Bill Naughton, Humphrey Spender, John Sommerfield, Mollie Tarrant, Julian Trevelyan and Woodrow Wyatt, with photographs by Humphrey Spender and Michael Wickham (Gollancz).
1966   *Long To Reign Over Us* (William Kimber). Based on Mass-Observation research by Mollie Tarrant.

Appendix Aii
Recent Anthologies and Edited Material

(Published since the establishment of the Archive in 1970)

Broad, R., & Fleming, S. (Eds.). (1981). *Nella last's war*. Bristol: Falling Wall Press. [Paperback published by Sphere in 1982] (Annotated version of a diary written for Mass-Observation).

Calder, A., & Sheridan, D. (Eds.). (1985). *Speak for yourself: A Mass-Observation anthology 1937-49*. Oxford: Cape. [Paperback published by Oxford University Press in 1985].

Cross, G. (Ed.). (1990). *Worktowners in Blackpool: Mass-Observation and popular leisure in the 1930s*. London: Routledge.

Harrisson, T. (1976). *Living through the blitz*. London: Collins. [Paperback published by Penguin in 1978. Re-published in the United States by Schocken Books in 1989 and in the United Kingdom by Penguin, 1990.]

Harrisson, T., & Spender, H. (1975). *Britain in the thirties: Worktown by camera*. London: Unicorn Press, Royal College of Art (limited edition).

Jolly, M. (Ed.). (1983). Dear laughing motorbyke: Letters from women welders of the second world war. *Mass-Observation File Reports 1937-1949* (in microform). Harvester Microfiche (Available for purchase from Primary Resource Media). The M-O File Reports are a separate publication listed by title as there is no author.

Richards, J., & Sheridan, D. (Eds.). (1987). *Mass-Observation at the movies*. London: Routledge.

Sheridan, D. (Ed.). (1985). *Among you taking notes: The wartime diary of Naomi Mitchison*. London: Gollancz. [Paperback published by Oxford University Press in 1986] (An edited Mass-Observation diary).

Sheridan, D. (Ed.). (1991). *Wartime women: A Mass-Observation anthology*. London: Heinemann 1990. [Paperback published by Mandarin in 1991].
Sheridan, D. (1993). Using the Mass-Observation Archive as a source for women's studies. *Women's History Review*, 5(1) 2-10.
Spender, H. (1977). *Worktown* (Catalogue to an exhibition of photographs at the Gardner Arts Centre with an introduction by David Mellor). Brighton: University of Sussex.
Spender, H. (1982). *Worktown people: Photographs from Northern England 1937-8* [edited by Jeremy Mulford]. London: Falling Wall Press.
Stanley, L. (1995). *Sex surveyed, 1949-1994: From Mass-Observation's "Little Kinsey" to the national survey and the Hite reports*. London: Taylor & Francis.
Ziegler, P. (1978). *The Crown and the people*. London: Collins.

Microfilming of sections of the Mass-Observation collection (including the Worktown project papers) is being undertaken during 2000 for future publication by Adam Matthew Publishers.

Booklets Published by the Archive

The Archive has produced three booklets on the Mass-Observation papers to help researchers use the collection: *Guide for Researchers*, *The Mass-Observation Diaries: An Introduction*, and an annotated catalogue to the *Mass-Observation File Reports*. A series of A4, spiral-bound booklets has also been produced for use by students aged 14-16 years. There are nine titles to date: *The Blitz, Tom Honeyford's Autobiography of a Spinner, Evacuation, Postwar Hopes and Expectations, Children at War, Bolton Working Class Life, The Falkland Islands Crisis 1982, Attitudes to AIDS 1987* and *Children's Essays 1937: "The Finest Person Who Ever Lived"*. All are only available directly from the Archive. Please enquire for prices.

Appendix Aiii
Mass-Observation Occasional Papers Series

The Mass-Observation Occasional Paper Series has been established to offer a public platform for some of the many original and creative research projects currently being carried out at the Archive. In accepting papers for inclusion in the Series, the editors would give preference to papers which:

1. are substantially based on research in the Mass-Observation Archive;
2. demonstrate a creative and original approach to the analysis and interpretation of material in the Mass-Observation Archive;
3. contribute to the wider debate on the theoretical and methodological issues involved in using the kinds of material encountered in the Archive-e.g., literacy practices, life history/auto/biography, ethnography.

Editors

Ms Dorothy Sheridan (Mass-Observation Archive, University of Sussex)
Professor Brian Street (Kings College, London)

Editorial Board

Professor David Bloome, Dr Angus Calder, Ms Joy Eldridge, Professor Liz Stanley, Professor Penny Summerfield and Professor Pat Thane

Mass Observation Occasional Paper Series

No 1. *Reading Mass-Observation writing: Theoretical and methodological issues in researching the Mass-Observation Archive* by David Bloome, Dorothy Sheridan and Brian Street, 1993. (£2.50)

Models of reading and their relevance in the process of interpreting M-O material with a particular emphasis on the M-O in the 80s/90s material. A final brief section is on doing case study work. David Bloome is Professor of Education at Vanderbilt University, USA, Dorothy Sheridan is the M-O Archivist at University of Sussex and Brian Street is Professor of Language in Education in the School of Education at Kings College, London.

No 2. *Observing the "other": Mass-Observation and "race"* by Tony Kushner, 1995. (£2.00)

The author's particular research interest is anti-Semitism and this paper makes use of early M-O studies of anti-Semitism, including M-O panel replies to the June 1939 directive on race, observational research undertaken by M-O in the East End of London in 1939, post-war material on Palestine and the establishment of the state of Israel, as well as more recent material derived from M-O in the 80s/90s directive replies in response to the "Social Divisions" Directive (Spring 1990). Dr Kushner is the Marcus Sieff Lecturer in the History Department at the University of Southampton.

No 3. *Weeping in the cinema in 1950: A reassessment of Mass-Observation material* by Sue Harper and Vincent Porter, 1995. (£2.00)

This paper involved a re-working of a 1950 study conducted by Mass-Observation on emotional reactions to sad films as described by members of the M-O volunteer panel. The re-analysis is compared to M-O original conclusions. Dr Sue Harper is a Lecturer in the School of Social and Historical Studies at The University of Portsmouth. Professor Vincent Porter is at the Centre for Communication and Information Studies, University of Westminster.

No 4. *Birth and Power. An examination of some Mass-Observation writing* by Claire Somerville and Helena Watson with Amy Fletcher and Anisha Imhasly, 1996. (£2.00)

Claire Somerville, Helena Watson, Amy Fletcher and Anisha Imhasly were undergraduate students in Social Anthropology at the University of Sussex 1993-96. The research for this paper was undertaken as part of their group project for the Social Anthropology major course: "Observation and Explanation". It is based on an analysis of the replies to a directive on personal experiences of giving birth (Autumn/Winter 1993).

No 5.   *Mass-Observation, gender and nationhood: Britain in the Falklands war* by Lucy Noakes, 1996. (£2.00)

One of the early directive themes of the M-O in the 1980s/90s Project was the Falklands/Malvinas War. Correspondents were asked for their reactions to the news in the media and to report on any direct experiences. In this paper, Lucy Noakes examines the ways in which the war was represented and perceived and looks at links with the Second World War. Lucy Noakes completed her D. Phil on gender and national identity during wartime (Sussex 1996).

No 6.   *The family in time and space: Personal conceptions of kinship* by Dorothy Jerrome, 1996. (£2.00)

This paper addresses the conceptual and methodological problems associated with the study of kinship through the words of the Mass-Observers writing in reply to the Winter 1984 Directive and develops a discussion of models of kinship. One of them, particularly popular among writers and interviewees, is linked to a popular pastime: working on one's "family tree". The paper also explores the motives of these amateur genealogists. The chapter ends with some conclusions about the nature of qualitative research and the value of Mass-Observation and life-history material. Dr Dorothy Jerrome is a Senior Lecturer in the Department of Social Work Studies and Geriatric Medicine at the University of Southampton.

No 7.   *"Damned anecdotes and dangerous confabulations": Mass-Observation as life history* by Dorothy Sheridan, 1996. (£3.00)

Consideration of some of the critiques about the "unrepresentativeness" of the Mass-Observers based chiefly on the M-O in the 1980s/90s Project. Discussion of appropriate methodology for the interpretation and use of the material, that is as case study rather than survey data. Dorothy Sheridan is the Archivist at the Mass-Observation Archive, University of Sussex. She directs the contemporary project.

No 8.   *Mass-Observation and civilian morale: Working-class communities during the blitz 1940-41* by Brad Beavan and John Griffiths, 1998. (£3.00)

One of the most difficult concepts in both contemporary and academic accounts of the Second World War is that of "civilian morale". This papers uses evidence from the Mass-Observation Archive to argue that understanding fluctuations in morale can only be achieved through an exploration of working-class culture during the 1930s and 1940s. The paper examines difficulties of defining "morale" and goes on to argue that the pattern of bombing in urban centres and the continuity of working class institutions helped shape and maintain morale during the critical period of 1940-41.

No 9. *Intellectual property, representative experience and Mass-Observation* by Jenny Shaw 1998. (£3.00)

This paper is based on doing research on the recent (post-1981) autobiographical material in the Mass-Observation Archive and examines the idea of intellectual property in relation to the use of the material for research purposes. It also explores Donald Winnicott's concept of the "transitional object", suggesting that the Archive may serve as a transitional object enabling both its contributors and the researchers to find the "other" in and through the "representative experience" stored in the Archive.

No 10. *Mass-Observation: A brief history* by Tom Jeffery, 1999. (£5.00)

This short history of Mass-Observation was first published as an Occasional Paper in 1978 by the Centre for Contemporary Cultural Studies. Although much work has been done on the Mass-Observation papers since then, Jeffery's paper remains one of the few overviews of the whole enterprise and gives a particularly good insight into the origins of the project and its social and historical context in the 1930s. The 1999 edition is over 60pp long and includes a new foreword by the editors and a postcript by Tom Jeffery.

Appendix Aiv
About the Mass-Observation Archive

The Mass-Observation Archive is located in the Library of the University of Sussex, close to Brighton on the south coast of England. The Archive holds all the papers generated from the research carried out by Mass-Observation into everyday life in Britain between the years 1937 and the mid-1950s. The new Project, initiated in 1981, has resulted in an additional collection of correspondents' responses to directives. These collections have been augmented by personal papers (diaries, letters, autobiographies).

The Archive is registered as a Charitable Trust in the care of the University of Sussex. The Archive Patron is Lord Asa Briggs. The Archivist is Dorothy Sheridan and the four trustees are Professor Ruth Finnegan (Open University), Mr A.N. Peasgood (University of Sussex Librarian), Professor Patricia M Thane (University of Sussex) and Professor Brian Street (King's College, University of London).

The Archive is open for public use by appointment. There are no charges for access to academic or freelance use; commercial researchers may be charged. To make appointments or for further information, please contact the Archivist at the address below.

The Mass-Observation Archive
The Library
University of Sussex
Falmer
Brighton BN1 9QL
UK

External phone. +44 (0)1273 678157
Fax: +44 (0) 1273 678441
e-mail: moa@susx.ac.uk

Website address: http://www.susx.ac.uk/library/massobs

Appendix Bi
List of Topics Covered in Directives Since 1981

The Directive number is shown to the left of the date; the part numbers in brackets.

1: Summer 1981
   Currency, Royal Wedding, Business Premises, Unemployment, Holidays, Food
2: Royal Wedding Special 1981
   Diary for the day
3: Autumn 1981
   Currency, Pet Food, Shopping Strategies, Business Premises, Unemployment, Liberal-SDP Alliance, Christmas.
4: Spring 1982
   House Prices, Unsolicited Mail, Weather in January, Railway Strike, Local Elections, Business Premises, Unemployment, Falklands/Malvinas War.
5: The Falkland Islands Crisis 1982
   War with Argentina
6: Summer 1982
   Public Services, Private Services, The Budget, Gas and Electricity Bills, Royalty, Inflation, Currency, Food, European Economic Community.
7: EEC Special
   Tenth Anniversary of British Entry into Europe
8: Autumn 1982
   Pocket Money, Business, Premises/Cheque Books/Currency
9. Falklands/Malvinas Postscript 1982
   Falklands War Aftermath : Reactions to Falklands Parade, October 1982.

10:   Winter 1982
      Food, Gardening
11:   Spring 1983
      The General Election, Waterworkers' Strike, Coinage, Viewing and Reading
12:   Summer 1983
      Work
13:   Autumn 1983
      Housework and Maintenance, Business Premises: Repeat Request.
14:   Winter 1983
      Christmas Cards, Buying British
15:   Spring 1984
      Social Well-Being
16:   Summer 1984
      Electronic Banking, Miscellany
17:   Autumn 1984
      Attitudes To USA
18:   Winter 1984
      Relatives, Friends and Neighbours
19:   Spring 1985
      (1) Morality and Religion, (2) Posters
20:   Autumn 1986
      (1) Self Portrait (Not yet open for research), (2) Major Events, (3) Christmas Day Diary
21:   Spring 1987
      (1) Waste, Thrift and Consumerism, (2) AIDS Campaign
22:   May Special 1987
      General Election
23:   Summer 1987
      (1) Holidays, (2) Day Diary: August Bank Holiday 1987
24:   Autumn/Winter 1987
      (1) The Car, (2) The Hurricane and Floods
25:   Spring 1988
      Clothing
26:   Summer 1988
      (1) Time, (2) Objects About the House
27:   Autumn 1988
      (1) Regular Pastimes, (2) Day-Diaries on Television Watching
28:   Spring 1989
      (1) Disasters, (2) Food News

29: Summer 1989
(1) Rules of Conduct, (2) Day Diary: For June 15th, European Election Day
30: Autumn/Winter 1989
(1) Relaxants And Stimulants, (2) The 'Backing Britain' Campaign
31: Spring 1990
(1) Social Divisions (2) Retrospective on the Eighties
32: Summer 1990
(1) Close Relationships, (2) Your Views on M-O
33: Autumn/Winter 1990
(1) Celebrations, (2) Gulf Crisis, (3) Organisations
34: Spring 1991
(1) Education, (2) The Uses of Reading and Writing and Literacy Diaries, (3) Taking Risks
35: Autumn 1991
(1) Women and Men, (2) Technology
36: Spring 1992
(1) Personal Hygiene, (2) The Pace of Life, (3) One Day Diary, (4) The 1992 General Election
37: Summer 1992
Nature and the Environment
38: Winter 1992
(1) Growing Older, (2) Looking Back at 1992, (3) Last Night's Dreams
39: Spring 1993
Growing Up, Reading, Community/Foreigners
40: Summer 1993
(1) Pleasure, (2) Security and Crime, (3) Current Issues
41: Autumn/Winter 1993
(1) Managing Money, (2) Birth, (3) The Title "Mass-Observation"
42: Spring 1994
(1) Death and Bereavement; Serial Killers, (2) Autobiography and Diaries
43: Autumn/Winter 1994
(1) Sport, (2) Drugs, (3) Current Events (Rail Strike, Ireland, Royalty, Criminal Justice Bill)
44: Spring 1995
(1) Day Diary (Meals), (2) The Countryside, (3) Television Soap Operas
45: Summer 1995
Shopping In Britain

46: Autumn/Winter 1995
(1) Images of Where You Live: Cities, Towns, Villages, (2) Mothers and Literacy in the Early 1900s, (3) Subject of Own Choice
47: Spring 1996
(1) The Lottery, (2) Menstruation, (3) Subject of Own Choice
48: Summer 1996
(1) Beef: BSE and "Mad Cow" Debate, (2) The Supernatural
49: Autumn/Winter 1996
(1) Using the Telephone, (2) Unpaid Work, (3) The Next General Election
50: Spring 1997
(1) You and the NHS, (2) The Next General Election (Cont.)
51: Summer 1997
(1) Doing a Job, (2) Being Overweight
52: Summer 1997 (Special)
The Death of Diana
53: Autumn 1997
(1) Music, (2) Dancing, (3) The Future
54: Spring 1998
(1) Gardens and Gardening, (2) Extra-Marital Affairs
55: Autumn 1998
(1) Present Giving and Receiving, (2) Staying Well in Everyday Life
56: Spring 1999 (Proposed)
(1) Researching the Millennium, (2) Keeping Animals as Pets (3) Ireland
57: Summer 1999 (Proposed)
Using Public Libraries
56: Spring 1999
(1) Going to the Cinema
(2) Current Issues
(3) Documenting the Millennium
57: Summer 1999
(1) The Public Library
(2) Body Piercing and Tattooing
(3) Current Events
58: Autumn 1999
(1) Sleeping and Dreaming
(2) Millennium Diary

Appendix Bii
Sample Directives

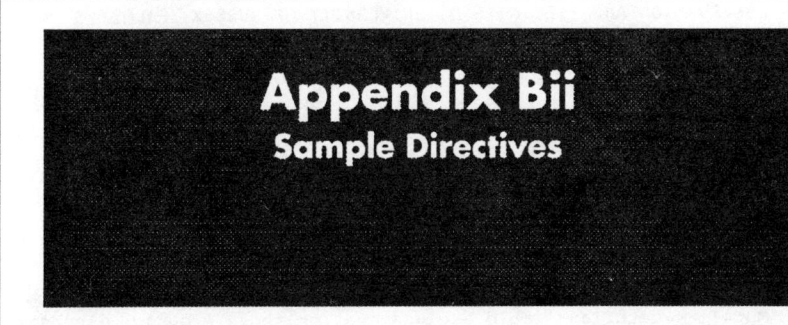

MASS-OBSERVATION SPECIAL   19 April 1982

THE FALKLAND ISLAND CRISIS

So many Observers have written in already about this that I thought it would be well worth asking for a wider reaction on what is the gravest development in our international affairs since Suez.

Was it mishandled from the start? If negotiations fail, should we act? And if so, how? If negotiations are to succeed, what do you think is the best solution? Is there a threat to world peace if we take any sort of military action, or is there a threat if we don't?

How does it affect domestic politics? How much support is there for the views of Tony Benn and Judith Hart? In general what do you think of the statements of politicians and other public figures on this matter?

Apologies for this barrage of questions. They should only be taken as suggestions.

As always I would be very grateful for your reactions. Please feel free to write in as your views develop or keep a separate diary of your reactions which you could send in later.

Because of all this and also because Dorothy will be on holiday in the first three weeks of May, I shall hold back the Summer Directive until the end of May.

Best wishes,

David Pocock

David Pocock

Special directive, April 1982 on the Falkland Island Crisis

MASS-OBSERVATION ARCHIVE, ARTS D, UNIVERSITY OF SUSSEX, FALMER, BRIGHTON BN1 9QN, SUSSEX

WINTER DIRECTIVE 1982

The theme is food, including drink. Please read the whole thing before you write anything.

1a. First the things that you, your family, your relations and friends do NOT eat and why.
Here are some of the reasons why you might not eat certain things:

Moral: vegetarians would exclude meat on these grounds; also some non-vegetarians avoid battery eggs or veal etc because of the way in which they are produced.

Health: this might also be a reason for vegetarianism, it would also apply to people on permanent or temporary diets and people with allergies. I would include here foods avoided because of preservatives, and additives generally.

Political: the products of certain countries are rejected because of the policies of their governments.

Religious: certain religions ban certain foods absolutely or occasionally (ie on certain days or at certain periods).

"Personal": some people refuse to eat or strongly dislike eating some things for none of the above reasons, eg some people will not eat offal, others have an entrenched loathing of 'greens'.

In replying to this section please be as specific as possible, eg specifying if you are a vegetarian, vegan, or modified vegetarian eating, say, fish. If you object to particular additives, please say which. Finally, please do add other reasons which occur to you for not eating things.

1b. What foods do you now buy rarely or never because of their cost which you used to buy (or as a child eat) regularly; butter, beef (other than minced), ground coffee and cod are a few of the items that some people no longer buy regularly.

1c. Do you regard meat in some form as an essential food in the sense that you feel you should eat it once a day or that any proper meal should include it?

2. Food for special occasions: what foods do you buy, which you would not normally buy, for entertaining, for celebrations and anniversaries of all kinds (the answer to this may well overlap with 1b above).

PLEASE TURN OVER..................

Winter Directive 1982 on Food Preferences

3a. New Foods: taking the food of your childhood as a baseline, what items of food have been introduced since, either regularly or occasionally eg vegetables, fruits, delicatessen products, Asian (including Chinese) Take-away, 'convenience' foods. I am reminded as I write of the look on the face of a grocer when I asked for olive oil in mid-December 1953.

3b. Does the phrase 'in season' as applied to food mean anything to you today? Do you, for example, buy tomatoes in February or avoid pork when there is not an 'r' in the month.

4. Like mother used to make.....Memories please of food which you particularly enjoyed as a child, not necessarily treats or special occasions but not excluding these. Also, frankly, childhood hates and a note on whether these have been overcome, eg as it might be for me : spinach, bread and butter pudding. I now like the former, the latter - never.

5. A project for home-growers only: in 1983 would you please cost the production of home-grown vegetables, cost of seed, fertilizer, pesticides etc from now until cropping time and then make a note of the approximate yield   Do not cost your labour but please do keep a note of the amount of time spent working in garden or allotment.

If you grow so large a variety that it would be a real chore to cost the lot, please keep details for one main crop.

Would you also make a list of all your equipment that relates directly to vegetable production, ie hoe, spade, fork etc but not lawn mower, and when you are next in the shop make a note of their replacement value.

IN CONCLUSION AND AS A CONCLUSION TO 1982 GRATEFUL THANKS TO EVERY ONE OF YOU AND CONGRATULATIONS ON THE COLLECTIVE WORK DONE THIS YEAR. VERY BEST WISHES TO YOU AND YOURS FOR CHRISTMAS AND THE NEW YEAR.

Dorothy Sheridan.   *David Pocock*

PS Be sure to read the enclosed notes!

Winter Directive 1982 on Food Preferences (con't)

MO

AUTUMN 1986 DIRECTIVE

This Directive is in three parts.

Part I   Please write a Self-Portrait, see Page 2 of General Information for more about this.

Part II   Mass-Observation has from the very beginning been concerned to record what people really experience and think as opposed to media assessments of the nation's mood or, for that matter, what politicians say 'people' or the 'British public' 'want', 'feel', or 'are fed up with'. Now, 1986 seems to have been an eventful year. But what have been the major national and international events, and how much do we really remember? As soon as you have read through this Directive and before discussing it with anyone else, please make a note both of the major events of 1986 in the order in which you remember them, and the month in which you think they occurred.

Again before discussing them with other people comment on your reaction at the time and the reactions of other people as you recall them. This would be the place to note comments overheard, remarks made in shops, etc.

Now, if the opportunity arises, by all means check your view of 1986 with the views of others. If you do report other people's reactions, please observe the anonymity rule (see Page 2).

I am quite ready, and so should you be, to hear that private and domestic events of all sorts have often pushed public events into the background. For one of our diarists, 1982 was a big year because her first grandchild was born; not surprisingly, the conflict in the Falklands came a poor second in her records of that year! It is essential that this sort of thing be recorded.

Part III   Among our most prized records are the Day Diaries. These are records of one day's events, from the moment of rising to going to bed. Any day in the Christmas Holiday period, preferably 25 December itself, is our target this time. Whether you celebrate Christmas or not, please write a Day Diary. One way of setting about it might be to write very brief notes every hour (or dictate them to someone else if your hands are full!) and then write up your notes when you have more leisure, but as soon as possible, of course, while memory is still fresh. If Christmas Day itself is quite impossible, then select any day during the period up to and including New Year's Day 1987.

DP

THE MASS-OBSERVATION ARCHIVE   UNIVERSITY OF SUSSEX   FREEPOST BR2112   BRIGHTON BN1 1ZX

Autumn 1986: Various

Mass-Observation in the 1990s

Summer 1992 Directive

Nature and the Environment

This directive asks you for your views about environment and development issues. 1992 is the year when the United Nations Conference on Environment and Development (known as the "Earth Summit") takes place in Rio di Janeiro during the first two weeks of June.

This directive has three main aims: (1) to ask you to express your feelings about the environment and development, (2) to ask you to describe how you find out about these issues; and (3) to ask you what you think can or should be done about such issues, if anything. If you don't feel able, for whatever reason, to answer this directive, or you can only answer briefly, could I ask you *please* to write and explain why. We would rather have a brief note of your reaction than no response at all.

Please answer the first two sections as soon as the directive reaches you but we would like you to wait until after 17 August to answer Section 4 (see page 4). You may like to take your time over Section 3. *Please send in your reply to all four sections of the directive together (to save on postage) after 17 August.*

Some helpful definitions

You should feel free to define what you mean by the words "environment" and "development". They can both cover a wide wide range of issues, but we thought it might help to get you thinking if we suggested some definitions:

"Environment" is simply the place where we live, our habitat, whether it is in the sense of our own neighbourhood, town, or country, or the planet as whole.

"Environment issues" include such well-publicised matters as atmospheric pollution, conservation of flora and fauna, ocean ecology, nuclear energy and radioactive waste, the thinning of the ozone layer, transportation and its impact, the introduction of toxic chemicals into the food chain, the destruction of the rain forests, the effect of environmental changes on climate, etc.

"Development" is a broad term which generally refers to the process by which a society or country expands economically. It is often taken to mean a progressive improvement in the standard of living. Historically the term "development" has been associated with what used to be called "Third World" countries (with the United States axis as the First World and the USSR axis as the Second World). "Third World" countries were typically "pre-industrial" or in the early stages of industrialisation, and later they become known as "developing countries". Increasingly, however, "development" is recognised as a process in which all societies are engaged and today the more common distinction is between the rich countries of the "North and the poor countries of the "South".

The issues and problems relating to development are also well publicised. They include malnutrition and under-nutrition, poverty, famine, debt and aid, public health provision, population growth, use of energy resources etc. Again, the list is long and interconnected.

This directive has been written in collaboration with Professor Colin Lacey, Dr John Abraham and Mr David Longman of the Institute of Continuing and Professional Education (Sussex) and Dr Peter Dickens of the Centre for Urban and Regional Research (Sussex).

Summer 1992: Nature and the environment

Section 1

It would help us a great deal if you could continue the practice of putting your sex, your age, your occupation (not just "retired" but your previous occupation) and your town or village of residence on the top right hand side of the first page under your M-O number.

Apologies to those of you who will have already provided the information in Section 1 in some form or other already. Please bear in mind that the researchers will be looking exclusively at this set of replies. We also have been joined by some new Mass-Observers who haven't yet provided this information.

1. What newspapers (weekday and Sunday), journals or magazines do you read?

2. What are your main reasons for choosing them?

3. What current affairs/news television programmes do you watch?

4. List any environment/development organisations of which you are a member.

Section 2

> Please complete the following section as soon as you receive the Directive

Recently the 'Earth Summit' took place in Rio di Janeiro. Even if you didn't hear about it, we would still like you to carry on answering where you can. Your views on the environment and media coverage of the environment and development issues are still very important to the success of this Directive.

1. The Earth Summit assumed that there are substantial environmental and development problems in the world. Do you agree?

2. Did you know about this event before receiving this Directive? If you did, what were your main sources of information?

3. Did you take a close interest in the event or would you have done so if you had known more about it?

4. What in your view were the main issues addressed by the conference?

5. Of all the sources of information available to you about the Summit which do you feel is the most reliable and trustworthy? Which is the least?

6. Do you have an opinion as to why these differences in reliability exist?

7. Do you feel that the press could have been more informative? Do you feel that television could have been more informative?

8. Do you think that there are any issues that were neglected by (a) the press and (b) television?

9. Has the coverage of the Earth Summit changed the way that you think or do things about these issues?

Summer 1992: Nature and the environment (con't)

Section 3

The next set questions are designed to get you thinking - and writing - but please feel free to answer them according to your own ideas of what is important and relevant. You may find them difficult at first, so don't agonise too long over your replies. Sometimes odd thoughts and "gut reactions" are as significant as carefully thought through essays. If you feel you can't answer any of the questions, please say so and explain why. We'd rather have a short explanation of this kind than no reply at all.

1. Nature and 'the natural'

We hear much nowadays about people's relationship to nature. But what does 'nature' really mean?

Should people see themselves as part of nature? Are people just another 'natural' species?

Similarly, the word 'natural' is very common. Many foods (muesli, for example) are now advertised as 'natural'.

Given that most 'natural' products are now produced in factories, does the word 'natural' have any useful meaning?

2. Nature and the Supernatural

Many people believe that nature was created by an all-powerful God or deity. Some also think that it is still controlled by supernatural forces. If we are subject to such forces it may be that the human race can do little to influence or change the non-human world. Perhaps we should surrender to fate?

Does the idea of nature carry any particular religious significance for you?

If so, do you think it worth changing our behaviour in order to protect resources and other species?

3. Identifying issues and problems

What in your opinion are the three most important environmental problems facing the world today? What are the three most important development problems?

Do you think future generations will face the same issues or will there be others that are more important for them?

Do you feel any of these problems pose a threat to you personally or to our way of life in the UK?

Or are they only relevant to remote areas of the world?

Do you feel that these problems are given too much or too little emphasis in what you read in the press or watch on television. Why do you think this is so?

Are environmental and development issues important enough to influence your choice of newspaper. If so, do you think there is an adequate choice available?

Summer 1992: Nature and the environment (con't)

326 APPENDIX Bii

4. What can we do about environment and development problems?

What do you think that people can do about these problems?

What sort of things do you do in your daily life that take environment or development issues into account.?

Do you think that individual action is the key to solving these problems?

Do you think it will require co-ordinated action by government or organisations such as the United Nations?

Do you think that richer societies such as Britain, USA and Japan should take more responsibility for these problems when they occur in poorer societies?

Would you be prepared to accept a lowering of your standard of living if this contributed to the solution of these problems?

If you are a member of any environment/development organisation can you explain what led you to become involved?

5. How useful is modern science?
We are still very dependent on scientists to tell us about the environment, our relationship with it and changes to our behaviour if we are going to protect the planet. Does modern science have an adequate understanding of our relationships to the environment?

How seriously should we take the explanations, predictions and proposals offered by modern scientists?

Section 4

Please complete the following section during the week beginning 17 August

It is now two months since the Earth Summit conference in Rio.

1. Do you feel that it has had an effect on the way governments or powerful organisations behave?
2. Are there any issues that you feel more strongly about as a result of the conference?
3. Are any of the issues raised by the conference still in the public mind? If so, can you say what they are?
4. Do you feel that the press has provided adequate coverage of the issues since the conference took place? What issues does the press concentrate on?
5. Do you feel that television has provided adequate coverage of the issues since the conference took place? What issues does television concentrate on?
6. Do you think this directive has increased your interest/awareness of the issues it covers or would you have been interested anyway?

DS 5.6.92/Dir. No. 37

The Mass-Observation Archive, The Library, University of Sussex, FREEPOST 2112, Brighton BN1 1ZX.

Summer 1992: Nature and the environment (con't)

Mass-Observation in the 1990s
Autumn Directive 1997

Part One: Music

Please remember to start with a brief (2-3 line) autobiography: M-O number (NOT name), sex, age, town or area where you live, occupation or former occupation

Please could you tell us all about you and music. Remember that you don't have to answer all the questions, or all of them in the same order. Many of your answers will overlap, and that's fine. Also, as always, please include anything you feel I should have covered.

Does music play an important part in your life? What kinds of music do you enjoy? Have your tastes changed over your life?

What kinds of music do you dislike? Can you explain why you get more out of some kinds of music than others?

Do you play a musical instrument or sing yourself? Do you perform in public? Now or in the past? (Please tell us if you are in a band or group or orchestra or choir).

Have you ever had music lessons (other than classroom music)? What do you feel about yourself in relation to performing music? Are you, or could you have been, good at it?

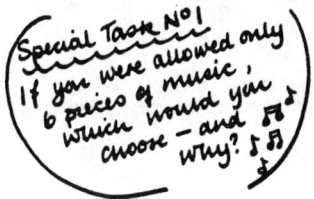

Special Task No 1 — If you were allowed only 6 pieces of music, which would you choose — and why?

Do you have special associations with music? Perhaps a piece of music reminds you of an important event, a film or TV show you like, a person you care about.

Do you have only positive associations, or are there negative ones too?

Do you use music in different ways? My mother used to play fast Greek music to get her going with the housework - do you have habits like this? Are they linked to particular times, places, activities or moods? For instance, you might use music in different ways at home, outdoors, or at work; in company or on your own; while you exercise, cook, study, make love, travel, or sleep; to cheer you up or calm you down. **PTO**

Autumn 1997 Music and Dancing

Music at home

Listening: if you listen at home, which room do you use, when and why? What kinds of music systems do you use? Where are they located? How have they changed over the years? Is the radio important to you for listening to music? Which stations do you prefer?

If you live with other people, how do your music habits fit with those of the others?

Storing your music: If you have records, tapes or CDs, please describe where they are kept and how you arrange them. Please include the collections of other people in your home.

Live music at home: Do you have musical instruments in your home? Where are they kept? When and by whom are they used? Who listens?

Music in public places

Do you go out to concerts or clubs for live music? Please describe the kinds of events you enjoy. Please include comments on the cost, the venue, the audiences at the kinds of places you are familiar with.

Please include any musical experiences you have had in other countries, especially any you would enjoy experiencing again.

Do you enjoy music in pubs? Restaurants and cafés? Supermarkets? Shops? Streets? Do you ever *dislike* music in public places?

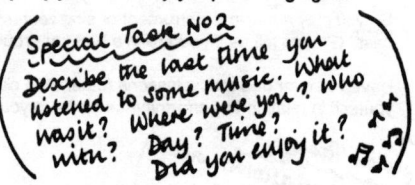

Special Task No 2
Describe the last time you listened to some music. What was it? Where were you? Who with? Day? Time? Did you enjoy it?

Do you belong to any music-related clubs, groups or societies? Or any fan clubs? Do you buy magazines or other publications (or other items such as t-shirts, badges, mugs) related to your musical activities and tastes?

Spending money on music

How do you budget for musical events or buying music?

Can you estimate how much you spend on:
    (1) tickets for public performances
    (2) on your sound system at home (or in your car or personal stereo system)
    (3) buying tapes, records or cassettes

Could you give a rough estimate of cost for all these *over the past six months*?

Finally, have you been listening to music as you answer this directive? If you have, what was it?

Autumn 1997 Music and Dancing (con't)

Part Two: Dancing

Please remember to start on a new page with a brief (2-3 line) autobiography: M-O number (NOT name), sex, age, town or area where you live, occupation or former occupation

What kind of dancing do you like? Think very widely and include everything from ballroom to ballet, from line-dancing to disco, from flamenco to morris dancing, barn dancing to the waltz, tap dancing to jigs, tangos to jive, belly dancing to tea dancing....... In the Archive we have accounts of people doing the "Lambeth Walk" and "Knees up Mother Brown". Does anyone remember these?

Please describe any dancing you do now or have done in the past? It would good if you could include details such as:
- the kind of dancing you do (dance names, steps etc)
- where you do it
- with whom (a partner, a group)
- the accompanying music (is it live?)
- the clothes and shoes you wear

Do you ever dance at home?
Have you had lessons?
Please include how your experience has changed over time.

Special Task N° 3
Supposing I had to edit a new M-O anthology of Dance Stories - experiences of Mass-Observers over the years.... what would you send in? Stories please of your experiences - good & bad, about dancing! Thanks. D.

Do you watch dancing - live on stage or in dance halls, in films or on TV? What kind do you enjoy?

Part Three: The Future

Please remember to start on a new page with a brief (2-3 line) autobiography: M-O number (NOT name), sex, age, town or area where you live, occupation or former occupation

Finally, three questions - please write as much as you feel able.

How far into the future do you usually plan?

What things do you usually plan for?

What does the "Millennium" mean to you?

DS/17 Nov 1997/Dir. No. 53

The Mass-Observation Archive ♦ The Library ♦ Freepost 2112 ♦ University of Sussex ♦ Brighton BN1 1ZX

Autumn 1997 Music and Dancing (con't)

Appendix Biii
Introductory Information for New Recruits

UNIVERSITY OF
SUSSEX
AT BRIGHTON

The Mass-Observation Archive
The University Library
University of Sussex
Brighton, BN1 9QL
Tel: 01273 678157
Fax: 01273 678441
Email: d.e.sheridan@sussex.ac.uk
Web: http://www.sussex.ac.uk/library/massobs

Thank you for returning your Self Portrait. We are very pleased you have decided to join the Project and we hope you will enjoy taking part.

You will find enclosed the following:

- **An orange card with your M-O number on it**
  Please keep this safely and remember to put your number clearly on the top right hand corner of everything you send us instead of your name. This number identifies you but preserves your anonymity when researchers look at your directive replies.
- **A copy of the latest directive**
  Please answer it as soon as you can and return it to us.
- **A copyright release form**
  Please complete and return.
- **A form asking for biographical details**
  Please complete and return. This might seem like a repeat of your Self-Portrait but it is a formal way for us to keep some basic information about you on file for researchers. Because it is in your own words, we can be sure of its accuracy.
- **Three labels**
  When you reply to the next directive, attach just one of them, with a paper clip, to your reply. *Please leave it on its sticky backing* and write your name and address on the paper side. (not the backing side) and we will use it on our acknowledgement letter back to you. Keep the other two safely, they are for enclosing with your replies to later directives. Please don't send all three back at once as this reduces their usefulness to us.
- **An appeal to you to become one of our Friends**
  In 1991, we launched an appeal inviting people to become a Friend of the Archive. The Archive is a Charitable Trust and relies on external funds for many of its activities. There is no obligation to become a Friend. We would be happy just to have you as one of our volunteer writers, but if you feel able to join (suggested annual subscription is £........... but less is certainly acceptable), we would be very pleased. All Friends receive an *Annual Newsletter*, invitations to Open Days and, where possible, discounts on M-O publications.

We look forward to hearing from you. Thank you again for joining the Project.

Yours sincerely

Dorothy Sheridan
Archivist & Project Director

Patron: Lord Asa Briggs
Trustees: Professor Ruth Finnegan, Mr Adrian Peasgood,
Professor Patricia M Thane, Professor Brian V Street
Archivist: Ms Dorothy Sheridan MA MBE
Charitable Trust No. 270218

Supported by the
Heritage Lottery Fund

The initial letter

The Mass-Observation Archive
M-O in the 1980s and 1990s

Copyright of your Mass-Observation writing

The material which we have collected as part of our new Mass-Observation Project has already attracted the interest and attention of researchers since we began in 1981. Although most of the research carried out at this Archive relates to our historical collection (from 1937 until the early 1950s) we are very keen to put access to the newly-gathered material on the same proper footing as the rest of the Archive.

It is very important for the Project to be seen as immediately valuable for social research so we do our best to ensure that directive replies are recorded and sorted as quickly as possible and they are made available to researchers usually within three months of receipt. Directive replies are only identifiable by your Mass-Observation number so your identity is not disclosed. Full diaries, self portraits, letters to us which have your name and address on them, and any other personal information, are all covered by an embargo which operates for 30 years from the day of receipt.

It would take us a great deal of time and involve us in a lot of expense if we had to contact you every time we needed permission from you for a researcher to quote from your directive replies. To avoid this problem, we invite you to share with us the copyright of your Mass-Observation writings. Your formal consent means that we can permit researchers to quote from your writing for up for 1,000 words of continuous text without having to contact you every time. Most of the requests that we receive come from academic researchers who wish to quote short extracts in their internal papers (dissertations, theses) or for articles in scholarly journals. If the request is to use quotations in a published book or programme, we make a small charge. The fees we receive for quotations make a small but important contribution to the Archive's funds.

There is no obligation on you to give us copyright but most people have been happy to comply and it helps enormously with our administration. Please note that this arrangement does not interfere with your own rights to publish your writing independently. You must, however, keep your own copies as the Archive will probably not be able to afford to provide copies in the future.

Please also note that unless we hear from you to the contrary, your Mass-Observation contributions will not be made available under your real name even to your nearest relatives and even after your death. If you want family and friends to see what you write for us, we will need a letter specifically stating your wishes which we can put in your personal file. If we don't receive such a letter, your contributions will remain anonymous.

Please complete the form below and send it with your next contribution to the Mass-Observation Archive, FREEPOST 2112, the Library, University of Sussex, Brighton BN1 1ZX.

Please cut off here ---

Name... M-O No. ....
Address...
....
....

I confirm that the Mass-Observation Archive holds the copyright of all my contributions to the Mass-Observation Archive.

Signed ....
Date.......................................

DS: 7.11.95
h:\mass-obs\moprojec\forms\copyrt.doc

Copyright form

APPENDIX Bii **333**

MASS-OBSERVATION IN THE 1990S: BIOGRAPHICAL INFORMATION

| Please fill in your M-O number here: | |

Please fill in this information sheet and return it to us with your next directive. Please *don't* include your name or full address as this sheet will be made available to Archive researchers.

The information here will only be available to researchers in an anonymous form.

MALE/FEMALE .... YEAR OF BIRTH..
YOUR **PRESENT** TOWN OR VILLAGE ....
COUNTY ....

MARITAL STATUS:
Please tick the appropriate box:

| single | married | separated | divorced | co-habiting | widowed |

If you would prefer to describe yourself in some other way, please do so below:

....
....
....

LIVING SITUATION:
Please tick the appropriate box:

alone	with a partner only	with partner & children	with children only
	with other adults not related to you	with adult relatives	

Please use the lines below to describe your situation in more detail especially if these categories are not useful.

....
....
....

OCCUPATION: *Please describe below (1) your current occupation and, (2) if relevant, the occupation of your partner. If either you or your partner is retired, unemployed, or has given up work to take care of children or other dependents, please also give the last main occupation. It would be helpful if you could provide full details. For example, describe exactly what you do, your level of reponsibility, and any other information which will fill out the overall picture. Some rough examples to help you (1): "Teacher of modern languages (1A "B") in large inner city comprehensive school, with special responsibility for careers advice", (2) "Assistant supervisor in large Marks & Spencers with responsibility for women's lingerie", (3) "Self-employed plumber, working from home". (4) "Heavy Goods Driver for large haulage company importing fresh foods".*

(1) YOUR JOB: ....
....
....
....

(2) YOUR PARTNER'S JOB: ....
....
....
....

PLEASE USE AN ADDITIONAL SHEET IF THERE IS NOT ENOUGH SPACE HERE FOR YOUR ANSWERS. THANK YOU.

H:\MASS-OBS\MOPROJEC\FORMS\BIOGINFO.DOC

Biographical information form

Appendix Biv
Pseudonyms and Numbers of Correspondents Cited

Men

Mr Barrow (B1106)
Mr Fisher (F1701)
Mr Muse (M381)
Mr Purcell (P2250)
Mr Reed (R450)
Mr Richards (M1593)
Mr Russell (R1671)
Mr Thwaite (T2222)

Women

Mrs Burgess (B1215)
Mrs Caldwell (C2079)
Ms Cleer (C2295)
Mrs Douglas (D2092)
Miss Early (E174)
Mrs Friend (F1373)
Mrs Martin (M1498
Ms McPhail (M2493)
Mrs Safran (B2197)
Ms Wright (W632)
Mrs Smith (S2207)
Mrs Williams (W2151)

Appendix C
The Spring Directive 1991

SPRING DIRECTIVE 1991

There's a lot here! Take a deep breath and read it through first. Answer at your leisure. Remember - this might be the last directive.

The first part of this directive is about education - your own experiences as a young person and in your adult life, as a parent (if you are one), and your observations and views on the current situation. The second part of the directive has been prepared in collaboration with Dr Br'an Street, a social anthropologist with a special interest in the practice of reading and writing in different cultures. There is a short Part III which is about the risks we take in everyday life. Professor Sandra Wallman, the Archive's new trustee, is especially interested in your answers to these questions.

Please bear in mind that these points are mainly for guidance. You should feel free to include additional points if you think it is important. And if you can't respond to a point, or you feel it isn't relevant to your situation, please say so.

PART I: EDUCATION
About you
Please start by listing your own schools and colleges with dates and your age. This is NOT another request for a Self Portrait! We just want the bare bones. You don't have to provide the full names of places but it would be useful if you could indicate what kinds of institutions they were. Please include a note of any qualifications you received. Don't forget to start right at the beginning (nurseries? playgroups?) and bring it right up to date with evening classes and adult education if it applies to you. Please include apprenticeships and day release and any other training schemes you can think of. The rule is - if in doubt, include it.

If you are (or have been) employed in education - in any capacity - please say so in block capitals at the beginning of your reply. You might also like to comment at some point on how your experience within education influences your views.

Looking back
What do you feel you got out of your education? What would you have liked to have got out of it? Do you have any regrets? Do you feel that your education prepared you for your adult life? Do you consider your education over?

Please write as fully as you as you feel able covering, if you can, the different stages of your schooling, your relationships with teachers and

Please turn over.

Spring directive part I

APPENDIX C

other pupils/students and the attutudes of your parents and other family members to your education.

The value of education
In your opinion, what should education be for? Who should decide what is to be taught? And who should pay for it? How important is it compared to other priorities in the national budget?

Education today
What are your views on the present situation in Britain? Please comment not only on schools but on the whole spectrum of education.

Obviously this is a vast subject and you won't be able to cover everything unless you are very enthusiastic! Can I suggest that you concentrate on those themes you think are the most important and relevant. Please illustrate with your own experience and observations whenever possible. You may want to compare present with past.

Parents: please comment, if you have not already done so, on your children's education, past and present.

****

PART II: THE USES OF WRITING AND READING
(Please remember to start this part on a new sheet of paper)

This section is about your everyday uses of reading and writing and your ideas about them. The yellow form enclosed with this directive is for use as a sort of diary. The form asks about all kinds of reading and writing. Instructions on how to fill it in are on the reverse side of the form.

The following twelve questions are mainly about your writing for Mass-Observation, whether it's a diary, a directive reply or a special report. People who have been writing for us for a long time will probably find it easier to answer than newcomers, but I'd be grateful if everyone would have a go.

You will probably find it easier to answer if you read the questions all through first and there will be some overlap.

1. Before you start writing for M-O, do you discuss your ideas with anyone else? If you do, who are they? Do people know that you are a Mass-Observer?

2. One you've written your contribution, do you read it out to anyone, or show them what you've written? Has any ever asked you not to write about them?

3. Do you need to be in a particular sort of mood to write for M-O? If you do, please describe it?

4. When you write, do you need to be in a particular place? Do you have a special chair, table or desk? Do you write at home or at at work? Do you ever write while travelling or away from home?

5. Do you need to have a particular pen or pencil or type of paper? Do you prefer to type or word-process?

6. Do you need privacy and silence to write or can you write with people and noise around you?

7. Do you get started as soon as a directive arrives or do you like to mull it over? Do you answer all in one go, or in different sessions? Do you make notes or do a draft first?

8. Have you kept copies of what you send us? Do you ever have afterthoughts?

Spring directive part I and part II (con't)

9. What do you think you get personally out of writing for Mass-Observation? Do you think writing for M-O has changed you? In what way?

10. In your opinion what is the value of this kind of writing and of the whole project?

11. Do you do other kinds of writing apart from your M-O work? Please describe. How are they different from your M-O writing? (style, place mood etc).

12. Lastly, we have had the honour of receiving your photographs but most of you have never seen us. Can you put into words what you imagine we are like at the Mass-Observation Archive? What do you think the Archive is like? When you write-do you have a reader in mind? If so, who is it?

****

PART III: TAKING RISKS
(Please start a new page)

1. Are you are person who likes to take risks? If so, what kinds of risks?
2. What is the most risky thing you do? How do you judge the risk? And why is it worth taking?
3. Is there anything you would never dream of doing because of the risk?
4. What do you think are the greatest risks to people in everyday life at the moment?

****

YOUR GULF CRISIS DIARIES
Please continue to record your reactions to the news. At the time of writing this directive, I have no way of knowing how things will develop. I suggest that you send in what you have done to date with your reply to this directive but that you continue for as long as the war continues and you feel able to write about it. Your reports have already attracted a great deal of interest. They comprise a unique, reflective, in-depth, record of how, over a period of several months, people responded to the news of the war which will be complementary to the more specific opinion polls which are being carried out all the time now. Please ensure that all your entries are dated and include your volunteer number. Many thanks.

ENDING PHASE ONE OF THE PROJECT
Please continue to send us replies, diaries, Gulf Crisis diaries, special reports as usual until the end of August 1991 when the present funding ends. We will do our best to acknowledge their receipt. If we are successful in obtaining funding soon, you will receive another directive in the Autumn. If you haven't heard from us by the end of 1991, you may have to assume that the Project is suspended. When we ran out of money before (1985-6) many of you continued to keep in touch with diaries or occasional special reports on subjects you consider important. It would be wonderful if you were able to do this but I'm afraid it would not be possible to pay your postage anymore (the FREEPOST system would cease) or acknowledge receipt. If an acknowledgement is important, you could enclose a self-addressed stamped postcard saying 'Your diary/report was safely received on.......... by............' and I will send it back to you. Your contributions would be much valued and would be safely stored as always.

LABELS: as before please return them with your name and address on them and we will use them to acknowledge your contribution.

Please return to: The Mass-Observation Archive, The Library, University of Sussex, Brighton BN1 9QL (stamp needed) or, The Mass-Observation Archive, FREEPOST 2112, The Library, University of Sussex, Brighton BN1 1ZX.

[DIR. 34 1.2.91]

Spring directive part II and part III (con't)

The Tom Harrisson Mass-Observation Archive

THE LITERACY DIARY   28 Feb - 2 March 1991

We are interested in finding out what we all actually do with reading and writing in everyday life. On the reverse of this sheet, there is a 'literacy diary' which we would like you to keep by recording the 'literacy events' you are involved in over the three day period, 28 Feb, 1 March and 2 March. By 'literacy event' we mean simply any situation in which reading and writing are used (eg taking notes when answering the telephone, reading a book, using a recipe book, helping children with homework and so on).

For each day, put the date and your number at the top. Under 'TIME' write the time of day and length of time this event lasted (it may only be a brief moment or an hour or two). There will be periods of the day of course when no literacy events are happening but this is of interest to our research too.

Write under 'PERSONS', a description (eg friend, daughter, customer, patient, boss) and age of the person(s) also involved.

Under 'LITERACY EVENT' describe the nature of the activity (eg notes for telephone, reading a book).

If you are unsure about what counts as a literacy event, then make a note in the COMMENTS section. Err on the side of including everything rather than leaving things out because they are not normally associated with 'literacy' (eg reading road signs or a map, listing the shopping, reading labels on goods in shops). When the enclosed form is full up, please draw up your own using the same format and number it page 2 (and 3 and 4 if necessary).

We hope you will find this exercise interesting, as others have done in previous research projects. Please use the COMMENTS section to tell us what you thought of the exercise - whether you learned anything about your own literacy practices, how it related to what you wrote in the first part of the directive about education.

Please return your literacy diary to the Archive with the rest of your directive reply. Thank you very much for your time and effort.
DS
23.1.91

Please turn over.....

Spring directive literacy diary

APPENDIX C **341**

MASS-OBSERVATION LITERACY DIARY

For 28 February, 1 March and 2 March 1991

Date..................   Vol. No..............

TIME	PERSONS	PLACE	LITERACY EVENT

COMMENTS

IF YOU RUN OUT OF SPACE, PLEASE DRAW UP YOUR OWN CHART AS ABOVE

Spring directive literacy diary (con't)

Appendix D
Interview Guidance Sheet

ESRC Research Project: "Literacy Practices and the Mass-Observation Project"

Guidance sheet for interviews

This sheet is intended as a guide to topics to be covered for both the interviewers and the interviewees. At the start of the recording, the interviewer should say:

> "This interview is part of the ESRC-funded research project: Literacy Practices and the Mass-Observation Project. It is with [Interviewee's M-O number] at his/her home on [date]. The tape will be used as part of the research, and the tape and any transcript from the tape will be stored in the Mass-Observation Archive and will receive the same protection as that given to all other written contributions."

The aim of the research project is to investigate:

1. Reading and writing (literacy) practices and processes in everyday contexts

2. Where these practices and processes fit with other parts of people's lives

3. How a person's past life, (especially their educational experiences) has influenced both the above.

4. The relationship between personal/private expression and more public social commentary in the writing process.

Topics especially as they relate to the Spring 1991 Directive:

1. What are the conditions for writing and reading: mood, practical arrangements (place, rooms, chairs & tables, location of reading matter including bookshelves), material needs? **Including** details for opening post, reading newspapers & magazines, TV Times etc.

   Questions 3 - 6.

2. The writing process: drafts and/or discussions, image of reader/archive. keeping copies, afterthoughts, self censorship.

   Questions 7, 8, 9, 12.

Guidance sheet for interviews

3. Reflexivity: identity as a "Mass-Observer", citizen, social commentator, reasons for writing, personal expressions, understandings of value, other writing and reading. Sometimes people describe themselves as being "ordinary", what does this mean to you?

Questions 1,2,10,11

Topics as they relate to the literary events diary:

1. What did you take to be a "Literacy event"?

2. What, if anything, did you learn about the role of reading and writing in your life from doing the Literacy Events diary?

Further questions & themes:

1. Does being a man/woman affect your writing? How? Is it easy to find time/space to write in relations to partners, other family members, friends?

2. How do you decide what M-O wants? What clues? What guidance? What do you think the expectations are? Do you think you get it right? Does it matter to you? What do you leave out why?

3. What would stop you writing for M-O? Not only your own circumstances but what, about the Archive and the way it operates, might discourage you?

4. Do you recommend M-O to other people? What kinds of people? What kinds of people would you definitely NOT recommend it to?

5. What counts as "Literacy": Correctness? Being grammatical? Spelling? Style? Being "literary"?

6. How far are you concerned about these issues when you write? Do you feel self-confident? What are your fears/concerns?

7. What kinds of different styles are called on: in M-O writing (eg different directives: diaries, one-day diaries. short questionnaires, open-ended directives, self-portraits, looking back over your life, or questions about the here and now?

8. And in other writing apart from M-O?

At this point, it might be useful to refer to your Education Directive and your Literacy Events diary to discuss or expand on any points you raised in your answer, also to pick on anything you feel differently about now, or want to discuss further.

Other questions or issues not covered above which you might like to raise?

Guidance sheets for interviews (con't)

Author Index

A
Abrams, M., 27, 37, *293*
Addison, P., 38, *293*
Agar, M., 165, *293*
Althusser, L., 262, *293*
Anzadula, G., 262, *293*
Asad, T., 103, 105, 107, *293*

B
Bakhtin, M., 116, 133, *293*
Barton, D., 6, 9, 109, 223, 238, 241, 283, *293*, *297*
Basso, K., 235, *293*
Bauman, R., 108, *293*
Baynham, M., 109, *293*, *294*
Bell, S.G., 38, *294*
Benjamin, W., 107, *294*
Bertaux, D., 73, *294*
Besnier, N., 4, 242, *294*
Bloome, D., 6, 14, 69, 76, 82, 100, 121, 121*n*, 217, 254*n*, 289, *293*, *294*, *297*
Bohman, S., 73, *294*
Bourdieu, P., 127, 239, 268, *294*
Broad, R., 54, *296*
Brodkey, L., 4, 121, *295*
Bruce, B., 121, *295*

C
Calder, A., 26, 27, 38, 40, 54, 56, *295*
Cameron, D., 1, 100, 111, *295*
Clanchy, M.T., 255, *295*
Clark, R., 4, 5, 9, *295*
Clifford, J., 85, 103, *295*
Collins, J., 11, *295*
Comber, B., 237, 241, *299*
Conquergood, D., 223, *295*
Coupland, J., 277*n*, *297*
Coupland, N., 277*n*, *297*

D
de Certeau, M., 262, 288, *295*
Dixon, J., 105, *293*
Dumont, L., 80, *295*

E
Easthope, G., 38, *295*
Egan-Robertson, A., 5, 242, *295*, *296*
England, L., 37, *296*

F
Fairclough, N., 4, 127, 262, 289, *296*
Fardon, R., 103, *296*
Farrell, E.W., 36, 133, *296*
Ferraby, J., 36, *296*
Finch, J., 41, *296*
Firth, R., 33, 88, 90, 93, 282, *296*

Fleck, L., x, *296*
Fleming, S., 54, *296*
Foucault, M., 239, *296*
Frazer, E., 100, 111, *295*

G

Gee, J.P., 3, 108, 289, *296*
Geertz, C., 107, *296*
Giddens, A., 262, *296*
Giles, H., 277*n*, *297*
Gilmore, P., 259, *297*
Gilyard, K., 263, *297*
Giroux, H., 262, 263, *297*
Goffman, E., 79, *297*
Graff, H., 223, *297*
Gramsci, A., 262, *297*
Green, J., 82, 100, *297*
Grillo, R., 87, *297*
Guerra J., 263, *297*
Gutierrez, K., 262, *297*
Gullestad, M., 73, *297*
Gumperz, J., 108, *297*
Gurney, P., 27, 39, *297*

H

Halliday, M., 224, *297*
Hamilton, M., 6, 9, 223, 238, 241, 283, 293, *297*
Harvey, P., 100, 111, *295*
Harris, L., 45, *298*
Harrisson, T., 9, 21, 22, 24, 34, 36, 83, 90, 281, 282, *298, 299*
Heath, S., 4, 108, 121, 223, 238, 248, *298*
History Workshop Collective, 39, *298*
Howard, U., 7, *298*
Huxley, J., 104, *298*
Hymes, D., 108, *297*
Hynes, S., 21, 27, *298*

I

Ivanic, R., 4, 5, 6, 9, 109, 223, 293, *295, 297*

J

Jahoda, M., 33, 34, *298*
Jeffery, T., 26, *298*
Jennings, H., 28, 33, *298*

K

Kent, R., 38, *298*
Kertesz, M., 36, *298*
Kinzer, C., 217, *294*
Knobel, M., 241, 283, *299*
Kress, G., 241, *299*
Kulick D., 110, 111, *299*
Kuper, A., 81, 83, *299*

L

Laing, S., 27, *299*
Lankshear, C., 217, *299*
Larson, J., 262, 263, *297, 299*
Lemke, J., 127, *299*
Luke, A., 237, 241, *299*
Lyons, J., 86, *299*

M

Mace, J., 8, 73, 223, *299*
Madge, C., 9, 21, 28, 29, 32, 33, 34, 90, 102, 281, 282, *298, 299*
Maguire, P., 73, 223, *300*
Malinowski, B., 79, 81, 85, 86, 87, *299, 300*
Mangelsdorf, K., 263, *300*
Marcus, G., 85, 103, *295*
Marshall, T.H., 33, *300*
Mass-Observation, 28, 38, 44, 84, *300*
McDermott, R., 259, *300*
McLaren, P., 217, *299*
McLaughlin, M., 248, *298*
Mitchell, J.C., 14, 106, 132, *300*
Morley, D., 73, 223, *299*

O

O'Brien, J., 237, 241, *299*
OECD, 8, *300*
Olson, D., 11, *300*

P

Parkin, D., 40, *300*
Plummer, K., 73, *300*
Pocock, D., 43, 44, 80, 96, 97, 97*n*, 99, 100, 101, 102, *300*
Poster, M., 239, *300*
Pratt, J., 87, *297*
Pyke, G., 22, *300*

Q

Qualitative Solutions and Research Pty. Ltd., 128, *300*

R

Rampton, M.B.H., 100, 111, *295*
Richards, J., 37, 57, *300*
Richardson, K., 108, 111, *295*
Robinson, J.L., 213, *300*
Rockhill, K., 5, *301*
Rosen, H., 137, *301*
Rowbotham, S., 39, *301*

S

Shaw, J., 70*n*, *301*
Sheridan, D., 6, 14, 26, 37, 38, 41, 54, 56, 57, 58, 69, 72, 76, 121*n*, 134*n*, 188*n*, 216, 254, *293, 294, 295, 3300, 301*
Sherzer, J., 108, *293*
Silvey, R., 73, *301*
Smith, D., 240, 249, *301*
Spender, H., 28, *301*

Spradley, J., 128, *301*
Stanley, L., 26, 38, *301, 302*
Stanley, N., 26, 40, 42, 76, 79, 87, 111, *302*
Steedman, C., 38, *302*
Stocking, G., 105, *302, 303*
Street, B., 3, 6, 7, 8, 11, 14, 69, 76, 87, 121, 121*n*, 235, 238, 254*n*, 259, 263, 283, 288, *293, 294, 297, 302*
Street, J., 7, 69, 108, 259, *302*
Stroud, C., 110, 111, *299*
Summerfield, P., 26, 41, 282, *303*
Swindells, J., 38, *303*
Szwed, J., 235, *303*

T

Terkel, S., 119, 133, *303*
Thornton, R., 104, *304*
Todorov, T., 104, 108, *303*

W

Willcock, H.D., 35, *303*
Williams, R., 74, *303*
Williams, W.C., ix, *303*
Worpole, K., 73, 223, *299*
Wray, D., 8, *303*

Y

Yallom, M., 38, *294*

Z

Ziegler, P., 44, *303*

Subject Index

A

Abrams, Mark, 37–38
Access issues, 77–78
Adams, Mary, 29
Addison, Paul, 38
Advertising and recruitment, 52–60
Al Khalidi, Alia, 69
Among You Taking Notes: The Wartime Diary of Naomi Mitchison, 54
Analytical induction, 106–107
Anonymity, 139
Anthologies, 307–308
Anthropology, 9. *See also* Ethnography
  British, 80–82
  British Social, 96–97
  combining with social psychology, 101–102
  critiques of Mass-Observation, 93–95
  Mass-Observation and, 79–111
  "of our own people," 1, 19, 25, 82–85, 102
  Personal, 46, 99, 110
  split among different branches of, 96

Archive. *See* Mass-Observation Archive
Archivist, letters to, 125
Audience
  Mass-Observation as, 229–232
  sense of, 196–197
Authorisations, 4
  scientific, 11
Authorship, 120–121
Autobiographical writing, 38, 42

B

Barrow, Mr (B1106), 139, 156–163
BBC Television, 51–52, 175
Benjamin, Walter, 107
"Big Brother," 74–75
Biographical information form, 62, 333
Bloome, David, 130–131, 140, 145, 163, 173, 201, 309
Bohman, Stephan, 73
Books, of correspondents, 200–201
Briggs, Lord Asa, 38, 313
Britain by Mass-Observation, 90
British anthropology, 80–82. *See also* Writing Britain
British Institute of Public Opinion, 40
British Social Anthropology, 96–97

British Sociological Association, 38
Burgess, Mrs (B1215), 216–217

C

Calder, Angus, 38, 40, 98, 309
Caldwell, Mrs (C2079), 263–264, 289
Case studies. *See also* "Representational cases"; "Telling cases"
  Mass-Observation as, 106–108
Changes, in Mass-Observation Project, 71–78
Churches, 3, 89
Civil disobedience, 126, 255
Civil rights campaigns, emergence of, 38–39
Class system, 174
Classification of data, 70–71
Classrooms, 3, 7. *See also* Schools
Cleer, Ms (C2295), 222, 276
Coldstream, William, 28
Communication, ethnography of, 108
"Communicative competence," 108
Construction, of dialogues, 132–135
Contested social practices, reading and writing as, 126–127
Contradictions, among disciplines, 2
Conversation, nostalgic, 158
Copyright Act of 1988, 72
Copyright Form, 332
Coronation of 1937, 28, 33, 83
Coronation of 1953, 45
Correctness, 134–135
Correspondents. *See also* Interviewees
  B1106, 139, 156–163
  B1215, 216–217
  B2197, 163–172, 266–267
  books of, 200–201
  C2079, 263–264, 289
  C2295, 222, 276
  D2092, 250
  defined, 76, 243–49
  diversity among, 162
  E174, 220
  F1373, 6, 145–56, 217, 219–20, 224, 229–230, 232, 260–261, 268–270, 289
  F1701, 227
  how they write a response to directives, 233–235
  leaving Mass-Observation Project, 56
  limiting, 59
  listed, 335
  losing contact with, 71
  M381, 249
  M1498, 173–180, 233
  M1593, 180–187
  M2493, 187–194, 274, 276–277
  P2250, 215, 225
  publicity generated by, 55–56
  R450, 139, 201–207, 219, 270–272, 274–275
  R1671, 195–201, 234
  recruiting new, 60–63, 331–333
  reshaping dialogues, 116, 128, 235–236
  S481, 134–135
  S2207, 219, 221, 249–250
  submitting unsolicited reports, 69
  T2222, 229
  thinking of selves as writers, 172, 176–178, 206
  W632, 139–144, 218–219, 221, 251–257, 261, 272–273, 275, 289
  W2151, 227–28
Courtrooms, 126
Cross-cultural conception, of literacy practices, 109
Crossings, 262–268

Crown Film Unit, 29
Cultural models, shared, 3
Cultural practices, reading and writing as, 124–126
Cultural processes, 238

D

Daily Mirror, 22, 47–48
Dancing, 329
Data, 94
  claimed novelty of, 90–91
  coding, 128
  gathering, analysing and writing up, 127–132
  interpretation of, 119
  organisation and classification of, 70–71
Data Protection Act of 1984, 72
Day Survey, 83
Decontextualised processes, 13
"Delegation," 242
Description, thick, 107–108
Desks, 178
Developments, in Mass-Observation Project, 71–73
Dialogues, 137–207
  constructing, 132–135
  conventions in representing, 139
  defined, 116, 128–129
  framing, 116, 119–135
  reshaped by correspondents, 116, 128
  and writing practices, 111–207
Diaries, 28, 34–36, 69, 74, 141, 149, 183, 189
  as impenetrable, 36
  literacy, 340–341
  one-day, 45
Directives, 35, 50–51, 64–70
  defined, 75
  how correspondents write a response, 141–42, 233–235
  responding to, 122, 164–165, 173–174, 181–182
  samples, 319–29
  Spring 1991, 123, 127–129, 139, 257, 337–341
  themes of, 169–171, 175, 184, 190, 315–318
  Uses of Writing and Reading, 214, 223
Dissent, 166, 178, 252
"Distancing," 104–105
Documents of Life, 73
Douglas, Mrs (D2092), 250

E

Early, Miss (E174), 220
East End, writing in, 206–207
Economic and Social Research Council, 52
Edited material, 307–308
Education, 228–229
  de-railed, 13, 258–259
  and writing and identity, 257–262
Edward VIII, abdication of, 22–23, 44
Eldridge, Joy, 309
Élites, 7–8
Elizabeth, Queen, 44
England, Len, 37
Enumerative induction, 106
Environment, Nature and, 323–326
Espionage, home front, 29
ESRC grant, 128–129, 131
Establishment institutions, 9, 282
Ethical responsibilities, in Mass-Observation Project, 71–72
Ethnocentrism, avoiding, 106
Ethnographic perspective, 82
Ethnography, 81–82, 110–111
  of communication, 108
  factual, 8–9
  fundamental contradiction within, 104–105
  reflexive, 9, 103–106

352 SUBJECT INDEX

subjectivity of, 87
tools of, 82
European Community, 65
London Office, 51
Events covered. *See* Directives;
Literacy events
Everyday Literacies, 283

F

Factual ethnography, 8–9
Falklands War, 65, 67, 319
Fascism, 21
Feminist social theory, 290
Feminist sociology, 240
Ferraby, John, 35–36
Fiction writing, 153–154
Fieldwork, 104, 110–111
Filing systems, 190
Finch, Janet, 41
Finnegan, Ruth, 313
First Year's Work, 79, 86
Firth, Raymond, 33, 79
and Mass-Observation, 88–93
Fisher, Mr (F1701), 227
Food Preferences, 320–321
Foucault's models of power, 239
Frazer, Sir James, 81
Friend, Mrs (F1373), 6, 145–156, 217, 219–220, 224, 229–230, 232, 260–261, 268–270, 289
Future, 329
of Mass-Observation, 153

G

Geertz, C., 107
Gender factor, 55–60, 243–247
Gollancz, Victor, 27
GPO Film Unit, 22, 24, 29
Grammar, 186–187, 275–279
Granada Television, 50
Grierson, John, 22
Guardian, 59, 142, 164, 273
Gulf War, 67–68, 141

H

Harrisson, Tom, 22, 24, 26–27, 29–32, 35–38, 43–44, 48, 79, 82–84, 89, 281
High Culture view of writing, 8
Historical context, of Mass-Observation, 19–111
Historical origins, social and political contexts, 21–32
Historical reality, 165–166
History. *See also* Self-history
contributing to, 155–156, 182
History Workshop, 39
Home front espionage, 29
Housewives Register, 55
"How To Take Part" booklet, 62–63
Huxley, Julian, 83
Hynes, Samuel, 21

I

Induction, 106–107
Indulgence, Mass-Observation as, 167
The Inflation Project, 45, 47, 49
Influences, life stories and, 199–200
Institutions. *See* Social institutions
Interpretation, 137
authorised, 4
contexts of, 4–5
Interviewees, selection of, 129
Interviews, 129–132
protocols for, 129–130, 343–344
styles of, 131
Invisibility. *See also* Transparency
of literacy practices, 5–8, 288

J

Jahoda, Marie, 33–34
Jeffery, Tom, 98
Jennings, Humphrey, 22, 24, 26, 28, 32, 101, 181, 281
Jewish, being, 171–172

K

Key Words, 74
Knobel, Michelle, 283
Knowledge
  contesting, 11
  kinds of, 119–120
  nature of, 121–127
  relativity of, 105
  representation of, 120, 138, 285–286
  traditional claims to, 10
  transmission of, 122
Knowledge construction model, of reading and writing, 123–124

L

Layers, of writing practices, 117
Legal status. *See also* Copyright Form
  of material collected in Mass-Observation Project, 71–72
Legitimacy, defined, 7
Lesbian/gay, being, 158–160
Letters, 6, 145–148, 160–161, 175–178, 202–204, 279
  to new recruits, 331
  to the newspapers, 143
  saving, 163
Life and Letters, 32
Life stories
  and influences, 199–200
  thematic, 69–70
Lists, 69, 194
Literacy
  defined, 3
  falling standards of, 8
  schooling of, 7
Literacy diaries, 340–341
Literacy events, defined, 4, 108
Literacy practices
  cross-cultural conception of, 109
  defined, 5, 19
  dialogues about, 137–207
  framing the dialogues, 119–135
  invisibility of, 5–8
  Mass-Observation as, 8–12, 108–111
  relationship to social life, 3–5
Literacy Practices, 109
Literacy theory
  and mass-observation, 1–16
  Mass-Observation Project as a "telling case" of, 13–15
Local Literacies, 283
Logs. *See* Diaries
London School of Economics, 81

M

M-O. *See* Mass-Observation
Madge, Charles, 22–24, 26, 32–35, 39, 86, 94, 101, 281
Malinowski, Bronislaw, 79–81
  and Mass-Observation, 85–88
Man Appeal, 56
Marshall, T. H., 33
Martin, Mrs (M1498), 173–180, 215, 233
Mass media
  coverage by, 53–54
  images of literacy in, 6
Mass-Observation. *See also* Correspondents; Observers
  1937-1981, 21–42
  1950-1980, 38–39
  1986-present, 51–52
  advertising and recruitment, 52–60
  as an historical phenomenon, 46
  and anthropology, 79–111
  as audience, 229–232
  as case studies, 106–108
  critiques of, 89–90, 93–95
  defined, 15–16
  diverse motivations reflected by, 26–27, 99–100, 103
  early days of, 9–10, 84
  exaggerated claims made about, 93

Firth and, 88–93
future of, 153
hiatus in, 43–51
historical context of, 19–111
historical origins of, 21–32, 95
as indulgence, 167
as literacy practices, 8-12, 108-111
literacy theory and, 1–16
Malinowski and, 85–88
original books on, 305–306
Pocock and, 95–103
possible abandonment of, 50–51
publications 1950-1970, 306
purpose of, 189–190, 195
reading, 121–127
recent anthologies, 307–308
rehabilitation of, 39–42
revival of, 43–78, 80
"Specials," 98
value of, 196
Mass-Observation Archive, 2, 12, 43–44, 48, 109, 115, 144
booklets published by, 308
described, 250, 313
open day at, 61
surviving papers in, 91, 284
users of, 34–35
Mass Observation at the Movies, 57
Mass-Observation Bulletins. *See* Directives
Mass-Observation Occasional Paper Series, 309–312
Mass-Observation Project
beginning of, 1–2
changes and developments in, 71–78
connections with other projects, 73
defined, 12–13, 144, 155–156
ethical responsibilities in, 71–72
gender factor, 55–60, 243–247
getting started with, 140, 148–153, 157, 164, 181, 188, 197

long-term interests of, 52
reductionist accounts of, 97
as a "telling case" of literacy theory, 13–15
uses and genres of writing associated with, 223–35
writing for, 6, 205–206
and writing from positions, 249–57
Mass-Observers. *See* Correspondents
May the Twelfth, 33, 44, 83, 100–103
McPhail, Ms (M2493), 187–194, 274, 276–277
"Meandering," 133
Media. *See* Mass media
Men, and writing, 185–186
Microfilmed publications, 306, 308
Minorities, recruitment of, 162
Models. *See also* Knowledge construction model; Shared cultural models; Theoretical models; Transmission model of power, 239
Muse, Mr (M381), 249
Music, 327–328
Music industry, 28

N

Narratives, embedded, 127
National Lesbian and Gay Survey (NL&GS), 139, 156–157
National Panel, 28
Nature and the Environment, 323–326
Negotiating among social domains, 11
Nella Last's War, 54, 74
New Literary Studies, 3–4, 108. *See also* Literacy practices
New London Survey, 92
The New Statesman and Nation, 22–26, 48
Nineteen Eighty-Four, 75

SUBJECT INDEX 355

NL&GS. *See* National Lesbian and Gay Survey
Nordiska Museet, 73
Nostalgic conversation, 158
Novelty, claimed of data, 90–91
Nuffield Foundation, 51–52, 58

O

Observers. *See also* Correspondents
  being, 171
  defined, 33–34, 48, 83
  untrained, 32
Occasional Paper Series, 309–312
Opinions, writing to express, 174-175
Ordinary people
  being, 158, 174–175, 184–185
  defined, 214–215, 285
  writing by, 211–291
Organisation of data, 70–71. *See also* Provenance
Orwell, George, 75
Other writing. *See* Writing, not for Mass-Observation
Ownership, 290. *See also* Copyright Form

P

Panel. *See* National Panel
Parkin, Diana, 40
Participants. *See* Correspondents
Peasgood, A. N., 313
People
  anthropology "of our own," 1, 19, 25, 82–85, 102
  ordinary, 211–291
  use of written language by, 3
"The People's War," 57
Personal Anthropology, 46, 99, 110
Personhood, 242–243
Pickering, Judy, 71
Plummer, Ken, 73
Plus magazine, 59

Pocock, David, 43, 45–48, 58, 62, 65–67, 70, 80, 85, 159, 174
  and Mass-Observation, 95–103
Poetry, 176, 202–204
Political contexts, and the historical origins of Mass-Observation, 21–32
Poll Tax, 251–257
Positions, 241–242
  Mass-Observation Project and writing from, 249–257
Potts, Ian, 57
Power, 238–241
  models of, 239
Press, unrepresentativeness of, 22
The Professional Stranger, 105
Provenance, 77–78
Pseudonyms, 335
Psychology. *See* Social psychology
The Pub and the People, 27
Publications on Mass-Observation, 305–312
Publicity. *See also* Mass media
  generated by correspondents, 55–56
Purcell, Mr (P2250), 215, 225
Puzzled People, 195
Pyke, Geoffrey, 22–23

Q

QSR NUD*IST software, 128

R

Racial discrimination, 142
Radicalism, emergence of, 38–39
Raine, Kathleen, 24
Rambler, 57
Reading
  as contested social practices, 126–127
  in decline, 8
  embedded in social practices, 4
  as knowledge construction, 123–124

as knowledge transmission, 121–123
as social and cultural practices, 124–126
Reading Mass-Observation Writing, 76
Reality, historical, 165–166
Recruitment, 52–60, 60–63
 of minorities, 162
Reed, Mr (R450), 139, 201–207, 219, 270–272, 274–275
Reflexive ethnography, 9, 19, 103–106, 287
Relationships. *See* Social practices
Representation, of knowledge, 120, 138
"Representational cases," 129
Research
 defined, 9, 100
 not limiting, 36
Research and Policy, 41
Richards, Mr (M1593), 180–187
Robinson, Jay, 213
Rowntree, Seebohm, 92
Royal Weddings, 45, 64, 98
Russell, Mr (R1671), 195–201, 234

S

Safran, Mrs (B2197), 163–172, 233, 266–267
Schools, 125
 and visibility and invisibility, 7
 writing at, 160, 178–179, 259–260
Scottish, being, 191–194
Second World War, 35
Self-history, 162, 322. *See also* Autobiographical writing
Self-indulgence, Mass-Observation as, 167
Self-Portraits, 61–62
Shared cultural models, 3
Shaw, Jenny, 59

Sheridan, Dorothy, 59, 66–67, 69–71, 98, 157, 164, 180, 290, 309, 313
Silver Jubilee, 44
Simpson, Wallis, 22–24
Smith, Mrs (S2207), 219, 221, 249–250
Social contexts
 creating, 212
 dynamic play of, 262
 and the historical origins of Mass-Observation, 21–32
Social domains, negotiating among, 11
Social institutions. *See also* individual social institutions
 co-mingling of, 5
 establishment, 9, 282
 influence of, 3
Social issues, emphasis on, 29
Social life
 continuous evolution of, 14
 relationship to literacy practices, 3–5
Social position, 4–5, 11, 237
Social practices
 new, 278
 reading and writing as, 124–126, 268–275
Social processes, 238
Social psychology, combining with anthropology, 101–102
Social Survey, 37
Social Surveys and Social Action, 37
Social theory, feminist, 290
Sociological Abstracts, 38
Sociological Review, 34
Sociology
 feminist, 240
 qualitative work in, 36
 subject matter of, 92
Spanish Civil War, 21

SUBJECT INDEX 357

Speak for Yourself, 54, 56
Speaking, writing rather than, 160
Spelling, 186–187, 275–279
Spender, Humphrey, 28, 30
Spring 1991 Directive, 123,
   127–129, 139, 257, 337–341
Stanley, Liz, 38, 76, 309
Stanley, Nick, 39–40, 42, 87, 98, 111
Stopping writing, 163, 187
Stories
   embedded, 127
   life, 69–70, 199–200
"Stranger than Fiction," 57
Street, Brian, 80, 156, 187, 195, 309,
   313
Subjectivity, 135
Summerfield, Penny, 40, 98, 309
Sunday Times, 181
Sutton-Spence, Kerry, 139, 156

T

Taxonomic analysis, 128
Television
   writing about, 149
   writing while watching, 153,
      161, 173
"Telling cases," 13, 20, 129
Thane, Patricia M., 309, 313
Themes
   of directives, 169–171, 175, 184,
      190, 315–318
   for life stories, 69–70
Theoretical models, 13
Thick description, 107–108
Thwaite, Mr (T2222), 229
Time, finding for writing, 154
Todorov, T., 104–105
Transcripts, 132
Transmission model, of reading
   and writing, 121–123
Transparency, 133
   pretense of, 116
Trevelyan, Julian, 28
Truth, 207. *See also* Reality

Turmoil, reading and writing as
   sites of, 127
"Typical cases," 129

U

Understanding Social Anthropology,
   96, 103
Uniqueness, 218
Unsolicited reports,
   correspondents submitting, 69
Uses of Writing and Reading
   (UWR), 214, 223

V

Vantage points, 34
Visibility and invisibility
   countering structure of, 7–8
   part schools play in, 7
Voice, 162

W

Wartime Social Survey, 37
Wartime Women, 54, 58–59, 216
Watermans Arts Centre, 57
Willcock, H. D. (Bob), 35–36
Williams, Mrs (W2151), 227–228
Williams, Raymond, 74
Women, and writing, 144, 154–155
Work schedule, 179–180
Workplaces, 3
Worktown Survey, 39, 83–84,
   92–94
World War II, 35
Worthiness. *See* Legitimacy
Wright, Mrs (W632), 139–144,
   218–219, 221, 251–257, 261,
   272–273, 275, 289
Writer, not being, 188
Writing
   about television, 149
   autobiographical, 38, 42
   conditions of, 161
   as contested social practices,
      126–127

to create social relationships, 268–275
creating space for, 263–268
directives influencing, 224–229
embedded in social practices, 4
to express an opinion, 174–175
by family members, 155, 187, 191
feeling of, 198–199
fiction, 153–154
finding time for, 154, 166–167, 265–266
High Culture view of, 8
invisibility of, 7
as knowledge construction, 123–124
as knowledge transmission, 121–123
materials for, 182
men and, 185–186
not for Mass-Observation, 143–144, 153–154, 168–169, 182–184, 264–265
of ordinary people, 211–291
a place for, 140, 145, 190, 198, 264–265
place in correspondents' lives, 142–143, 182
proper, 134–135, 275–279
rather than speaking, 160
responses to directives, 233–235
at school, 160
as social and cultural practices, 124–126
stopping, 163, 187
uses and genres of, 219–235
uses of, 213–236
women and, 144, 154–155
Writing Britain, 279
writing ourselves and, 281–291
Writing Culture, 103
Writing ourselves, and writing Britain, 281–291
Writing practices
data evidencing, 94
dialogues and, 111–207
layers of, 117
Writing process, people's ideas about, 110, 157
Written language, people's use of, 3

Z

Ziegler, Philip, 44, 47